MYTH OF THE WELFARE QUEEN

A PULITZER PRIZE–WINNING JOURNALIST'S PORTRAIT OF WOMEN ON THE LINE

DAVID ZUCCHINO

A Touchstone Book
Published by Simon & Schuster

⩚

TOUCHSTONE
Rockefeller Center
1230 Avenue of the Americas
New York, NY 10020

First Touchstone Edition 1999

TOUCHSTONE and colophon are registered trademarks of Simon & Schuster Inc.

DESIGNED BY ERICH HOBBING

Set in Goudy Oldstyle

Manufactured in the United States of America

1   3   5   7   9   10   8   6   4   2

Library of Congress Cataloging-in-Publication Data is available.

ISBN 0-684-81914-7
ISBN 0-684-84006-5 (Pbk)

For Kacey

MYTH
OF THE
WELFARE
QUEEN

"None of them knew the colour of the sky."
—Stephen Crane, "The Open Boat"

Acknowledgments

This book is a work of journalism. It would not have been possible without the cooperation of its subjects. I am indebted to Odessa Williams and her family, and to Cheri Honkala and other members of the Kensington Welfare Rights Union for their willingness to share with me the most intimate details of their lives. They demanded nothing and delivered everything.

The events described in this book were either witnessed by the author or related in interviews with the people involved. It would not have been possible to portray this book's characters against the backdrop of daily life in Philadelphia without the sustained excellence of a great American newspaper, *The Philadelphia Inquirer*. I have drawn heavily on the reporting of my colleagues at the *Inquirer*, particularly reporters Ralph Cipriano, John Woestendiek, Dan Rubin, and George Anastasia.

I am grateful to my colleagues on the foreign desk of the *Inquirer*—Nancy Szokan, Lisa Karoly, Bob Filarsky, and John Lubell—for their professionalism and dedication during my long absences from the desk while reporting and writing this book. I am grateful, too, to Max King and Robert Rosenthal of the *Inquirer* for their patience and support.

I am thankful to Pastor Tony McCreary, who showed me the way to what is true and real in North Philadelphia, and to Rick Nichols, who knows well the ways of this world. I also thank my agent Flip Brophy, for believing in this book, and my editor, Leigh Haber, for conceiving it and nurturing it with skill and imagination.

Most of all, I am grateful to my beloved wife, Kacey, for holding our lives and our family together with love and caring while this book project was underway. She made it happen in a thousand ways that I can never repay.

Contents

Introduction

On August 22, 1996, President Clinton signed into law the "Personal Responsibility and Work Opportunity Reconciliation Act," better known as the welfare reform act. The new law revoked the federal guarantee of welfare cash to low-income families with dependent children, ending sixty-one years of entitlement for the poorest of the poor in America. The President's signature set adrift 13 million people, including 8 million children, who had come to rely every fortnight on a welfare check from the Aid to Families with Dependent Children program.

While the transfer of welfare programs from Washington to state capitals was likely to take months, and probably years, people on welfare felt threatened and abandoned by the impending withdrawal of guaranteed federal aid. Their concerns went unheeded in official Washington, where few of the senators and congressmen who voted for the welfare bill had ever met a person on welfare, and even fewer had attempted to find out precisely what welfare recipients did with their government checks.

In the months preceding the passage of the welfare reform act, from Independence Day 1995 to New Year's Day 1996, I followed the lives of several unmarried welfare mothers living in the ghetto of North Philadelphia. I wanted to answer an elemental question: What did welfare mothers do all day? I wanted to know how they spent their checks, how they managed their finances, how they fed and clothed their children, how they obtained medical care, and whether they had realistic possibilities of finding jobs. More than anything else, I sought to discover whether anyone among a class of women so despised by mainstream America attempted to improve their circumstances and to raise their children for lives beyond poverty. I wanted to know whether such women were worthy more of contempt or compassion, or something in between.

If there were any Cadillac-driving, champagne-sipping, penthouse-living welfare queens in North Philadelphia, I didn't find them. What I found instead was a thriving subculture of destitute women, abandoned by their men and left to fend for themselves and their children, with welfare and food stamps their only dependable source of income. Their lives were utterly dominated by subsistence concerns. They spent hours each day foraging for food and clothing and securing safe housing for themselves and their children through punishing heat waves and bitter cold snaps. Out of sight of mainstream America, they survived from one welfare check to the next, making ends meet by picking through trash cans, doing odd jobs, borrowing from relatives, and shopping at thrift stores. They lived at the mercy of the welfare bureaucracy, which demanded documents and economic updates, while sometimes cutting off payments with little warning. Through it all, they struggled to stay alive in one of the most dangerous places in America. North Philadelphia is cursed with one of the highest violent crime rates in the nation; its main industry and chief source of employment is the sale of illegal drugs.

Under these conditions, few of the women I met were in a position to find employment. They had little formal education and few job skills; they were skilled primarily at raising children. In the economic wasteland of North Philadelphia, deserted by commerce and industry a generation ago, there were virtually no unskilled jobs that matched the income from welfare and food stamps—and certainly none that offered the health care benefits provided by welfare. Even if such jobs had existed, these women were so consumed by the business of securing housing, food, and health care that taking a job and leaving their children alone at home was not a viable option.

In this setting, and during this difficult period, these single mothers lived with the knowledge that their lives were about to undergo profound changes. They knew all too well that President Clinton had campaigned on a promise to "end welfare as we know it." They tried to follow the national welfare debate by catching snippets of television news and by exchanging fact and rumor on the street. They were buffeted by changes in the welfare bureaucracy at the state and city levels. They lived each day knowing that the lives they had fashioned would change drastically, and soon, but in ways still unknown to them.

This book is the story of survival by single mothers during the dying days of the American welfare state.

CHAPTER ONE

Trash Picking

The long and rambling drive down Allegheny Avenue took Odessa Williams past Bob's Crab House. The big red cartoon crab on Bob's sign invariably got her to thinking about her son Darryl. Sometimes, sitting behind the wheel of her rattletrap 1984 Chevrolet Caprice Classic, Odessa had to laugh out loud, remembering the time Darryl got caught breaking into another crab place, the Crab Shack over on Seventeenth Street. Darryl was on the pipe then, smoking crack and swilling beer. He broke into the Crab Shack one night, so high on crack that he did not realize he had set off the burglar alarm. And as soon as he saw what was inside, he forgot about robbing the place. All he could think of was the platters of steamed crabs left over from the evening crab plate specials. Darryl may have just about lost his mind to drugs and drink, but he had not lost his appetite. By the time the police arrived, they found him fast asleep beside a small mountain of crab shells and crab guts.

Odessa had four grown sons, but none of them could make her laugh the way Darryl could. He didn't mean to. It was just that crazy things seemed to keep happening to him, like the time he couldn't even get himself arrested. He had stopped seeing his probation officer shortly after he was convicted of breaking into the Crab Shack. He was strung out on crack, desperate for help. He figured that prison would be the best place to clean himself up. So Darryl went up to the 25th Police District, the station nearest his mother's row house, and told the officer at the reception desk that he wanted to turn himself in. He was high at the time, but he managed to tell the man about the bench warrants out on him for missing court dates on drug possession charges and for failing to report to his probation officer. The cop told him to sleep it off. Darryl did as he was told. He took a two-hour nap on a court bench. Then he came back to the front desk, but was sent away again. On his third try, he persuaded a different officer to look up his bench warrants on the court computer. When the officer saw the long computerized list of Darryl's outstanding warrants, he whistled softly to himself and said: "You're going away."

And that is how Darryl got himself sent to the roughest prison in the state, to the State Correctional Institution at Graterford, which turned out to be, fortuitously, a mere fifty-minute drive from his mother's house in North Philadelphia. But that is also how Darryl got himself cleaned up. He got off drugs in a prison rehab program and started teaching Bible classes in the prison ministry. He became a vegetarian and began preaching to everyone who would listen about the evils of drug addiction and sloth and godlessness. And though everyone in prison still called him by his nickname, Four D, they did not know that it stood for Deep Down and Dirty Darryl. Darryl did not tell them, because that was his street name, and his street days were a long way behind him now.

Odessa loved to read the letters that came every month from her renewed, refreshed, sober, God-fearing son. She was especially pleased when Darryl told her he had petitioned for a new bunk mate because the one assigned to him was a foulmouthed man; Darryl did not tolerate profanity from anyone these days. And just when everybody thought Darryl was punking out and going soft, he punched out a white inmate who called him a nigger. Darryl got away with a mild reprimand because the authorities ruled that the punch was warranted on account of Darryl's having been unduly provoked. Odessa considered the ruling a sign from God that her son was headed in the right direction.

Odessa was a woman who tried to see the best in everything and everybody. She could drive down Allegheny Avenue, through some of the worst slums in North America, get to thinking about her recovering drug addict son in prison, and still laugh out loud. She found humor in many things, including her own meager circumstances. She was on welfare. She lived off food stamps. She had four grandchildren and two great-grandchildren to feed and clothe. She lived in a tumbledown row house so crammed with relatives that every morning she had to step over the sleeping forms of her grandsons spread out like corpses on her living room floor. She joked about squashing them like little bugs.

She had to laugh at herself. Otherwise she might dissolve into tears at the futility that sometimes nearly suffocated her. She owed $3,250 to the gas company, which had cut off her service, leaving her dependent in winter on foul-smelling and dangerous kerosene heaters. She was several months behind on her electric bill. Her phone service was about to be cut off. There was a gaping hole in her dining room ceiling because she had lost her temper and ripped out the ceiling tiles while searching for the source of the leak that sent water dripping onto her dining room table. She could not afford to have the hole repaired because she barely survived from welfare check to welfare check every two weeks. There were many times when she was literally down to her last dollar and she had to spend it on an eight-pack of bony chicken backs that she boiled into a pasty stew over rice. And the next day her grandchildren would have to go off to school without their snack money.

Odessa did not complain. She was beyond that. She was fifty-six years old, with a lifetime spent making do. That was what her mother had taught her: you make do with what you have. When there was a problem in the family, or even in the neighborhood, Odessa did what she could to solve it. She had raised eight children of her own. But she also had raised two of her grandchildren when her own daughters failed as parents because they were mere children themselves. Sometimes she felt like a mother to the world.

In addition to caring for the children of her own children, Odessa had taken in three children from the neighborhood whose parents had beaten and starved them. Those children, too, she raised as her own. One of them was a little white boy named Michael, who was now a grown man who called her "Mama" whenever he telephoned from his army post, in Georgia. For three years Odessa had cared for four children of crack-addicted mothers because she could not bear the thought of them being taken away by the child welfare people and raised by strangers. And now, when Odessa should have been a grandmother who spoiled and coddled her grandchildren on weekend visits, she was a seven-day-a-week mother to her daughter's children and to her granddaughter's children. She was raising four of her thirty-two grandchildren and helping to raise two of her seven great-grandchildren. Their own mothers had failed them, so Odessa did as her own mother had done. She made do.

She did not believe in waiting for things to come to her. She waited on God and no one else. That is why she was driving her Caprice Classic down Allegheny Avenue one sweltering August evening in the summer of 1995, thinking about Darryl as the red crab on Bob's Crab House faded in her rearview mirror. On many evenings, especially in summer, she climbed behind the wheel and drove out to Northeast Philadelphia for a long, leisurely night of trash picking at suburban curbsides. She always looked forward to rummaging through other people's trash, especially white people's trash, because white people threw away the damnedest things. She once found an entire set of china still in its original packing box. She had found perfectly usable TV sets, VCRs, vacuum cleaners, suitcases. In fact, she had furnished her entire house via this method. Trash picking had clothed her grandchildren and helped stretch her meager welfare check by enabling her to apply it solely to the sort of essentials that you couldn't trash-pick, such as food.

Sometimes sifting through other people's throwaways so relaxed her that she could almost feel her blood pressure dropping. She cherished each new treasure she dragged home: a bed, a sofa, a cabinet, a child's snowsuit, a bouquet of plastic flowers. But she cherished even more the hours she spent away from home—as Odessa the woman, not Grandma the caretaker. She called it her trash therapy. It gave her time to reflect on her life, away from the clatter of children and the demands of squalling babies and meals uncooked and clothes unwashed. And each long drive on Allegheny Avenue was like a journey through her past, for she saw at each passing block a reminder of a family member or some long-ago event that either filled her heart with gladness or pierced it with a pain that felt like it would never go away.

Each trip began at 714 Allegheny, a drab brown row house that is one of the first structures that comes into view on the Amtrak trip from Philadelphia to New York. The elevated tracks soar high above Allegheny Avenue, where it breaks hard to the north at Eighth Street. Anyone gazing out the train's south windows can see Odessa's worn wood porch with its rickety metal railing and slanting cement steps. They can see her trash-picked metal lawn chairs, lashed to the railing by a trash-picked steel chain that snakes through the rear grill of the trash-picked air conditioner jutting from the filmy living room window. The row house is distinguished from other homes on the block by its singular lack of graffiti and by the artful way that tiny mirror chips have been affixed to the brick facade to form the numerals *714*.

On any evening a passenger looking out the train window can see groups of young black men clustering on the two corners that frame the home at 714. At Eighth and Allegheny, just outside John's Deli, there is a billboard smeared with graffiti that advertises a hair straightener called Tender Headed Relaxer. The face of a lovely model, half obscured by the words *I've Been Burned So Many Times*, smiles sweetly down on the young men, who lean into cars at the curb to sell white-cap and blue-cap plastic vials filled with gummy gray crack cocaine. They also sell a potent brand of heroin, packed in blue glassine bags, nicknamed Tyson for its punch.

A block east, at the corner of Wendle and Allegheny, other young men peddle drugs to passersby just down from what the neighborhood people call the Chinese store but which has actually been run by a progression of Koreans named Sun, Moon, Kim, and Lee. The young men routinely shout, "C.D! C.D!" to tout a new form of crack packaging known as a "cooked dime." A C.D. contains a sliver shaved from a rock of crack cocaine and is sold not in the customary plastic vial for $5 but in a tiny square glassine bag for $10. It is the same old drug, but marketed in a simple, elegant way that seems almost exotic. It was the hot new drug item in North Philadelphia that summer.

Between the two drug corners, in the middle of the block, a group of younger black boys gather every afternoon along the cracked sidewalk. From the train windows, they, too, appear to be selling drugs. They huddle in small groups, and from time to time they scatter out toward the street. Their sudden bursts of movement attract the attention of cars that cruise slowly past. But if someone on the train were to watch the boys for a few moments, it would become apparent that they are not selling drugs. They are playing football. That is what the grandsons and nephews of Odessa did almost every night that summer in front of row house number 714. Odessa forbade them to stray beyond that small patch of sidewalk. She demanded that they stay close enough to see her as she sat in her trash-picked lawn chair on the porch—close enough to hear her shout, "Get down!" whenever gunshots rang out from the drug corners at either end of the block.

On this evening, Odessa had shouted out another order: "Everybody inside!" Dusk was falling, and it was time for everyone in her family to be off the streets. She wanted to go trash picking, but she could not leave until everyone was safely settled inside. Her little nephews ran to their dark row houses up and down Allegheny Avenue. The three grandsons who lived with her, Jim, Kevin, and Brian, stomped up the porch steps, fatigued and sweaty, and into the sanctuary of their grandmother's house.

Jim ran in so quickly that the heavy glass door slammed shut in his wake, causing Kevin's forehead to crash into the door frame. Kevin stopped and brought his hand to his head and let out a soft moan just as Brian, running full steam, plowed into him, burying his cheek into Kevin's spine. Jim turned around and saw his brothers howling in pain and laughed, which enraged the two boys all the more. They charged their older brother. But Jim was agile and stepped aside as Kevin and Brian sped past him and tumbled onto their grandmother's trash-picked sofa.

Odessa saw what happened and shouted, "Jim! Stop tormenting your brothers!" She ordered Brian and Kevin upstairs and told Jim to have the entire downstairs cleaned up and swept by the time she got back home from trash picking. Jim stopped laughing and mumbled, "Okay, Grandma."

Jim could stir up trouble, but he could also be responsible and reliable. At thirteen, he was the man of the house. Odessa depended on him. She trusted him to watch his brothers and sister, and any other children who happened to be in her charge. Jim had lived with her since he was five, and was already growing into a handsome young man. He had high, bold cheekbones and a square jaw, and was taller and more solidly built than most of the boys in his class. He was a quiet boy who kept to himself and tended to avoid confrontation, but he did not shrink from a challenge.

*   *   *

When a boy on Lehigh Avenue punched Kevin in the back of the head that summer, Jim hunted the boy down and smacked him so hard that the boy fell to the pavement and stayed there until Jim stalked off.

Kevin, at ten, was almost big enough to take care of himself. He wasn't as big boned or as well muscled as Jim, but he was rangy and well proportioned. He had lived with his grandmother since he was a two-year-old baby who demanded to be held on her lap day and night. Odessa was tempted to nickname him Seven Twenty-four because he wanted to be coddled seven days a week, twenty-four hours a day. Now, as a young boy, Kevin was fascinated by football. He was out on the sidewalk every evening, catching passes and crashing into the trash cans that marked the sidelines in the street games. He had begged his grandmother to sign him up for one of the recreation football leagues, but Odessa had said no because the registration fee could not be accommodated by her bimonthly welfare check. Kevin often pictured himself in brilliant white plastic shoulder pads and a crimson-and-gold San Francisco 49ers jersey, looking fierce and dashing and even bigger than Jim. It was only August, but already he had given his grandmother a one-line Christmas list: "Football stuff."

Brian, at seven, was still Odessa's baby. That's what she called him: "My little bitty ol' baby boy." She had raised him since he was a thin, sickly newborn. He was born two months premature, weighing just two pounds. When Odessa first saw him at the hospital, he looked to her like some helpless baby bird that had been shoved to the bottom of the nest. He all but disappeared inside his baby blanket. His diaper was bigger than he was. Even now, Brian seemed to be swallowed by his clothes. His arms were thin and bony. His big oblong head seemed too heavy for his tiny neck, and it wobbled when he walked. He was the smallest child in his class, and the way his big dark eyes shone under black eyelashes that curled up like ribbons gave him a soft, cherubic look.

The three boys' sister, Delena, was nine years old, a demure, respectful girl who almost always obeyed her grandmother. She had a round, delicate face and expressive brown eyes that often stared up at the sky when she was thinking of what to say. Unlike the other girls on the street, whose speech was punctuated by sharp shouts and squeals, Delena rarely raised her voice. She would often join the other girls in pretending to be cheerleaders at the boys' street football games, but she poured her energy into jumping and twirling, not shrieking. She was introspective and self-aware for her age. She spent a great deal of time in her closet-sized bedroom upstairs, for she was the only one in the house with a private room. When she wanted to get away from the racket on the street or in the crowded living room, she climbed upstairs and flopped down on her bare mattress to read a book or play a video game on the bulky old color TV her grandmother had trash-picked for her.

Downstairs on this August evening, Odessa stood in her narrow living room with her hands on her hips and hollered, "Where is my flashlight?" She could not go trash picking without her flashlight—the very flashlight, in fact, that she had plucked from somebody's trash pile earlier that summer. Jim walked to the dining room table and lifted a pile of baby clothes and said, "Here it is, Grandma," and handed her the flashlight.

Odessa flicked the switch and a beam of light cut through the dim room at dusk. As the light ricocheted around the room she realized that most of the things it illuminated had been thrown away by someone else. It seemed to her that her whole house was trash-picked. Her big green refrigerator was trash-picked. So was her white upright freezer. So were the VCR and the color TV and the magnificent brass-and-glass home entertainment system, which was so massive that it had taken two of Odessa's grown sons to muscle it into a pickup truck and haul it up the steps into her living room, where it was now the downstairs centerpiece.

Odessa prided herself on the quality of her trash picking. She had a discerning eye. She did not bring home junk. And for her there was no stigma attached to the base origins of these objects. Each item she dragged home represented to her a form of independence. She might be on welfare, but she wasn't dependent, and she certainly wasn't helpless. She did not expect anyone to give her anything, but she saw no reason not to take advantage of what was available. Just as she qualified for welfare, she was also entitled to root through people's trash cans and seize for herself those things that others lacked the common sense or initiative to put to good use. When people visited her home, Odessa would point out her latest find and describe in detail how she had unearthed it and extracted it and cleaned it and hauled it home. Often she would cock her head and admire the new item and ask, "What kind of fool threw *that* in the trash?"

In a way, the very house that held her trash-picked treasures was itself trash-picked. Odessa had noticed the place while driving down Allegheny one day in 1986. It was a wreck. Junkies had been shooting up inside, and the downstairs was smeared with filth and crammed with trash, but the house remained strong and solid. Odessa knew her sons could help her fix it up. She went down to city hall and looked up the the name of the owner, who agreed to rent her the place for $185 a month.

It took three pickup truck loads to haul off all the trash inside, but in a mere matter of weeks Odessa and her grown sons had made the house habitable. They put up drywall, fixed the roof, laid in a new bathroom, replaced broken pipes, updated the kitchen. The owner dropped by one day to check on the place and was so impressed, according to Odessa, that he asked her: "You want this house? It's yours."

But before he could sign the place over, the man was killed in a car crash. When his widow came by to reclaim the house, Odessa told her of her husband's promise. The widow was skeptical. She later confided to Odessa that she thought Odessa was one of the kept women her husband apparently had set up in houses around town. But soon she realized that Odessa could not possibly have known her husband in that way, and she relented. She signed over the house to the city, which in turn handed it over to Odessa under a special donor-taker program on the condition that she pay transfer fees and other costs. Odessa ended up paying about $125 to own the house.

In the nine years since then, Odessa had grown as comfortable and secure in the old row house as in anyplace she had ever lived, and it was the only home she had ever owned. It was also the only true home her grandchildren had ever known, except perhaps for Jim, who was still trying to bury the painful memories of the cold and filthy row houses in which he had spent his first five years. The children felt safe and special in their grandmother's house. It always smelled of rich food—pancakes and syrup in the mornings, grilled cheese sandwiches for lunch, and in the evenings, fried pork chops or pigs' feet with turnip greens and rice and pink beans. In summer the house had the close, pungent odor of mildew and wood rot. In the winter it was cozy and warm, and the kerosene heater gave off a slick, oily scent that seemed to calm the children the minute they rushed in from the frigid air and tossed off their coats.

It did not bother the children that their grandmother was an indifferent housekeeper. Odessa tried to clean up every day, but the demands of the children often overwhelmed her. She had neither the time nor the energy to wipe down the greasy kitchen walls or to clean what remained of the grimy and tattered linoleum squares on the dining room floor. Sometimes scraps of food fell from the table and remained on the floor for days, turning hard and sticking to the bare wood beneath the torn linoleum. On some days cockroaches feasted in the corners of the kitchen and did not bother to scurry away when people passed by, and in the late afternoons they could be observed marching single file up and down the living room walls. In the summertime the flies gave off a steady hum, like a small generator, and sometimes they sought out the moisture of the children's eyes and noses. Odessa hung fly strips from the ceiling, but they quickly filled up, and still the flies came. The children scarcely noticed, for this was home, and for the most part they were safe and happy at Grandma's.

Now, as the low rays of the dying day lit up the Amtrak overpass and streamed into the living room, Odessa made her way to the door. She tripped over a black trash bag full of wrinkled children's clothes—the residue of last week's trash picking—and yelled to Jim to put them away. As she opened the front door, there was a clinking sound, like ice skittering across a frozen sidewalk. Some of the white tiles on the foyer floor had broken loose and were scattered across the breezeway. Odessa had meant to have somebody replace the tiles, but how would she pay them? Maybe one of her sons could do the job. And perhaps they could also put a latch and lock on the outside screen door, which did not close properly and was an invitation to thieves.

Odessa sighed and walked carefully across the bare wood porch and down the cement steps. She turned her big body sideways, holding the rail and placing both feet on each step before lowering herself down the next one. She was a big woman, whose weight at times approached 240 pounds. She had a heavy torso and broad hips and soft, fleshy arms that easily could encircle Brian's skinny waist. She had a round face and deep brown eyes that registered kindness most of the time but hardened into bright little stars behind her spectacles when she was provoked. Spattered around her eyes were tiny black moles that gave her a sunny, freckled look. She smiled easily and often, revealing strong white teeth that had survived a lifetime of poor dental care. Though Odessa was approaching sixty, her hair was still black except for little wisps of silver. Even in summer she wore a cap, except on those occasions when one of her nieces would braid her hair in tight little cornrows that made her look young and carefree. But the cap could not hide the dark crease across her brow left by intersecting furrows of worry and exhaustion. Even when she smiled, the lines only deepened.

Long ago Odessa had taught herself to move slowly, for she was not an entirely healthy woman, despite her robust frame. She had suffered a stroke in 1986. Before that she had endured what her doctors called nervous breakdowns—one in 1957, another in 1962, and a third in 1967. Now she took Valium to keep her nerves in check. Whenever the children riled her, she shushed them by shouting, "My nerves are going, kids, they're going!"

There were other infirmities that were beyond repair. As a young woman Odessa had sliced open her ankle on a broken bottle. The wound had not healed properly. Sometimes the ankle would collapse as she walked, and she would have to balance on her good ankle to keep from toppling over. In 1968, she had broken her pelvis in a car accident, but the fracture was not diagnosed until a doctor noticed it on an X ray in 1991. The injury still gave her pain and slowed her gait, and she could not walk or stand for more than a few minutes without sitting down to rest.

Odessa also had severe asthma. Sometimes she would be talking and suddenly her voice would trail off into a high squeak, like a cartoon character's. She would try to keep talking, but then her eyes would close involuntarily, her chest would clutch, and her voice would trail off into a faint wheeze. For that reason she always carried an inhaler, and inside the house she kept a nebulizer that she shared with Kevin and Delena, who also suffered from asthma. Odessa also had high blood pressure, which shot up whenever the kids raised a ruckus in the house. And it was usually during those tense times that she made for the old Caprice and sought sweet solace in the drive to trash picking.

Odessa walked across the sidewalk to the curb and bent low to pick up two plastic trash barrels that someone had knocked over, then fished out the car keys from her purse and unlocked the Chevrolet. The car was a thirdhand piece of junk, but it was in many ways her most valued possession. Without the car, she would be trapped at home, certainly not free to trash-pick; she laughed at the thought of trying to lug home some bulky cabinet or bed frame on a city bus. She would not be able to drive to the thrift stores and discount outlets and dollar stores and butcher shops to find the best bargains on food and clothing. Without a car, in fact, she would have no means to make the most important trip she took every fortnight: the one to pick up her welfare check.

The Caprice had been a gift from Odessa's second-oldest daughter, Bertha, who had bought a minivan to replace the Chevrolet, which she had bought used from the owner of the Chinese store up the street. Odessa was proud of Bertha. She regarded her daughter as a person of substance—what people on the street called "thorough." Bertha had graduated from high school and had worked her entire adult life. Bertha was, in fact, the only one of Odessa's four daughters who had not relied at some point on welfare. Unlike the other daughters, Bertha was married to the father of her children, who worked as a counselor at a school for troubled boys. Bertha lived in a fine house in West Philadelphia and worked as a medical assistant. She was a stabilizing influence on the entire family. Odessa did not mention it to other family members, but secretly she favored Bert— that was the special nickname Odessa had given her—for another reason. She was the one daughter who looked just like Odessa.

Odessa gunned the engine and pulled the Caprice onto Allegheny Avenue. She drove in the shade of the sycamore trees, which drooped like bent old men in the midsummer heat. It was only August, but already the leaves were turning brown and dropping to the street. The man on the car radio was saying it was the hottest and driest summer in Philadelphia history, or at least since they started keeping records of such things. In July alone, the temperature hit ninety degrees or higher on twenty-two of thirty-one days. Odessa could not remember the last time it had rained. Now she rolled down the car window as far as it would go. The Caprice's air conditioner was trying to pump out cool air, but it wasn't doing enough.

In the rearview mirror Odessa could see the white front door of the row house occupied by her eldest daughter, Joyce. Joyce lived a block west on the same side of Allegheny Avenue as her mother, in a battered row house a few steps up the street from the cacophony of the corner drug market. Odessa watched Joyce's front door fly open and slam shut as Joyce's boy Elliott—nicknamed Geedy—ran inside. She was relieved to see him safely home, for some of the drug dealers were already arriving for the busy evening shift. Odessa was relieved, too, that Joyce had set down for her children the same rules Odessa laid down for her grandchildren: everybody home by dark.

Odessa admired Joyce's obstinate ways. She was serious and determined, and so single-minded that she had decided while still in high school to become a successful career woman. Joyce had always worked, despite raising four children on her own and then getting swept up in the neighborhood crack epidemic of the late 1980s. She had managed to overcome her addiction and to rid herself of the crack-addicted man who had fathered one of her children and nearly dragged her life down to the low, desperate level of his own. Joyce had an entrepreneurial spirit, and for a time she had run a small restaurant at Sixth and Allegheny. After that she worked for ten years as a nurse's aide, but had to quit after wrenching her back lifting a heavy patient, after which she was no longer able to meet the physical demands of the job.

After her injury, for the first time in her life Joyce had had to fall back on welfare. It was an unpleasant experience, and her self-image suffered. She did not think of herself as a dependent person, and despised people who could not or would not rely on themselves. And she knew more than a few welfare recipients who could have found work but preferred to lie around and collect "aid," or "fixed income," or "the check," or "DPW" (for Department of Public Welfare), as welfare was variously known in North Philadelphia. Yet now Joyce was taking her own easy money. She tried to justify it because of her bad back and the responsibility of feeding and clothing her children, but still it ate away at her.

By early summer, Joyce had decided she wanted off welfare. She went to see her caseworker, who helped her enroll in a business administration course in Northeast Philadelphia, near the very neighborhoods where Odessa did some of her most productive trash picking. Soon Joyce was learning all the latest computer programs, even Windows 95, which wasn't commercially available yet. Odessa was pleased. She knew how much Joyce hated to take charity—that's really all welfare was, she thought—

and she knew Joyce would blossom once she was supporting herself again. Her heart went out to her daughter every time she saw her thrust out her jaw and declare, "I'm a person who *needs* to work."

Even if Joyce did one day return to work, it would not end her troubles. The tensions Joyce felt between work and welfare extended to her entire family, and she was especially dismayed by the reluctance of her own daughter, Iesha, to take charge of her life and end her passive reliance on welfare. Iesha was just eighteen, but already she had given birth to three children. There were the twins, Danielle and Darryl, who turned two years old that August, and the baby, Khalil, almost a year old.

Iesha had dropped out of high school and immediately applied for welfare. Now her check and her food stamps seemed to insulate her from responsibility. Joyce despised the politicians in Washington, who seemed to be on the news every night that summer, suggesting that people on welfare were lazy and shiftless. Most people she knew on welfare were, like herself, using it as a springboard to a better life. She regarded welfare as a temporary crutch to feed and clothe her children, not a permanent means of support. Even so, Joyce had to acknowledge that her own daughter fit the politicians' stereotype—welfare was becoming a way of life for Iesha. And though it pained her to admit it, Joyce herself was contributing to Iesha's sloth. She gave her daughter a place to live and paid the house bills, so the $248 in cash Iesha received every two weeks and the $288 in food stamps she picked up every month were sufficient to sustain her. All summer, Joyce and Odessa had been carping at Iesha to register for classes for the high school year beginning in September. Iesha did speak vaguely of going back to school, but Joyce had doubts about her sincerity. It didn't help that Iesha was overweight and that she spent many afternoons that summer on her front porch, eating potato chips. "I hate to say this about my own daughter," Joyce said one day, "but she's just plain lazy."

It was little solace for Joyce that she had warned Iesha to stay away from the young man who eventually fathered her three children. She told Iesha the boy was irresponsible and would disappear as soon as he was called on to act like a father. Joyce wanted Iesha to learn what she had learned only after a lifetime of pain and miscalculation. Her own four children were fathered by four different men, none of whom contributed anything of consequence to her children's upbringing. But Iesha said her boyfriend was not that way. He loved her, she told her mother, and he would stand by her. But as Joyce had predicted, the young man took off shortly after Khalil was born. Later she learned that he had become a drug addict and was serving prison time for robbery.

The young man's abandonment of Iesha had profound consequences for

Odessa. It seemed to her that Joyce had lost control of Iesha. So Odessa, as she often did, felt obliged to step in. She took in Danielle, one of the twins. The little girl had severe asthma and was prone to seizures. Odessa did not trust Iesha to care for the child; Iesha could barely be trusted to change her babies' diapers regularly. So for most of her young life Danielle lived with her great-grandmother, curling up every night next to Odessa's big warm body in the king-size bed that took up most of her cramped upstairs bedroom. On many nights, little Darryl slept over, too, and every day it was Odessa, not Iesha, who made sure the twins got their shots, wore clean clothes, visited the clinic, got their bottoms wiped properly.

As Odessa drove east up the hill and approached Wendle Street, she saw the usual parade of eager boys gathering on the corner, waiting for people to drive up and buy drugs. She held the boys in such contempt that she refused even to acknowledge them when she drove by the corner, though most of them knew her by name and called out when she passed. One of them knew her quite well. He was her grandnephew Boo-Boo. His reckless ways—it was said he carried a gun—were one more reason that Odessa banned her grandchildren from the corner except to buy a quick snack at the Chinese store. She hated that corner. The sight of it always reminded her of the great tragedy of her life—her second-youngest daughter's slow descent into drug addiction.

Brenda had been Odessa's sweetest and most respectful child. She was such a dutiful little girl, so helpful and trusting, that Odessa had longed for her to grow up and have children of her own. But just after Brenda turned thirteen, her personality abruptly changed. She got cheeky and talked back, and started staying out late at night, in defiance of Odessa's strict curfew. She threatened to run away from home. "Brenda went bad," Odessa often said, "and she stayed there."

Odessa blamed her ex-husband, Willie, who had been no help with Brenda. He had refused to discipline her. The very first time Brenda, at thirteen, stayed out all night, Odessa had whipped her with a belt. Brenda promptly telephoned her father—Willie and Odessa had split up in 1967—and told him she did not want to live with her mother anymore. The next day she packed up and moved in with her father, and it was then that Odessa knew that she had lost her. The way Odessa tells it, Willie let Brenda do whatever she wanted, and soon she was smoking marijuana. When crack hit the streets of North Philadelphia, in the mid-1980s, Brenda tried it and liked it. She became hopelessly addicted. To raise money, she began to prostitute herself. At the same time, she began having sex with a series of drug-addicted boyfriends. One of them fathered Jim, Kevin, and Delena. Another fathered Brian.

Odessa tried to keep up with her grandchildren, trailing Brenda from one filthy crack house to the next. She would take the children for a few days, feed them, bathe them, give them clean clothes. Then Brenda would beg to get them back, promise to clean herself up, and Odessa would relent. Brenda would enroll in a drug rehab program for a time, then drop out and sign up for another. Each time she ended up back where she had begun, smoking crack and pulling tricks under the elevated train tracks along Frankford Avenue. She spent her welfare checks on drugs, sold her food stamps for cash or crack.

By 1987, when Jim was five, Brenda had taken Jim, Kevin, and Delena to live in a shabby row house a few miles from Odessa's home on Allegheny Avenue. Odessa was repulsed at the filth that surrounded her grandchildren. Brenda tried to keep her mother away from the place, but Odessa often barged in and cleaned it up. One day, as Odessa rested at her own home, worrying about Brenda and the children, the phone rang. It was Jim.

"Grandma," he said, "we hungry. We been here all day but we haven't ate nothing. Mama said she be back in a jiffy, but she ain't back."

It was 3 P.M. Jim told Odessa that he had managed to open two cans of green beans to feed Kevin and Delena, but everybody was still hungry.

"Stay right there, baby," Odessa said. "Grandma's coming right over."

Odessa did not have a car in those days, so she caught a bus on Allegheny and reached Brenda's row house a half hour later. On the bus, she prayed that Jim was exaggerating, that Brenda had just stepped out for a few minutes. But when she got inside she was staggered by what she saw. The children were smeared with filth. Kevin and Delena wore soiled, soggy diapers. The house reeked of urine. The floor was carpeted with trash. Odessa tried not to cry. She cleaned up the children, gave them some food she had brought along, and sat down to wait for Brenda.

At 8 P.M., Brenda walked through the front door, high on crack. Odessa wanted to smack her. She screamed at her. Brenda screamed back. Odessa told her she was taking the children away—for good this time. Brenda said nobody, not even her mother, was taking her kids away from her. They were her kids, and she would raise them anyway she damn well pleased. Odessa began to gather up the children. "You just try and stop me," she said.

Brenda said, "I'm gonna call the police on you," and she ran to the phone and dialed 911.

Two officers arrived. Brenda told them Odessa was trying to kidnap her children. Odessa told them to ask Jim what had happened. The cops questioned Jim, who told them about being left alone all day with no food. The officers listened intently and looked around the house. Finally they told Brenda she had two choices: the child welfare people or Grandma.

And that is how Odessa, at age forty-eight, became a mother all over again. It is also how she ended up back on welfare long after she had thought she was through with welfare forever. After she went to court and obtained legal custody of her four grandchildren—Brian was born during that process—Odessa took over Brenda's welfare benefits. Now she received $201.50 every two weeks, plus $87 per month in food stamps, to support the four children. She also received $490 a month in Supplemental Security Income under a federal program for the disabled; she qualified because of her stroke.

Through Brian, Odessa received a second SSI check for $490 a month. In the eyes of the Social Security Administration, which administers SSI, Brian was disabled. He was what came to be called, during the great crack cocaine epidemic that devastated America's inner cities in the 1980s, a crack baby. Health care people preferred the term "crack-affected baby" because it shifted the onus for crack use away from the child. But whatever the term, Brian was indeed a child of cocaine.

Brenda had been on the pipe almost daily during her seven-month pregnancy with Brian. She was hardly an anomaly. In Philadelphia during that period, one of every six babies was born to a mother who had cocaine in her system at the time of delivery. Brian weighed just two pounds at birth, with a head so enlarged that he was four before he could walk without keeling over from its disproportionate burden on his thin neck.

Even now, at age seven, the effects of the cocaine lingered. Brian had been diagnosed with hyperactivity and attention-deficit disorder. He was disruptive in school and required constant attention. He had been transferred out of a regular class and into a special education class. At home, he often erupted in volcanic temper tantrums, during which he would fall to the floor and flail and scream until Odessa could tolerate it no longer. She would then hold him in her arms until he stopped, murmuring his name again and again, "Bryant, Bryant," for that is how she pronounced "Brian." Every week she drove him to a medical center on Lehigh Avenue for an hour of behavioral therapy.

For all of Brian's problems, his SSI check was a godsend. Without it, the family simply would not have been able to survive. But even with it, Odessa's monthly income was just $1,382, not counting food stamps. That came to $16,584 a year, or about $1,000 short of the federal poverty line of $17,449 for a family of five. Odessa laughed at the notion of a poverty line. She did not need a number from the government to tell her she was poor, nor did it surprise her to learn that fully half the families in her neighborhood were, according to the 1990 census, officially living in poverty. In fact, she would have guessed that the number was even higher. It seemed to her that just about everyone she knew was on the check.

As the big Chevy lurched up the hill where Allegheny crests at Sixth Street, Odessa passed the row house of her youngest daughter, Elaine, at the opposite end of the block from her own. Elaine was a big, open-faced, good-natured woman who walked slowly and deliberately and seemed to take life as it came, with few complaints and little comment.

Like Joyce, Elaine was on welfare but wanted off. She had enrolled twice in job training courses, but each time some emergency with her children or some calamity at home caused her to drop out just before graduation. She found it hard to properly care for her children while away in class all day, even when the welfare department paid for her child care. She needed to be there for them. They didn't need a baby-sitter, she thought. They needed their mother.

But after Joyce signed on at the business school, Elaine felt pressure from the family to keep abreast of her sister. She went to see her welfare caseworker, who helped her enroll in yet another job training class at another trade school, in Northeast Philadelphia. She signed up to study hotel management and food services. She would begin the six-week course in October. By New Year's, she hoped, she would be working in a motel or restaurant somewhere.

Elaine was only thirty, but already she had six children. Her first child was born when Elaine was just twelve. She had been raped by the seventeen-year-old brother of one of her playmates, an episode so traumatic that no one in the family ever spoke of it. By the time a doctor at a public health clinic had diagnosed Elaine's upset stomach as pregnancy, it was too late for an abortion—not that Odessa would have gone through with it anyway. The child was born and they named him Raysonno, and Odessa had raised him as her own. His face was so round that Odessa nicknamed him "Pie Face," later shortened to "Pie." Raysonno was followed by four more children born to Elaine, who all lived in a weather-beaten row house that Odessa could see out of her passenger window each time she drove out to go to trash picking. All five children were being raised by Elaine without benefit of their biological fathers.

Sometimes Elaine got so overwhelmed that she let the house fall into disrepair. She had bought it for $11,000 five years earlier and was still paying off the mortgage. The house was in woeful condition. Several months earlier one of the neighbors—Elaine never found out which one—had telephoned the city Department of Human Services and said Elaine's children were living in an unclean and unsafe environment. A woman from DHS had inspected the home and subsequently declared it unfit for raising children. She gave Elaine twenty-four hours to clean up the place or risk having her children remanded to the custody of DHS.

Elaine went immediately to Odessa, who got on the phone and called everyone in the family. The next day more than a dozen family members marched into the place and went to work putting up new drywall, patching the holes in the ceiling and walls, repairing the plumbing in the bathroom. They washed down the kitchen, deep-cleaned the living room and bedrooms, replaced broken windowpanes, and painted all the walls. When the DHS woman returned to inspect the house, she was speechless. "That poor lady just broke down and cried. She kept bawling and wiping her eyes and saying she'd never seen a family come together like that," Odessa remembered. Elaine kept her children.

Now Odessa picked up speed as the Caprice crossed Sixth Street and rumbled down Allegheny toward Front Street. She drove on, past Bob's Crab House and past a garish mural honoring a recently deceased local drug kingpin, to the intersection of Allegheny and Howard. She could not drive past Howard Street without thinking of her mother, who also was her best friend. Bertha Boone, now eighty-one, had been the first black person to move onto Howard Street, three decades earlier. She still lived in the same brick row house that had been a focal point of white rage when Bertha set up house there with her two handicapped sons in 1965. The whites screamed curses at her, called her "nigger" and worse. They threw garbage at her house, threatened to burn the place down.

According to family lore, several dozen Boones—her mother's relatives were scattered across North Philadelphia—had marched over to Howard Street. They called the whites out of their houses and announced that serious trouble would follow unless the harassment of Bertha Boone ceased immediately. The white people listened and went back inside and shut their doors. The way Bertha told it, from that day on she didn't have a single problem with those white folks. In fact, she said, some of them became good friends, who would drop in on her even years later, long after they had moved away from North Philadelphia. Bertha liked to brag that she had outlasted the whites, for today there wasn't a single white person living on her block. Howard Street, like most North Philadelphia neighborhoods, is virtually 100 percent black and Hispanic these days.

Bertha Boone was the reason that Odessa and everyone else in her vast extended family, from Joyce all the way down to Danielle and little Darryl, found themselves in Philadelphia. The history of the Boones stretched the length of Allegheny Avenue, from Odessa's home on Seventh Street to Bertha's place on Howard Street. In between, there were some sixty-five people of Boone blood, many of them branched out along the Williams and Hill family lines. Each one was inextricably tied to the summer day in 1950 when the Red Cross had spirited Bertha Boone away from a sharecropper's patch in Georgia to escape a drunk and abusive husband.

Bertha Boone had always assumed that her children and grandchildren would be raised, as she had been, in the red dirt country of Georgia. She had grown up in a sharecropper's shack, and from the time she could walk she had worked the fields, stacking peanuts, suckering tobacco, chopping cotton, and pulling green beans for $1.25 a day.

Her husband, Shellmon, like most black men of the rural South in those days, was obsequious toward whites. He let them call him Mister Sonny, a condescending name he hated but still tolerated. He moved from farm to farm, working as a sharecropper on one spread until the work ran out and he was sent on to the next one. His wife and children followed him, always hungry, always on the bottom edge of poverty.

To help make ends meet, Odessa began working the fields with her mother at age five. She was seven before she owned her first pair of sneakers, for which her father paid three cents. To make school shoes for her children, Bertha traced their feet on cardboard, cut out the shapes to make soles, and then wrapped them with an open flour sack. To make dresses, she stitched together flour sacks. To this day Odessa can still remember how shrunken and beaten her mother looked in those days, now a half century ago, and how she wept in the corner of their shack one winter's day, her tears freezing on her cheeks.

Bertha's own early memories were of being sent to the general store by her mother to beg the shopkeeper for credit. She remembers her mother walking the fields with her head down, gathering up peas the farmworkers had missed, and then boiling them in salt for dinner. She recalls being sent into the woods to pick blackberries, and the sharp prick of their thorns on her fingertips. She could then sell the damp, dark berries on the street for a nickel a pint, money her mother would use to pay off the white shopkeeper for food she'd bought on credit.

These were the memories that Bertha Boone brought to Philadelphia, to a vast, strange, cold place unlike anyplace she had ever known. She did not realize it at the time, but she was caught up in the greatest American migration of the century. Between 1940 and 1970, some 5 million Southern blacks left farms and country shacks to seek steady work in the factories of the big Northern cities, arriving just in time to stand helplessly by as the American urban manufacturing economy collapsed. For the European immigrants who had arrived a generation or more earlier, the factories and warehouses had provided a wealth of unskilled and semiskilled jobs that lifted them into the working class and catapulted their children into the middle class and upward. But by the 1950s, those jobs had begun to drift away, first to American Sunbelt states with low wages, low taxes, and few unions, and later to foreign lands with still cheaper wages and no unions at all. Black unemployment rates hit a historic low of 4.5 percent in 1953, but that was temporary, and then the rate soared back upward in the late 1950s as the economic urban cores of Northern cities began to disintegrate. The historian Roger Lane has written of black urban migrants: "they were in effect being piped aboard a sinking ship, welcomed into the urban-industial age only as it was beginning to die."

Bertha Boone arrived in Philadelphia in 1950 with three children. She moved in with her sister Leola on Melon Street in North Philadelphia. (Leola had been brought to Philadelphia from Georgia in 1940 by her husband, an army man who hailed from the city.) Two of Bertha's young sons, Junior and Charles, were severely handicapped. Junior was confined to a wheelchair, unable to speak or move his legs. Junior's brother, Charles, suffered from deformed hands. He could walk only with a metal walker, and he spoke in grunts. Odessa was eleven years old and healthy.

Somehow, Bertha made do. She drove to the farms of southern New Jersey and told the boss men that she was a hard worker who had worked on farms all her life. One of them told her she could pick tomatoes for ten cents a bushel, and so she went to work beside migrant workers, following the seasons. She picked blueberries for thirty cents a tray, picked strawberries, cut collard greens. When school let out, she took Odessa with her. The girl spent her summers working with her mother, then was sent back to relatives in Georgia to attend school.

Farmwork helped sustain Bertha and her children year after year. Bertha picked up a few extra dollars by taking in sewing and by cleaning people's houses. But by 1967, all the bending and lifting and sweating of farmwork had begun to wear her down, and her health began to fail. She was fifty-four years old. She had two grown handicapped sons to lift and bathe and feed. She had never thought of herself as dependent, and had always shunned charity. But now she resigned herself to accepting help. She decided to go on welfare. She signed up for $90 every two weeks, and somehow she survived.

That same year—the first year any Boone ever went on welfare—Odessa also signed up for public assistance, also out of desperation. From the age of thirteen, Odessa had essentially taken care of herself, and it distressed her to now have to go on public relief. She considered herself a worker, not a dependent. Once, when she was a young girl in Georgia, she had been ordered by the father of a white girlfriend to address the girl as "ma'am." Because the white girl had just turned thirteen, her father said, she was old enough to be shown the respect due a white woman of the South. Odessa could not understand why her good friend should suddenly be treated as a superior. She refused to call her "ma'am" or anything other than her name. The girl's father summoned Odessa's own father and warned him to get his uppity daughter out of Georgia. If not, he said, she might end up hanging from a tree one night. The next day Odessa was sent to stay with her aunt in Philadelphia.

After a few weeks, Odessa was sent back to Georgia, but she did not call her girlfriend anything close to "ma'am." Instead she shunned the girl and settled in with relatives in the countryside. For the next two years, she helped with the housework and worked the fields for $3 a day. There she met a sharecropper named Willie Williams. On August 20, 1955, she and Willie were married. Odessa was fifteen years and eight days old.

Odessa would give birth to eight children, four girls and four boys. She and Willie moved to Philadelphia in 1956 to be near Bertha. Willie found work as a mechanic, and later as a burner who cut up scrap metal with an acetylene torch. Odessa took an eighteen-month mechanic's course and found a job repairing cars at a garage at Fifth and Allegheny, just two blocks from where she would one day make her home, near Seventh and Allegheny. After two and a half years, she was laid off, but found a job working in a lamp factory in downtown Philadelphia. The job lasted five years before she was once again laid off. She then moved on to a job in a factory that made gift candles, and when that factory shut down, she worked in a toy factory. Later she took a job as a seamstress.

By 1967, she had been laid off once again. Willie was still working, but he had become increasingly abusive and jealous, and began to demand that Odessa stay home all day with the shades drawn and the door locked. He accused her of seeing other men and began to beat her. The beatings got so bad that Odessa began to fantasize about killing her husband, who had threatened to kill her. She knew she had to leave him, so one day she took the children and moved into a tiny row house at Twelfth and York. She tried and failed to find work. The trauma of the separation and the move and the shortage of money culminated in what her doctor called her third, and most severe, nervous breakdown. When she got back from the doctor Odessa went down to the Department of Public Assistance and signed up for welfare. To support her eight children, she received $150 every two weeks.

Now, as Odessa drove down Allegheny Avenue past Howard Street, she thought about how little welfare had increased in the twenty-eight years since she'd first gone on public assistance. To support her four grandchildren, she now received just $51 more every two weeks than she'd once received to raise eight children. She told herself that she was not complaining, but merely observing. The paltry amounts that welfare provided made it clear to her that it was not designed to support anyone. It was meant only to supplement the various means that families in North

Philadelphia utilized to scrape up money—from family members and friends, from part-time jobs that never got reported, from odd jobs performed for neighbors, from dealing drugs, and from letting drug dealers hide their stashes in their homes. She was proud that she had never done anything seriously illegal, that she had never touched alcohol or drugs, that no one in her immediate family sold drugs, that she never sold her food stamps for fifty cents on the dollar as some people did.

Odessa considered welfare a precious gift. When she said her prayers at night, she thanked God for welfare. She promised him that if she ever came into serious money—if she won the Pennsylvania lottery or hit a lucky slot machine in Atlantic City—she would pay back every cent that welfare had sent her way. She could not have raised her children without welfare. And in her mind, it was the children who were on welfare, not her. The money went straight to them, for food and clothes and shoes and school supplies. That is why, when she took in her grandchildren and went back on welfare in 1987 after being off public assistance for so many years, she was not ashamed or defensive or even depressed. She was merely making do.

As the Caprice passed Howard Street, Odessa thought about what fine sons she had raised on her welfare checks. They were so different from the men who seemed to dominate her neighborhood—the men who fathered child after child with one woman or another, then abandoned them to a life of welfare and dependency. Her sons supported their children. They spent time with them, counseled them, disciplined them. You would never see *their* kids selling drugs or running wild. They all went to school and brought home good grades, and they showed the utmost respect for their parents and especially their grandmother, who tolerated no cheekiness.

Fred, Odessa's youngest child, lived near Bertha on Howard Street. Just twenty-nine years old, he was already the half-owner of a prosperous neighborhood garage on Front Street. Fred was so skilled a mechanic that a transmission company in Delaware, where he had once worked, was constantly trying to hire him back. Fred wanted to concentrate on his garage work, but he did manage to set himself up as a well-paid consultant. Every few days, the transmission company would phone him and ask him to talk one of their mechanics through some vexing transmission problem. Most months, Fred pulled down several hundred dollars giving advice. Whenever Odessa lectured her grandchildren on the importance of learning a skill, she cited Fred: "Uncle Fred gets paid *just for talking on the phone!*"

Fred had not married any of the three women who had given birth to his five children, but at one point all three women lived with him on Howard Street. They shared the household duties and child rearing, and even cared for one another during pregnancies. But not even a charmer like Fred could balance the needs and demands of three women in one small row house, and after two years together the women went their separate ways. That was fine with Odessa because she had realized since Fred was a teenager that he was not the marrying kind. It was not of great importance to her that her sons married their women. What mattered to her was whether they took care of their children, and Fred did. Whether they were living with him or their mothers, Fred supported his children financially. He saw them regularly. One child still lived with him. Three others had moved with their mother into a row house just around the corner from Fred's place on Howard Street. The kids were in and out of Fred's house almost every day, and he made sure they stopped in to see their great-grandmother Bertha up the street.

You could not walk more than a few feet in any direction around Howard Street without stumbling across a Boone or a Williams. In addition to Bertha and Fred, Odessa's second-oldest son, Israel, also lived on Howard Street. He was staying that summer with his girlfriend of long standing, Anita, in a row house directly across the street from Bertha's redbrick row house. Israel had three children by another woman, all of whom lived with him and Anita. It gave Odessa great satisfaction that Israel took his role as father so seriously that he had fought for and obtained custody of his three boys when he and their mother had split up. Israel had since adopted a fourth boy, Ray-Ray, a playmate of his sons' who spent so much time under Israel's roof that he decided he might as well raise him as his own.

Israel was a big, powerful, playful man of thirty-eight, who loved to box and wrestle his boys. He stood over six feet tall and weighed more than two hundred pounds, but he was fast and nimble. In a flash he would grab one of the boys in a headlock and pin him to the floor with the weight of his big chest and belly until the boy begged for mercy. When his sons and nephews played street football outside Odessa's place, Israel was often in the middle of the huddle, mapping out plays on the sidewalk and winging passes so hard that they stung the boys' hands. It was important to him that boys in the ghetto have a safe place to play, without interference from the drug dealers and gun-toting hoodlums who dominated so many street corners. Israel was, in fact, something of a legend around Howard Street for the way he had taken back the neighborhood playground from pipers and drug dealers.

In the spring of 1992, the Waterloo Playground, just a few doors down from Israel's front door, was essentially a garbage dump. It was supposed to be the neighborhood playground, but the city had abandoned it years earlier. A drug gang calling itself the Dauphin Street Posse had taken the park over in the mid-1980s. With the acquiescence of a drug addict who happened to be a recreation official (according to Israel), the gang turned the park into a drug transfer point. The only people they allowed inside were pipers, who bought their crack from the gang and smoked it inside the ruins of the playground's tiny recreation building. The neighborhood children, including Israel's boys, were ordered by their parents to stay clear of the place. When they played outside at all, it was in the middle of Howard Street.

As the gang's drug business flourished, Howard Street became a sort of all-purpose drug-shopping throughway. Addicts and pipers raced down from Allegheny Avenue, scattering children playing on Howard Street, and parked on the sidewalks. Israel called the police. He was directed to Lt. John Gallo, chief of the narcotics unit in that part of North Philadelphia. Gallo promised to make drug busts at the playground, but he warned Israel that arresting dealers wouldn't shut down the operation. The people who lived there would have to help reclaim the playground.

Week after week, Gallo sent his undercover narcs to make buys and bust dealers at the playground. But as Gallo had predicted, Dauphin Street persevered. Drug sales continued around the clock. Every few weeks, somebody got shot or stabbed. In the previous seven years, five people had been shot dead, by Israel's informal count. By early 1992, it wasn't just the playground that was being taken over. Howard Street itself was under siege.

That spring, Israel had seen enough. He decided to call in the Boones. Twenty years earlier, they had stared down the white people on Howard Street. Now, he decided, they would take on the Dauphin Street gang. He gathered up his brothers and cousins. Together, they marched into the playground and demanded a meeting with the Dominicans who ran Dauphin Street. The Boones told the dealers they didn't want any trouble, but if they did not vacate the park within a week, there would be trouble. "This is *my* playground. Nobody messes with *my* playground," Israel told them. The following week, Dauphin Street cleared out. Later, one of the dealers told Israel that they had left out of respect—respect for the way the Boones had confronted the gang head-on, no bullshit.

After the Dauphin Street Posse was gone, Israel and some of his neighbors hauled away several truckloads of trash from the playground. They shoveled out human waste and crack vials from the recreation building. They got neighborhood kids to paint the building, covering up years of graffiti. And Israel figured out a way to get rid of a wrecked Toyota beached on the dry bed of the swimming pool. The way he tells it, he climbed down into the pool, braced himself behind the car, and single-handedly pushed it up an incline to the shallow end and on out of the pool. The story of man versus car spread through the neighborhood. Soon community groups and antidrug crusaders based nearby began to offer support and to raise money for rebuilding the playground.

The city's new Recreation Department commissioner, Michael DiBerardinis, began hearing about the man on Howard Street who had run the drug dealers out of Waterloo Playground. One story making the rounds came from a recreation maintenance man, who told of passing by the Waterloo pump room one morning and hearing Israel screaming at four pipers inside: "If you don't get the hell out of there, I'm going to shove my foot right up your butt!"

DiBerardinis had people in his department scavenge an old pool pump and install it at Waterloo. Somebody donated playground equipment. The man who owned Roy's Ornamental Metal Work across the street from the playground donated iron gates. By Independence Day 1992, the playground had reopened with a working pool. Later that summer, DiBerardinis hired Israel as Waterloo's part-time summer park director.

As Odessa drove past Howard Street three summers later, she wondered what people would think if they knew that the man who had saved Waterloo was raised by a welfare mother. For one week in the summer of 1992, Israel had briefly been a celebrity, at least in Philadelphia. The papers had run feature stories about his success at Waterloo, and one of the local TV stations showed the new playground on the evening news. Israel became known as the man who pushed a Toyota out of a swimming pool. It was the first time Odessa could remember reading anything about Howard Street that didn't involve some drug dealer shooting somebody. But now, three years later, the TV news (she didn't read the papers very often) was hammering away at people on welfare. They were running stories about Congress ending welfare and putting people back to work. Odessa wanted to fly down to Washington and tell everybody that a son she'd raised on welfare had just about single-handedly cleaned up the drug problem on his street—and got a paying job out of it, too. She still had the newspaper articles to prove it.

While she was at it, she could tell the Washington politicians about her oldest son, Willie. She thought of Willie every time she drove east on Allegheny Avenue toward the Interstate 95 overpass on her way to trash picking. If she took I-95 to the Ben Franklin Bridge and over to New Jersey, she would end up at Willie's immaculate suburban home in the little town of Beverly. Willie was a successful contractor, practically middle class. He put in bathrooms, decks, additions, and he could fix anything. One of his specialities was metalwork. He had designed and installed one of the metal subway-stop coverings on the Broad Street line in downtown Philadelphia, and every time she drove past it with her grandchildren in the car, Odessa would cry out, "Look, kids, your uncle Willie built that! It's a permanent part of the city!"

Now Odessa drove down Allegheny across Kensington Avenue. She headed into the gloom beneath the elevated train tracks at the crowded

corner known as K and A, for Kensington and Allegheny. If she were to
turn right and follow the El tracks south, toward the center of Philadelphia, she would approach Brenda's workplace. It was along Kensington
Avenue, beneath the black shadows cast by the El gridwork, that Brenda
stood and waited for men cruising in cars to stop and negotiate with her for
sex. Each time Odessa drove across Kensington Avenue she thought about
Brenda. Each time, she became more reconciled to the awful realization
that her daughter was lost to her forever, that crack had seized Brenda and
would not let go until she was dead. It was no consolation to Odessa that
Brenda was joined by dozens of other women of all ages and races, each
one strolling under the El, bending low in a miniskirt or tight spandex
slacks to solicit men in cars. Odessa wondered if the mothers of the other
women felt the same pain and despair that she felt.

The Caprice emerged from under the El and was again bathed in the
low orange sun at dusk. The sunlight seemed to light up the pale faces of
the whites who walked the streets on the east side of Kensington Avenue.
It was always a shock to suddenly encounter whites after passing so many
blacks and Hispanics for miles along Allegheny west of Kensington. It is
sometimes said that Kensington Avenue is where white and black
Philadelphia meet. It is an unspoken but acknowledged line of demarca-
tion. To the west lies black West Kensington and Odessa's neighborhood of
Fairhill, and beyond that the vast bleak landscape of crumbling row homes,
graffiti-tagged factories, abandoned warehouses, and shabby bodegas
known generically as North Philadelphia. To the east lies white Kensington, Port Richmond, Fishtown, and the low river wards, home to more
decaying factories and dilapidated row houses and trash-strewn lots.

Odessa had never encountered problems in these white neighborhoods,
but she had heard many tales over the years. She knew that many of the
working-class and unemployed whites there deeply resented the gradual pen-
etration of their crumbling neighborhoods by black working-class families.
An incident in Fishtown the previous summer had epitomized this. Late one
night, two young white men and their mother burst into the home of the only
black family on their block, screaming, "We've had enough of you niggers!"
Inside, a black woman named Joan Smith did not hear the intruders, for she
was deaf. Smith was beaten with a baseball bat until blood gushed from her
head. Her hand and foot were smashed and broken. It took twenty stitches
to close her wounds. Long before the white attackers were convicted and
jailed a year later—the judge called their crime "a family outing"—Joan Smith
had moved out, restoring the block to all-white status.

Odessa regarded such unfortunate incidents as aberrations. She
believed that white Kensington was no different from black Kensington.

Both were populated in large measure by good, decent people, along with a few nasty, hateful souls. All people, she believed, had God in their hearts, but only the good ones listened to Him. As for white Kensington, no one had ever bothered Odessa in those tight, cramped neighborhoods. Indeed, she had encountered only profit there. Once, while driving past Ed's Tap Room at Allegheny and Jasper, she had seen a white man with long silver hair and a bushy beard burst from the bar and toss money into the street, laughing madly. Odessa pulled over and joined a crowd of people on their hands and knees, scooping up dollar bills and quarters and dimes. Someone told her the man emptied the bar's tip jar this way every few weeks. Odessa had come away with $6, and from that day on she always drove slowly past Ed's Tap Room.

And that wasn't the only good fortune she had encountered there. Once, while Odessa was trash-picking at the curb, an elderly white woman called her aside and offered her bags of neatly folded clothes that her grandchildren had outgrown. The clothes looked so clean and fresh that Odessa's grandchildren assumed they were new, and Odessa let them think so. Now the woman telephoned Odessa every few weeks to announce: "It's the grandma on Aramingo, and I got some more clothes for you."

Odessa drove onto I-95 north, which cut through the heart of Northeast Philadelphia. The Northeast seemed to her a paradise, with its tidy little duplexes and neat square lawns and curving sidewalks. It was home to working people—policemen, firemen, city workers, mechanics, plumbers, electricians. There were drugs and graffiti, of course, but they were kept to a manageable level. The schools were cleaner and better run than those in North Philadelphia. The Northeast was, in fact, everything that North Philadelphia was not. The streetlights got fixed. The trash got picked up on time. The potholes got filled. The snow got cleared. The cops came right away when you called, or so Odessa imagined.

High above the Northeast, on the elevated portion of the interstate, Odessa looked down at the the sea of brown and gray rooftops and began to sing. It was a gospel song she had written on a scrap of paper one day:

> If you ever have a problem
> There's a person who will understand
> You can call on Jesus
> He's the man.

If Israel had been with her, he would have covered his ears and said, "Mama, if God had wanted you to sing, he would have given you a voice." But the only person with her this evening was Lorraine, her sister-in-law.

Odessa did not have much to do with Willie Williams these days, but she considered his sister one of her dearest friends. Lorraine was a squat woman with a gentle nature and easy disposition. She was the ideal trash-picking companion—better than Israel, who complained about Odessa's selections and always wanted to go home early. Lorraine had patience and fortitude. She loved to trash-pick as much as Odessa did, and she was healthier. Lorraine would get out of the Caprice and patrol the sidewalks while Odessa drove slowly along, pulling the car close to the curb to trigger the security-light sensors that bathed the trash piles in bright silver light.

Odessa spotted a promising trash pile and pulled over. Lorraine got out and poked at three large black trash bags. She knew by touching them whether they contained household trash or useful clothing. Trash was irregular and lumpy. Clothes felt smooth and neat. These bags contained trash. "Nothing," Lorraine said, and walked on.

On the sidewalk, Lorraine bent down and picked something up. It was an electric weed whacker. It appeared to be in good working order. All that was missing was the string.

Odessa drove on to the next street, where Lorraine disappeared around the corner. It worried Odessa when Lorraine got out of her sight. It was nearly dark now. She had never been seriously threatened while trash picking, but she had experienced a few unpleasant moments. In some townships, the police would stop her and tell her she needed a permit to pick trash. In others, the town watch people would ask her to move on because they knew she did not live there. Once, in the very neighborhood where she was now driving, a white boy hit Odessa in the back with an egg. And more than once in the Northeast, kids would holler, "Trash picker!" and, very rarely, "Nigger!"

"That's all right," Odessa said now. "I'm not ashamed of who I am, and I'm not ashamed to go after what I need."

As she turned the corner, Odessa saw Lorraine beckoning her. She pulled up to a trash pile at the curb, where Lorraine was looking down at three cardboard boxes. Odessa leaned across the seat and saw Lorraine hold up a beautiful navy blue sweat suit, top and bottom intact. Inside the boxes were more clothes, neatly pressed and folded.

"I think we got something here, Dessa," Lorraine said. She pulled out girls' dresses, children's sweaters, and women's pantsuits.

"We hit the jackpot," Odessa said. She got out and unlocked the trunk. Lorraine loaded all three boxes without inspecting them fully. They could do that at home.

Back on Allegheny Avenue, Odessa parked the car in the space in front of number 714 that was informally reserved for the Williams family. She was so weary that she left everything in the trunk. She would have Jim and

Kevin haul it out in the morning. She said good night to Lorraine, who was yawning herself, and the two women agreed that it had been a very good night of trash picking.

Inside the house, Odessa saw that Jim and the other grandchildren had cleaned up the living room. She was pleased but hardly surprised. Jim usually did what he was told, except when his brothers and sister aggravated him. He must have kept them under control tonight, because it was quiet upstairs. Everyone was asleep.

Odessa sat down on her trash-picked sofa to watch the eleven o'clock news on her trash-picked TV. She turned the set on and saw a baby sitting on a dirty blanket in the hot sun. She thought it must be a report from Haiti or Somalia or one of those countries with all the poor refugees. But the announcer was talking about North Philadelphia. He mentioned Fourth and Lehigh. Odessa leaned closer to the set. Fourth and Lehigh was only a few blocks away.

The announcer said a group of homeless people on welfare had set up a camp on an empty lot at Fourth and Lehigh. They called it Tent City. They were protesting the way the city was treating poor people. Odessa saw video clips of babies being washed in a fire hydrant, of people squatting on threadbare sofas under tarps.

She turned off the TV. It pained her to see people suffering, especially children, and especially so close to home. She went upstairs and looked into the two back bedrooms. In one room Delena lay curled on her bed, asleep. In the rear room Jim and Kevin were sprawled on a mattress, their legs entwined. Brian was asleep on a portable mattress along the back wall.

Odessa left them and went into the front bedroom, where Danielle lay sleeping on the pillow at the head of her grandmother's vast king-size bed. Odessa gently moved the girl to one side of the mattress. Then she sat down heavily and opened a small safe that was set against the wall. She reached in and withdrew a tiny Colt semiautomatic pistol. She tucked the gun under her pillow, as she did each night. She had never shot anybody in her life, but she would surely shoot anyone who threatened her or her grandchildren.

She sat on the edge of the bed and, as she did every night, read half a chapter in her Boone family Bible. Then she lay down beside Danielle and listened to the child breathe. Her shallow wheezing sounded like a little teapot. Odessa stroked her granddaughter's cheek and lay her own head on the pillow in such a way that she could not feel the pistol underneath. She closed her eyes and thought about all the children in the world, and about her own grandchildren safe in their beds. She thought about the babies on the sunny lot at Fourth and Lehigh, and just before she fell asleep she wondered: Why doesn't someone help those poor children?

CHAPTER TWO

Quaker Lace

From the fourth-floor window of the old Quaker Lace factory, it was possible to view the whole worn and faded face of North Philadelphia as it sagged toward the horizon. The rooftops were a muddled gray and brown, and the brick row houses leaned like drunks down into the narrow streets. A wild tangle of power lines crossed at severe angles overhead, creating the tight, intricate effect of a weaver's loom. Some of the wires were bowed from the weight of old sneakers that hung by frayed shoelaces, and others were decorated with colorful flags like those commonly seen in used car lots. But even with the jumble of wires and flags, the view from the fourth floor of Quaker Lace was essentially unobstructed. It was not difficult to observe the movements of every single person who passed by the intersection of Somerset and Orkney Streets, which lay just north and west of the towering factory.

On summer afternoons the corner took on a festive air. Mothers wearing T-shirts and tight shorts sat on their stoops and watched their children run madly up and down the sidewalks. Invariably, someone would open up a fire hydrant, and children would rush headlong into the torrents of water, slipping and sliding into little ponds that formed at the curbs. Idle men whose soft bellies spilled over the tops of their short pants pulled out lawn chairs from their living rooms and sat down in the shade next to the stoops. They guzzled beer from quart bottles, and a few of them smoked the crack-laced marijuana cigars known as blunts. The young men of the neighborhood stood on the sidewalk, smoking their own pungent blunts and doing what thousands of young men do in North Philadelphia every day. They sold drugs, chiefly crack in $5 plastic vials and heroin in $10 and $20 blue glassine bags. They stood across from the factory's northwest wall, so close that their cries of "*Perico!*" and "Butter!"—the street slang for cocaine—floated up and through the gutted window frames on the fourth floor.

The big factory—it was actually a fortress of eight connected structures—had been quiet since the Quaker Lace Company had declared bankruptcy, in 1992. But like most of North Philadelphia, it had been dying for many years before that. Quaker Lace was a half century past its glory days, when Philadelphia was the nation's textile center and factories like Quaker Lace provided steady work for European immigrants. Irish, English, and French artisans made doilies and lace inside the complex. Hundreds of people worked the factory, most of them walking to work from row houses nearby. Quaker Lace made curtains and tablecloths sold in department stores across the country. As recently as the 1950s the company was asked to produce a massive tablecloth for a White House dinner. But by 1993, a full ninety-nine years after fine lace was first produced at Fourth and Lehigh, the factory's furnishings and most of its equipment had been sold at auction.

A year later, in the summer of 1994, new life was stirring inside Quaker Lace. The main building, useless as a factory in a part of the city long past its industrial prime, still had value. It was an ideal observation post. And no one needed to observe the activities at Somerset and Orkney more than the narcotics agents charged with controlling the flourishing drug trade in North Philadelphia. It was a simple matter to climb up to the fourth floor from the south end of the factory, set up a surveillance camera, and film the hundreds of drug sales that began with each morning rush hour (many functioning heroin addicts picked up a day's supply on the way to work) and continued well into the long, hot summer nights.

Virtually every drug unit in the city took a turn at the camera. The Drug Enforcement Administration people were there. So was the DEA's hated rival, the federal Bureau of Alcohol, Tobacco, and Firearms, which irritated everybody in law enforcement by horning in on the drug trade when it was supposed to focus on firearms violations. The state attorney general's drug team was there, too, but nobody really complained, because the state narcs were from a small agency desperate for filmed evidence.

One of the people caught by the camera that summer was Osualdo Robles, a huge, lumbering, three-hundred-pound man known on the street as El Gordo, the fat man. The camera loved Robles. He filled up a frame. At age forty-seven, he stood in stark contrast to the skinny teenagers who sold drugs for him. He wore his black hair long and combed it straight back, shiny with hair oil. He had a menacing black mustache and goatee. He wore bold tattoos on both arms. He looked like a criminal, and in fact he had served sixteen months of federal time for selling heroin near a school. The agents knew that El Gordo not only sold drugs but dipped into his own stocks. He smoked crack and shot up heroin. People on the street said his big body soaked up $2,000 worth of drugs a day. What the agents didn't know as they watched El Gordo run the corner that summer was that El Gordo was watching them watch him.

Some of El Gordo's drug workers had spotted the surveillance teams and told their boss. El Gordo found a pair of binoculars, trained them on the fourth floor, and saw the agents camped there. The sight of the narc outpost infuriated him. If the cops stayed there with their camera, he was ruined. How could he run a business with every narc in North Philly filming his operation? The building had to go. It was going to burn.

At Fourth and Lehigh, a block away from Somerset and Orkney, Ray "Trigger" Rodriguez ran a crack cocaine operation. He, too, had heard about the surveillance nest inside Quaker Lace. One day in September 1994, a kid from the neighborhood named Christopher Hernandez told Trigger that El Gordo and some of the Dominicans who sold drugs nearby were taking up a collection to pay to have Quaker Lace torched. Trigger said he'd chip in. In fact, according to Hernandez, Trigger offered him and two of his teenaged homeboys $600 to burn the place to the ground. One afternoon that September, according to one of the teenagers, El Gordo convened a meeting at his row house on North Orianna Street. There he paid one of the three boys $100 as a down payment on the arson.

That night, Christopher Hernandez and two friends collected a milk carton, a soda bottle, and an old antifreeze bottle. They took the containers to a gas station at Fifth and Lehigh and filled each one with gasoline. It cost them $3. Lugging the gasoline, the three boys walked a block to the rear gate of Quaker Lace, forced it open, and crawled inside. They climbed to the fourth floor, where they poured the gasoline over the floor and around the window, spreading the fluid here and there across the entire fourth floor. Hernandez leaned down and flicked his lighter. The gasoline erupted in a wall of flame that nearly engulfed him. As the fire shot across the floor, the boys ran back down the stairs and out toward the roar of evening traffic along Lehigh Avenue.

The fire at Quaker Lace was one of the most spectacular in Philadelphia history. It rapidly consumed not only the main, five-story factory building but the entire complex. There was nothing to stop the advance of the fire because the factory's owner had removed the structure's fire walls just two weeks earlier. Within minutes, the flames shot so high into the night sky that a deep orange glow was visible from miles away. For several blocks in each direction, flaming embers rained down on rooftops. At Third and Cumberland, four blocks away, a building burst into flames. On Lawrence Street, bricks tumbling from the collapsing building crushed a Honda. Thousands of people poured into the streets and watched as the flames leaped from Quaker Lace west across Lawrence Street, north to Orianna Street, and east along Fourth Street. The fire raged across El Gordo's drug corner at Somerset and Orkney, and past Trigger's cocaine operation at Fourth and Lehigh. The people living in the row houses on all sides of the factory ran for their lives and took refuge at Episcopal Hospital, a half mile away.

The first alarm was struck at 9:14 P.M. By ten-thirty, the fire was a beast—eight alarms. Firefighters rushed to the factory from across the city, more than 190 in all. The fire commissioner had to call in eleven off-duty fire companies to protect the rest of the city in the event that another fire broke out. It took until 12:21 the next morning to bring the Quaker Lace fire under control. By then, eighteen row houses, a church, eleven cars, and one corner store had been destroyed. Quaker Lace burned to the ground.

The sight of an abandoned building going up in flames was a daily event in North Philadelphia. The Quaker Lace lot lay at the heart of what the fire department considered a target zone for arson. During the previous year, the fire department had been called to 831 fires in the target zone, or nearly three a day.

A few days after the Quaker Lace fire, in the enduring tradition of Philadelphia lawyers, an attorney named Bruce Marks, who happened to be running for reelection to the state Senate seat in North Philadelphia, invited to his district office the families who had lost their homes. Grieving family members were greeted there by members of Marks's law firm, who urged them to sign fee contingency agreements that guaranteed the firm one-third of any damages awarded in lawsuits.

The following summer, after El Gordo had been sentenced to ten years in federal prison and Trigger Rodriguez to six years, and after they were ordered to pay $3,000 each in restitution from their prison wages, the people who lost their homes to the fire were asked to fill out restitution forms describing their losses. Clara Sims from Lawrence Street wrote: "My home and everything in it, even my Bible." Margarita Echevarria, also from Lawrence Street, wrote: "Total lost."

The lot where Quaker Lace once stood evolved into what urban sociologists call a brownfield, an urban prairie as flat and desolate as the high plains of Nebraska. The row houses that survived the fire now looked naked and exposed, and strangely out of place in a neighborhood where row houses literally leaned on one another for support. People who lived in the surviving homes at the edge of the lot complained that with the massive factory gone, their homes were left exposed to the elements. The winds in summer blasted their walls with dirt and grit, and in winter beat on their doors and windows like a storm across the steppes. But for all the suffering the fire had brought to the factory's neighbors, the charred site was not a total loss for everyone in the neighborhood. For some, the tragedy meant opportunity. For some, even a brownfield had something to offer.

*　　　*　　　*

The first shack to go up belonged to the Gonzalez women, Mariluz and Elba. It rose from the dark dirt near the spot where, one year earlier, the three teenagers had climbed through the rear gate at Quaker Lace to spread their gasoline. The new structure had wood pallets for floors and scraps of lumber for walls. The roof was fashioned from a tarp stretched between a frame formed by several two-by-fours. Inside was a single room, which Mariluz and Elba furnished with a flowered sofa, two portable cribs, two mattresses, and a plastic cooler. It was an altogether unsightly shack, but it was the sturdiest and most dependable accommodation the two women had lived in for many weeks.

Mariluz and Elba were not related, but they had much in common beyond their surname and their Puerto Rican heritage. Each woman had three small children. Each had been plunged into homelessness that summer by a complex set of events that boiled down to a simple lack of cash. Each woman had been abandoned by the fathers of her children. Each lived a life measured in fortnights, the intervals between welfare checks and food stamp allocations they picked up at the state welfare office a few blocks down Lehigh Avenue at Front Street. The proximity of that office, in fact, was one reason they were setting up camp on the Quaker Lace site. The other reason was the fire. It had forced the city to raze and clean the lot. What remained was a flat, cleared expanse along a busy thoroughfare in the middle of a poor but vibrant neighborhood—the ideal location for homeless people on welfare to live together and make a very public statement about their circumstances.

It had been Cheri Honkala's idea to set up on the lot. Cheri, a young welfare mother herself, was a woman who loved to create dramatic and politically charged spectacles. That summer she was at war with society over its treatment of the poor. She sought ways to dramatize how city, state, and federal policies had set destitute people adrift. The lot at Quaker Lace was to be Cheri's boldest tableau yet. She envisioned a small city of the poor rising from the fire's ashes, populated by struggling welfare mothers like Mariluz and Elba, whose meager lives would be on public display.

Whatever Cheri said was fine with Mariluz and Elba. They had known Cheri only a few weeks, but already they looked to her for guidance and even inspiration. Cheri got things done. It was Cheri who got them off the street, Cheri who straightened out problems with their welfare checks, Cheri who kept the child welfare people off their backs, Cheri who made sure their children got food and a place to wash up, Cheri who asked some of the homeless men in the camp to help build the shack.

It was Cheri, in fact, who was responsible for the entire encampment of thirty or forty or fifty ragged, homeless people—the number changed daily—that began spreading out across the Quaker Lace lot that July. Cheri called it Tent City. She set it up to provide a sense of community for the homeless, but more important, to shove homelessness and poverty down the city's throat. The camp was an ugly sore that festered and cried out for attention, even in blighted North Philadelphia. The local TV stations loved it. Their cameras focused in on people washing up at the fire hydrant on Fourth Street and on the homemade signs Cheri had drawn up with messages like *No Housing, No Peace* (in English and Spanish), *House Our Children*, and *Tent City—2 Legit 2 Quit.* The cameras always found the children, too, and it was the dirt-smeared face of Mariluz's baby boy, Demitre, that Odessa Williams had seen on TV the night she came home from trash picking.

This was not Cheri's first Tent City, but it was certainly her most impressive one. It didn't have just tents; it had actual shacks, like the one Mariluz and Elba had built, complete with floors and furniture and even children's. drawings tacked to the wooden walls. Cheri had been setting up encampments across North Philadelphia for four years, ever since she arrived from her hometown of Minneapolis and set up something called the Kensington Welfare Rights Union.

The KWRU was basically Cheri and a phone. She called herself the union's executive director, but she was not paid. She did, however, preside over what she called the group's war council, an ever-shifting band of her dozen closest supporters, most of them homeless Tent City denizens. The group's membership—dues were $5 a year for people on welfare, $10 for everyone else—consisted of people recruited from the streets and homeless shelters and welfare offices, along with well-intentioned college students and churchgoers and well-to-do homemakers from Philadelphia's Main Line suburbs who volunteered to do grunt work and write donation checks. The KWRU, through Cheri's constant if sometimes unfocused agitation, argued that society had a sacred obligation to care for its poor.

Cheri felt abundantly qualified to speak on behalf of the dispossessed. She was a welfare mother. She worked off the books at odd jobs to supplement her welfare check, but she did not report the income to the welfare people as required, because she didn't think it was any of their business. She lived in a $600-a-month row house on Randolph Street a few blocks south of the Quaker Lace lot. That July her phone bill was past due and the electricity was in constant threat of shutoff. She relied on a $158 welfare check every two weeks, plus $200 each month in food stamps, to help feed, house, and clothe herself and her fourteen-year-old son, Mark. She had given birth to Mark when she was seventeen and living in a Camaro. Mark's father was a heroin addict who had abandoned them, much to

Cheri's relief, a month after Mark was born. With that kind of résumé, Cheri thought, she could top any tale of hardship and woe any other welfare mother handed her. Her past was a chit that she played with the poor, and it bought her credibility.

The newspapers called Cheri a homeless rights advocate or a welfare rights advocate. The most common adjectives applied to her were "controversial" and "unorthodox." The bureaucrats responsible for welfare, housing, and the homeless in Philadelphia said worse things about Cheri, chiefly that she was a publicity hound, that she lied and schemed, that she was all mouth and no results. It was not surprising that they said such things about Cheri, for she woke up almost every morning with a new plan to confront and embarrass some poor city functionary. She would gather welfare mothers in a city office and chant and scream until the bureaucrat in charge came out to take a painful and very public tongue-lashing from Cheri. After the city spent millions to build a new convention center next to a soup kitchen, Cheri led a group of homeless welfare recipients who bedded down for the night on the center's polished marble floors. Later, she and a gang of homeless people camped out on the front lawn of a city housing official. That same year, Cheri wrote out and issued an arrest warrant for the governor, saying he had committed crimes against the poor. Earlier that summer, she had chased the mayor down a City Hall corridor and engaged him in a rousing shouting match as press photographers snapped away.

One focus of Cheri's wrath was the city's shelter system. No homeless person could receive housing assistance without first going through the system, which the city used as a vast but tattered net to collect the homeless so that they might be more easily sorted and catalogued. Only then were they eligible to be placed on waiting lists, containing thousands of names, for scarce rent-subsidy vouchers. By requiring all housing voucher applicants to enter the shelter system, the city was able to determine not only whether the applicant was truly homeless but also what mix of social pathology—drugs, alcohol, mental illness, job loss, fire, domestic abuse, AIDs, desertion by a spouse—had contributed to their condition. This process was called certification.

Cheri despised the notion of a bureaucrat's certifying someone's homelessness. She believed people knew damn well whether they were homeless or not, and that the last place they needed to go was a homeless shelter. She regarded shelters as dirty, dangerous, noisy, crowded internment camps. In a city with twenty-seven thousand abandoned properties (thirteen thousand of them in North Philadelphia), she argued, the homeless should be placed in homes, not shelters. For the previous four years, Cheri had stubbornly tried to bypass the shelter system. She and the "war council"—as she called the union's ruling committee— had recruited homeless people from the shelters and helped them break into and take over abandoned houses. In 1993 and again in 1994, she had forced the city to back down and award about three dozen KWRU families vouchers for their takeover houses—without going through the shelter system. But by the summer of 1995, the city had tired of Cheri's tactics. It was taking a stand. There would be no more exceptions. Cheri's people had to go through the shelter system like everyone else. Cheri responded by building Tent City.

Most people who met Cheri thought she had an attitude. She didn't deny it. Who could think more than a minute about the way the richest nation on earth treated its poor and needy, she wondered, without copping a serious attitude? She was one of those people who answered a question with a question. When anyone asked her why she had welfare mothers and their children living on a vacant lot in the broiling sun, Cheri always shot back: "Where the fuck do you expect them to live? These—people—are—homeless! Get it?"

One thing that struck people about Cheri was that she didn't look like a welfare mother, or what people who have never met a welfare mother imagined one should look. She was thirty-two, but she looked younger. She was slender, with long legs and narrow hips and a generous bosom. Mariluz thought she looked like a model. Cheri had long chestnut hair that formed an elegant peak at her crown, where it parted and flowed in thick waves down her back. Her nose was strong and straight. She had high cheekbones (she was part American Indian), a tapered chin, and deep brown eyes set far apart under arched eyebrows. Her lips seemed somewhat full because of a slight overbite and her prominent upper teeth. When she smiled, she looked faintly bucktoothed, but in a cockeyed and intriguing way.

On most days on the lot, Cheri arrived wearing makeup and eyeliner and brilliant red fingernail polish. She looked glamorous, at least in comparison to the sweating, rumpled women living in tents and shacks. But even after Cheri had spent the night asleep in an easy chair on the lot and her hair was mussed and her makeup faded, she looked like a college girl on a sleepover in her neatly pressed denim shirts and tight stonewashed jeans and tan hiking boots. On the hottest days she wore tank tops and cutoff jeans rolled up to the top of her thighs, which exposed her tanned legs and drawing whistles and hoots from young men rushing past in cars.

On this day in August of 1995, the very day that Odessa Williams was driving her Caprice on her trash-picking sojourn down Allegheny Avenue just five blocks north, Cheri was having problems. She sat on a garish, orange-over-green plaid sofa beneath a blue tarp, smoking a cigarette and holding her head in both hands. She had listed each of the day's pressing hassles in a black steno notebook. The word *Problems* was written on the cover.

Problem: cops. They were writing parking tickets for cars that pulled to the curb at Lehigh and delivered donations of bread, canned food, ice, sodas, and sandwiches, stacking them beneath signs that read, *Feed Us,* and, *We Need Donations.* The police also were checking the registration of the rusty red pickup truck that served as the group's unofficial staff vehicle on the rare days that it was up and running. Cheri was convinced the police were part of a covert city plot to cut off her public support. She told somebody to park or push the truck to a hiding spot a few blocks away.

Problem: bees. Two children had been stung by yellow jackets that afternoon. Cheri told their mothers to put ice on the stings and to stop giving the kids sodas. Didn't they know bees love sodas?

Problem: heat. It was the hottest summer in Philadelphia's history. Already, forty-five people had died from the heat. Some of them were homeless people. At Tent City, the heat rose up in shimmering waves from the dirt and rock surface of the lot. The sun produced a yellow haze that settled on the white stones, reflecting a light so bright that it stung the eyes. The effects of the heat and humidity were intensified under the plastic tarps, and the wood walls and pallet floors of the shacks were slick with moisture and grime. Cheri ordered everybody to stay in the shade of the big tarps that were strung across the camp's common areas, even though the yellow jackets tended to lounge there, too. She told mothers of small children to scrape up bus fare and take the children to shopping malls or emergency rooms—anyplace with air conditioning.

Problem: eviction. A man claiming to have bought the lot from Quaker Lace was coming by every day, telling Cheri she had to get her people off his property or he'd have the police do it. Each time, Cheri told the man to either produce some kind of paperwork proving ownership or leave. And each time, the man left, but then returned the next day. "Lying jerk," Cheri said after the man's most recent visit.

Problem: illness. Elba was sick. She lay curled in a folding beach chair under the tarp. Her face was pale and clammy. Beads of perspiration were collecting along her forehead and soaking her black hair. Elba was the third person on the lot to fall sick that week. Cheri dug into her jeans pocket and pulled out a crumpled $5 bill. She handed it to one of the women standing on the green indoor-outdoor carpet beneath the tarp and said, "Go to the drugstore. Buy a thermometer. Not a rectal one." The woman frowned. "Rectal?" she asked. Cheri shook her head. "For the mouth, not the ass," she said. The woman nodded. "Got it," she said.

Problem: food. Enough food had been donated to feed everyone, but most of it had to be prepared. There were rice, beans, flour, and canned meats and vegetables. Cheri had set up a rotation of people who were supposed to make sure the camp's barbeque grills were kept clean and that the charcoal supply was replenished. Other people were supposed to take turns cooking simple communal meals in the camp kitchen, which was a shack with food stacked along three sides and one side left open for ventilation. But no one had shown up to cook dinner this afternoon, and the kids were complaining of hunger. Cheri looked up from her problem list at people lounging in easy chairs and recliners under the tarp. "Any volunteers?" she asked. Everyone stared down at the carpet. Finally a man wearing a T-shirt that read, *Don't Ask Me 4 Shit,* raised his hand and said, "I can cook." Cheri smiled at him and said, "You're hired."

Problem: bureaucrats. Every day, somebody in a suit showed up on the lot, looking ill at ease and trying not to get the gray dust of the lot on his office shoes. There were people from the child welfare agency, from the city office for the homeless, from city License and Inspections, from the mayor's office. They all delivered essentially the same message: The encampment was illegal, not to mention unsafe and unhealthy. Everybody would have to leave, sooner or later.

There was even a midnight visit from a man in charge of the new federal empowerment zone. He told Cheri the city had just received a federal grant of $29 million to help revitalize that section of North Philadelphia. He said it really didn't help him sell the neighborhood to business investors when he had to explain to them why a prime business location like the Quaker Lace lot was overrun with shacks and tents and ragged-looking homeless people. He suggested that Cheri consider "the larger picture of economic development and community revitalization" and, well, leave. He asked her when she planned to move her people out of the empowerment zone. Cheri told him, "When you decide to empower *us.*" Cheri knew the city powers were determined, for reasons both political and altruistic, to get her people off the lot.

Looking down at her problem list, Cheri saw where she had written a single word: "Neomi." Neomi was indeed a problem. She was a homeless welfare mother of six who had brought Tent City unwelcome media attention in July, when the child welfare people showed up with a judge's order. They took Neomi's five youngest kids away from her and put them in a foster care shelter. The city Department of Human Services, citing confidentiality rules, would not say specifically why the children were taken. But Neomi had admitted using crack cocaine. That admission disturbed Cheri. She believed drugs represented the biggest threat to her group's struggle; the war council had put up signs all over the camp: *No Drugs, No Alcohol* and *This Is a Drug-Free Zone.* Cheri knew that accusations of drug use would enable people to dismiss everyone in the group as drug addicts unworthy of concern. But she also knew that many people in Tent City, and even the war council, had past or current drug or alcohol problems. Neomi wasn't the only secret piper on the lot.

The dramatic and public way that Neomi had lost her children sent a wave of terror through the women at Tent City. Welfare mothers were often confused by the mysterious acronyms of various agencies that intruded on their lives, but they all knew what "DHS" represented. Though DHS could not remove children from homes without a court order based on documented evidence of abuse or neglect, most of the women in Tent City believed the agency could arbitrarily snatch their children from them. From what they could see, the kids in Neomi's tent had been faring just as well as any of their own. And they saw what had happened to those kids. "If they can take Neomi's kids, they can take ours," Mariluz told Elba inside their shack one night.

Cheri decided to improve facilities at the lot in order to deprive various city agencies of any pretext to shut down Tent City. But once she walked through the lot, she realized that she and the war council had already done everything possible to make the site habitable. They kept meat and fruit in coolers full of donated ice. The huge loads of bread and bagels that arrived every morning, donated by bakeries and sympathizers, were wrapped in plastic and stored in the shade of the makeshift kitchen, where a hand-made sign read, *Warning! Please. If You Like to Eat, Keep the Table Clean. I'll Be Watching You.* All cooking and eating utensils were washed with soap in water collected in buckets from a hydrant at the corner of the lot. People took sponge baths at the hydrant, and those willing to make the long walk to Cheri's apartment took showers there.

Residents of Tent City were responsible for keeping their living areas clean. Some people pitched sturdy camping tents, then attached additions made of scrap wood and tarps. They had beds with bedspreads and sofas with throw pillows and dressers decorated with little lace doilies very much like the ones Quaker Lace had once produced. Most people dug trenches around their makeshift homes to divert rainwater. They marked their perimeters by lining them fastidiously with the many white stones strewn about the lot, creating the appearance, from a distance, of neat suburban yards. A few people raked the bare spots in front of their homes, leaving careful lines in the dirt that suggested tidiness. Almost everybody put down a mat in front of doors or tent flaps. Most mats had *Welcome* written on them, and on a few were written the words *Home Sweet Home.*

At the western edge of the lot was a shack with pallet floors and a blue awning, called "the school." In the mornings, before the sun began to bake the lot, the children of Tent City gathered there to be read stories and to be served breakfasts of cereal, bananas, and Pop-Tarts. Along one wall of the shack were cardboard boxes filled with used toys and books. Outside, in the full sun, lay a donated plastic wading pool filled with hydrant water that often turned a murky brown from the gray dust that coated the children's little bodies.

Sanitation was the most serious problem facing Tent City. But like so many other needs at the camp, this one was met by someone who magically appeared one day and offered to help. In this case, it was a rumpled little man who called himself Les the Pretzel Man. He had pulled up to the lot in an old gray sedan one day in July and announced that he would be installing two portable toilets. He mentioned that he had been sent to Tent City by the Lord himself.

According to Les, whose full name was Les Hall, he had been watching a TV news report about Tent City when God's voice spoke to him and told him to go there and help the poor. That Sunday, he spoke at his church in the hamlet of Trappe, Pennsylvania, about twenty-five miles north of Philadelphia, and asked for donations. The following week, he walked from door to door in his neighborhood, and then in the neighboring towns of Collegeville and Schwenksville, to collect more donations. Les knew from the news report that Tent City had no toilets, so he used the several hundred dollars he had collected to rent two portable toilets for $150 a month each. He strapped them to the top of his car and delivered them to the lot. Some of the women there, who had been begging merchants to let them use their toilets or had been squatting on the lot at night to pee, grabbed Les and hugged him.

Les called himself the Pretzel Man because it was pretzels that got him off welfare. He had once owned a small rigging business that moved factory machinery. But by the early 1990s, most of the old factories in the Philadelphia area had been shut down or had moved. The rigging business failed, and Les applied for welfare. He received $128 every two weeks, plus $400 in food stamps, to support his wife and child. It shamed him to take welfare, and he hid his new status from friends and neighbors. He had been raised to believe that people went on welfare because they were lazy and refused to work. But as hard as he tried, he could not find anyone to hire a middle-aged rigger.

After a year on welfare, Les said, he asked God to help him find a way to make a living. The Lord directed him to the Bible, where he happened to read a verse that described a recipe for baking bread. That got him to thinking about the people he saw by the side of the road when he walked to the welfare office to pick up his check and stamps. They sold Philadelphia-style soft pretzels from the highway shoulder. If they could make a living selling pretzels, Les figured, so could he. He used his food stamps to buy flour and salt. He experimented in his kitchen with different ways to mix and bake and boil the pretzels. He took some of them to local shops and arranged to sell them there, splitting the profits with the merchants.

In just a few months, he sold enough pretzels from enough stores to get off welfare and expand his pretzel operation. Still baking pretzels in his kitchen, Les began to ship boxes of pretzels to convenience stores and supermarkets under the brand name Les' Pretzels. Later he branched out into specialty pretzels. He sold chocolate-covered pretzels, Star of David pretzels, Christmas pretzels, Easter pretzels, pretzel nuggets. In 1994, the year Les turned fifty, he was awarded the honor of a lifetime. *Philadelphia Magazine*, in its annual "Best of Philly" issue, gave Les' Pretzels the Best of Philly Soft Pretzel Award.

You could see the award on the rear window of Les's car now when it pulled up to the Quaker Lace lot every week. It was a square of yellow-and-green cardboard with a bright gold star that said, *Best of Philly.* People on the lot began to look forward to Sunday mornings, when Les would drive down from Trappe with boxloads of fresh pretzels. Some were for eating, Les told everybody. The rest were for selling on the street. He wanted to provide the Tent City people with a way to raise cash. Some of the welfare mothers sold Les's pretzels on Lehigh Avenue. When Les won the Best of Philly Award again for 1995, they were the first ones to rush up and congratulate him.

There were many volunteers like Les that summer, and they helped keep Tent City alive. Every morning, people would pull up to the curb and unload clothing, ice, canned foods, fresh fruit, and bread. A few churches mailed checks to the post office box Cheri had taken out in the union's name. A young man everyone called Truck Boy showed up to offer the use of his truck. Several well-to-do women from Philadelphia's Main Line, known on the lot as the Main Line ladies, called Cheri and offered to raise money and send provisions. College students from a university-based coalition called Empty the Shelters volunteered their time and vehicles. They were on the lot almost every day, collecting and sorting food, building shacks, offering rides to emergency rooms and welfare offices.

With all the attention Tent City was receiving, Cheri took care to build a certain image for the lot. She didn't want her people to appear helpless and dependent. She welcomed donations, but she wanted the people who contributed to know that the Tent City people were in transition from helplessness to activism. Cheri had some of the Tent City people fashion tiny tombstones out of scrap lumber and set them up in neat rows in the dirt at the front of the lot. On each tombstone they painted their names and the letters *R.I.P.* Cheri said the tombstones represented people who had died "at the hands of the system." They were being "reborn" at Tent City, she said. Through the KWRU, she told everyone who visited the lot, the welfare mothers and the others were transforming themselves from passive victims to people who demanded and received attention.

Cheri regarded welfare as an entitlement in the strictest sense of the word. She believed poor people, particularly single women with children, were entitled to the care and support of a prosperous society. In return, the poor were obligated not only to better their own lives but to contribute to the uplifting of other poor people. Cheri's favorite slogan was "Up and Out of Poverty Now," the name she had given to the first antipoverty group she formed, back home in Minneapolis in the mid-1980s. That principle applied to the KWRU. Cheri required each person who received a benefit from the group—help with the bewildering welfare bureaucracy, food, or shelter—to perform volunteer work for the poor. Every Wednesday, for instance, Tent City residents were required to help with the distribution in the neighborhood of excess food left by donors. And after the group had broken into and taken over abandoned houses the previous two years, the families receiving housing vouchers were obligated to help the union move more Tent City people into more takeover houses.

In Cheri's view, affordable housing was the key to easing the strains of poverty, and thus ending dependence on welfare. People could not consider getting off welfare, she believed, unless they could afford to pay their rent. And with the cheapest rents for roach-infested North Philadelphia apartments in the $400-to-$600 range, who could pay the rent from monthly welfare payments that rarely topped $600 a month even for a woman with three children? Most of the people in Tent City were home-less, in large measure, because there was nothing left from their welfare checks after food, clothing, and other daily necessities were paid for. The most severe cases were single women with children. Cheri saw in them a familiar, repeating pattern: Woman gives birth. Father disappears. Woman looks for work, can't find child care. Woman goes on welfare, can't afford rent. Woman and children become homeless.

Mariluz fit the pattern. The two fathers of her three children had aban-doned her soon after the children were born. She had been receiving AFDC checks for five years (Aid to Families with Dependent Children), since her oldest daughter, Destiny, was born. By now, with three children, her welfare checks had reached $299.50 every two weeks, plus $342 per month in food stamps. She survived, but she felt trapped and stunted by her circumstances.

That spring Mariluz had taken a two-bedroom apartment at B and Indiana Streets, just east of Quaker Lace, for what the landlady said would be $65 per week. But as soon as she moved in, the woman asked for $200 every two weeks, plus a $200 security deposit. Mariluz didn't have it. Her year-old baby, Demitre, was costing her a fortune in Pampers. Desiree, the two-year-old, was growing up fast. She constantly needed new clothes. Destiny, the five-year-old, would soon need clothes and supplies for kindergarten. And Mariluz insisted that her children have new toys, not used ones, so she spent lavishly at Caldor's discount store. When the rent came due on June 1, Mariluz didn't have it. The landlady showed her the door.

Mariluz took the kids to her girlfriend's apartment on Somerset Street. That lasted only a few days because Mariluz, who was not one to back down from a fight, screamed at her girlfriend's live-in boyfriend in a dispute about a grocery bill. Mariluz gathered up the kids and moved next door to an abandoned row house. There she tried to set up housekeeping with the scraps of furniture and kitchen utensils she had salvaged from the apartment on Indiana. But the row house smelled of rot and urine, and the kids complained. So Mariluz got them out of the house early every morning, and they spent their days under shade trees in a park.

One afternoon Mariluz was pushing the kids in a stroller along Fifth Street when a Puerto Rican man handed her a flyer. It read: *Angry About Being Poor? Join the Kensington Welfare Rights Union.* She told the man she was homeless. The man, who introduced himself as J.R., told her the union would find her a place to live if she attended a meeting that night. Mariluz thought J.R. was charming, and she wanted to believe him. She decided she had nothing to lose. She walked that night to the union's walk-up office, on Fifth Street. At the meeting, two things happened that would change the way she lived and the way she thought about herself. She heard about Tent City for the first time. And she met Elba.

Elba, despite her circumstances as a Puerto Rican mother of three on welfare, was quite different from Mariluz. Elba was thirty-one, with a plump, matronly aspect that made her seem much older. She was quiet and diffident. Often her soft brown eyes did not seek out the faces of people who spoke to her. Instead she would stare down at the ground with a humble, expectant expression. She seemed to accept her lot without complaint. And her English was poor. She often did not understand what people were trying to tell her. Instead of asking questions, she withdrew, and sometimes she broke down in tears out of frustration. At the KWRU meeting, she seemed to Mariluz to be on the verge of tears.

Mariluz wanted to shake Elba and tell her to stand up for herself. She believed in confrontation. She had a sharp tongue, in English and Spanish, and she did not care whether people liked her so long as they provided what she demanded. At twenty-nine, she felt much older and more experienced than Elba. She certainly attracted more attention than Elba, with her slim figure and high cheekbones, her dark brown eyes and straight black hair. Where Elba was soft and rounded, Mariluz was hard and angular. But the two women had shared goals: both of them wanted desperately to raise their children in a decent house, to find day care, get some sort of job, and get off welfare.

That night Mariluz decided she would take Elba under her wing. The two women were offered a space at Tent City, with a promise from Cheri that the union would try to find them affordable housing if they agreed to join in the political struggle. Mariluz and Elba were willing to do just about anything to get a house, so they joined the union. Their $5 membership fee was waived because they were homeless.

The two of them decided to share living quarters and pool their welfare checks and food stamps. Elba was getting $248 every two weeks in AFDC payments, plus $277 a month in food stamps. She used the money to raise Yazmenelly, seven, Keishla, three, and Edgardo, two. She had been on welfare since mid-May. It had taken her only about three weeks to receive benefits after arriving in Philadelphia from Puerto Rico in late April. She had left Puerto Rico for the same reason she had ended up in Tent City: she lost her house.

In Puerto Rico, Elba and the children had lived with the parents of the children's father. The man had fathered Elba's children, but he'd shown no inclination to marry her. Elba did not force the issue. She assumed that they would live forever as a couple, whether formally married or not, and raise the children and grow old together. To help make ends meet, she took a job in a laundry.

That spring, the children's father told her something that stunned her. He had another woman. He was moving out to go live with her. Elba was devastated. Not only was she losing her main source of financial support, she was also losing her house. The man's parents told her that, with their son moving out, there was no reason for Elba to remain there.

Elba called her aunt in North Philadelphia, who told her to come north and live with her. She sent the airfare, and by June Elba and the children had settled into her aunt's narrow row house on Diamond Street. But the row house was not big enough to accommodate four more people, and Elba longed for her own place. One day in July a friend showed her a KWRU flyer written in Spanish and urged her to attend one of the union meetings on Fifth Street. Just one week later, she and the children were living in Tent City.

The original Tent City, where Elba and Mariluz shared their first tent, was several blocks east of Quaker Lace, on a cramped lot at American and Berks streets. It lasted only a few days. Cheri decided to shut down the location after several homeless people camped there fell ill. Someone told her that toxic chemicals had been dumped on the lot. She saw dark, oily spots in the dirt next to some of the tents, and she knew it was time to move.

Cheri had been eyeing the Quaker Lace lot all summer. She was particularly intrigued by the concrete stanchions the city had erected around the perimeter of the lot. She envisioned them as billboards for political slogans. Once the stanchions had gone up and the city had cleared most of the debris off the lot—earlier that month—Cheri made her move. She ordered everybody on the American Street lot to pack up their tents and belongings onto the rusted red Tent City pickup. In a matter of hours, the first tents went up at Quaker Lace.

In many ways, the arrival of welfare mothers at Quaker Lace was a fitting coda for the old factory and everything it represented about North Philadelphia's ongoing industrial decline. The collapse of manufacturing and the evaporation of blue-collar jobs had helped give rise to the illegal drug trade. Those who sold drugs had torched the Quaker Lace ruins, which in turn had provided a new home for another unfortunate byproduct of the area's economic collapse—welfare recipients. It was like a forest fire that cleared out old growth and made way for new vegetation. But in the case of the Quaker Lace lot, the new growth was stunted, and it was only scavengers who brought new life to the grounds.

The Quaker Lace fire and the jailing of El Gordo and Trigger had little lasting effect on the drug trade around Lehigh Avenue. The Dominicans who dominated the narcotics operations in that part of North Philadelphia merely put someone else in charge of the corners once run by the two men. Business was as brisk as ever. There was black-cap crack and red-cap crack, "Mercedes brand" heroin and TNT heroin. All day and deep into the night, cars swung off Lehigh Avenue toward the warrens of row houses behind the Quaker Lace lot. Inside, drivers and their passengers clutched $10 and $20 bills. Those who wanted crack asked the boys on the corners for "ready rock," and those who needed heroin asked for a certain brand name, or for generic "dope," or simply for heroin, pronounced "harrow-wine."

Just south of the lot, in the ruins of a city park across Lehigh Avenue, pipers and junkies sat in the shade and smoked crack and shot up their veins with milky gray heroin. It seemed to the people at Tent City that they were hemmed in by drugs. The mothers were particularly distressed. No matter which way they chose to walk their children, whether east toward the welfare office or west toward Hoagie City or the San Juan Meat Market, they had to make their way past either drug dealers or drug abusers. Sometimes mothers like Mariluz would curse them, but they did not seem to notice. The pipers and junkies were lost inside their own heads, and the dealers were busy collecting cash in bulging wads that they wrapped tight with rubber bands and stuffed into their jeans.

Day after day, welfare and drugs coexisted. They were the two largest sources of income in North Philadelphia. They touched everyone. There was hardly a family in all of North Philadelphia that did not have someone on welfare, or involved somehow in the drug trade, or both. In a part of urban America with virtually no functioning economy, two shadow economies had evolved to fill the vacuum.

By the reckoning of the Drug Enforcement Administration, street drug sales pumped at least a quarter-billion dollars a year into a three-square-mile swath of North Philadelphia that includes parts of Lehigh and Allegheny avenues. Like a thousand tiny creeks feeding a raging river, each $5 and $10 and $20 sale built inexorably into a multimillion-dollar empire. Some drug gangs raked in $15,000 to $20,000 a day from a single corner, virtually all of it in small bills.

The cash seeped down into the neighborhoods. The gangs paid elderly men and women to hide their drug and cash stashes in their homes. They hired neighborhood children as "scopes," who stood watch for approaching police. They paid armies of local teenagers to sell drugs on commission, typically $1 for each $5 vial of crack sold. The boys and girls took the money home, where more than one meal or schoolbook or pair of sneakers was paid for with drug money. It was trickle-down capitalism at its purest. Even some of the retail outlets that managed to survive—bodegas, mom-and-pop groceries, video stores, hair salons, hoagie shops—were tainted by drugs. Many of them were simply money-laundering fronts set up by dealers to funnel drug cash.

The neighborhood fed off the drug trade in more oblique ways, too. People charged pipers and junkies a couple of dollars each to use their homes for smoking and shooting up. Longtime addicts set up shooting galleries in abandoned buildings, where they helped junkies mix and cook their heroin, and helped them locate veins suitable for injecting, all in return for a cut of heroin. Drug-addicted prostitutes not only bought their drugs on the corners, but also earned cash by servicing drug dealers and buyers alike. "Needle men" sold syringes and "glass men" sold homemade glass crack pipes. Local artists earned hundreds of dollars from drug gangs, who paid them to paint In Memory ofs, the elaborate, two-story wall murals that paid tribute to gang members killed in shootouts.

One day in 1991, Lieutenant Gallo—the same cop who had helped

Israel Williams clean up the Waterloo Playground—was driving through the neighborhood with a DEA agent. The two men got to talking about how wild and desperate and reckless it all seemed. They looked at the spectral remains of factories and the row houses streaked with graffiti and the strutting corner dealers, and somehow it reminded them of the Wild West. One of them mentioned the Badlands of South Dakota. That was it—"the Badlands." Soon beat cops picked up the nickname and it spread to the press. The newspaper ran a series on the Badlands drug trade. After that even the dealers the cops arrested were calling home and saying they had been busted in the Badlands. Someone opened the Badlands Bar across from a busy drug corner on Clearfield Street. By the summer of 1995, the people at the Quaker Lace lot knew all too well that they were living in the Badlands.

The Badlands, in addition to offering the largest concentration of street drugs between New York and Washington, housed the poorest neighborhoods in Philadelphia. In the census tract that included the Quaker Lace lot, 64 percent of the population lived below the federal poverty line. Per capita income was $4,367. Nearly one out of every three households was headed by a single woman with children. Fully half of all households in the tract received public assistance.

More than $2.4 billion a year in welfare benefits poured into Philadelphia, much of it directed to North Philadelphia. At least 550,000 people, or one-third of the city's population, received some form of public assistance. This meant that Philadelphia's welfare outlay was bigger than that of thirty-eight states.

The chances of moving those huge numbers of people from welfare to work were not good, given the economic realities not only in North Philadelphia but throughout the city. Philadelphia's three-decades-old economic slide was accelerating, continuing to drain the lifeblood of the poor—blue-collar and service industry jobs—from the urban core. Since 1970, Philadelphia had lost a quarter-million jobs. Since 1979, it had lost more than half its factory jobs. Between 1985 and 1994, the city posted sixty-eight consecutive months of job losses. In 1974, Philadelphia provided 27 percent of the region's tax base; by 1994, its share was 18 percent.

Every week, it seemed, another company shut down or moved away, taking with it the very entry-level and semiskilled jobs that welfare recipients were seeking. Botany 500 closed its clothing plant on Broad Street, electing to pay Costa Ricans 70 cents an hour for the same sewing work Philadelphians had performed for $8.50 an hour. Breyers closed its ice cream plant after seventy-one years in the city, saying it was laying off 340 workers in order to "consolidate operations to stay competitive in the marketplace." The Fleer Corporation, makers of chewing gum and baseball cards, shut down its plant, laying off ninety workers. Scott Paper Company, a Philadelphia-area landmark for 116 years, was merged with a rival company, triggering massive layoffs. These and other closings punctuated a long, slow slide in which Philadelphia lost manufacturers that had made brand-name products familiar to every American, from Stetson hats to Flexible Flyer sleds, from Whitman's chocolates and Schmidt's beer to the U.S. Navy warships that once clogged the now-closed Philadelphia Naval Yard. Each shutdown seemed to heighten the sense of desperation among Philadelphia's poor. On those rare occasions when a company opened or expanded in the city, throngs of low-income people lined up to apply for jobs. When a new Marriott hotel prepared to open downtown, the company announced that it would hire 550 workers. Nearly 10,000 people applied, waiting all day in lines that stretched for blocks in subfreezing temperatures. Most of the applicants were on welfare.

At the bottom of the welfare pipeline were single mothers like Mariluz and Elba and the other inhabitants of Tent City, none of whom constituted a census "household." They were the poorest of the poor, the people that passersby saw on the street and hurried past with a look of pity or contempt. Suffocated by the drug culture, beaten down by poverty, they felt isolated and forgotten. Sometimes Cheri would walk into their tents or shacks and shake her head and say, "I'm looking at the most hated women in America—welfare mothers."

Poor, single mothers were not yet the objects of widespread public scorn in 1935, when the modern form of American welfare was institutionalized as a federal entitlement. Mothers of that era typically fell into poverty and dependency not because they had given birth out of wedlock but because their husbands had died, deserted them, or become incapacitated. Their children were deemed worthy of public charity, usually provided by churches or other philanthropic groups. But as the Great Depression deepened, advocates for women and the poor began to demand federal assistance for children deprived of a breadwinner—invariably their fathers. The goal was the opposite of what welfare reform politicians would demand sixty years later. The welfare advocates of the 1930s did not insist that single mothers "earn" their welfare checks by finding a job. On the contrary, they sought cash "relief" payments as a way to keep single mothers at home with their children. The primary beneficiaries of such payments were to be impoverished widows or abandoned wives. These women were objects of sympathy, and sometimes pity, but rarely of contempt, for they were regarded as having stumbled into calamity through no fault of their own. Society did not demand that they find jobs. It insisted that they stay home with their children, supported by welfare payments.

By the first term of President Franklin D. Roosevelt, the concept of federal responsibility for the poor and deprived had evolved dramatically from the days of the Elizabethan Poor Laws. Those sixteenth-century laws had been adapted from England by colonial settlers. They required towns and villages to care for poor women, children, and the infirm, but they demanded work from the able-bodied poor. In Pennsylvania, the first General Poor Law was enacted in 1705; it required people who received "poor relief" to wear on their sleeves a red or blue *P* for pauper. The spirit of the Poor Laws dictated the nature of public assistance in Pennsylvania and most other states until the turn of the twentieth century, when private charities began to provide for the poor.

In 1934, at the height of the Depression, Roosevelt asked Congress to create a "safeguard against misfortunes which cannot be wholly eliminated in this man-made world of ours." A year later, the New Deal was launched with the passage of the Social Security Act, a truly revolutionary piece of legislation. For the first time, the federal government assumed direct responsiblity for the social welfare of its citizens. Even then, critics warned of the potential for fraud, waste, and mismanagement. Roosevelt answered them: "Better the occasional faults of a government that lives in a spirit of charity than the constant omissions of a government frozen in the ice of its own indifference." The key portions of the act provided for old-age pensions and unemployment compensation, along with federal assistance to the blind and other handicapped citizens. But the act also sent federal dollars to help states care for poor and dependent children in their own homes rather than in institutions. The Aid to Dependent Children program was born.

By the autumn of 1995, when Mariluz Gonzalez and Elba Gonzalez were raising their children on welfare checks, the federal welfare program (renamed Aid to Families with Dependent Children in 1962) was deeply entrenched in Philadelphia. Forty-four percent of the state's AFDC recipients lived in the city, most of them in North Philadelphia. Pennsylvania (largely because of Philadelphia) accounted for more than 5 percent of the nation's AFDC recipients.

In Washington that autumn, the political debate over welfare often focused on unwed mothers, who were viewed as the primary drain on the nation's welfare system. Politicians of both major parties tended to portray out-of-wedlock births as a phenomenon largely confined to black teenagers in the nation's inner cities. In fact, the typical unwed mother in America was neither black nor a teenager. She was a white woman in her twenties. Although the out-of-wedlock birth rate for black women was 3.5 times higher than for white women (down from seven times higher in 1970), 60 percent of all births outside marriage were to white women. While teenagers accounted for 30 percent of out-of-wedlock births, women aged twenty to twenty-four were responsible for 35 percent of such births, and women twenty-five and older another 35 percent. And the rate of out-of-wedlock births to teen mothers actually dropped between 1960 and 1995—from 89 to 57 births per 1,000 girls.

Nor was the typical welfare recipient an unwed teen mother. In fact, by far the largest single group of AFDC mothers was comprised of women in their thirties, who accounted for a third of all welfare mothers. Just 7.6 percent of AFDC mothers were teenagers, and a minuscule one-tenth of 1 percent were aged fourteen or fifteen.

In Pennsylvania, the typical welfare recipient was hardly a young, black, unwed mother. Fifty-seven percent of the state's AFDC recipients were white, and 32 percent were black. Just 5 percent of the state's AFDC mothers were under nineteen years old; four out of ten were in their twenties; and two out of ten were in their thirties. Nor was the state's typical AFDC mother a woman who refused to work. Fully a third of AFDC mothers in Pennsylvania had worked within a year of receiving benefits. Only 11 percent had never worked at all. Nor did these women give birth to inordinate numbers of children. The average number of children per AFDC family in the state was 1.6. And the state's AFDC mothers had hardly turned welfare into a way of life. One in four had been receiving AFDC checks for a year or less. Just 7 percent had been on AFDC for more than three years. More than half had never been on AFDC before.

Nationally, the typical AFDC recipient was as likely to be white as black: 38.3 percent white, 36.6 percent black, and 18.5 percent Hispanic. She was anything but a teenaged mother; eight of ten AFDC mothers were in the twenty-to-forty age bracket. She did not give birth to huge broods of children; the average number of children per AFDC mother was 1.9, and the average AFDC family decined from 4 people in 1969 to 2.9 in 1992. She did not make welfare a way of life; three out of four AFDC recipients got off AFDC within two years. And while 42 percent of AFDC women returned to welfare within two years of leaving it, half of them were back off welfare a year later. Only 15 percent stayed on AFDC for more than five years. And the typical welfare mother did not shirk work; one study of women who received welfare at any time over a two-year interval found that the typical mother held 1.7 jobs during that period. Forty-four percent held two or more jobs.

During the 1976 presidential campaign, Ronald Reagan drew roars of approval at rallies by telling the story of a Chicago welfare mother who cheated the system. "She has eighty names, thirty addresses, twelve Social Security cards and is collecting veterans' benefits on four nonexisting deceased husbands," Reagan told one rally. "And she's collecting Social Security on her cards. She's got Medicaid, getting food stamps, and she is collecting welfare under each of her names. Her tax-free income alone is over $150,000." Reagan had a name for the woman: Welfare Queen. He did not coin the term—newspaper headline writers in Chicago had used it in stories about the woman—but he drove it deep into the public consciousness. Although the slur has all but vanished from the political theater today, welfare mothers still hear it from time to time from fellow citizens convinced that welfare dependence is a path to riches.

Reagan was referring to a forty-seven-year-old Chicago woman named Linda Taylor, who had indeed been charged with welfare fraud in 1976. But reporters who looked into the case that year found that Reagan had lavishly embellished a tale of petty fraud. Taylor was charged with defrauding the state of $8,000, not $150,000. She was charged with using four aliases, not eighty. But few voters paid attention to the facts. The image of the big-spending, lavish-living, Cadillac-driving welfare queen was by then thoroughly embedded in American folklore. (Reagan later added a fillip to the welfare queen caricature, spinning a tale of an unnamed young man—presumably black—who purportedly used food stamps to buy an orange and then spent the change on a bottle of vodka).

By the summer of 1995, welfare fraud and abuse were certainly a serious problem; in North Philadelphia, the black market sales of food stamps and the failure to report outside income was widespread. But few people were getting rich from welfare, legally or illegally. The drug dealer or merchant who traded illicitly in food stamps might earn a few hundred or a few thousand dollars a month, not millions. The typical welfare recipient who failed to report outside income was hiding a few hundred dollars a month, not thousands or millions. And a welfare mother with two or three children to feed and clothe might find it difficult to buy a fur coat or champagne with her fortnightly AFDC check whether or not she had squirreled away illegal outside income. She would not likely be able to squeeze enough cash from her welfare checks to buy a new bicycle, much less a Cadillac.

For all the talk in Washington of welfare largesse, welfare checks were shrinking, not growing. Since 1970, inflation had eroded the purchasing power of the average welfare check by 45 percent. In 1970, the average monthly welfare check was $676 in 1993 dollars. By 1993, it had shrunk to $373. Even a family receiving maxium AFDC benefits earned just 42 percent of the federal poverty line. The typical family of three receiving welfare and food stamps averaged $8,000 a year, well below the poverty line.

Even with subsidized housing assistance added to AFDC and food stamps, fewer than one welfare family in five lived above the poverty line.

With Cheri's prodding, Mariluz and Elba began to consider their lives in a different light. Cheri was indoctrinating them. She was insisting that they attend war council meetings and leadership classes. She told them not to be ashamed of being on welfare. Until society created conditions where the poor were provided with housing and jobs, she said, they had every right to take the government's money. They also had a responsibility to ease the plight of all poor people, not just their own.

The KWRU philosophy was literally all around them. Next to their shack Cheri had posted a Tent City information board listing *Diarios Trabajos & Eventos/Daily Chores & Events* in both languages:

1. Drink 6 to 9 glasses of water to stay alive. No joke!
2. Clean up at 9 A.M. and 7 P.M. daily.
3. Go to your scheduled educational classes.
4. Attend daily noon Tent City meeting.
5. Check the schedule for planned demonstrations and meetings.
6. Have petitions signed and pass out flyers.
7. Fight for UNITY at all times.
8. Say at least one nice thing to a brother or sister in the struggle.

Mariluz took the listings seriously. After drifting helplessly for so long, she believed she had found a home at Tent City. When she listened to Cheri, she was filled with a sense of purpose she had never felt before. She began to believe that she might one day live the life she had always dreamed of—as a working mother who lived in a roomy house on a tree-lined street in a safe neighborhood, where her children walked to school and there was enough money for nice clothes and home-cooked meals.

At Cheri's suggestion, Mariluz began to keep a diary. In her shack late at night, when the children were sleeping on their mattress laid out on the pallet floor, she wrote in longhand into a spiral notebook. Though she had dropped out of school in the tenth grade, she was able to express herself clearly. She had never learned to spell properly, but she tried to write the words the way they sounded. She intended to improve her spelling by taking remedial reading classes Cheri said would be starting soon inside one of the shacks at Tent City.

That night Mariluz wrote about Elba and Cheri and the union:

> Elba had been with me from the beginning at the Tent City. Even though we went up and down, we managed to get along and became real close, not only her and me but everybody in the Organization. Even Ms. Honkala. She

show me a lot. I even look up to her because she had a heart. God bless her and her son. Since I started in the Organization I learned how to struggle, organize, politics, attitude and getting a long with other people.

But the hardest thing is being out there with your children trying to learn how to survive and manage to keep safe and happy. But its hard to be happy!

. . . But we manage to get along great. There were 35 of us. How did we survive? People saw the way we were living and felt pity on us, especially for the children. They began to bring food and water to us. And that's how Donation started to come on the lot from neighbors and people who find out about us in the newspaper and on TV and started bringing clothing, pampers, rash cream, baby powders, stuff for women and stuff for men. Dish, pots and charcoal, fold chairs, bed and baby crib, and more.

Sometimes we went with out eating 1–2 day. You know how hard it is when donations didn't come with food. But we manage to struggle.

As one of the hottest Augusts of the century dragged on, Cheri began to realize that life on the lot was growing untenable. The heat was sapping everybody. She feared someone would collapse and die of dehydration or sunstroke, bringing the full wrath of the city down on the union. She knew the city was waiting for a reason to shut down the lot, and the heat was as good as any. During most of the day it was impossible to get anything done because everyone walked off the lot to find a store or public building with air conditioning. At night it was too hot to sleep—not that anyone could think about sleeping with rats scratching at the garbage piles and mosquitos buzzing at the tent flaps and babies squalling from heat rash.

One morning that week, two cops approached Cheri and told her they had caught one of the Tent City men in a stolen car. They described him as a homeless white man driving a late-model Nissan Pathfinder. Ah, Cheri thought, that would be Phil, an intense, ruddy-faced man in his thirties, who lived in a tent at the back of the lot with Amanda, his thin, pale, cropped-haired girlfriend. Cheri had given Phil and Amanda a place on the lot after Phil lost his job and the couple ended up sleeping in a Mercury Cougar. She was surprised that Phil would steal a car. He seemed the quiet, respectful, resourceful type. Every day, he and Amanda walked to a small mail order company in South Philadelphia, where they stuffed envelopes five hours a day for three cents an envelope.

The next day, Phil emerged from police custody with an oozing red wound across his forehead and a decidedly different version of events regarding the stolen car. The way Phil told it, the Pathfinder had been loaned to him by a friend at a car dealership. When Phil pulled the car to the hydrant at the lot to wash up one morning, he accidentally knocked a stereo speaker from the car door. As he bent down to replace the speaker, he said, he felt a hand on his shoulder. He looked up and, as he put it, "All I saw was stars." A uniformed police officer had smashed him across the forehead with a nightstick. As he crumpled to the ground, Phil said, the cop stood with his foot on Phil's neck while a second officer kicked him in the ribs. He was arrested for car theft and taken to Episcopal Hospital, where, he said, the cops told the nurses that Phil was struck while resisting arrest. Then he was booked at police headquarters and charged with car theft and resisting arrest. The next day, after the car dealer appeared and verified that he had loaned Phil the car, Phil said, he was released on a signature bail. But he still faced charges of resisting arrest.

As Phil stood on the lot with the August sun baking the six crimson stitches that held together the wound on his forehead, he poured out his troubles to Cheri. He told her he understood now what she meant when she told Tent City people that society regarded them as less than human. Until he became homeless himself, he had little empathy for destitute people. A few months earlier, he was the property manager for a luxury town house, with a company car and an apartment. Then he injured his knee, got laid off, lost his apartment, got divorced—"one disaster after another," he told Cheri. Now he was homeless, but not until the cops descended on him did he fully realize the implications.

"If I'd been my former self, with a job and clean clothes and all, the cops wouldn't have suspected me of anything," Phil told Cheri. "But they see a poor, homeless person, he's washing in a fire hydrant, driving a nice car— and suddenly he's a dangerous car thief."

Cheri sympathized with Phil, especially after studying the gash on his forehead, but she heard stories like his all the time. She advised him to get a lawyer and file suit. While he was at it, she said, he might as well get a lawyer for her. She was certain the city was about to shut down Tent City.

If eviction came, she thought, it would be as a result of the neighbors. They were complaining more than ever now. In July, some of them had donated rice and beans and the use of their bathrooms. But now they were tired of the noise, worried about the increasing numbers of homeless people arriving daily, and weary of the attention Tent City was attracting from the police.

One afternoon, a woman named Marie Murphy, who lived in a row house at the eastern edge of the lot, leaned out of her front door and unleashed a long diatribe loud enough for people in Tent City to hear. She had been there thirty-five years, she said, and never had she seen such filth and squalor. She had thought things could not possibly get worse after her husband, son, and daughter had lost their jobs at Quaker Lace and after the factory was torched. But they had.

"The whole lot is a pain in the neck," Murphy said, squinting in the bright white light that reflected off the stones in the lot. "I'm sick of smelling garbage and shooing flies. These people throw all their crap around, their bottles and crap. The other day, seven-forty-five in the morning, a lady comes out with her baby, pulls down her pants, and takes a pee on the street in front of my house. And the men. The men are too lazy to pee in the Porta Potti's. They pee right on the ground. They don't have to live here. Why can't they go to shelters?"

Cheri did not want to lose the support of the neighbors. She called everyone together and urged them to keep their trash picked up and to use the portable toilets. But she knew she could not hold on to the lot forever. She began to consider other locations.

That afternoon, as Cheri stood next to Lehigh Avenue and wrote in her notebook the topics she wanted to discuss at the war council meeting that evening, a car drove slowly to the curb. Cheri looked up and saw a big woman driving a station wagon. The woman stared hard at her and screamed, "Yo, bitch! Why don't you take care of your kids? Get a fucking job and put 'em in a house!"

The woman pulled away, and Cheri was too shocked to scream back at her.

That morning, Cheri had found herself at the center of another minor crisis. She had been drinking coffee at the Lehigh Avenue McDonald's, discussing the day's schedule with some of the Tent City people, when three boys grabbed an elderly customer and yanked a gold necklace from her neck. As the boys bolted through the front door and into the parking lot, everyone inside the restaurant tried to pretend nothing had happened. Nobody moved. Cheri leaped up, ran outside, and chased after the kids. It was quite a sight—a woman in a white T-shirt and blue jeans and hiking boots trying to run down three skinny kids in sneakers. Cheri wondered what she would do if she caught them, but they were too fast and soon she gave up and stopped. Back inside the restaurant, she saw the old woman sobbing and saying the necklace had been a gift from her son. Cheri felt like weeping, too.

The same day, Cheri got a notice from the welfare department. She was being cut off. It was the latest in a series of notices informing her that her welfare benefits were about to be terminated. Cheri was hardly surprised. On her last visit to her caseworker, she had seen in her file a thick set of newspaper clippings about her work with KWRU and Tent City. It was during that visit that she was first told she was being terminated for (1) failing to show for her last appointment and (2) failing to provide her son's birth certificate.

The latest notice listed a third reason: the department had learned that Cheri had withdrawn money from her son's college account. Cheri could not deny that. The rent was past due, so she had taken $600 from Mark's $2,000 college fund to pay it. She did not report the withdrawal, and now she was caught. She decided not to fight it. She had been wanting to get off welfare anyway. It wasn't worth the few dollars a month to have to play by rules that required her to report to total strangers the most personal details of her life. She was tired of hiding her income, tired of worrying about getting caught.

Cheri was worried about her son, Mark, too. The kids at school ridiculed him and called him Shelter Boy. He cringed every time his mother was interviewed on TV or in the newspapers, screaming about injustice to the poor. Mark refused to accompany Cheri to the grocery store because he didn't want anyone to know his mother got food stamps. Once, when Mark and Cheri were homeless and moving from shelter to shelter, his teacher asked the kids in his class to draw pictures of their homes and neighborhoods. Mark drew an elaborate fantasy house and neighborhood full of happy, prosperous people.

For months, Cheri had wanted to prove to herself and to Mark that she could support him and Tent City without welfare. She was concerned about the loss of her welfare medical benefits, especially if she or Mark fell ill. But in the long run, being freed of welfare's constraints made it easier for her to help others challenge the system. Without the welfare bureaucracy holding the threat of termination over her head like a sword, she would no longer feel like a hostage.

But Mariluz had plenty to fear; the welfare department was closing in on her. She, too, had received a notice from the welfare people. She, too, was threatened with a cutoff. And her notice was more than a week old. It had been mailed to her last known address, the abandoned row house on Somerset Street. Mariluz had found it when she walked to Somerset that morning to check her mail.

The notice said Mariluz was being cut off because she had missed her last appointment. But she didn't even know she had had an appointment because the letter notifying her of the date and time was stuck inside the doorway of the abandoned house, unopened. Mariluz showed both letters to Cheri and asked her what to do.

Cheri hugged her and said, "Don't worry, they can't cut you off." She told Mariluz to go down to the welfare office and make an appointment to appeal the ruling. She should tell them the truth: She was homeless. She couldn't get her mail. She couldn't be cut off for something she had no control over. They would be compelled to reinstate her benefits, Cheri told her, plus reimburse her for any missed checks.

As much as Mariluz needed her welfare check, she put off the trip to the welfare office. She had more pressing emergencies. For one thing, a hurricane was bearing down on her family's village in Puerto Rico, and all the phone lines were down. For another, a woman had run onto the lot that morning with a message that Mariluz's sister had hanged herself in prison. Mariluz spent the entire morning riding buses to reach the prison, only to be told that her sister was very much alive. "Somebody's sick idea of a joke," Mariluz said when she returned.

As soon as she walked back into her shack, Mariluz was stunned to see Neomi baby-sitting all six children. She didn't trust Neomi with Neomi's kids, much less her own. Where was Elba? "Hospital," Neomi said. The Tent City truck, by now repaired, had rushed Elba to Episcopal Hospital after she fainted inside the shack. As it turned out, it was nothing more than heat exhaustion and a bad urinary tract infection. But Mariluz could not help wondering what would happen to the kids if both she and Elba fell sick and somehow DHS got wind of it.

Mariluz sat down in a heap, feeling fatigued and beaten. Neomi looked up, her face slick with sweat, and told Mariluz that someone had stolen a tape recorder from her tent. She seemed to expect Mariluz to solve the burglary. Mariluz thought about Cheri's lectures on working together and helping others. She thought, too, about how sad and empty she felt. She sighed heavily and said to Neomi, "Get out of here and leave me the fuck alone."

For the rest of the day, Mariluz sat sweating inside the shack. Soon Elba came back from the hospital, looking gray and drawn. The two of them sat on their mattress all afternoon and listened to the babies cry, watching helplessly as the older kids ran in and out of the shack, tracking dust and trailed by flies.

Cheri found them sitting there that evening when she came to tell them that she was calling a war council meeting. Mariluz and Elba were not formally members of the war council, but Cheri usually invited them to meetings. This was an important meeting, she told them. People were beginning to lose interest in Tent City. The TV crews had stopped coming by and the newspaper stories had dried up. Tent City couldn't afford to become irrelevant. And so, Cheri told them, the union was planning a major public demonstration that would jolt the entire city.

That evening, the war council brought together the main KWRU leadership at the lot. Among them was Chicago, a thin, wiry black man with a bushy black beard and no front teeth. He was wearing violet-tinted sunglasses and a T-shirt with a message that read, *I'm Stoned and I Can't Get Up.* Chicago, whose real name was Leon, had been with the union for some time. He was a veteran of many tent cities. He had become homeless, he said, because he was unable to work due to frequent epileptic seizures. He had applied for Supplemental Security Income but was turned down because, as he put it, "They said I was capable of doing little ol' jobs like stuffing sunglasses into plastic envelopes." While recent changes in state welfare laws meant that single, childless men could not receive public assistance, Chicago did receive medical assistance. He often showed people his Greater Atlantic Health Service ID card, telling them, "Same medical plan as city workers!" Cheri considered Chicago reliable and loyal, and often she left him in charge of the lot in her absence. He was also a valuable worker, for he was gifted at building sturdy shacks out of absolute junk. It was Chicago who had helped design and build the snug shack where Mariluz and Elba slept with their children.

Crouched next to Chicago under the tarp, squatting on her haunches, was Katie. Some people in Tent City called her Grandma. At forty-nine, Katie was by far the oldest person on the war council. In truth, she looked older than forty-nine. Her thin face was a maze of deep wrinkles and crevices. Her hair was pale and lank, and on most days it clung to the sides of her head in a damp lump. Her bony frame and missing front teeth gave her the look of a frightful hag, but actually she was quite gentle and soft-spoken. Cheri admired Katie not only for her willingness to help with any chore, but also for her steadfastness. Katie, along with her daughter and grandchildren, were among the homeless families who had been awarded housing vouchers as a result of the union's home takeovers the year before. They lived now in a subsidized apartment, but Katie spent her days and many of her nights on the lot.

Katie was flanked under the tarp by a Hispanic couple, who sat holding hands. Tara was a plump young woman with a soft, pleasant face and bright hazel eyes. Her boyfriend, J.R., was a fast-talking, wisecracking young man with thick curly hair and a rakish smile. It was J.R. who had charmed Mariluz when he saw her on Fifth Street and gave her the KWRU flyer. Cheri had encountered J.R. and Tara earlier that summer, when Tara wandered into the union offices one night and broke down in tears. The abandoned house where she and J.R. had been living had been sealed by the city and declared unfit for human habitation. After sleeping a few nights in a park, Tara had become separated from J.R. after J.R. left to find work. Cheri agreed to help her find her boyfriend. They drove around all night until they found J.R. on Frankford Avenue, unloading salt for $5 a day. Cheri took both of them to Katie's house, where they camped out until they were able to set up their own place at Tent City.

Now Cheri told the war council of her plans. She began by saying that while the city might be willing to tolerate a Tent City in North Philadelphia, it could not abide a KWRU encampment in downtown Center City, home to office towers and upscale shops and yuppies living in town houses. Think of it, she said—a Center City Tent City. That would get everybody's attention.

"If the city wants us to escalate the struggle to another level, that's what's gonna happen," Cheri told the group. "And the way we do that is to create the illusion that Tent City is moving to Center City on a permanent basis. The city knows we have a history of crazy stunts, so they just might believe it."

Cheri conceded that she had no intention of moving permanently to Center City, and everyone under the tarp looked relieved. But she was more than willing to threaten the city with an unsightly Tent City faux camp. And she had just the place in mind. It was a flat expanse, just like the lot, but it was manicured and verdant. It was a place that attracted tourists from around the world. And while Philadelphia might not care about its poor people, Cheri told them, it damn sure cared about its tourists.

When she announced the site for the new, temporary Tent City, it sounded so audacious that everyone sat in silence for a moment. You could hear the children splashing in the wading pool and the dull drone of mosquitos attacking the tarp. Then everyone began to laugh and stomp their feet, and even the crackheads in the park across Lehigh Avenue looked up from their pipes at the sharp sound of applause and war whoops erupting from Tent City.

CHAPTER THREE

Check Day

All that night Odessa was seized by a nightmare. It was dark and violent and so disturbing that the strength of it woke her. She sat up in her bed and tried hard to drive it from her mind. She wanted desperately not to remember it. She buried her head in her hands and prayed to God to reach down and draw the visions out of her. She began to feel sick to her stomach, and deep inside she sensed something being pulled from her. Then she felt light-headed. At that moment she knew that God had cleansed her and made her forget. She lay back down and pulled Danielle's hot body close to her. She felt empty, and soon she let herself be pushed back into the deep void of sleep. By morning, when I called on her, she was not able to recall a single detail of the nightmare that had so terrorized her just hours before.

I had come to take Odessa to the welfare office. It was check day. Under the numerical system set up by the Department of Public Welfare, Odessa was a Number Three. The numbers ranged from zero to ten, determined by the last digit of a recipient's welfare account number. Each digit assigned its owner to a certain day on which a welfare check was to be issued. Number Three happened to fall on this particular Wednesday, a late August day so hot and still that even by early morning a fine yellow haze had begun to suffocate Allegheny Avenue.

Odessa was sitting in the shade of her front porch, rocking gently in a rusted metal lawn chair. She was sipping hot coffee from a Dixie cup. She had bought it, as she did most mornings, for fifty cents from the Spanish man around the corner who sold fresh coffee from his porch. Buying the coffee was part of a daily routine that settled Odessa's nerves and added a certain tenuous structure to her life. In the afternoons she would pay another Spanish man a dollar for a *pincho* dripping with spicy grilled meat. And toward evening, when the hint of a breeze had begun to insinuate itself along the sidewalk, she would send one of the boys with a dollar to buy a bag of hot peanuts from Donald the Peanut Man. The rich aroma of charcoal and smoldering peanut shells at dusk was Odessa's regular reminder that another day was dying.

That morning, Odessa blew on her coffee and described to me the saving way that her nightmare had been driven from her by prayer. She sensed that the dream was somehow woven around a threat to her grandchildren. Beyond that, she could not remember anything about it. Even so, a vague dread clung to her. She debated whether to leave the children alone in the house while she went to pick up her welfare check.

She loved her neighborhood, but she was the first to admit that it could be a menacing place. Danger struck in strange ways, and at the oddest moments. One day her daughter Elaine was walking along the sidewalk toward Odessa's porch when a neighborhood man named Willie looked at her and said, "What's going on?" Elaine answered, "I don't know, Willie, what's going on?" Willie said, "*Here's* what's going on," and he sliced open Elaine's forehead with a hunting knife. Another time, her nephew Stanley asked the Puerto Ricans at Seventh and Allegheny not to sell drugs while neighborhood kids were walking to school. They smashed his skull with a baseball bat. When Odessa's niece Robyn went to help, one of the dealers punched her in the face, breaking her nose.

"Nothing in this neighborhood surprises me anymore," Odessa said from her porch, pointing to the spot at the curb where the dealers had attacked her niece and nephew.

A person could get killed just walking down Allegheny Avenue. She had seen it happen: One night she overheard some boys on the sidewalk plotting to kill someone over a drug dispute. The next night, a boy from across the street was, in the terminology of the neighborhood, shot dead "outright." From her porch Odessa could see the boy's bloody face pressed against a darkening pool that spread across the pavement.

Murders were as common as car wrecks in her neighborhood. Fairhill, which incorporated Odessa's stretch of Allegheny Avenue, had by far the highest murder rate in Philadelphia—123 per 100,000 people, or nearly double the rate of the city's second-most-murderous neighborhood. The rate for Philadelphia as a whole was 28 per 100,000. The national rate, so historically high that politicians in Washington were demanding more prisons and tougher sentencing, was about 9.5 per 100,000.

In Fairhill, many among the dead were children. On a row house wall along Susquehanna Avenue, a few blocks south of Odessa's home, some people from the neighborhood had painted a towering mural on a white row house wall. Printed above four lists of a dozen names each was the message *End Your Silence, Stop the Violence.* The names belonged to local children who had died violently, listed alphabetically from Sultan Jihan

Ahmad to Stanley Zuber. Odessa told herself that there was no room for anybody else named Williams in the space on the wall between the names of Shawn Wells and Chedell Ray Williams. No child of hers would ever have his name on a death mural. The most important thing she did every day was to keep her grandchildren safe and alive.

In a way, it was the neighborhood's violent patterns that had brought me to Odessa's row house door. I had passed her home many times over the years. For almost four years, I had reported on the Badlands drug trade and the lethal street codes among the young men who lived there. I had written extensively about four people whose lives brushed the periphery of the Williams clan. There was Lieutenant Gallo, the cop who helped Israel drive out the Dauphin Street Posse. There was Junior, a cocaine corner boss who ran a drug crew a block north of Odessa's house. There was a young street dealer named Boo Sampson, who sold and smoked crack on the same corners as Odessa's nephews Boo-Boo and James. And there was Bernadette, also known as Chocolate, a drug-addicted prostitute who shared syringes, sex partners, and jail cells with Odessa's wayward daughter Brenda.

All four people had ties to the man who introduced me to Odessa: Tony McCreary, a driven, charismatic young street preacher who was a legendary figure on the streets of North Philadelphia. Pastor Tony, as he was known to thousands of neighborhood residents, knew most of the narcs and corner bosses in the Badlands. He had helped wean Bernadette and Boo from drugs for a time. He had tried and failed to persuade Odessa's son Darryl to stop smoking crack. All three addicts—Bernadette, Boo, and Darryl—had joined McCreary's New Life storefront church on Sedgley Avenue, where the pastor ran a drug recovery program and delivered thundering sermons on Sundays.

Odessa, too, had joined New Life, primarily because of her grandchildren. The pastor had recruited Jim and Kevin into his truck-bed gospel show, known as *Super Snoopy*, performed by a traveling children's Bible troupe that set up on street corners throughout the Badlands. Jim and Kevin had heard the pastor's amplified voice one afternoon, reverberating from the truck bed and bouncing off the row houses along Allegheny Avenue. The boys wandered over to watch, drawn by the pastor's voice and by the huge cartoon Snoopy character painted on the side of his truck. Within a week the pastor had persuaded the boys to help him pass out candy and toys as prizes for his children's games. Odessa was intrigued by the pastor's energy and his detailed knowledge of the Bible, and soon she was attending his Sunday services.

It was during that period that Odessa's row house caught fire. One morning in 1987, her grandson Kevin, who was four at the time, sat on a bed in the rear upstairs bedroom. He was amusing himself by striking matches and flipping them beneath the bed. One of them smoldered and ignited a rug, which went up in flames that spread across the entire floor and up into the roofline. Most of the top floor and roof was destroyed. The next day, the pastor showed up with volunteers from the church. They brought hot food and bottled water. They also brought lumber and drywall, paint and furniture. Within days they had rebuilt and refurnished Odessa's top floor.

Odessa still remembered how the pastor and the church people were smeared with grime when they had finished. "You talk about some black white folks when they were done with that mess," she said. She emerged from the disaster with a renewed fear of fire, and she tried to instill that same fear in her grandchildren. She made them watch as she pressed a smoldering match to each fingertip on Kevin's right hand, the very hand that had struck the match that burned his grandmother's home. Kevin howled in pain, and Odessa felt like crying herself. But she believed extreme measures were required to drive home the danger of fire. Kevin's fingertips blistered and healed, and he never touched a match again.

Odessa came away with something else from the fire: an enduring respect for Pastor McCreary. Never in her life had someone stepped forward so boldly to help in a time of crisis. Now, eight years later, the pastor was suffering through his own crisis. After counseling hundreds of addicts, he himself had succumbed to crack. In the midst of a divorce and a bitter internal struggle over control of his church, he had begun buying crack from Badlands dealers and smoking it in his car. Soon both his marriage and his ministry collapsed. He underwent drug rehabilitation, took a job as a construction laborer, and set about rebuilding his ministry. Among the parishioners who continued to support him was Odessa. She knew through Brenda and Joyce that it was the drug that was evil, not the user. Whenever someone in the neighborhood spoke badly of the pastor, Odessa would stand up for him. She told everyone that Pastor Tony had redeemed himself, that his ministry was coming back, that every person could benefit from his teachings. Often she wore a red satin windbreaker the pastor had given her, the one with the cartoon dog and the words *New Life Church*.

On this Number Three check day in August, the pastor dropped by to see Odessa. The two of them chatted on her porch, reminiscing about their days together at New Life and remarking on how the top floor had been so thoroughly rebuilt that you would never know it had once been gutted by fire. The mention of the fire prompted Odessa to reach out and hug the pastor and thank him again for what he had done. And she promised, as she had many times before, that if she ever came into serious money, she would give him enough cash to build a new church. Even now, she told him, she was willing to donate a few dollars from each welfare check to his ministry.

"That check is for your grandchildren," the pastor said, squeezing her hand. "But when you come into a big pot of money, I'll be right over to get my share."

"And you better believe I'll have it waiting for you," Odessa said. "I wish I could give you a million dollars right now."

The pastor smiled and hugged her. He was a fit-looking man of thirty-six, with wiry blond hair brushed straight back, a strong jaw, and piercing blue eyes. Some people thought he looked like a young Paul Newman. He was a fixture on the streets of North Philadelphia, where children trailed in his wake as he walked the Badlands on his door-to-door rounds. He stood out like a beacon in the black-and-Hispanic neighborhoods, a young, vigorous white man dressed in baggy hip-hop slacks, a sport shirt, and the latest in high-top sneakers. At the sight of the pastor, people would shout from their stoops, "Yo, Snoopy!" and, "Yo, Pastor Tony!" And Pastor Tony would grin and slap palms and shout, "What's up, what's up?"

To Odessa, the pastor was like a son and a mentor. She fussed over him, chided him about his diet of junk food, worried that he was trying to do too much for too many people. But she also listened to him when he quoted to her from the Bible. She had never met anyone who could draw so many pointed lessons for her life from the scriptures. Often, when she read her Bible verse by verse late into the night in her upstairs bedroom, she thought of Pastor Tony. She felt blessed by his concern for her, by the intensity of his attempts to help Darryl break free of crack, by the moving ceremony he had conducted when he presided over Joyce's wedding.

Now the pastor laughed and thanked Odessa for her million-dollar promise. "Odessa, you are good people," he told her. "The Lord is watching over you."

"Well, right now," Odessa said, rising from her porch chair, "He's gonna watch me pick up my check."

The financial exchange was located inside a squat green building smeared with white graffiti. It was a check-cashing business, one of many in the city that contracted with the state Department of Public Welfare to disburse bimonthly welfare payments. The bulk of the cash went to recipients of Aid to Families with Dependent Children, or AFDC, which is what citizens and politicians alike mean when they refer to "welfare." Odessa and her four grandchildren were among some 240,000 people in Philadelphia receiving AFDC cash. That meant at least 15 percent of the city's population was dependent every two weeks on a trip to a financial exchange center.

Inside the exchange, Odessa saw four lines of people waiting to be served by four women who sat behind thick Plexiglas shields, looking bored and vaguely put upon. The lines were long but orderly, and they moved quickly. Virtually everyone in line was black or Hispanic, for the exchange was in the heart of North Philadelphia. Most of the recipients were women trailed by sleepy-eyed children. They scolded their kids, took thumbs out of their mouths, wiped their snotty noses. The long, dark room was filled with the sounds of idle chatter. Many of the people in line knew one another, at least by sight, connected month after month by their shared Number Three. With the quiet conversation, the sudden squeals of children, the slow shuffle of feet moving forward, and the steady *snap, snap* of the clerks counting currency, the place had the look and sound of a bank.

Odessa selected the shortest line and, to pass the time, read the signs on the walls. One showed a drawing of Uncle Sam below the message *We Want to Cash Your Income Tax Check.* Another sign read, *Count All Money and Food Stamps Before Leaving Window.* Others read, *Children to Be Kept at Side or Outside,* and, *Today Is Number Three.* It seemed to Odessa that the welfare people spent too much time making signs and not enough time issuing checks. She hated waiting in line; it made her legs ache and her feet swell, especially on days as hot and miserable as this one.

As the line inched forward, Odessa saw a neighbor woman and waved at her. The woman smiled and waved back. Nobody minded being singled out in the welfare line, because so many people from the surrounding neighborhoods were on welfare. In the next line, in fact, was one of Odessa's nephews, who was waiting to pick up his food stamps. Odessa yelled his name. He looked back and grinned and shook his fist at her.

Odessa made a fist back at him. She loved to clown with all her relatives. The Boones were a roughhouse kind of family.

"Let's go at it right here!" she hollered, and she feigned a move toward her nephew. "Or would you rather go outside where all these people won't see you get a butt whipping from an old lady?"

Everyone in line was laughing now and watching the nephew, who raised both fists in a boxer's pose and yelled out, "Just let me get my stamps and I'll fight you for your check!"

"I'll whip you, and take your stamps, too!" Odessa said, but then she turned away and moved to take her place at the window, where the woman behind the glass was beckoning her forward.

Odessa produced her state welfare card with her color photo, which she hated because her hair looked flat and ragged, and because she was only half smiling. The clerk punched Odessa's welfare account number into the computer, which spit out a pink slip of paper containing Odessa's name and the cash amount due: $201.50. Odessa signed it. The woman counted out ten crisp $20 bills, a single dollar, and two quarters, and handed the whole amount to Odessa. She also passed her a tan coupon book stamped with a drawing of the Liberty Bell and the words *U.S. Department of Agriculture Food Coupons*. Inside was $84 worth of food stamps.

Odessa stuffed the coupon book into her purse. She folded the $20 bills and tucked them under her blouse and beneath her bra. The money had to last her the next two weeks, and thieves were everywhere.

She walked outside, where a stocky young man blocked her way.

"Stamps!" he yelled out. "Stamps! Seventy!"

Odessa pushed her way past the man, staring at him with contempt. The man shrugged and shouted "Stamps!" at the next woman who walked through the doorway. Just inside, a security guard was bent over the *Daily News*, ignoring the stamp man as he offered to pay cash for people's food stamps.

Odessa despised stamp men. They were neighborhood hustlers who bought food stamps for less than their face value. This particular stamp man was offering a good price—seventy cents on the dollar. Some offered just fifty cents. Odessa knew some welfare recipients who sold their stamps this way, usually to raise cash for drugs. Her daughter Brenda had done it before Odessa took over her AFDC payments and stamps. Odessa knew, too, that it wasn't only stamp men who bled the system. Plenty of merchants paid cash for stamps at discount, then turned them in for the face amount.

Even some drug dealers accepted food stamps, though at steep discounts. Over on North Hutchinson Street, a few blocks from Odessa's place, the Rivera gang accepted food stamps for green-cap crack, though at just twenty cents on the dollar. Some gangs offered to sell drugs on credit to welfare recipients; they required addicts to hand over their welfare ID cards until check day, when the dealers would accompany them to the financial exchange to recover their cash—plus interest.

The whole wicked business sickened Odessa. People like the stamp men only fed the notion that welfare recipients were cheats and drug addicts, when in fact most of the welfare people she knew played by the rules. She thought of welfare as part of God's bounty. To cheat the system would be to cheat the Lord.

The drug dealers were the worst offenders, she thought. Many of them had wives and girlfriends on AFDC, though Lord knows they didn't need the money. But there was no way for the welfare people to know that the women were supported by their drug-dealing men. Dealers did not exactly report their income. So as far as the welfare department knew, it was providing checks to needy women with dependent children. Odessa would feel her blood pressure rise whenever she drove by the dealers' row houses and saw the elaborate new iron grillwork that had transformed their homes into fortresses against police raids. She would shake her head at the sight of a new BMW or Lexus parked out front.

"They ruin it for people who really need welfare—and there's plenty that do need it," Odessa said as she left the exchange center.

With the cries of the stamp man still ringing in her ears, Odessa walked to the deli next door. Inside she ordered the same treat that she allowed herself every time she picked up her cash. She sat down and ate the $1.75 special—a spicy hot sausage with relish, catsup, and onion, plus a cup of coffee with a free refill. It seemed extravagant, but she needed it to help steel herself for the next two weeks. There would be many days ahead when she did not have $1.75. So now she luxuriated in the sweet, hot spray that filled her mouth when she bit into the steaming sausage. As she ate, she told herself that she was actually saving money. The sausage so satiated her hunger that she decided she would forgo her usual lunchtime *pincho* and her dollar bag of roasted peanuts that afternoon.

Back home, Odessa climbed the steps and collapsed into the lawn chair on her porch. Her legs ached from the long wait in line. She was out of breath. The heat and humidity aggravated her asthma. She needed her nebulizer. She reached behind her and banged on the living room window and shouted, "Jim! Bring me my machine!" Jim hauled the contraption out to the porch and plugged it in. Odessa took the mouthpiece from him and inhaled deeply. Soon the knot in her chest faded and she began to breathe normally. Now she could think about money.

She tried to set up a budget for the next two weeks. The way she figured it, with her AFDC check and stamps, and with $980 she had received on the first of the month for Brian's and her SSI payments, she would have $216 left to pay for food and incidentals. Most of her income was already allotted for the phone bill, which was fattened by Darryl's collect calls from prison and her own calls back home to Georgia. She had to pay for gas for the Caprice, Pampers for the twins, sneakers for the boys, snacks for the kids every afternoon, and her past due gas bills from the previous winter.

Her biggest outlays were for the electric bill, which usually ran $280 a month, and for past due bills. She tried to cut back on electricity, but she needed at least two hours a day to prepare meals on her electric stove. And the kids needed hot water from the electric water heater for their baths. She had taken enough cold baths as a child; her grandchildren deserved better. She also ran her trash-picked air conditioner all day long in July and

August. The device seemed to drink up electricity, but she needed it to help control her asthma, and Kevin's and Brian's too.

Odessa reached beneath her blouse and withdrew the welfare money from her bra. She counted out $60 for Integrity Meats on Front Street and tucked it beneath her left thigh. Integrity had the cheapest bulk meat in the neighborhood. For $60, she could buy a case of turkey wings, a case of turkey legs, twenty pounds of chicken wings, a package of oxtails, a box of chicken backs, and four packs of pork chops. Most of it she would store in her big upright trash-picked freezer.

She took another $20 bill and slipped it beneath her right thigh. That was for Murray's food store. Murray's was having a special—buy one pack of frozen meatballs, get one free. For $20 she could buy the meatballs, plus frozen beef patties and several boxes of mashed potato mix.

She counted out another $120 and dropped it on the chair between her legs. That was the amount she had spent the previous month at SAV-A-LOT, the big discount food center. The money would have to pay for another month's supply of nonperishables, such as canned goods, toilet paper, barbeque sauce, catsup, tuna, and dried beans.

There would be new expenses this month, with school starting the following week. The kids would need snack money for school—fifty cents a day each for Brian and Delena, a dollar each for Jim and Kevin. On the other hand, Odessa would save a small amount on breakfasts. The schools provided free breakfasts for low-income children, which included just about every child in the neighborhood. Even so, her kids sometimes ate breakfast at home *and* at school.

Odessa looked at the three little mounds of cash around her lap and wondered whether to promise the kids their regular monthly trip to Stacy's, the all-you-can-eat family restaurant in the Northeast. The kids loved driving up on a Sunday afternoon and gorging themselves on shrimp, pork chops, and fried fish at the all-you-can-eat buffet. Sometimes they refilled their plates half a dozen times. But last month Odessa had miscalculated; she had thought the price was $1.99 per child. When the family arrived, she saw that it was $2.99. She did not want to disappoint the kids, so she paid the higher price. But now, thinking about it, she knew she would have to forgo Stacy's this month. Movies were out, too. She normally let the kids go see a movie once a month. Not this month.

This was probably not the right month to try to help the people at Tent City, either. She had been thinking about the children living there in squalor since the night she saw the TV news report. She wanted to offer them something. Money was out of the question, but she had had a good summer trash-picking. She decided she would poke through some of the trash-picking finds she stored in her basement. It was like a little department store down there, piled to the ceiling with items she planned to use or sell one day. She would look for extra pots and pans, small pieces of furniture, children's clothing, lunch boxes—anything of use for someone living in tents and shacks. And perhaps, she thought, she would cook up a pot of stew or soup and drive it up to Tent City if she had a few extra dollars at the end of the month. She also tried to think of ways to raise donations for Tent City. Maybe she could have the grandchildren go door-to-door and ask people for fifty cents each. She figured people on welfare living in houses might sympathize with welfare folks living in tents and shacks.

Odessa scooped up the three cash piles tucked around her lap. She folded the money into a little roll and tucked it back beneath her bra. She had allocated the entire $201.50, including the $1.75 she had spent on the hot sausage. She had picked up her welfare payment less than an hour ago, and already she felt broke.

And then there was Christmas. It was only August, but Odessa's Christmas planning had already begun. Christmas was the highlight of the year for her and the grandchildren. She planned for it like a miser, tucking money away here and there, month after month, to pay for layaway gifts. In fact, the frozen turkey legs she planned to buy at Integrity Meats that week were for Christmas dinner. She would pack them in the freezer and resist until December the temptation to thaw them and cook them up.

She had begun paying for her grandchildren's first Christmas gift back in March. Ollie, her late sister's husband, had bought on layaway a Hooked on Phonics set containing audiotapes and books designed to improve reading ability. Ollie did not read well. He was determined to become literate. But that spring he was laid off from his job as a substitute custodian for the city school district. He couldn't make the Hooked on Phonics payments. They were $58 a month for four months, and he still owed for three months. Odessa offered to take over the payments. Her grandchildren were all good readers, but she wanted to give them an advantage the schools did not offer. And she wanted to improve her own stunted reading ability; just reading the electric bill was a struggle for her. By August, Odessa owed only one more payment. Soon Hooked on Phonics would be hers.

Once she got her hands on the set, she decided, she would hide it at her mother's place on Howard Street. One reason was to keep the grandchildren from finding it; they loved to root around in her closets. But the main reason was to keep it away from Brenda, who still dropped by the house whenever she needed food or a place to sleep. Two years earlier, Odessa had spent months paying for the grandchildren's Christmas toys and then hid them in her bedroom closet. Just before Christmas, Brenda stole every last gift and sold each one for cash to buy crack. She stole Odessa's trash-picked VCR and TV set, too.

Odessa vowed she would never again let Brenda ruin Christmas. Now she hid everything at her mother's house. Already that summer, she had bought two other Christmas gifts. That Saturday, she had driven up to the flea market on State Road and paid $50 from her SSI check for a used stereo for Jim. She had it tested by her son Fred, who pronounced it fit. That same day, she also had gone to a pawn shop and paid $7 for a used video game to give Brian for Christmas. The game cost $75 new, so Odessa was quite pleased with her savings.

She had many ways to cut corners and save money. She did not clip coupons, because few stores in North Philadelphia honored coupons. But she did drive to dollar stores and grocery stores and meat markets every few days, checking prices and asking about sale days. She was a regular at the Salvation Army donation centers, too. She would wait in the parking lot for people to pull up in cars to drop off donations. If she saw something she liked, she would ask for it. People almost always obliged her. Most of them, in fact, told her they admired her initiative. She got her favorite mop that way—one of those high-tech mops that allow you to wring out the sponge without bending over. It came with a brand-new replacement sponge, too. She also got an entire set of stainless steel cooking pots one day from a man dropping off donations.

To earn extra cash, Odessa relied on the old Caprice. A car was a luxury for many people in North Philadelphia. Several of her neighbors relied on buses and subways, which were usually reliable but often required great outlays of time for the most basic errands. Odessa figured that most people would rather travel by car to pick up their welfare checks instead of taking public transportation. She began charging people a $5 round-trip fee to drive them to the financial exchange, wait outside at the curb, and drive them back home. She knew no one would complain about the price; she always felt flush and ready to spend money when she picked up her check. Everybody did. It was the highlight of most people's week. What was $5 at a time like that?

The same principle applied to grocery shopping. Many people took the bus to Cousin's supermarket on Allegheny Avenue, but they dreaded tak-ing the bus back home while loaded down with bags of groceries. Odessa would stand at the store exit and offer rides to shoppers struggling with heavy bags. People on the street called this "hacking." Like most hackers, Odessa charged between $5 and $10, depending on the distance. Most people were glad to pay. On most days she earned at least $50 for a few hours' work.

Odessa found ways to stretch her food budget. Sometimes her sister-in-law Lorraine gave Odessa cornmeal, flour, and rice that she had earned for helping distribute food to the needy in West Philadelphia. During hunting season, Odessa filled her freezer with squirrel, rabbit, and venison that her sons Willie and Israel shot on their hunting jaunts. She helped clean the meat herself. And all spring, summer, and fall—and just about anytime the temperature crept above fifty degrees—Odessa went fishing. She called herself a fishing fool. On certain summer mornings she would drive to Howard Street, pick up her mother, drive to West Philadelphia to dig worms at a vacant lot, then speed across the Ben Franklin Bridge to a secluded fishing spot hidden behind willow trees at a narrow bend in Woodbury Creek in southern New Jersey. On good days they would return home with fifty good-sized perch. Bertha Boone didn't eat fish, so Odessa would clean the whole load of perch and stuff them into her freezer. Most summers, she and her mother caught enough perch to last Odessa's family most of the next winter.

As Odessa sat on her porch, thinking about her bimonthly budget, she was struck by a sudden urge to go fishing, but she felt too tired to go that day. She heard someone shout her name. She looked up and saw one of her nieces, Betty, running toward the house, screaming. The young woman's eyes were glassy with tears.

"What's wrong, baby?" Odessa asked.

Betty ran up the steps and buried her head in Odessa's bosom. Odessa hugged her and wiped her tears. Betty looked up and said, "James shot Boo-Boo."

James was the son of Betty's sister-in-law. He was also Odessa's nephew. Boo-Boo was the son of Betty's brother. He, too, was Odessa's nephew. Odessa was hardly surprised by this turn of events. Both teenagers had gone bad long ago. That was why she forbade her own kids to have anything to do with them. But for her niece's sake, she professed shock.

"What? What happened?" she asked.

Betty sniffled and wiped her arm across her eyes.

"Some kinda drug thing," she said. "They was arguing and they went at it with their guns. James shot Boo-Boo all in the belly. He's at the hospital."

Betty mentioned that it was Boo-Boo's sixteenth birthday. It was the thought of her brother's boy turning sixteen in a hospital bed with a bullet hole in his pelvis, she said, that had triggered her tears.

Odessa tried to listen to the rest of her niece's tale, but all she could think about was her own grandchildren. Thank God they were not like James or Boo-Boo. She imagined Jim or Kevin lying on the street with the Boone family blood pouring from them, and she felt sick. Then she made herself think about the way her kids came straight home when she called them, and how they never lingered at the corner store with Boo-Boo and the dealers, and how she always knew where they were late at night—in their beds, where they belonged.

Soon a debate raged within James and Boo-Boo's wing of the family. Everybody knew James had shot Boo-Boo, but people disagreed over what to do about it. A few relatives wanted to tell the police what had happened. Most favored following the street code that said keep your mouth shut and let the cops figure it out. So James remained on the loose.

The Boones and Williamses, like many people in North Philadelphia, displayed a healthy cynicism toward the police. While they knew and liked many officers on a personal basis, they considered the police force something of an occupying army. In their view, the police regarded crime in North Philadelphia in the same way they regarded the weather—it was something that changed from day to day, but it was always there, and there was little they could do about it. In the estimation of the residents of North Philadelphia, the police gave low priority to crimes against blacks and Hispanics. At the same time, people on the street believed, the cops were all too quick to lock up a black or Puerto Rican on the slightest pretext. For years, both drug dealers and law-abiding residents had been telling me that cops routinely robbed dealers of their cash and drugs, or planted drugs on innocent people, but I had dismissed the tales as some sort of urban myth, like alligators in the sewers.

That summer, six cops from North Philadelphia pleaded guilty to robbing drug suspects of cash and drugs, and planting drugs on innocent people. Detailed newspaper accounts described the officers' actions not as isolated opportunities but as systematic and sustained patterns of predation. As a result of the arrests and guilty pleas, more than sixty criminal convictions were reversed. Another fourteen hundred arrests were being reviewed by federal authorities, and the city faced a flood of civil rights suits. With testimony from the six guilty cops, the FBI began investigating other officers for corruption in North Philadelphia and elsewhere. At the same time, another North Philadelphia cop was charged with running a massive fencing operation for stolen goods from a corner store on Allegheny Avenue. Families in North Philadelphia greeted news of the burgeoning police scandal with a sense of righteousness and vindication. Maybe now, people on the street said after news of the cops' misfortune had spread from row house to row house, the city would listen up when folks said North Philly was thick with crooked cops.

In the case of James and Boo-Boo, the scandal only reinforced their relatives' contempt for the police. No one turned James in. For weeks after the shooting, James would appear here and there on the street—more than once, someone claimed to have seen him on his old drug corner—but no one tipped off the police. Odessa saw Boo-Boo after he got out of the hospital, hawking crack at Eighth and Allegheny, wincing from the pain, hobbling on crutches, his whole midsection wrapped in bandages.

Later, Odessa said she thought that Boo-Boo's misfortune had made an impression on Jim. Her grandson tended to take life seriously, even at thirteen. She was proud of his maturity.

"If Jim wants to sell drugs on the corner when he's sixteen, that's up to him," Odessa said, sitting on her porch at dusk. "I won't be able to stop him then. The time to stop him is now, and I think I got enough control over Jim at thirteen that he won't stray. He's been brought up right since I got him away from his mama. He's seen the wrong way from his mama and the streets, but he's seen the right way from his grandma. And I think he'll choose Grandma's way."

Odessa believed the current generation of young mothers and fathers was too permissive. Somehow, through drugs or TV or rap music, they had been stripped of the capacity to know right from wrong and to pass that certainty of belief down to their children. White people were the worst, she thought. They didn't spank their kids, the way black people of a certain generation spanked theirs. In her mind, it all went back to the days when prayer and the Bible were taken out of schools. It was then that kids started to run wild and turn violent and live by their own codes of behavior and morality, which Odessa considered no codes at all. She had never heard the term "nihilism," but the concept seemed to encapsulate her understanding of the prevailing attitudes of her children's and grandchildren's generations.

Some of her neighbors had been telling Odessa that she was too strict with her grandchildren. They thought the kids should be able to wander farther from home, not have to stay within their grandmother's sight, like toddlers. They suggested to Odessa that she was stifling them.

"You know what I tell them?" Odessa said. "I say you can't be *too* strict. And I tell them: *I know* where my kids are. Do *you* know where your kids are? Some of them, I know where their kids are."

She craned her neck and looked west down Allegheny Avenue, toward the thick throng outside the corner store. She adopted a mock pose of superiority, raised her eyebrows, and said, "They're over on Eighth Street, selling drugs."

The next morning, Odessa put Brian and the baby, Danielle, into the Caprice and drove over to the row house of Lorine, her sister-in-law's daughter. Lorine, whom Odessa had nicknamed Niecee, had agreed to pay

Odessa $10 to take her to the financial exchange on Parkside Avenue to pick up her welfare check. Odessa needed the cash. She didn't have any meat for dinner, and she didn't want to dip into the freezer for meat that was already allocated for the rest of the month. With the $10, she could buy enough chicken backs and chicken necks to make a hearty stew with onions and rice that would feed her and the kids, with enough left over for Joyce and her kids.

Odessa parked outside the financial exchange while Lorine went inside to wait in line. After a while, Odessa felt the need to use the toilet. She tried to stifle it. She did not want to have to haul the children inside, where she would have to take Danielle into the toilet with her and find someone to watch Brian. But the urge grew too great, so she decided to risk leaving the children in the car. It would be for only a few minutes. And Parkside Avenue was in a relatively safe part of North Philadelphia, with plenty of people outside enjoying the warm summer sunshine in the park next to the welfare office. Odessa told Brian to entertain Danielle and keep her happy until Grandma got back. Then she walked inside.

Odessa was gone for less than five minutes. When she walked back out the office door and into the parking lot, she saw a copper-colored car parked so close to the Caprice that the bumpers of the two cars were nearly touching. She walked as quickly as she could, struggling with her weak ankle and stiff legs. As she got closer, she saw a young white man with a light mustache and long, stringy hair. He was sitting behind the wheel of the copper-colored car. He was leaning forward, staring into the backseat of the Caprice.

Danielle! He was staring at Danielle! Odessa made her way to the Caprice, screaming at Brian to lock the doors. Through the windshield she could see Danielle's cornrowed little head popping through the back window to see what was going on outside the car.

"Get your head back inside the car!" she yelled at Danielle.

When Odessa reached the Caprice, the man backed his car away and then stopped it a few car lengths away. He leaned forward again, staring at Danielle and then at Odessa. He had mean little eyes.

Odessa climbed into the front seat of the Caprice and slammed the door. "Get your heads down! Now!" she screamed at Brian and Danielle. The children ducked down below the rear window. Odessa stared hard at the man, wondering what he planned to do next. She thought about yelling for help from someone in the park. She wished she had brought her Colt pistol.

Suddenly the man threw his car into gear and sped away. The vehicle disappeared down Parkside Avenue and was swallowed up by the row houses that shimmered in the hazy sunshine.

Odessa's hands were shaking. Her throat was seizing up, and she found it difficult to speak. She needed a nebulizer treatment. She could also use one of her Valium pills. But her pills and her handheld asthma inhaler were back at home. She sat in the car and tried to calm herself. She told Brian everything was fine. He sat happily in the backseat, watching Danielle pull herself up to look back out the window.

By the time Lorine returned with her welfare money, Odessa had collected herself. She told Lorine what had happened, and the two of them decided to forgo grocery shopping and drive straight home. Odessa needed her nebulizer.

Odessa did not tell anyone in the family about the incident. She did not want to alarm them. There was enough to worry about in North Philadelphia without getting people worked up about some fool white man staring at children in a parking lot.

That night, as Odessa watched the TV news, she saw something that sent a stab of fear through her. She saw the white man from the parking lot. A drawing of his long, pale face filled her entire TV screen. His eyes had the same intense stare she had seen that morning. Odessa brought her hand to her mouth. She was afraid she would scream and wake the children.

The TV newscaster called the man a child molester. He said the police had drawn up a composite picture of him based on descriptions provided by children he had tried to abduct in Northeast Philadelphia. The Northeast? He went all the way up there, too? Odessa was convinced it was the same man she had seen that morning.

According to the newscaster, the man had abducted two twelve-year-old girls from the Northeast that Saturday. He drove them around for three hours, then released them unharmed in Center City. On Tuesday, he tried to snatch an eleven-year-old girl on her way to school, but she pulled free and ran. The girls told the police the man was white, with reddish brown hair and a mustache. He drove a red or brown car.

There was one more thing: the girls said the man had a gun.

Odessa tried to breathe and swallow at the same time. A gun? If he had made one move toward Danielle, she thought, he would have had to use that gun on her. And if she'd had her Colt, she would have pulled the trigger on the man.

Odessa turned the TV off. She usually waited for the weather forecast, but she couldn't bear the man's likeness staring at her a single minute longer. She wanted to call the police and tell them she had seen the molester on Parkside Avenue, but she was too upset to call. They might not believe her anyway. She would call them in the morning.

She walked slowly upstairs, her legs aching from her clumsy run to the

Caprice on Parkside Avenue that morning. She wanted to sit on the bed and listen to Danielle sleep, if only to reassure herself that the girl was all right. She knew she would not be able to sleep herself, for the man's image on the TV screen seemed to have infiltrated the entire house. She could not shake the feeling that he was somehow watching her.

Odessa opened the Bible and tried to read. She kept seeing Danielle's head poking from the window of the car. She closed her eyes. The house fell silent. The dark nightmare returned to her clearly, vividly, and this time it had a face.

CHAPTER FOUR

An Historic Square Mile

Few of the tourists waiting to enter the Liberty Bell pavilion that after-noon noticed the decrepit red Toyota pickup truck that pulled into the no-parking zone on Chestnut Street directly across from Independence Hall. Most of the people in line were shading their eyes from the midday sun, trying to see through the smoked glass enclosure that made the Liberty Bell appear to be draped in a shroud. It was only when a crowd of people gathered around the truck and a park ranger began to engage them in an animated conversation that the tourists began to sense that it was not going to be an ordinary day at Independence Mall.

Passersby on the street were stopping to stare at the truck, which was loaded with boxes, crates, and placards streaked with florid lettering. The ranger was waving the truck on, which seemed to agitate the crowd assembled there. As the tourists watched, the truck pulled away, leaving a crowd of people standing at the curb. The people were poorly dressed—worse, even, than most of the tourists. They wore jeans and T-shirts so rumpled that they appeared to have been slept in. They were carrying ice coolers and boxes of food, as if they were on their way to a picnic.

In the Liberty Bell line, tourists began to shift nervously as it became apparent that the people were walking directly toward them. As the little throng drew closer, the tourists could see bedraggled women trailed by noisy children and street-hardened men with unkempt hair. Suddenly the group stopped and began unloading coolers and boxes on the exquisitely manicured expanse of grass halfway between Independence Hall and the Liberty Bell pavilion. Everyone waiting in line seemed relieved that the odd little procession had halted a safe distance away.

On Chestnut Street, the red truck appeared again at the curb, having circled the block after being sent away by the ranger. Now more people unloaded more gear and hauled it to the grass. Two men hoisted placards that read, *House Us Now!* and, *Affordable Housing Now!* It was possible now to read the message painted on the truck: *Tent City.* On the grass, some of the women began unfurling what appeared to be a camping tent.

The tourists read the signs and looked again at the shabbily dressed group. "My God," someone in line said, "homeless people? Here?"

Willie Bowman, the assistant chief ranger for the Independence National Historical Park, stood at the curb and tried to figure out what was going on. If this was some kind of protest, these people had picked the wrong place. No demonstrations of any sort were permitted on this end of Independence Mall. Protesters were supposed to use the Judge Lewis Quadrangle, an open expanse on the far north side of the Liberty Bell, but only if they'd first obtained a permit. Bowman had heard nothing about a permit. He stopped one of the women unloading the truck.

"Who's in charge here?" he asked her.

Mariluz Gonzalez, toting an orange milk crate loaded with bread, jerked her head toward a slender woman wearing a brown T-shirt, tight jeans, and tan hiking boots. "Talk to her—Cheri."

Bowman walked over to Cheri Honkala, who was unfurling a black banner that read, *Kensington Welfare Rights Union*. He smiled and introduced himself. Cheri shook his hand. Before Bowman could say anything more, she told him, "These people are demonstrating for affordable housing." When dealing with authority, Cheri liked to take the initiative.

Bowman tried to explain the regulations against unauthorized demonstrations on that part of the mall. Cheri did not appear to be listening. She was saying something about First Amendment rights and rights of free assembly. Bowman interrupted her to say that he would try to get the park's public relations lady to drop by. Maybe she could explain the policy.

Cheri turned away and told Chicago and J.R. to set up a tent as quickly as possible. The two men were unrolling a tarp and laying out sections of scrap lumber. They were reasonably certain they could fashion a tent out of the materials. The same tarp and wood, in fact, had formed the main communal structure at Tent City, until it was torn down and hauled over to the mall that morning.

"Just got to remember how we had it up before," J.R. told Cheri. His black beard was glistening with sweat. "It was sorta half tent, half shack. Now we gotta figure out how to make it a tent."

To Bowman, the mass of wood and plastic certainly looked like the beginnings of a tent, which suggested an extended stay. He couldn't allow that. Camping on the mall was against Park Service regulations. Bowman looked around and spotted Levi Rivers, a criminal investigator for the National Park Service. He walked over and told Rivers that a homeless demonstration was under way. Rivers sighed. He didn't need this. He was three months from retirement. This was his third protest in two weeks. He had already dealt with one group of irate demonstrators protesting the city's policy toward a radical group known as MOVE and another complaining about the courts' handling of the politically charged case of a convicted cop killer named Mumia Abu Jamal. Now it was homeless people.

It did not make it any easier that women and children were involved in this demonstration. Rivers noticed that the protesters had already set up a portable playpen on the grass. A baby boy was sitting in it, happily sucking on a pacifier. Women were opening up jars of baby food. Rivers shook his head. How were they going to evict mothers and babies?

Rivers and Bowman spoke with Dennis Reidenbach, the park's chief ranger. Rivers said rangers should photograph and videotape the protesters in case the whole affair ended up in court. It was agreed that Reidenbach and ranger Hollis Provins should carefully explain to this woman Cheri the prohibition against demonstrations on the grass between the Liberty Bell and Independence Hall. It was all there in the park regulations: "The association between the Liberty Bell and Independence Hall is one of the most important and symbolic anywhere. It is important to the visitor experience that the association between these two icons remain undisturbed."

Reidenbach and Provins approached Cheri and introduced themselves. They did not know what to make of the woman. She did not appear to them to be homeless. Her hair was lustrous and carefully combed. She wore makeup and eyeliner. Though she was dressed in jeans and a T-shirt, the clothes were clean and pressed.

Before the rangers could begin their explanation, Cheri spoke up and, as if reciting an announcement, told them: "We're citizens of Philadelphia. We're visiting our Liberty Bell, the symbol of free speech. We're not obstructing anyone's view of the bell, and we're not going to be disruptive."

Reidenbach said it appeared to him, from the tent that was going up, that the group intended to do more than exercise its free speech rights. It looked to him as if they were planning to camp out on the mall.

"There's a prohibition against camping," he told Cheri.

"They're not camping," Cheri said. "They're going to be living here. They don't have anyplace else to go."

"Well, they can't live here, either," Reidenbach said. "There's a prohibition against that, too. If you want to exercise your First Amendment rights, we'll provide the proper location."

"What's wrong with right here?" Cheri asked. "What better place to exercise your First Amendment rights than the Liberty Bell, the symbol of America?"

Cheri's voice grew higher in pitch, to the flat, nasal tones of her native Midwest. When she was agitated—which was frequent when addressing people in authority—she spoke in a rapid whine. "Who are you to tell American citizens where they can sleep or stay?" she asked.

"The Park Service is here to maintain the park for everyone's enjoyment," Reidenbach said. He pointed north, to the open expanse beyond the Liberty Bell pavilion. "You might try the Judge Lewis Quadrangle. Numerous First Amendment activities take place there."

"Why not here?" Cheri asked.

"Because," Reidenbach said, "you're impacting on Park Service operations. You're obstructing citizens' views of the Liberty Bell and blocking their ability to contemplate the meaning of the Liberty Bell. I want you to know that you are in violation of Park Service rules and regula—"

Cheri cut him off and said, "I want *you* to know that you're in violation of our First Amendment rights."

Reidenbach shrugged. "Well, we disagree on that."

Cheri nodded. "Yeah, we do."

As Cheri turned and stalked away, local TV crews began arriving. A reporter asked Reidenbach what he intended to do.

The ranger thought for a moment and said, "We'll take the appropriate action at the appropriate time." As long as the protesters didn't build any campfires or dig holes in the sod, he said, they might be allowed to spend the night. And because they were on such symbolic turf, he said, "we're very sensitive to their First Amendment rights."

Cheri retreated to the grass, where J.R. and Chicago had managed to erect a makeshift tent. Building a tent was a more difficult process on the lawn than on the lot, because Cheri had told them not to use stakes. She didn't want any holes in the ground; that might trigger their instant eviction for damaging park property, she thought. So the tent was held up by ropes attached to an easy chair, a portable bed frame, and plastic milk crates weighted down by bricks and old newspapers. Two heavyset homeless women had to sit on the chair and bed frame to keep the whole flimsy structure from collapsing.

While Mariluz translated for Elba and other Spanish speakers, Cheri sat on the grass inside the tent and addressed her supporters. There were about two dozen of them; the rest of the Tent City people had been left back on the lot to guard the site from theft by pipers or eviction by the city. Cheri told everyone that if they did not wish to risk arrest, they should leave right away.

"Based on what Ranger Rick over there is saying," she said, gesturing toward Reidenbach, "they may start locking people up if we don't get off their precious little lawn here."

Katie, the oldest of the war council members, reminded Cheri that several people on the war council had outstanding bench warrants. Katie, Cheri, and Mariluz, among others, had been arrested outside City Hall during a street protest in July. They had all missed their subsequent court dates. They were, technically, fugitives from justice. But in a city with roughly forty-eight thousand outstanding bench warrants for assorted drug dealers, killers, and rapists, it was not likely that the cops were actively seeking welfare mothers charged with blocking the highway. Even so, several plainclothes officers from the police Civil Affairs unit were conferring with the rangers on Chestnut Street at that very moment.

"Our Civil Affairs friends are here, and they all know who we are," Cheri said. (Civil Affairs cops had carried out the City Hall arrests in July.) "If you're scared, Katie, you ought to get out of here."

Katie said she was staying, but she crouched down behind an ice chest.

"Listen, people, there's no reason for anybody to get locked up," Cheri told the group. "If they come in here and order us to leave, you should go to the sidewalk and ask if we can get our stuff back. But I don't think they'll push it with all these Middle Americans watching." She pointed to a small band of tourists who were standing in the shade, gawking at the tent.

"But whatever happens, there will be no fighting with police officers or rangers, no pushing or shoving," Cheri said. "Our goal isn't to get locked up. It's to force all these fine Middle Americans to think about what it's like to be poor and homeless, and what our own government is trying to do to us. All we have to do is be here, in plain sight."

Cheri looked over at the gathering force of rangers and plainclothes cops. "If they move on us and we get split up, just meet back at the lot," she said. She didn't say so, but she was wondering whether the city might be shutting down Tent City while she was preoccupied at Independence Mall.

Cheri ordered everyone to continue filling the tent with sleeping bags, lawn chairs, coolers, and boxes of food. She intended to spend at least one night, perhaps two. She knew the authorities would have to evict the group at some point. Even she had to admit that this makeshift Tent City was an eyesore. It might be tolerated in North Philadelphia, but not at the city's biggest tourist attraction. The mall was so green and tidy, with graceful sight lines connecting the Liberty Bell and Independence Hall. She thought how much it must gall the Park Service people, not to mention city officials worried about tourist dollars, to have to look at a lumpy tent full of homeless people on so idyllic a site.

Cheri loved to make people uncomfortable. That was the whole point of Tent City—whether on the lot or at Independence Park. She wanted people to squirm and recoil when they saw poor people. She was convinced that America sought desperately to keep its poor out of sight so as not to be reminded of the social policies she believed exacerbated poverty. If the country was going to turn its back on the poor, she was not going to let anyone feel ambivalent about it. She would assault people with her high-pitched nasal voice—in public demonstrations, in confrontations with elected officials, in media interviews, and in front of a ragged tent on Independence Mall.

All that summer, it seemed to her, Congress was plotting to drive millions of Americans deeper into poverty. Congress was writing a welfare reform bill that would end sixty years of entitlement to welfare. Its goal was to end the historical assumption that people were eligible for assistance solely because they were poor. That assumption was built on the principle that the federal government had an inherent responsibility for the welfare of its weakest and most vulnerable citizens, particularly children. But the bill would let the states decide what, if anything, to do to assist the poor. It also imposed a five-year limit on welfare benefits and required recipients to work after two years. But it provided virtually no money for job training, job development, or child care. If you were going to throw people off welfare, Cheri thought, at least help them find work, take care of their children, and provide an affordable place to live. If they had all that, she reasoned, they wouldn't *need* welfare.

Cheri saw a direct and quite obvious correlation between welfare cuts and homelessness. The connection had emerged dramatically in Philadelphia the year before. The state had enacted a law, Act 49, that removed or reduced state general assistance benefits to poor but able-bodied people aged forty-five and older. As a result, more than five thousand people in Philadelphia were suddenly cut off from their main source of income. It was no coincidence, Cheri thought, that almost immediately more homeless people began turning up on the streets. City officials in charge of dealing with the homeless noted the connection, saying Act 49 had created a sudden upsurge of hundreds, perhaps thousands, of new homeless people in Philadelphia. There were now some twenty-four thousand homeless people seeking shelter space each year in a city with just twenty-six hundred shelter beds.

It was those kinds of numbers that motivated Cheri. In her view, they underscored her contention that people were better off living in tents and shacks, using their welfare money for food and other essentials, rather than fighting their way through the city's beleaguered shelter system. Why submit to a system that openly acknowledged that it could meet the needs of only a fraction of the city's poor? And if the city wanted Tent City off its lot at Fourth and Lehigh, it made sense to Cheri to air her grievances on federal property. It was the federal government, after all, that provided the bulk of the money for welfare and housing for the poor.

Now, squatting in the shade of the tent on Independence Mall, Cheri tried to explain her position to the reporters and TV crews that had set up on the grass. Attracting the press was not difficult. She knew that if reporters were tired of the same old story at Tent City, their appetites for cheap drama would be whetted by the same old story in a new location. That is why she'd chosen Independence Mall. It provided the most dramatic stage in the entire city. The place was weighted with symbols of defiance and resistance to tyranny and injustice. The media feasted on such obvious symbolic connections, and Cheri was more than willing to play out her role as rabble-rouser and champion of the dispossessed.

"The main thing we want to accomplish today," Cheri said, addressing the camera crews, "is that these families *will* be heard. They have dreams much larger than a bed in a crowded shelter somewhere."

After the reporters left and the TV crews packed up, Cheri walked over to the edge of the mall to smoke a cigarette and collect her thoughts. As she smoked, she thought she recognized a man in a dark suit walking across the mall. He had a square, tanned face and wavy black hair streaked with silver. The man looked up and seemed to recognize her, too. He introduced himself as Jeff Lindy, and then Cheri remembered. She had served with Lindy on a bar association panel on legal aid to the poor. He was a lawyer.

"Hey, I could use a good lawyer right about now," she told him. She described the demonstration and recounted her discussion with the park rangers. Lindy said he would represent her pro bono. He enjoyed a good legal challenge. Cheri told him she'd sell the Liberty Bell and pay him with the proceeds.

Satisfied that she had legal backing, Cheri went back to the tent and told everyone they were spending the night. She told Mariluz and Elba to prepare dinner—canned tuna on white bread—and asked Katie to walk toward the Liberty Bell pavilion and talk to tourists. Cheri thought it was important to seek support and understanding toward the poor from people who had traveled from around the country and the world to visit the symbols of American democracy.

Not all the tourists seemed receptive. Many, in fact, were repulsed by the rickety tent and the scattered piles of blankets and bottles. "Looks like a goddamned rock concert," said a man from South Carolina. A Korean couple asked whether the demonstration had been organized by the government; they didn't think so because the people seemed so dirty. A woman from Lancaster County said the homeless people might get a better reception if they cleaned themselves up and wore nicer clothes. An elderly man from Trenton, New Jersey, said, "If I wanted to see homeless people, I would've stayed home."

As a tour group left the Liberty Bell pavilion, the tour guide told them the collection of tarps and signs was a demonstration on behalf of the homeless. "That don't look too good," one of the tourists said. Another said, "I'll bet they're all on welfare. That's how they have the time to do something like this."

Katie overheard the comments and walked quickly toward the group. She tried to contain her anger, but her face reddened. With her stringy hair and baggy jeans and missing teeth, she was not a welcome sight for people accustomed to warding off homeless people who approached them, usually to ask for money.

Katie stared hard at the tourists and said, without smiling, "Hi, I'm with the Kensington Welfare Rights Union, and we're here fighting for affordable housing and welfare reform. I'm not a bum. I worked for seventeen years before I had two heart attacks and lost my job and my house. It could happen to youse, too. But that wouldn't mean you didn't have a right to get help from the government."

As Katie spoke, the tourists recoiled. They averted their eyes and walked faster, trying desperately to get away from what seemed to be a crazy, babbling homeless woman. They were halfway to Independence Hall before Katie stopped talking and let them go.

Cheri walked over and hugged Katie, who stood with her hands on her hips, gazing at the shadows that darkened the pale bricks across the front entrance to Independence Hall. "Always good to touch base with Middle America, isn't it?" Cheri said.

Just before midnight, Calvin T. Farmer of the National Park Service arrived for night duty. Farmer, a stocky man with a mustache and spectacles, had been assigned to follow the protesters through the night and report on everything they did. His neatly typed criminal incident record was a model of investigative acumen.

"At approximately 0010 hours on September 8, 1995, I began an investigation of the group's activities," Farmer's report read.

> I observed several conditions which appeared relative to the establishment of some extended length of stay. I saw a bar-b-q grill; tent with stakes; staked canvas type canopy; three coolers; several types of beddings including pillows, quilts and sleeping bags; and people sleeping in those beddings.

After his investigation concluded that the protesters were indeed spending the night, Farmer began a surveillance of Cheri Honkala. Three times between 1 A.M. and 5 A.M., his report said, he saw her move around the tent area. "I noticed her because she wore a dark colored jacket and dark colored pants," Farmer wrote. "Her dress seemed different from the others in the crowd who wore mostly T-shirts, shorts and more casual type clothing."

There was not much more for Farmer the investigator to report. The group's activity for the bulk of the night consisted largely of sleeping, with occasional trips to the bus station toilets.

At 5:30 A.M., after a long and restless night, the sound of rushing water awakened everyone inside the tent. Water was gushing everywhere—down from the rooftop tarp, across the support beams, and up from the grassy sod inside the tent. The spray seemed to be coming from both the sky and the ground.

Cheri woke and saw water bubbling up from beneath the portable playpen where Mariluz's and Elba's babies were still asleep. She lifted the playpen, rolling the babies into a corner, and found the source of the water. A sprinkler head had popped up from the ground and was spurting water everywhere. Now she remembered. The park rangers had warned her that the sprinkers were set off by a timer at certain intervals.

Mariluz and Elba scooped up the babies and left the tent. Everyone else crawled out of sleeping bags and off mattresses, sputtering and cursing. Everything was soaked, including the trays of fresh bread and rolls a baking company had dropped off in the middle of the night. Everybody moved off the grass and onto the sidewalk, shivering and stamping their feet as water rained down on their temporary home. After a while, the ever-vigilant ranger Farmer walked over and asked Cheri to move her people from the sidewalk because they were blocking what he called "the pedestrian traffic flow." Cheri complied, moving everybody back onto the grass next to the tent.

Cheri didn't tell anyone, but she decided at that moment that the demonstration would end that day. People were miserable. Even before the sprinklers went off, everyone was complaining about the lack of food, the cold stares of the tourists, the long walks to the bus station to use the toilet, and the threat of arrest. She had made her point. The local TV stations had run reports on the protest. They portrayed homelessness as a serious issue, and even mentioned the proposed federal cuts in welfare that likely would contribute to more homelessness.

That morning, the newspapers ran prominent stories. One article quoted Mayor Ed Rendell as saying the city had offered shelter space to Cheri's people and had been turned down. The mayor said the protesters would not get housing ahead of people who had entered the shelter system. "If we did that," the mayor said, "we'd have a riot on our hands." Cheri had to admit that Rendell was probably right. But she thought people in the shelter system should target their anger at a system that forced poor people to compete for limited services. The riot should erupt at City Hall, not Tent City.

As Cheri read the mayor's quotes in the paper and tried to dry off, she wondered what sort of riots the welfare cuts would trigger if they went through. Her thoughts were interrupted by the approach of a shadowy figure walking across the wet grass. She looked up and recognized one of the park rangers from the previous day. He was not wearing his Park Service uniform. He was dressed in civilian clothes, which made him appear smaller and less threatening. He asked if he could speak with her off the record.

The ranger warned Cheri that the federal government planned to arrest the protesters later that day. He said he was torn between doing his job and his concern for the children inside the tent. He had considered asking permission to make a statement to the press that his job should not require him to evict children from an historic area, but he did not because he knew he would be turned down. He was on a committee for the homeless at his church, he said, and he often donated money to groups that helped the poor.

The man seemed on the verge of tears. He asked Cheri if there was any way she could make her points about society's responsibility to the poor—sentiments he personally supported—without risking a confrontation. He wasn't sure he could bring himself to arrest women and children, he told her, even if his job depended on it.

Cheri told the ranger she would talk to her lawyer about ways to end the protest without evictions or arrests. She thanked him for approaching her "as a human being." He shook her hand and left.

Later that morning, Jeff Lindy appeared at the tent, looking out of place in a double-breasted gray suit and black tasseled loafers. He told Cheri that the U.S. Attorney's Office across the street had contacted him. Some of the staffers in the office wanted to arrest every protester on the spot and haul them off. But the assistant U.S. attorney handling the case proposed a compromise: because Cheri seemed determined to get arrested in order to prove a point, he would be happy to oblige. But he did not want to deal with the children, particularly because it was a Friday, which meant that DHS would have to take custody of the children of jailed mothers for the entire weekend. Why not move the mothers and children off the mall and issue Cheri a citation that would keep her out of jail but require her to appear in court, where she could explain her actions in a public forum?

The U.S. Attorney's Office, working through the night, had typed up a ten-page temporary restraining order. It was clearly intended as a club to force Cheri to accept the government's offer. Lindy said the injunction had not been filed—and would not be filed if Cheri agreed to the deal proposed by the U.S. Attorney's Office. He handed a copy of the document to Cheri.

Cheri saw that the order named as defendants herself and Mariluz. It said each of them "presently resides at 5th and Chestnut Streets"—the location of Independence Mall. She did not know whether the reference was intended as a joke, but it amused her that the federal government acknowledged her home address, however temporary, to be what the injunction called "America's most historic square mile."

The injunction pointed out that Cheri had been offered a chance to demonstrate—but not camp—on the far north side of the Liberty Bell. Cheri had declined the offer because she knew that a demonstration out of sight of the Liberty Bell robbed her of the symbolic, historic weight she craved. Poverty in the shadow of the Liberty Bell was dramatic. Poverty on a lawn in downtown Philadelphia was not.

The document said the National Park Service had made adequate allowances for freedom of speech near these two important symbols of American liberty. At the same time, it said, demonstrations could not be permitted to block the "important vista" between the Liberty Bell and Independence Hall.

Cheri read on:

> As the Supreme Court found in 1984, there is a substantial Government interest, unrelated to suppression of expression, in conserving park property that is served by the proscription of camping in an area like Lafayette Park and Independence National Historical Park. . . . Visitors to the Liberty Bell Pavilion can look through the glass wall across an uninterrupted grassy vista to Independence Hall as the Park Ranger interpreters explain the historic relationship between the Liberty Bell and Independence Hall.

"If they remain," the injunction said of the protesters, "there will be increasing security, sanitation, and health concerns, rising to a significant injury to the United States."

Attached to the injunction was a four-page, single-spaced list of "Federal Laws Which Have the Potential to Be Violated by the Homeless Advocacy Group Setting Up In Between the Liberty Bell Pavilion and Independence Hall." The laws covered everything from camping to picnicking, fires to radios, digging to soliciting money.

After Cheri had read the documents, she was impressed by the government's detailed effort. All this for a few homeless welfare mothers pitching a tent? She wished someone in the federal government would make the same sort of effort to find jobs and housing and day care for the poor. Even so, she did not regard the Park Service as the enemy. She was fighting the people who made and enforced laws governing services to the poor—members of Congress, the welfare bureaucracy, the city officials who decided how dwindling federal money was spent on the poor. By creating a public spectacle on such a symbolic site, she thought, she might somehow awaken sympathy from the voters who elected the congressmen and city leaders. For at least a day or two, she hoped, she had accomplished that.

Lindy put the injunction back in his briefcase and told Cheri he thought the government had made an acceptable offer. No one would benefit from mass arrests. Cheri had made her point. It was time to pack up.

Cheri agreed. She would move everyone off the site, take down the tent, and stay put on the site long enough to be issued a citation. At least it would give the TV crews a dramatic climax. Beyond that, she was tired and edgy. She had not slept much during the night. Her hair was knotted and her makeup was smeared. She had long ago stopped worrying about how she looked, but she did not think as clearly or as quickly when she felt unwashed and bedraggled.

As Cheri and Lindy huddled together at the edge of the tent, TV crews and reporters and tourists began to crowd around them. A TV reporter poked a microphone toward Lindy and asked him for a statement.

Lindy adjusted his tie and said: "KWRU will continue their act of civil disobedience. But with the cooperation of the U.S. Attorney's Office, we will make sure the children and their parents are taken care of. . . . KWRU has a legitimate statement to make. If this is the only way to get the attention of the federal, state, and city governments, then this is what they will do."

A TV reporter asked Cheri: "What do you want people to do?"

Cheri looked at her and said: "We want to be allowed to fix up abandoned houses and let poor people move into them and continue to fix them up. There are twenty-seven thousand abandoned properties in this city, just sitting there going to waste."

Cheri finished the interview and Lindy left to consult with the U.S. Attorney's Office. As Cheri walked back to the tent, she saw Mariluz running out from beneath the tarp. She sprinted across the mall toward her five-year-old daughter, Destiny, who was talking to a woman in a red blouse and white polyester slacks. The woman was holding the child by the arm, peering intently into her face as Destiny looked up at her.

"Did you see anyone take it?" the woman asked.

"Nooooo," Destiny told her. She was a round-faced girl with soft brown eyes and dark, wavy hair. She seemed small and fragile next to the woman, who was tall and big boned.

Mariluz ran up and screamed at the woman: "What are you doing to my daughter?"

"I'm not doing anything to her," the woman said. "I just asked her if she saw anyone take my bag. It was here a minute ago. Now it's missing."

Mariluz snatched her daughter's arm away from the woman and stalked back toward the tent, dragging Destiny by the hand. The woman pursued them, asking again whether Destiny knew what had happened to her bag.

At the edge of the tent, Mariluz whirled and shouted: "My child didn't take your damn bag!"

"I didn't say she did," the woman said, her voice rising. "I just asked if she saw anything. I wasn't—"

"Get away from me!" Mariluz screamed. The woman turned and walked away.

Mariluz tried to pursue the woman, but Cheri grabbed her and held her tight. "Cool it, Mariluz!" she said. "Let her go."

"I ought to sock her!" Mariluz said, balling both fists. "She called my child a thief. We're poor, but we ain't no thieves."

Cheri was disappointed in the tourists. She had thought the protest would elicit more sympathy, if not encouragement. It seemed to her that the tourists were more interested in being tourists than in learning what it was like to be poor. A few had turned the tent into a regular stop on the tour between the Liberty Bell and Independence Hall, asking questions and listening politely to Cheri's complaints. But most of the tourists walked past quickly, avoiding eye contact. Cheri realized that they were all on vacation. But being on vacation didn't mean suspending your responsibilities to society, she thought. Not that she would know. She never took vacations.

Cheri gathered everyone inside the tent and told them the protest was ending. Katie and Mariluz had tears in their eyes. Everyone joined hands and said a prayer. Outside, a team of park rangers was setting up a rope barrier like the ones outside movie theaters.

Mariluz stood up and shouted: "All the kids move out—now!" She and Elba and the other mothers rounded up their children and walked over to the rows of benches at the edge of the mall. J.R. and Chicago and the rest of the men kicked out the support beams and let the tarp collapse. It fluttered to the grass, emitting a final gasp of hot, stale air. Everyone gathered up the coolers and food and mattresses, and hauled them to the benches. J.R. folded the tarp and carried it away.

All that remained in the matted grass was an upholstered bucket seat someone had torn out of a car. Cheri sat down in it and lit a cigarette. Katie came over and hugged her and stuffed Marlboros and matches in Cheri's socks in case she was taken to jail.

The rangers, standing in single file behind the rope, rolled their eyes. They knew nobody was going to jail. Ranger Farmer knelt in the grass and filled out an incident report. In the box for "offense code," he wrote the numbers 33-99-00 and the words "Residing in park." He left blank the spaces for types of weapons confiscated, including "shotgun," "poison," "knife/cutting instrument," and "blunt object." The TV cameras zoomed in as Farmer wrote.

Cheri snuffed out her cigarette and waited. With the rangers lined up and facing her beyond the rope, she felt like a death row prisoner waiting to be strapped into the electric chair. She had been arrested fifty-four times, by her latest count, but still she was nervous. At one point she felt like crying, but she bit her lip.

On the sidewalk, the Tent City people struck up a chant: "No Housing, No Peace!" They tried to unfurl the black KWRU banner, but Lindy stopped them, saying it was not permitted under the agreement with the authorities. Instead, as Farmer and another ranger ducked under the ropes to approach Cheri, everyone shouted: "Shame! Shame! The whole world is watching."

Actually, it was just a few local TV stations and a handful of newspaper and radio reporters, plus a crush of tourists. But it was a decent audience anyway, Cheri thought. And it was only late afternoon, plenty of time to make the 6 P.M. newscasts.

As Cheri sat in the car seat, her legs tucked up beneath her chin, ranger Farmer kneeled down and explained that he was issuing a citation for illegally residing in the park. He handed her a white form that looked like a parking ticket. He told her she would be notified by mail of her court date. Cheri said she would plead not guilty. Farmer shrugged, stood up, and strode away as the TV cameras focused on the citation in Cheri's hand. The Tent City people chanted "Shame! Shame!" In his report, Farmer wrote, "The incident ended without physical violence or arrests."

Cheri folded the paper and put it in her pocket. She walked over to the cameras and said, "We've basically been told that we don't have the right of freedom of speech on Independence Mall in Pennsylvania, U.S.A. . . . We pray we won't have to deal with this same situation back at Fourth and Lehigh."

Cheri lit a cigarette and hugged Mariluz. Everyone waited for her to say something. The children were restless. Destiny told her mother she wanted to go home—home being the shack at Tent City. Cheri looked down at the loads of lumber and food and mattresses. The wind was picking up. Long shadows were creeping across Independence Mall, making the lush grass appear black and flat. Cheri wondered what had become of the red Tent City truck.

"Well," she said finally. "It's getting late. Nothing to do now but go back to the lot." Everyone nodded. After two days on the grass at America's most historic square mile, shacks and tents on an urban brownfield seemed more than ever like home.

CHAPTER FIVE

Scratching Matches

O dessa was on the sofa, trying to keep Danielle quiet so that she could hear what Victor Newman was saying on the episode of *The Young and the Restless* that lit up the screen of her trash-picked TV set, when Elaine came through the front door. Elaine looked as if she were about to cry. She told her mother that she had just taken a phone call from the people at the job training institute she had arranged to attend. It was bad news—the worst news Elaine had heard all year. The course she had planned to take was being canceled. "Lack of funding," someone had told her over the phone. It had something to do with budget cuts.

Elaine sank down into the sofa across from her mother and stared blankly at the TV set. She had just finalized her plans to begin her first class the very next morning, at 9 A.M. sharp. She had checked the bus schedule, filled out the forms for the course, made sure all her kids would get to school on time. She had allowed herself to dream of holding down a job, cashing a paycheck, setting up a checking account, telling the welfare people to cancel her checks and stamps. The six-week course at the institute was to have taught her the rudiments of hotel management and food preparation. It was a field that appealed to Elaine. It meant dealing with all kinds of people, which she knew she could handle. It meant accepting responsibility, which she craved. It involved cooking, something she loved so much that she would have done it for nothing. And the best thing about the course was that, upon completion, the institute promised to help find her a job at a hotel or motel. The timing was perfect, too. For the first time, all six of Elaine's children were attending school. She was free to work during the day.

Now it had all come crashing down. Elaine was not certain she could find another training course. Various problems and crises at home had compelled her to drop out of two previous welfare-to-work training programs—a GED course and a computer course—both of which had provided child care and transportation costs. In most cases, welfare recipients were limited to two such benefit programs. It was only through the intervention of her welfare caseworker that Elaine had been given a third opportunity, with the hotel management course, though child care and transportation were not covered. But now the course had been canceled.

"Oh, they busted my bubble good," she told Odessa. "I was telling everybody I was getting off welfare. I was so sure it was gonna happen. Right now, I should be up at the school, taking their math and reading test, finding out which hotel in Center City they were gonna train me at."

Odessa reached over and patted her daughter's arm. Elaine tried to smile. "Seems like just when I start to rise up," she said, "something comes along and—bam!—it knocks me back down."

As much as she sympathized with Elaine, Odessa had to save her concerns and her energy for her grandchildren. Elaine was a grown woman. She would find a way to cope. The grandchildren had no one but Odessa, and they were keeping her busy late that summer. Every day, it seemed, one of them did something to aggravate her. With all her worries about money and food enveloping her like a thick summer smog, the last thing she needed was disobedient children in her home.

Brian was acting up in school, interrupting his teacher and throwing temper tantrums whenever his classmates teased him. His teacher, Ms. Chisholm, had called Odessa that week. She told her that when she warned Brian she was going to call his grandmother and tell her he was misbehaving, he begged her not to. When Ms. Chisholm asked why, Brian said his grandmother would punish him by telling his new friend not to give him fifty cents anymore. I had been giving Brian two quarters every time I saw him, with the understanding that he would not spend the money but instead put it in an aluminum container Odessa had given him. By December, I had told him, he would have saved enough to buy himself—and perhaps his grandmother—a Christmas present. Now Odessa told Brian that she would ask me to stop giving him money if his teacher called again to complain about his behavior. Brian promised he would "act right."

Delena, meanwhile, was having her own problems in school. The week before, she had arrived home with a note from her teacher, Mrs. Harley. It read:

Dear Mrs. Williams:
    Delena socked Sierra in the face after school. I'm sure this will be a problem when they get back to school tomorrow.

    P.S. Delena has been better in class lately.

This bit of news had surprised Odessa. Delena was not an aggressive girl. Odessa thought she must have been provoked. She had taught Delena what her own mother had taught her: Girls should not look for fights, but they should not run from them, either. It was okay for girls to fight, but only if someone hit them first.

The day the note arrived, Odessa had questioned Delena closely on the front porch.

"Why'd you hit her?" she asked.

"She threw paper at me," Delena said.

"Why didn't you tell the teacher?"

"I did," Delena said. "She didn't do nothing."

"So what did you do?"

Delena lowered her eyes and answered, "I smacked her."

"Mm-hmm," Odessa said. She was disappointed. Delena knew she should never, ever be the first to throw a punch, regardless of the provocation.

"I'm through warning you," Odessa said evenly. "You get a whipping this time. And I want the living room cleaned up, plus you got three days on punishment in your room."

As Delena stood facing her on the porch, Odessa smacked her three times with her thick hand across the back of the girl's legs. Delena bit her lip to keep from crying. Then she stalked off the porch and went inside to clean up the living room, stopping in the vestibule to bend down and kiss the cheek of Danielle, who was bawling at the sight of Odessa spanking her cousin.

That same week, Odessa had to put Kevin on punishment, too. He had been walking in the street one day, daydreaming about football, and he wandered into the path of a city bus. The bus screeched to a stop just as one of Kevin's cousins pulled him out of harm's way. Kevin did not tell anyone about the near miss, but Odessa found out anyway. The bus driver was one of her many nephews. He called and told her he had nearly run over her grandson. Kevin was shocked when Odessa asked him about the incident; he couldn't figure out how she knew. But he was not surprised when she punished him by banning him from the street football games for three days.

Pretty soon, Odessa thought, everybody in the house would be on punishment. But at least Jim wasn't worrying her. He was as steady and dependable as ever. Odessa never heard a word of complaint from Jim's teachers. In fact, they adored him. Jim was in the gifted program at the Julia de Burgos Bilingual magnet school on Lehigh Avenue, just four blocks from Tent City. Odessa knew that the school was among the worst in the city, attended almost entirely by desperately poor children from deprived backgrounds. Only 10 percent of the school's students tested at or above the national average on standardized reading tests. Nearly 70 percent were from welfare families. The school itself looked more like a prison than a school, with its forbidding walls coated with graffiti and its windows sealed by metal bars. Jim had to walk a circuitous route to bypass the many drug corners on the way to school.

Even in this distressed environment, Jim flourished. Bilingual Magnet might not be the best school around, Odessa told people, but her grandson Jim was one the very best students there—and popular, too. Odessa showed everyone a letter that had arrived for Jim that week from President Clinton himself. Jim, asked by his teacher to dream up a special project, had decided to write the president and describe the violence in his neighborhood.

The president's reply arrived in a crisp white envelope with the return address, *The White House, Washington, D.C.*, embossed in blue lettering beneath a golden eagle.

"Dear James," it read,

> Thank you for writing to me. I share your concern for the safety of our communities. You can do your part in America's fight against crime. By staying away from drugs, helping your community, and treating others with respect, you can help to move America in the right direction. Together we can build a safer future.
>
> Sincerely,
>
> Bill Clinton.

Odessa knew the president himself had not written this sample of boilerplate rhetoric, but she decided to have it framed anyway. It had the president's signature. How many kids in North Philadelphia had that?

Distressed by Elaine's setback at the training institute that afternoon, Odessa tried to focus her mind on positive thoughts. She made herself think about the president's letter, which she tucked into the Boone family Bible for safekeeping, and about Jim's scholastic performance and her daughter Joyce's determination to graduate from her job training course. Soon her state of mind improved, and she tried to maintain her equanimity by imagining the day the following spring when Joyce would graduate and find a job.

Things were going well for Joyce. Every weekday, she got up and fed her children. Then she took the number 60 bus to K and A, where she transferred to the El, which took her to the stop for the number 14 bus, which in turn took her to a job training center in Northeast Philadelphia. Even with discounted tokens, the trip cost her $1.90 each way, not to mention more than an hour spent riding buses and the El. But the effort was worth it to Joyce. She was studying medical administration. She learned computer databases, medical terminology, billing, and graphics.

After seriously injuring her back lifting patients while working as a nurse's aide, Joyce wanted a medical job in an office, where she could sit down and work at a computer. The administrative work was in keeping with her vision of herself as a young professional. She was thirty-nine years old, a mother of four, and a grandmother of five, but she felt youthful and vigorous. And she was still an attractive woman, with her lean frame and high cheekbones and sharp, refined features.

Joyce was motivated by something her fifteen-year-old son, Curtis, had said to her recently: "Mama, why don't you go back to work and make some money? I'm tired of being poor." Curtis was right. They were poor. Joyce brought in just $201 every two weeks from welfare, plus $287 in food stamps each month. She was tired, too—tired of doing without until check day, tired of relying on a welfare system that dictated the narrow parameters of her household budget.

"I don't want to live this way, with my kids wanting and needy, and me having to tell them they can't have what they want," Joyce said one day, sitting on her mother's porch, holding a cutoff notice from the gas company and wondering how she was going to pay her overdue electric bill. "That's why I like this school so much. They try to eliminate any excuse for why you can't get a job. They even pay you to go to driving school and help you get a driver's license so you can't say you don't have any way to get to work. And if you don't have a car, they'll pay your transportation to work."

Riding the number 60 bus home that afternoon, Joyce had daydreamed about her future. She wanted to use her computer and graphics training to start up a specialty magazine devoted to exotic dancers. It could run features on male and female dancers. It could have provocative foldouts, club notes, a Q-and-A column on dating and safe sex. There were enough young, single, urban club hoppers in Philadelphia, New Jersey, and Delaware, she thought, to support such a hip and breezy treatment of exotic dancing. The magazine might be a big seller in nightclubs. It was something she wanted at least to consider after she had worked at a hospital job for a while and saved up her money.

As the bus bounced past the bodegas and hoagie shops along Allegheny Avenue, Joyce thought about what a friend had suggested to her: she should write down her idea for the magazine, have it notarized, then mail it to herself. That way, her friend had said, Joyce would have proof that the magazine was her original idea in the event that someone else tried to cash in on the same concept. This suggestion so occupied Joyce's thoughts that she scarcely noticed the fire truck that sped around the bus, its siren wailing, and disappeared down Allegheny Avenue toward the train overpass.

As Joyce rode home, her daughter, Iesha, was napping on the living room sofa in Joyce's row house just down Allegheny Avenue from Odessa's place. At nineteen, Iesha was, like many teenagers, perpetually lethargic and bored, particularly on a hot, still afternoon like this one. Often she would leave high school early and come home to watch soap operas and care—haphazardly, Joyce thought—for her three small children.

That afternoon, Odessa had sent the twins, Danielle and Darryl, and their infant brother, Khalil, to be with Iesha for the afternoon. Odessa wanted a break from the babies so that she could watch "the stories"—her favorite soap operas. In addition, she was waiting for a lady from the electric company to drop by. She had made an afternoon appointment to discuss setting up a payment plan to pay off some of the several hundred dollars Odessa owed.

Odessa had sent Brian over for Iesha to watch, too. If Iesha was going to skip school, Odessa thought, then she could help her baby-sit. Odessa did not want Brian interrupting her discussion with the electric company lady. Brian had been pestering her to let him play with Joyce's youngest boy, Elliott, age seven, who was known to everyone in the neighborhood as Geedy, from the word "greedy," in deference to his ravenous appetite. Brian and Geedy were like twin shadows—two thin, manic, garrulous little boys.

While Iesha dozed, her three small children crawled across the floor at her feet, yapping over the roar of the TV set tuned to the stories. Brian and Geedy, left unsupervised, went upstairs to look for something that might entertain them on a drowsy late summer afternoon. They had been forbidden by Odessa to go outside while Odessa was inside; Joyce's house was only a half block from the crack and heroin sales point outside the corner store.

Bored and stuck indoors, Geedy pulled out a set of matches he had found. Geedy loved to strike matches—"scratching," he called it. He was an impish boy, lanky and bony like Brian, with deep-set dark eyes and his mother's brilliant white teeth. Geedy's entire being seemed shot through with unfocused energy, and sometimes it led him to trouble. Around Joyce's house, he was a notorious pyromaniac. Twice Geedy had been caught playing with matches. Once, he started a fire in a trash can, which smoldered until Joyce discovered it and put it out. Another time, he caught a bed on fire and the fire department had to rush over and put it out. Both Joyce and Odessa had lectured Geedy on the dangers of playing with matches. Geedy knew he risked a whipping if he was caught, but now he was bored. And Brian was urging him on.

Geedy found a newspaper and lit it. It was soggy from the humidity. It smoldered until Geedy dropped the smoking heap into a trash can. Two more times, Geedy lit a wad of newspaper and watched as it went up in smoke inside the can. Soon the newspaper fires lost their appeal. Brian wanted to see something more stimulating. He looked at a mattress in the room. It was covered with a bedspread.

"Geedy, stick it to the bed," Brian said. "We can put it out."

Geedy struck a match and held it to the bedspread. For a moment, nothing happened. Then a flash of orange flame burst out. Within seconds the bedspread was consumed by fire and smoke. The two boys looked at each other.

"Get some water, Geedy!" Brian shouted.

Geedy ran to the bathroom. He returned with a tiny Dixie cup dripping with tap water. He threw the whole thing at the bed. The water evaporated in a sizzle of steam and smoke.

Brian knew from watching TV that you could smother a fire by bundling up a blanket or bedspread. He reached out and grabbed the bedspread and tried to shake it to put the fire out. The bedspread twisted and flapped across the bed, brushing against a set of curtains. The flames seemed to leap from the bedspread to the curtains, which disappeared in a haze of smoke and crackling fire.

Brian dropped the bedspread and ran from the room, followed by Geedy. The boys stumbled down the stairs. In the living room they saw Iesha dozing on the sofa. Geedy shook his sister awake. "Iesha, you better go upstairs and see what's going on!" Geedy said. "There's big trouble upstairs!"

Iesha dragged her big body off the sofa and looked up the dark stairwell. She saw smoke and knew instantly that her little brother had been playing with matches again. She punched Geedy in his bony chest and ran upstairs. When she saw the flames, she went into the bathroom and filled a plastic bucket with water. But the water evaporated with a loud hiss when it hit the flames. Iesha gave up and ran downstairs. She dragged the babies outside to the porch and stretched the phone cord out the front door and punched in 911.

Brian knew he had to tell his grandma what was going on. He ran out the front door and, without pausing to look for cars that often turned swiftly onto the street from busy Allegheny Avenue, he sprinted across narrow Franklin Street. He leaped up the front steps of Odessa's row house. He burst through the front door and shouted, "Grandma! Grandma! Geedy's done something bad!"

Odessa looked up from the soaps and asked, "What is it, baby? Tell me."

Brian, breathing hard, said, "Grandma, Geedy burnt the upstairs at Aunt Joyce's!"

Odessa rose from the sofa and stumbled past the piles of trash-picked clothes spread across the living room floor. She pushed past Brian and hurried across the porch and down the front stairs toward Joyce's. She made her way to the porch, where Iesha was talking frantically on the phone to the fire department. Odessa gathered up the three babies and grabbed Geedy's arm and got everybody away from the house. Iesha hung up the phone and followed them out to the sidewalk to wait for the fire department.

The first fire engine arrived within minutes, but most of the top floor was by then in flames. Working quickly, the firemen managed to confine the flames to the top floor. But the three upstairs rooms and the bathroom were badly burned. The rear room, where the fire had begun, was gutted. The top of the back wall was left exposed, and anyone standing in the back room could see the entire trash-flecked back alley spread out below. Smoke and water poured down through the floor and spread across the downstairs. The living room and kitchen walls were blackened, and the carpets and furniture turned dark and damp.

The firemen were still soaking the smoldering fire with their big hoses when the silver-and-blue number 60 bus pulled up to the gentle rise where Allegheny crests near Sixth Street. On board, Joyce was thinking about what a fine, productive day she had had in school. She had just been told that she had passed one of her toughest efficiency tests. She had joked and clowned with her girlfriends as they worked on computer programs. They had all discussed what they planned to wear to the graduation ceremony that spring, and they had debated what sort of information to include on their résumés.

Now, riding home, Joyce pictured herself gliding down an aisle in a cap and gown, with Odessa taking photographs and her children applauding. She imagined herself taking a hospital job, buying a new car and smart new clothes, and moving into a new apartment. Then she saw a fire engine chugging slowly up Allegheny near Franklin Street and she thought: Oh, my God, no, not my house.

Joyce got off the bus and saw two firemen rolling up hoses on her block. Another fireman was loading gear onto a fire engine. She smelled a sharp chemical odor, and the damp, dirty scent of wet wood. She saw Geedy and Iesha walking up the sidewalk toward her. She tried to form the words in her mouth—"Is it our house?"—but when she parted her lips, nothing came out. Geedy and Iesha looked at her with hurt in their eyes, but they said nothing. Then Joyce looked at the black rings around the upper windows of her row house and at the little funnels of gray smoke seeping from her front door, and she knew.

As Joyce stood on the sidewalk, staring at the remains of her house and holding her school papers limply in her hands, Geedy burst into tears.

"What are you crying about, Geedy?" she asked him.

"They said you was gonna kill me when you got home, Mama," Geedy said, blubbering. "Don't kill me, Mama, please don't kill me."

Geedy looked so small and vulnerable that Joyce could not work up any anger toward the boy. She knew she should spank him, but she felt too empty and beaten. Odessa came over and hugged Joyce and told her that Geedy had already been spanked twice—once by Odessa herself and once by Odessa's nephew Prince, who happened to be walking by and recognized the need for a man's firm discipline. Odessa approved; a man's whipping was different from a woman's, she thought.

Joyce walked into her smoking house to assess the damage. Her first concern was where she and the children would sleep that night. Then she saw everyone's waterlogged clothes, and the collapsed ceiling, and the kids' schoolbags and homework papers scattered across the floor, smeared with grime and firemen's boot prints. The tears wanted to come, but she held them back. All her life, Joyce had taught herself to meet disaster and disappointment with stoicism and determination. She decided to get busy, to smother her shock and sorrow with work and concentration. She began to poke through the rubble, performing a sort of triage by dividing her worldly possessions into three categories: salvageable, borderline, and gone.

As Joyce went to work, Odessa set about making sure Joyce and her children had a place to sleep and food to eat. She had seen the damage to Joyce's place, and she knew they could not stay there. Their beds were ruined, and so were most of their clothes. Odessa pulled out comforters and quilts, many of them plucked from people's trash, and set up places to sleep in her living room. She went to the freezer and pulled out some of the frozen pork chops she had bought on sale at Integrity Meats. She had not planned to eat the meat until later in the month, but the fire had changed everything. She would worry later about how to stretch her food budget until her next welfare check and stamps arrived.

Now it was time to deal with Brian. When it came to playing with matches, Odessa turned deadly serious. She had lost more than one home to a fire caused by a child's careless ways. Darryl alone had burned three of her houses when he was a young boy. After the third time, Odessa went to the dollar store and bought a big box of kitchen matches. She struck them again and again, pressing their burning heads to each of Darryl's ten fingers as the boy wailed and struggled. The burns raised blisters the size of dimes, but the punishment produced the desired effect. Darryl may have ended up in Graterford prison, but it wasn't for arson. He never burned down another one of his mother's houses.

Odessa sat Brian down in the living room and asked him what had happened at Joyce's. She did not tell Brian that Geedy had already told her of Brian's role in urging his cousin to set fire to the bed.

"Baby, are you sure you didn't have nothing to do with that fire?" Odessa asked. "You sure it was just Geedy all by himself?"

"Uh-huh," Brian said. "It was Geedy."

"Well, Geedy said you told him to stick it to the bed and see what happened," Odessa said.

Brian studied the dark stains in the shag carpet beneath his sneakers. "I didn't," he said.

Odessa reached over and lifted Brian's chin so that the boy was forced to look into her face. "Brian, don't tell me a tale, or else I'll sit on you hard and I'll half kill you," she told him.

Brian looked away and shrugged.

"Now, tell me the truth," Odessa said. "Did you tell Geedy to stick it to the bed?"

Brian let his lower lip droop. "Yeah," he said.

It was then that Odessa told her grandson that he was going to get a warning and a whipping. The warning was for playing with matches. She told him how close he had come to killing himself and his cousins and the twin babies. She warned him that if she ever caught him with a match again, she would burn every finger on his hand, just as she had done with Kevin after he had torched her entire top floor.

The whipping Brian was about to receive was not for playing with matches, Odessa said. It was for lying about what he had done. She demanded that her grandchildren always tell her the truth, she told him. Then she spun Brian around and smacked him hard on his narrow rear end. Brian squeezed his eyes tight and bit his lip, but as hard as he tried to fight the tears, they came anyway and wet his cheeks and dripped down his cheeks and onto his wobbly little neck.

For the next several days, Odessa was consumed by the aftershocks of Joyce's fire. She took it upon herself to tie together the many fraying strands of her daughter's life. She did not want Joyce to use the fire as an excuse to drop out of school. Getting a degree and a job and getting off welfare was more important, Odessa thought, than such prosaic concerns as eating and sleeping. She told Joyce to worry about staying in school, and to let her worry about keeping her and the children housed and fed and clothed.

Joyce had no intention of allowing the fire to interrupt her job training. The first phone call she made after the fire was to the school. She told them she would have to miss one day, perhaps two. But under no circumstances, she told them, would she drop out of school because of the fire. The school's administrators assured her that they would hold her place in class and arrange for her to make up any missed work.

By the morning after the fire, Joyce felt resigned but also resolute. She and the children had spent the night sleeping on comforters spread out on Odessa's living room floor. Now Joyce sat on Odessa's porch, dressed in the only decent clothes she owned now—the same dress skirt and blouse she had worn to school the day before.

"If it's not one thing, it's another," she said. "Bad things happen, I guess, and I've had more than my share. But I'm not one of those people who gets down and stays down. I'm not going to sit here and cry about what happened. Maybe some people would use this as an excuse to give up and quit trying. Not me. I've got to keep pushing ahead. I have a goal, and that's to graduate and get a job. It's gonna take more than a little old fire to stop me from getting there."

Joyce was not even angry at Geedy. In fact, she felt a twinge of guilt for not being home every day to watch over him. She thought a seven-year-old needed his mama at home, though that certainly was not possible in Geedy's case, given Joyce's circumstances.

"I guess my little boy was bored being left home, and he needed something to amuse himself with," she said.

Joyce had sent Geedy off to school with a kiss and a hug that morning, and now she set about putting her life back together. The Red Cross had given her a $373 voucher to buy clothes at Kmart and another voucher for $88 to buy food at the Thriftway market. Odessa dug through her big plastic garbage bags of trash-picked clothes and found something for everyone in Joyce's family. She found a school outfit for Joyce, tiny shorts and T-shirt sets for the twins, and jeans and sport shirts for Geedy. She also dug into the set of trash-picked clothes she was saving because they were a size too big for Brian. She gave them to Geedy even though they were too big for him, too.

That morning, a Friday, Odessa drove Joyce to Kmart and the Thriftway. She wanted to get Joyce's food and clothing needs satisfied so that Joyce could be back in school the first thing Monday morning. At Kmart, Joyce used the vouchers to buy herself two more outfits for school, and socks and underwear for Geedy. She spent the voucher on meat and vegetables at the Thriftway, and Odessa gave Joyce a few dollars' worth of her food stamps for bread and milk.

Then Joyce told her mother about the only small bit of good fortune that had befallen her that week. It was check day. Her welfare check was to be issued that day, and it could not have come at a more opportune time. Joyce was flat broke. Odessa drove her to the financial exchange, and then over to the SAV-A-LOT. There Joyce spent $55 from her welfare check on ground hamburger and fresh tomatoes, cucumbers, and onions. It was enough food for several dozen hot meals, which she intended to serve on paper plates and sell door-to-door in the neighborhood that Saturday. That was what people in North Philadelphia did when they needed to raise quick cash. They sold dinners. On Saturday afternoon, Joyce sold enough dinners at $6 each to raise $220.

That same Saturday, Odessa drove to the Home Depot outlet, where she showed the manager a letter from the Red Cross verifying that Joyce had been burned out of her home. She suggested that Joyce's calamity qualified her for a discount. The manager agreed, and Odessa used part of that month's SSI payment to buy enough discounted drywall to repair at least one of Joyce's upstairs rooms. Then she telephoned her son Willie, the New Jersey contractor, and told him to come inspect Joyce's place. She wanted Willie to tell her how much it would cost to buy the materials necessary to repair the place. She intended to take up a collection from every extended family member in North Philadelphia to pay for materials. Labor costs were not an issue. The unwritten family code required that Willie do the work for free, assisted by the many Williams and Boone cousins and nephews with their assorted self-taught skills in carpentry, plumbing, and electrical wiring.

Later that day, Odessa drove to a warehouse on Indiana Avenue, where the shelves were stacked high with home building supplies. The warehouse was run by the Building Materials Exchange, which sold surplus and salvaged building materials to low-income families. Odessa had discovered the warehouse when she was renovating her row house. The paint on her walls, the cabinets in her kitchen, the tiles in her bathroom—all of it had come from the warehouse, at half the price she would have paid in a retail store. Now Odessa searched the shelves for low-cost drywall, paint, and plywood for Joyce's repairs. She was only pricing the items. She didn't want to buy anything yet because she was going trash picking the next week—and she never knew what she might find in somebody's trash pile.

All that weekend, Odessa made phone calls. She telephoned her children, her nephews and nieces, her in-laws—the entire Boone clan. She told everyone that she needed one of two things from them: cash to buy building materials for Joyce, or labor to help Joyce put her house back together. She said she would soon set an upcoming weekend as the date for a two-day rebuilding party at Joyce's, a sort of urban barn raising to make the row house habitable again.

Next, Odessa tried to find a temporary home for Joyce and her children. After two nights together in her cramped row house, both Odessa and Joyce realized that the house could not hold so many people. They sent Iesha and her three babies up the street to stay at Elaine's place. Then they made plans for Joyce to move temporarily into the row house next door, at 712 Allegheny. The place had been empty since the owner moved out years earlier. Odessa had sought the man out and asked his permission to use the row house, pointing out that he had shown no interest in holding on to the property or keeping it up. The man gave her the house keys, and Odessa held on to the row house as a hedge against calamity. It had since evolved into a storage facility, where Odessa stacked trash-picked furniture and clothing until she figured out what to do with it.

Number 712 was dirty and grim, but it was habitable. Odessa asked her nephew Clarence, an unemployed handyman who lived around the corner, to clean the place. Clarence—everybody called him Bo—sometimes succumbed to the temptations of the streets, and occasionally he disappeared for days at a time. But he was intensely loyal to Odessa. She relied on him for odd jobs and errands. Bo quickly cleaned up number 712 and, without being asked by Odessa, hauled out Joyce's TV set, VCR, and home entertainment center from her charred row house. They had survived the fire. Bo cleaned and dried the items, then set them up inside number 712. With Odessa's trash-picked armchair and sofa, a few spare mattresses and comforters, an old bureau, and Joyce's salvaged home entertainment center, the place looked like a Salvation Army showroom. But it was clean and dry. Joyce, Geedy, and Joyce's fifteen-year-old son, Curtis, moved into their temporary new home that weekend.

On Monday morning, Odessa drove Joyce to the job training institute. She did not want to rely on the bus. She insisted that Joyce arrive early, with enough time to reestablish herself in class. She did not anticipate any problems, but she was also a person who left little to chance. "If you're there early," Odessa told Joyce, "they see how serious you are, and they'll put you right back in the routine."

Joyce nodded in agreement, but she was preoccupied with her outfit. She was wearing a new black-and-white sport coat and plum slacks she had bought at Kmart. On one leg of the slacks were dark smears. Joyce looked at them closely and realized that Danielle had wiped her buttery fingers there when she hugged her at breakfast. Joyce dabbed at the spots with a tissue as her mother told her not to worry about how she looked.

As the old Caprice pulled away from the curb, Elaine watched from her porch. She was concerned about Joyce's state of mind.

"With her being a recovering addict and all, when something like this hits, it would be easy for her to backslide," Elaine said. "My priority right now is to take care of all the little things worrying her, so she can concentrate on staying in school. That's what I'd want her to do for me."

Elaine had washed a load of smoke-filled clothing recovered from

Joyce's house. Among them were Iesha's school clothes. Elaine wanted to salvage Iesha's clothes so that the girl did not have an excuse to miss school. She had laid them out to dry across the back of an old sofa on her porch, and now she sniffed at them.

"They're not too bad," Elaine told Iesha, who was sitting on the porch eating a bowl of cereal while managing simultaneously to smoke a ciga-rette. "You can wear them."

Iesha shook her head. "I'm not wearing those," she said. "They smell like smoke."

Elaine didn't care to argue with Iesha. It was obvious she had no inten-tion of going to school that morning. She had slept in past 9 A.M. Now Iesha begged her aunt to write a letter to the high school saying Iesha wouldn't be attending classes for a couple of days because of the fire. Elaine consented. If Iesha wanted to miss school, there wasn't much she could do about it. She was Joyce's child, not hers.

Elaine sat on the bare wood porch and wrote on a piece of notebook paper:

> To whom it may concern:
>   Iesha won't be able to attend class for about 2 days because she
> and her mother had a fire in there house and her clothes and every-
> thing else was ruin.

At least, Elaine thought, Iesha could stay home and take care of her own children for a change. Odessa had left the babies in Iesha's care while she took Joyce to school. For the rest of the morning Iesha sat on the porch, smoking and chatting, as her children played at her feet.

On her way into class, Joyce stopped and looked at a small exhibit on a bulletin board titled *Success Stories.* The board contained dozens of color photos of smiling faces—graduates of the institute who had found full-time or part-time jobs and had broken free of the welfare system. Joyce scanned the names of their new employers: Meridian Bank, Temple University, Q.V.C., the U.S. Postal Service, the University of Pennsylvania, the Social Security Administration. Below the photos was a message: *Thought for the day—To reach the peak of a mountain, you have to begin at the bottom.*

Joyce tapped one of the photos with her finger and said, "I may be at the bottom now, but I'll be right up there at the top come spring."

On the drive back home, Odessa drove through the tidy working-class neighborhoods of Northeast Philadelphia. She loved to daydream about moving her entire family away from the crime and privation of North Philadelphia, to a place in the Northeast with a lawn and shade trees. As she drove down Rhawn Street, she noticed a *For Sale* sign on the sidewalk. Beyond it was the most beautiful house she had ever seen. It was a stone mansion with gabled windows flanked by towering oaks and a row of tall spruces encircled by a graceful stone wall. To Odessa, it looked like a country house in the middle of the city. It was the kind of place with enough bedrooms for her four grandchildren, with plenty of room for her mother and her handicapped brothers and whatever stray children she took in. "My dream house," she said, staring at it from her car window.

Odessa wrote down the telephone number of the real estate agent. She knew it was preposterous for someone like her to consider buying such a place. Surely it would cost at least $100,000, she thought, maybe more. But she would call the agent and inquire anyway, in the event she miraculously came into a fortune. "I believe the Lord gives you what you deserve," she said. "If the Lord thinks I deserve this, I'll get it somehow."

The next morning, Odessa was awakened by a loud banging on her front door. She dragged herself out of bed and made her way downstairs. She squinted through the filmy yellow haze on the living room window and saw a tall white man standing on the porch. She opened the door and heard the man say, "Good morning, ma'am, do you have any used furniture you'd like to sell for cash?"

Odessa did not know what to say. The man looked like something out of a dream. He handed her a business card that said, *Cash Today for Any Furniture, Dishes, Rugs, Lamps, Pictures, Jewelry*. At the bottom was a phone number and the man's name, Bill Douglas.

Odessa told the man to wait a minute. She shut the door and left him waiting on the porch. She wanted to collect her thoughts. Of all the houses in North Philadelphia, she wondered, what had brought Mr. Bill Douglas to her front door? Had someone on the street told him that the lady in 714 had a basement full of old furniture? Or was it pure chance?

She looked again at Mr. Douglas on the porch and reread his card. Then she walked as quickly as her heavy body would allow, down the basement steps to her furniture stockpile. She saw a curio case she had retrieved from a trash pile in Northeast Philadelphia the week before. She dragged it out to the porch and asked Mr. Douglas what he would pay her for it.

Odessa took $50 from the man and mentally deducted $40 to pay her overdue water bill. She heard him ask if she had any old lamps or dishes. No, she told him, but she knew where to look for them. She told him she had more furniture downstairs. He promised to return soon and look it over.

After Mr. Douglas had left, Odessa sat down and looked at the money in her hand. She thought about her prayers from the night before, and she wondered if Mr. Douglas was a Christian sort of man.

On the front porch that afternoon, Odessa engaged me in a long discussion about religious faith. She outlined her belief that all good deeds are eventually rewarded for those who are patient and giving. She told me about the furniture man and the $50 payment for the weather-beaten curio case she knew was not worth that amount. She reminded me that God gives people what they deserve, and sometimes more.

"God knew I was broke, so he heard my prayers and he sent Mr. Bill Douglas directly to me," she said. The slanting afternoon sunlight was reflected from the windshields of passing cars onto Odessa's face, and it lit up her eyes behind her spectacles. "Looks to me," she said, "like I'm living right."

CHAPTER SIX

Don't Stand Here

All that summer, the rains did not come. The hard white earth of the Quaker Lace lot cracked in the sun, and fine gray dust settled like sand into the little fissures that snaked out across the brownfield. The walls of wood scrap that formed the shack belonging to Mariluz Gonzalez and Elba Gonzalez changed in hue from brown to gray and finally succumbed to a brilliant white patina that gave the shack a whitewashed look. When the fire hydrant was opened up, the water flowed over the pale dust and ran like milk to the gutters. Sometimes Mariluz would bathe the children at the hydrant, but very quickly their soft skin turned stiff, and dark creases formed inside their elbows and across their necks.

It was the worst drought in the recorded history of Philadelphia. No rain had fallen on the lot since July 16. Now it was mid-September, and even the pipers in the park across the street were heeding the public health warnings blaring from their radios. They moved into the narrow band of shade beneath the park's tired old elms, where they sucked greedily from plastic milk jugs filled with filmy water collected at the hydrant. Mariluz heard the warnings, too, and she forced the children to drink every hour from gallons of bottled water that arrived by the boxload at the donation pile each morning.

On the hot, still night of Saturday, the sixteenth of September, Mariluz and Elba shooed the flies from the children's mattresses and put the six kids down to sleep. Everyone slept fitfully because of the Saturday night traffic and the wild shouts and screams of the pipers and winos in the park. Mosquitos buzzed in the children's ears and flies hovered over the tiny supply of food at the rear of the shack.

The first drops of rain began to tap at the rooftop tarp sometime after midnight. It was a gentle sound, and it soothed the children. But soon the rain fell harder, and toward morning it sounded like a waterfall. Great waves of water crashed down on the roof and against the walls, jolting Mariluz and Elba awake. Already their clothes were damp. They looked around and saw that the water had seeped up through the dirt, penetrated the pallets on the floor, and was now soaking the bottoms of the mattresses. They woke the children and tried to get the mattresses up off the ground, but the sudden flurry of activity seemed to destabilize the flimsy shack. The tarp above them suddenly shifted and collapsed, unleashing a torrent of water that broke over them in a single, soaking wave.

Everything they owned was ruined. The two women's clothing and their children's, too, which they had stacked so neatly the night before on shelves made of scrap lumber, was stained and soiled. The children's boxes of cereal were soggy. The mattresses and sheets and blankets were stained brown with muddy water. Even in the hazy warmth of early morning, the children shivered in their wet clothes.

Mariluz got everyone outside, where they were shocked at how naked and exposed the shack looked with its roof gone and its walls leaning weakly inward. All around them, Tent City seemed to be sinking into a lake. The tents where people had so carefully dug ditches to divert rainfall were crumpled from the force of water that overflowed the ditches and poured inside. Most of the shacks were still standing, but they had lost their tarp roofs and were flooded inside. The mountain of donated clothes, which everyone had intended to cover with scrap lumber one day soon, was soaked through. The wind had blown away the plastic sheeting that had covered the fresh bread and bagels and Les' Pretzels, and now it was all dissolving into dull brown clumps of dough.

Mariluz cursed in English and Spanish, and she beat her fists on the walls of her shack. She saw one of her shoes lying in the mud. She picked it up and threw it against the shack, and it made a splattering sound like a melon dropped on the sidewalk. She stomped over to the main tent, where she knew a fresh load of children's clothing had been delivered the day before. She found that some of the clothing had stayed dry beneath a set of wooden shelves. She picked out dry clothes for Elba's children and two of her own, but she could find nothing to fit Destiny, her five-year-old. Destiny came over and dug through the pile and found something in her size. It was a green clown outfit, apparently a Halloween costume someone had donated. She put it on and danced in the mud, crying out, "Look at me! Look at me! I'm a clown!"

Mariluz had to laugh, but the disaster could not have come at a worse time. She had big plans for the next day. She was determined to walk down to the welfare office the first thing in the morning and try to get her check and stamps renewed. She had put it off long enough. She was running out of both cash and stamps. She also intended to register Destiny for kindergarten. School had started nearly three weeks earlier, but Mariluz had been so preoccupied with helping Cheri run Tent City and plan for the Center

City demonstration that she'd put that off, too. Now she hated herself for it. She wanted Destiny in school and learning, not wearing clown clothes on a vacant lot.

Later that morning Cheri arrived and took charge of cleaning up. She ordered everyone living in tents to spread them out to dry and then set them up again. She inspected the shacks and decided to rebuild some and tear down others. She conferred with Mariluz and Elba about their shack. The three of them decided that it was no good trying to house children in such a damp, muddy hovel. Cheri invited Mariluz and Elba to move into the third floor of her row house on Randolph Street until they figured out where to go next.

Mariluz and Elba salvaged what they could from the shack and spent the rest of the day packing their belongings into Cheri's old Renault and helping others to clear the lot of soggy debris. Toward evening, J.R. and Chicago found a hammer and a crowbar, and in less than thirty minutes they had torn the Gonzalez shack apart, until all that remained was a neat stack of boards, tarp, and pallets. Next to the bare, flattened spot where the shack had stood, someone had arranged the women's sofa, easy chair, and folding table in such a way that it looked like a living room display in a department store. As Cheri's car pulled away to take everyone to Randolph Street, Mariluz noticed that her furniture was set up precisely the way it had been inside her shack. Somehow, the sight of it comforted her.

Everyone was so tired that they slept hard and long at Cheri's house. The next morning Cheri had to poke at Mariluz several times to wake her. Mariluz heard Cheri chanting, "Big day, Mariluz! Big, big day! Get your butt moving!" Cheri told her she was going to see to it that Mariluz got her welfare check and food stamps reinstated, if Cheri had to personally carry her down to the welfare office. There was no excuse not to, Cheri said. Elba would watch the children. Cheri would handle things on the lot.

Cheri had helped Mariluz set up an appointment with a welfare case-worker for 1:30 P.M. that day. By the time she woke and dressed the children, washed their faces, and fed them cereal and milk in Cheri's kitchen, it was late morning. Mariluz insisted on going back to the lot to check on the rest of her belongings. She had left behind clothing, canned food, and some of the children's toys. She persuaded Cheri to drive her to the lot, where she spent an hour rummaging through the ruins of the shack, collecting toys and food and disposable diapers. At some point she checked the time and saw that it was nearly one-thirty. She threw everything into damp cardboard boxes and began walking in the stifling midday heat to the welfare office at Front and Lehigh.

As she walked, Mariluz began to dread the visit. On the days that she picked up her AFDC cash, the time spent inside the dingy welfare office was almost tolerable, despite the long waits in line. On those occasions she associated the place with cash, and thus a sense of reward, if not pleasure. But her other visits—the ones in which a caseworker asked probing questions about her personal affairs—were painful ordeals. She felt defensive and exposed. She never grew accustomed to sharing intimate details of her life with a stranger. And her life, she knew, was rich in the sort of details that piqued the interest of caseworkers.

Mariluz had been born in Puerto Rico twenty-nine years earlier. As an infant she was taken by her mother to live in North Philadelphia, to a row house only a few blocks from the Quaker Lace factory. She hardly knew her father, she said, for her mother moved from house to house with a series of live-in boyfriends, who fathered five more children. Mariluz and her siblings were taken by their mother to live with men in North Philadelphia, and later to Massachusetts, to New York, and finally to Paterson, New Jersey. During that period, she said, she was repeatedly raped by one of her stepfathers. When she told her mother about it, she was told that she was mistaken, that such a thing could not possibly happen.

At age thirteen, Mariluz came home from school one day to her mother's apartment in New Jersey to find the apartment packed up and cleaned out. In the hallway was a suitcase packed with her belongings. From that day on, she said, she was essentially on her own. Her mother had arranged for her to live with members of a Pentecostal church in North Philadelphia, who raised her as a Pentecostal, and she adhered to their beliefs and practices until she was fifteen. That year, she decided she could not abide by the church's ban on the wearing of jewelry and makeup, so she ran away and returned to live with her mother, who had by this time moved back to North Philadelphia.

That year she dropped out of high school while attending tenth-grade classes. She began hanging out on the streets with her friends, smoking marijuana and drinking beer. When she was eighteen, she landed a job as a bartender in a nightclub. There she met a man named Cruz, who fathered her first child, a boy named Aaron, who was born the year Mariluz turned twenty.

"I didn't want a baby then," she recalled. "I always thought I'd have babies much later, when I was older—and married. But I got pregnant, and from then on nothing worked out the way it was supposed to. My life went out of control."

She divided her time between the nightclub and the streets. She wore heavy makeup and miniskirts, danced all night, dated drug dealers. Some of the people she associated with not only sold crack but smoked it. In fact, smoking crack was so common among her friends that she soon found herself smoking the stuff and liking it.

Some of her girlfriends were members of the Westmoreland Girls, a street gang that sold drugs at Fifth and Westmoreland. They invited Mariluz to join. As an initiation rite, she beat up a girl on the street. Soon she was smoking crack regularly and selling Satan brand heroin in $10 bags. On some days she earned several hundred dollars. But she was also neglecting her baby boy, and eventually he was taken away from her by DHS social workers.

Mariluz was addicted to crack and still smoking when she became pregnant with Destiny. The father was somebody named Willie, a one-night stand. Despite her cocaine use, Mariluz knew from pamphlets she had read at the public health clinic that she was endangering her baby's health. As her due date neared, she promised herself that if the baby was born healthy, she would never touch drugs again. Destiny was born as normal and healthy as a baby could possibly be, given her mother's circumstances. So Mariluz kept her promise and willed herself to stop smoking crack, and she insisted now that she had not touched drugs since.

By the time Destiny was born, her father was nowhere to be found, not that Mariluz cared. She wanted nothing to do with Willie. She knew that, as a single mother with a dependent child, she was eligible for welfare. She signed up. Later, after she gave birth to Desiree and Demitre, she watched their father, Alberto, go to prison on drug charges, and Mariluz decided she did not need him, either. With each new child, her welfare check grew.

Now, as she walked toward the low, gray welfare office, Mariluz was finishing her fifth year on welfare. She was weary of her own dependency. She had only herself to blame, and she accepted that. She was willing to pay for her many mistakes and bad decisions, but it pained her that her children were suffering because of her inadequacies. The longer she stayed on welfare, she thought, the more likely it was that she would condemn her children to the same sort of bleak existence.

Mariluz longed for a home and a job—the two stabilizing fulcrums of life she had denied her own children. She had worked as a grill cook at Burger King and a salesclerk at a thrift store, but those were minimum wage jobs that did not pay any more than welfare—and they did not provide medical coverage. If she ever found an affordable home, she promised herself, she would find day care for the kids and go back to school. She wanted to be a pediatric nurse, for she loved to take care of children.

But for now, she was wholly reliant on a welfare check. She felt helpless. It was all she could do to keep the children fed and clothed. She could not afford a decent place to live. In fact, she wondered how anyone on welfare could pay for housing, much less food and clothing. She could only imagine that they had family and friends to rely on, or husbands and boyfriends who gave them money under the table. Mariluz had no family, no boyfriend. Her only true friends were Cheri and Elba, who were as destitute as she was.

"So here I am," she said, walking into the hot, steaming parking lot of the Lehigh welfare office. "Here I am, begging for my check."

As she crossed the lot, Mariluz squinted in the hazy sunlight and saw that the line from inside the building spilled out the front door and down the steps. She was already half an hour late for her appointment. "Shit," she muttered, and she walked to the end of the line.

It took ten minutes for Mariluz to work her way inside the building. The welfare office was a plain, institutional place. It seemed especially dark and dull to Mariluz after her long walk in the bright sunshine. As her eyes adjusted, she looked around and saw people slumped into orange plastic chairs, looking sluggish and despondent. Cheri always made a point of telling Mariluz not to look beaten down like everyone else at the welfare office, but to present herself in a proud and determined manner. She tried to look erect and composed.

The people in line around her seemed agitated and impatient. They were shifting their feet and craning their necks to see what was happening at the front of the line. Some of them were cursing softly under their breath. Mariluz heard snatches of Spanish and English—white English and black English. The Lehigh office was close enough to white Kensington to attract a significant number of white welfare recipients, an unusual sight in most of North Philadelphia.

Mariluz heard a commotion at the rear of the line, where an elderly security guard was trying to keep the doors shut to ward off blasts of hot, moist air from the parking lot. But people outside thought the shut doors meant the office was closing for the day. They yanked them open and squeezed inside, ignoring the old guard, who kept saying, "Keep 'em shut, keep 'em shut."

Inside, another security guard was slumped in a chair, reading a newspaper below a sign that read, *Don't Stand Here.* He did not seem to notice that children were climbing onto the rack containing welfare and public health brochures, dumping the documents onto the floor. Out spilled detailed discussions of the issues presumed to dominate the lives of people on welfare.

There were brochures on AIDS and child nutrition, on homeless shelters and job training programs and safe sex. There were pamphlets telling how to nurse a baby, how to establish paternity for child support purposes, and how to keep your house from burning down. There were warnings about lead paint and instructions on how to report child abuse or neglect to DHS. There was information on how to get child support from someone living out of state. And there was a six-page brochure outlining the many sources of outside income that must be reported by welfare recipients, from alimony and black lung benefits to veteran's benefits and worker's compensation. This brochure also disclosed the penalties for failing to report outside income or lying to the welfare people—up to a $15,000 fine and seven years in jail. And at the bottom of that brochure, Mariluz noticed, was an advisory on promptly reporting any change of address. She wondered how she was supposed to report a change of address when she had no address.

By the time Mariluz reached the front counter, it was after 2 P.M. She gave her name to an Hispanic woman seated behind the glass partition. The woman ran her finger down a list and, without looking up, said: "Your appointment was at one-thirty."

Mariluz shrugged. "I been her since one-twenty," she said. "Been stuck in line all that time."

It was a lie, but it seemed to make the woman pause. She looked up at the line snaking out the front door, then looked across at Mariluz, who stood rigidly with an expectant look on her face. The woman snatched her appointment book from the counter and walked behind a partition to a set of cubicles in the rear of the office. After a few minutes, she returned and said to Mariluz: "Sit down and wait."

In a singsong, sarcastic voice, Mariluz said, "Ohhh, thank you sooo much." She walked to one of the plastic chairs and sat down. From her jeans pocket she withdrew her welfare ID card. She stared at the color photograph of her narrow face with its deep, dark eyes and pursed mouth. She thought the picture made her look old.

After a brief wait a black woman wearing a dark skirt and white blouse appeared from behind the partition and shouted, "Mariluz Gonzalez!" Mariluz shouted back, "That's me!"

The woman introduced herself as Mrs. Staley. She took Mariluz to a rear cubicle, where the two of them sat facing each other across a desk that held a computer terminal. Mariluz noticed how quiet it was in the cubicle. It was as though someone had flicked a switch that turned off the sound of squabbles and complaining from the crowded waiting room.

Mrs. Staley smiled at her, which relaxed Mariluz. Perhaps this would not be so difficult, she thought. Mrs. Staley punched up Mariluz's case file onto the computer screen and announced: "You've been cut off."

"Oh, I know that," Mariluz told her. "That's why I'm here."

"Do you know why you were cut off?" Mrs. Staley asked.

"Nope," Mariluz said. "That's what I want to find out."

"Well, you were cut off because you missed an appointment," Mrs. Staley said. "That's the procedure."

Mariluz took a deep breath and tried to explain all that had happened to her since she left the abandoned row house on Somerset Street. She wondered how much she should reveal, and whether certain details were important. She decided not to mention the fact that Alberto's wife had showed up on the lot the day before, challenging Mariluz to a fistfight over some imagined offense. But she did mention the argument with her roommate's boyfriend that got her evicted from the apartment on Somerset Street.

Mrs. Staley cut her off and said, "So you're homeless?"

"I guess so," Mariluz said. "I'm living on the lot."

"The lot?"

"Fourth and Lehigh."

"Oh, yes," Mrs. Staley said. She seemed to know about Tent City.

She asked Mariluz if she had brought "proof of past management."

"What?" Mariluz asked. She had no idea what the woman wanted.

"Something that shows how you get by. How you manage," Mrs. Staley said. "Do people help you with money? Do they give you food?"

"Oh, yeah, we get lots of donations on the lot," Mariluz said. "Food, old clothes, Pampers, furniture, ice, like that."

Mrs. Staley asked whether it was a structured sort of thing, with formal donations and signed receipts, or was it just people showing up and giving things away.

"Just people coming by every day and giving us stuff," Mariluz said.

Mrs. Staley asked if there was a mailing address at the lot. Mariluz said no, but she mentioned the Kensington Welfare Rights Union walk-up office, on Fifth Street. Other Tent City people got their mail there. She recited the address to Mrs. Staley, who wrote it down.

Mrs. Staley reached into a drawer and pulled out several forms. She showed them to Mariluz. One was titled *Appointment Notice and Verification Check List*. It had little boxes for cash assistance, food stamps, and medical assistance. In order to reapply for all three, Mrs. Staley said, Mariluz would have to bring in her Social Security card, birth certificates for her children, and a statement from her landlord.

Mariluz kept her Social Security card and the children's birth certificates at a friend's house. She knew better than to bring them to the lot, where they might be stolen, lost, or flooded. Just about everyone at Tent City kept important papers stored safely elsewhere. They were more valuable than cash. They were poor people's passes into the welfare system.

Though Mariluz had access to her primary papers, the landlord's statement was a problem. She had no landlord, much less a paper signed by one.

Before she could ask about the landlord, Mrs. Staley showed her another form. It was titled *Verification of Residence, Rent and Utilities (To Be Completed by the Owner or Landlord)*. It had spaces for the rent amount, the gas and electric bills, and a line that asked, "Does tenant buy and prepare own meals?"

Mrs. Staley told her to have "somebody from the organization," meaning KWRU, fill out the form. That person should also give written permission to use the KWRU mailing address, and verify that Mariluz was among the homeless people receiving donations on the lot.

Mariluz wondered why the welfare office needed all the forms and information, but she did not ask any questions. She decided to ask Cheri later. Cheri had told her she would fill out any forms she brought back.

Mrs. Staley handed her yet another form, titled *Absent Parent Verification*. She explained that Mariluz had to verify that the fathers of her children were not living with her. Someone would have to sign the form, which stated that Mariluz lived at a certain address without the children's father, and that she had "care and control" of her children. The person signing the form could be a "friend, neighbor, clergyman, social agency, et cetera, not a member of the household."

Cheri could sign that form, Mariluz thought. She certainly qualified as a friend, and she wasn't a member of the household, at least on the lot. She considered her and Elba's camping out on Cheri's third floor a temporary situation not worth mentioning to Mrs. Staley.

After Mariluz had looked over all the forms, struggling to comprehend some of the more difficult words, Mrs. Staley told her that her food stamps could be restored as early as the next day, and her cash benefits and medical assistance within a few days. But first Mariluz had to return the signed forms and provide the Social Security card and birth certificates. Could she bring everything at 8:30 A.M.?

"Tomorrow morning?" Mariluz asked.

"If you can," Mrs. Staley said. "You should take care of this as soon as possible."

"Okay," Mariluz said, but she doubted that she could find Cheri and have her fill out the forms so quickly.

Mrs. Staley smiled and looked Mariluz in the eye. "I know you must need it real quick if you're homeless. I'd really like to get your stamps and cash restored."

Mariluz folded the forms and got up to leave. She wasn't sure what to say to Mrs. Staley. She had not expected her to be so compassionate. Caseworkers usually seemed so bored and distant. She heard herself say to Mrs. Staley, "Thank you so much." She surprised herself. Never before had she said such a thing to a caseworker.

*   *   *

Back on the lot, Cheri was holding her head in her hands and trying not to cry. Someone had just told her that her friend and ally, Faith Evans, was dead. It didn't seem possible. She had just called Faith's answering machine the night before. His voice sounded so firm and strong. His recorded message told people who called to contact their congressman and complain about the proposed welfare cuts in Washington. The message ended as it always did, with the words "Keep the faith."

Now Faith was dead, killed in his sleep by a heart attack. His death removed for Cheri a powerful ally and inspirational force. Faith had been a national leader of the welfare rights movement. His base was Washington, D.C., but he had traveled often to Philadelphia to support Cheri's work. He had been deeply moved by Tent City, and his emotional attachment to the camp reassured Cheri that Tent City was the most effective way to keep the miseries of the poor in the public eye.

But it was more than Tent City that had drawn Faith to Philadelphia, and now his death created a delicate situation. Faith had been involved in a secret love affair with Cheryl Mucerino, who happened to be the president of the Kensington Welfare Rights Union, as well as Cheri's closest confidant. Faith had died in Cheryl's arms in the bedroom of Cheryl's house in Northeast Philadelphia. But this was not just any old house. It was a house obtained in 1994 after Cheri had led two dozen families on takeovers—breaking in and setting up households in empty houses owned by HUD. After threatening to evict the families, the city backed down and agreed, grudgingly, to provide vouchers for subsidized rents in other homes and apartments.

Because Cheryl was a single welfare mother with four small children, the war council had made sure she received one of the first vouchers. She moved into a small but comfortable house in the Burholme section of Northeast Philadelphia. In effect, Cheri's obstinacy in the face of the authorities' threats to evict Cheryl and others had permitted them to leap over thousands of other poor, welfare-dependent families on the waiting list for subsidized housing vouchers. Now, the death in the subsidized rental house of a man who did not legally live there—and in the arms of a single mother on welfare who was a leader of KWRU—was not the sort of publicity Cheri desired.

Worse yet, Faith's death triggered a deep and almost paralyzing depression in Cheryl. She was numb with shock. She was not capable of caring for her four young daughters. It was left to Cheri to deal with the police and the body—and with Cheryl's children, aged six, five, three, and eighteen months. Cheri had J.R. and Tara move into the house, where they fed the four girls, put them to bed at night, and got the two older girls off to school in the mornings.

In the days after Faith's death, it became obvious to Cheri that Cheryl would have to give up the house. She was helpless. She spent her days at Tent City, curled up on one of the flea market sofas, her face slack with grief, her heavy mascara smeared with tears. She was a tall, big-boned, handsome woman in her mid-twenties, and even in her mourning she carried herself with a certain dignity. But to Cheri, who knew her better than anyone, Cheryl was losing control of her life. She was in the process of being cut off welfare for failure to answer letters and meet appointments. She received $250 every two weeks, plus $375 in food stamps. Without that income, paying her subsidized rent of $203 a month was out of the question. And the eighteenth-month rent voucher was about to expire, with little chance that it would be renewed, given the union's intense political war with the city. Cheri would have to take in Cheryl and find a temporary site on the lot for Mariluz and Elba.

Giving up Cheryl's house was no great loss, Cheri thought. For one thing, Cheryl was about to lose it anyway. For another, the place seemed cursed. Cheri called it "the house from hell." From the moment Cheryl moved in, the neighbors had responded venomously. They'd circulated a petition demanding her eviction, and held a protest rally that sounded eerily like a Tent City protest, complete with angry chants and slogans and placards. They tossed dead fish in the children's wading pool. They threw garbage on the front steps, forbade their children to play with Cheryl's children, wrote down the license plates of Tent City people who visited the house. Several of them told Cheryl to her face that homeless people and welfare people belonged in North Philadelphia, not the Northeast.

The harassment intensified after Faith Evans became a regular house guest. Faith was black. Cheryl was white. The neighbors saw red. The neighborhood was virtually all white, a blue-collar enclave of firefighters and contractors and electricians. Some of them shouted "nigger lover" at Cheryl. Others, according to Cheryl, called the police to complain that "a big black man" was staring at them, trying to intimidate them. Cheryl began finding her mail already opened and read. She did not receive letters that her welfare caseworker said had been mailed to her, which poisoned her already strained relations with the welfare bureaucracy. Once, when Cheryl fell into a diabetic coma inside the house, rumors spread through the neighborhood that she had collapsed from a drug overdose. During this period, Cheryl continued to look for work, and she received several job offers. She had to turn them down, she said, because she was unable to find a baby-sitter willing to stay alone with the children while the house was such a focal point of neighborhood hostility.

Cheri considered Cheryl a soul mate. The two of them had lived parallel lives of poverty and abandonment, tracing the same arc from pregnant teenager to welfare mother to social activist. Cheri was both mentor and partner to Cheryl. Four years earlier, when the two women were neighbors in Northeast Philadelphia, Cheri had spent months persuading Cheryl to leave her abusive husband. At the time, Cheryl seemed passive and helpless, and so dependent on her husband that she was willing to tolerate his regular beatings. Several times, Cheryl and her children hid behind Cheri's locked front door. But each time, after Cheryl's husband beat on the door and promised he would never again harm her, Cheryl relented.

Finally, according to Cheryl, she summoned up enough courage to leave home and hide out with the children in a motel room. When her husband tracked her down and threatened her, she called Cheri. With Cheri's help, she filed charges against her husband and eventually obtained a protection order. Cheri's union helped find housing for Cheryl, who joined KWRU. Pushed by Cheri, she became a member of the war council, which elected her president, a nonpaying job but still a position of some influence within Tent City. Cheryl's metamorphosis from abused wife to social activist was startling even to Cheri, who had counseled many troubled young women. Sometimes she referred to Cheryl as a "beautiful, blossoming flower"—an endearment that would have made Cheryl retch, had she ever heard it.

Now Cheri was forced to take Cheryl under her wing again. She feared the woman was suicidal. Cheryl seemed to have no interest in living. Not even the mention of her children stirred her. The two oldest girls had missed several days of school, prompting a call from the Department of Human Services. Tara, camping out at Cheryl's home, fielded the call and promised to deliver the girls to school personally. At Cheri's row house on Randolph Street, Cheri stayed up with Cheryl late into the night, hugging her, caressing her, trying to talk her through her depression.

While Cheri was attending to Cheryl, Katie—one of the war council members Cheri considered the most reliable—was preoccupied with her own crisis. Like Cheryl, Katie had obtained a house in Northeast Philadelphia via one of the vouchers for subsidized rent so reluctantly provided by the city. The voucher was the war council's reward to Katie for her help in breaking into and taking over houses in 1994. It was those takeovers that had forced the city to back down from its requirement that voucher recipients go through the shelter system.

Katie had moved into a clean, sturdy, three-bedroom brick row house with her daughter Nancy and Nancy's young son and daughter. But the voucher would expire at the end of September, and it was not renewable. The landlord, aware that the city's share of the rent was about to dry up, ordered them to pay the full rent by October 1 or leave. That was out of the question. The rent was $625 a month, a huge increase from the subsidized $127 Katie and Nancy paid under the voucher plan. Nancy received $201 every two weeks from welfare, plus $292 a month in food stamps. Even with Katie's $497-a-month SSI check, they couldn't afford the full $625 rent. They would have to move back into North Philadelphia, where the housing was dirty and dangerous but cheaper.

As the family scrambled to find a new home, Nancy's food stamps were cut off. The letter purporting to explain the reason for her termination was indecipherable. Nancy couldn't understand why her stamps had been terminated. She had attended every scheduled meeting with her caseworker, provided every document demanded. She showed the letter to her mother. Nancy thought Katie, given her exalted position on the war council and her many confrontations with welfare officials, might make sense of it. But Katie was a seventh-grade dropout. She read well enough, but not *this*. It was gobbledygook:

> Your food stamps are being stopped because you failed to submit a timely PA 600 for recertification, or you did not complete the recertification interview scheduled by the CAO. These requirements were explained on the notice of expiration of certification sent to you in a prior month.

Katie folded up the letter and told Nancy to call the welfare office and demand an explanation. Katie had learned from Cheri to insist on answers, to take responsibility for solving her own problems; now she tried to teach her daughter to be more assertive. Nancy was a quiet, solemn young woman. She was slender and pale, with her mother's narrow face and limp blond hair. Like Katie (and like just about every woman at Tent City, it often seemed to Cheri), Nancy had fled an abusive husband. She had left their home in Florida, stealing away one night with the two children in tow, and made her way to Philadelphia to live with her mother. Also abandoned was the best job that Nancy, a ninth-grade dropout, had ever held—a $350-a-week position as a motel manager.

In Philadelphia, Nancy found herself with no job and few prospects. With two young children to raise, she could not afford child care, and thus she could not look for work. (Her husband had been abusive, but at least he had watched the children while Nancy worked.) Katie, still recovering from a heart attack, did not feel physically capable of caring for her grandchildren. And anyway, she was soon consumed by her work with Cheri and the union. So Nancy went on welfare, which fed and clothed her children but did not necessarily house them.

By the late summer of 1995, Gina was nine years old, a third-grader. Billy was an eight-year-old second-grader. Each child had been held back a year in school, which was not surprising, given the fact that they had attended eight different schools in Philadelphia as their mother and grandmother bounced from house to house and from shelter to shelter. Now, thanks to the voucher, they had spent an entire calendar year at the same school. They had made friends and earned perfect attendance awards. That, to Nancy, was the most devastating aspect of the family's impending eviction.

Katie, while distressed at having once again to uproot her grandchildren, held little affection for their current neighborhood. The neighbors knew the family was on welfare, and they sneered. Their attitude enraged Nancy, especially after she found out that some of her neighbors were secretly collecting welfare themselves.

"I see them down at the welfare office, picking up their checks, and they pretend they don't recognize me," Nancy said. "Then they go back home, where they live for free in their parents' houses, so they have enough money to buy their kids nice clothes and pretend they're not on welfare. And all the time they're looking down their noses at us."

Adults and children alike called Gina and Billy "squatter kids" and "shelter kids." The next-door neighbor, noticing one day that Gina's doll had a black face, asked Nancy: "What kind of mother would let her daughter have a nigger doll?" Other white neighbors rebuffed Nancy's attempts at friendship, and her only friend on the block was an Hispanic woman. One day Billy ran home crying because neighborhood kids had told him he was going to die because a black man (Chicago from Tent City) had visited the house.

And now Nancy's food stamps had been cut off. Even with the stamps, it was difficult to keep the family fed. Once a month, Nancy took a $6 cab ride to the Acme supermarket, where hot dogs and hamburger patties were sold regularly on a buy-one-get-one-free basis. She bought enough to last most of the month. But toward the end of the month, the meat was usually gone. Nancy was down now to one meal a day for herself, two for the children. They were eating peanut butter and jelly sandwiches and canned tuna.

At the end of months like this one, Nancy paid particular attention to the TV news reports about welfare reform in Washington. If life on welfare was this difficult now, she thought, what could she expect if the Republicans had their way? She had heard about their time limits and cutoff dates and work requirements. But she heard nothing about job training or child care or affordable housing. Nor had she heard much about food stamps. She could only assume that welfare reform would mean fewer stamps—and possibly none at all. She pictured herself on the street someday, begging for scraps of food for Gina and Billy. And if she didn't get her stamps soon, she realized, that day would arrive sooner than she had ever imagined.

For two days in early September, Nancy called the welfare office on Kensington Avenue. She was bounced from one caseworker to the next, up to a supervisor's office, back down to the supervisor's secretary, over again to a caseworker. Finally she reached a Mr. Hegarty, who told her that, despite the cutoff letter she had cited, her name definitely was not on his Blue List of people subject to food stamp termination. She wasn't supposed to get a cutoff letter.

"It's not your fault," Mr. Hegarty told Nancy over the phone. "It's not my fault. It's the system's fault."

He told her to come in the next morning at 10 A.M. to see a Mr. Hardigan, who would explain how to apply for reinstatement. Nancy was relieved. The next day was the Thursday before the long Labor Day weekend. If she did not get her stamps by then, she feared, she would have to survive without them until the following Tuesday.

On Thursday morning, Nancy gathered up the children's birth certificates, her birth certificate and welfare card, rent receipts, utility bills, and the children's school records. She wrapped a thick rubber band around the whole wad of documents and stuffed them into a plastic shopping bag for the long walk to the welfare office. Nancy always brought along every document she owned. Caseworkers were forever asking for paperwork. If you forgot just one document, your case ground to a halt until you could get home and fetch it.

The welfare office was a $5 cab ride from home, so Nancy and Katie set off on foot. It was a bright, cloudless, humid day, and they stopped along the way to rest on the shaded benches of bus shelters. By the time they reached the welfare office, they were panting like dogs. Their hair was plastered against their foreheads, and their faces were bright pink from exertion.

Inside the office, Nancy collapsed into a plastic chair and caught her breath. Then she got in line and waited to tell a receptionist that she had arrived for her appointment with Mr. Hardigan. She turned to walk back to her seat even before the receptionist sang out the familiar refrain "Have a seat and wait for your name to be called."

While they waited, Katie handed out flyers she had brought along. Cheri had given them to her. They said: "Angry About Being Poor? Join the Kensington Welfare Rights Union. The KWRU Gives a Damn! We are homeless people and unemployed people—we understand how hard it is. We are not part of the Welfare system, and we are not afraid to fight for what we need." People in line read the flyers, shrugged, folded them in half, and tucked them into the little caches of documents each of them carried.

Within ten minutes, Nancy's name was called. Katie walked with her to a cubicle in the rear, where a silver-haired man with a florid complexion and a bulbous nose sat hunched over a computer. He wore a T-shirt featuring a cartoon moose and owl. His alabaster legs poked from a pair of shorts. On his feet were white athletic socks and blue low-cut sneakers.

This, apparently, was Mr. Hardigan. The man looked up from the computer and saw that Katie and Nancy were staring at him with puzzled expressions. "Getting ready to go down the shore," he said, tugging at his T-shirt. "Vacation starts tomorrow."

Nancy gave the man her name. He looked at Katie and said, "I'm Mr. Hardigan. Who are you?"

Katie was tempted to say she was a representative of KWRU. But she decided instead to say, "I'm her mother."

Mr. Hardigan flipped through Nancy's case file and told her that her food stamps had been cut off by mistake. He described the long and complex process of terminating food stamps or other welfare benefits. Somehow, he said, the process had been short-circuited in Nancy's case, and she had been cut off. It wasn't her fault, he told her. It wasn't his fault. It was the system's fault. He would try to reinstate her food stamps as soon as possible.

Katie whispered to Nancy, urging her to ask for retroactive payment for any stamps she might miss. Nancy spoke up and asked about retroactive payments.

"What for?" Mr. Hardigan asked. "I just told you I was gonna reinstate you. You won't miss anything. They'll just be late."

Katie leaned over the man's desk. "Can I ask you a question? Can you tell me again why she was terminated in the first place? It doesn't make sense."

Mr. Hardigan slapped Nancy's case file down on his desk. "It's a long story," he said.

"I got all day," Katie said.

"Well, I don't," Mr. Hardigan said. "I got a long weekend coming up. I don't have time for all your questions."

"I have a right to ask," Katie said.

Mr. Hardigan's fleshy face reddened. "Get out of the booth!" he said. "Right now. I told her what happened. I don't need to tell you, too."

Katie's face tightened. She felt an urge to curse at the man, but she didn't want to ruin Nancy's chances. She knew how badly she needed her stamps. She got up and walked back to the waiting room.

Mr. Hardigan smiled weakly at Nancy. He told her he would put her paperwork through. She could come back the next afternoon, a Friday. Her stamps might be waiting for her by then, he said.

He saw a hopeful look cross Nancy's face. "Of course," he went on, "they might not be there. Then you have to call this number." He wrote a telephone number on a slip of paper and slid it across the desk.

"You can try it, but I don't know if anybody will answer," Mr. Hardigan said. "Holiday weekend, you know."

CHAPTER SEVEN

Fried Perch
on White Bread

L ate that night, after Odessa had drifted off to sleep despite tiny squalls of coughing and wheezing from Danielle, the phone rang. It was Israel. He was in trouble. He always called his mother when things went bad, and this was a truly bad night. Israel had had a nasty spat with Anita, his live-in girlfriend of nine years. Anita had retaliated by announcing that she was throwing Israel's four boys out of her house in the dead of night. Worse yet, she warned Israel that she would have him arrested for trespassing if he tried to come get them, despite the fact that Israel had lived in Anita's row house on Randolph Street for several years. Anita had already thrown Israel out of the house following an argument the previous week; he had been sleeping in his van ever since. Now Israel was begging Odessa to drive over to Randolph Street to rescue her grandsons from his soon-to-be ex-girlfriend.

"I'm coming over, baby," Odessa said, and she hung up the phone softly to avoid waking Danielle. Then it hit her: how in the world was she going to find enough space in her little row house for four growing boys, plus big old Israel? She had just moved Joyce and her children out from underfoot to the row house next door. The disruption had just about worn her out. And now this. How would she feed everyone? She barely had enough food by the end of each month now. And Israel and his boys loved to eat.

These were the questions that nagged at Odessa as she put on a pair of dark slacks and an old T-shirt and slipped on Pastor Tony's red Super Snoopy jacket. She walked down the hall and woke up Jim and told him to watch the other children until she got back. As she made her way downstairs to fetch her car keys from where she had hidden them inside a trash-picked dishwasher in the dining room, a single thought presented itself to her: The devil is sure busy tonight.

Odessa liked Anita, but she had always been wary of the woman's volatile personality. Anita was the jealous type. When Israel worked during the summers at his Recreation Department job, Anita would call the Waterloo Playground office and ask people there if Israel was with another woman. It was Anita's suspicious nature, in fact, that prompted her to kick Israel out of her house—which was actually owned by Anita's mother, though Anita had charge of the place. According to Israel, Anita pawed through his wallet one day and found several telephone numbers on slips of paper. She accused him of seeing other women and ordered him out of the house. She stayed inside with Israel's boys, who pretty much considered Anita their mother, even though three of them—Steven, thirteen, Anthony, eleven, and David, ten—were born to Israel's first wife, Joanne. Israel had obtained legal custody of the fourth boy, Ray-Ray, twelve, a family friend.

When Odessa arrived on Howard Street, the boys were waiting for her. They had packed their clothes and personal belongings. Odessa stuffed everything into the Caprice. Anita didn't have much to say, except that she planned to go to court the next day and get a protection order against Israel, who she said had threatened her. Odessa put the boys in the car and picked up Israel at her mother's row house across the street. Israel had managed to get his TV set, his shotgun, some clothes, his fishing rod, and the boys' set of encyclopedias out of Anita's house during the week. It all went into Odessa's trunk. Israel complained that Anita had hidden his key ring, which contained the house key, his van key, and the keys to the Waterloo Playground.

Odessa told him to worry about the keys the next day. She wanted to get the boys bedded down and off to sleep. They had school the next morning. Back home, she hauled out the same comforters and blankets that Joyce's family had used. She spread them in the living room on the stained carpet remnants she had taken from a Dumpster behind a carpet store in New Jersey. She put out trash-picked sheets and a blanket on the living room sofa for Israel to sleep on. Then she told everyone good night. She climbed wearily up the stairs and collapsed beside Danielle, who dozed fitfully on Odessa's bed.

The next afternoon, after Odessa had spent the morning getting all eight grandchildren fed, dressed, and off to school, the phone rang. Again, it was Israel. Odessa thought he was calling from Howard Street. But Israel said, "Mama, I'm locked up."

Israel was calling from the Roundhouse, the drab, circular police headquarters building in downtown Philadelphia. He had been charged with violating a protection order. As Anita had promised, she had obtained the order against Israel that morning. When he arrived that afternoon and demanded his keys and other possessions, she ordered him to leave. That is when the altercation had erupted.

The way Israel told it, he'd simply walked into the house and asked Anita for his belongings. When she refused and clutched the key ring in her hand, Israel said, he lunged at her, grappled with her, pushed her, and wrested the keys from her hand. Then he'd stalked outside. He may have cursed her, he said, but nothing more.

Anita called the police. When they arrived, she offered her version of events. Israel did more than just shove her, she told the officers. She described how he had punched her in the mouth, knocking two of her teeth loose, and kicked her, too. Anita provided a vivid and quite public description of the fracas, delivered in her high-pitched voice as she stood on the sidewalk outside her row house, waving her arms wildly in the sunshine.

Israel was yelling, too, trying to give the officers his version. Some of his relatives and a few of the old heads on the street advised him to control his temper, but this just made him scream louder. He hollered at the police to check Anita for blood or bruises or swelling or loose teeth—anything that would prove he had struck her. She looked perfectly fine to him. The police said Israel could deal with those issues in court. Right now, they told him, they would have to arrest him for violating the protection order, which prohibited him from approaching Anita. They put handcuffs on Israel, right there in the middle of Howard Street in front of all his friends and relatives. They led him to a squad car, where he sat shaking with rage and shame.

At the Roundhouse, Israel was so agitated that he could not eat—not that he would have been able to stomach the stale bread and processed cheese he was offered. He fantasized about ways to get back at Anita, and he devised complex schemes designed to make her suffer. He did not regain his composure until one of the old heads in the holding cells told him, "Be cool. She's not worth it. Get out a protection order on her, then just leave her alone and forget about her."

It was then that Israel called Odessa and asked her to raise the cash to pay his bail. He had been assigned a nominal bond because he had no criminal record. It was only $1,000, which meant Odessa had to come up with $110—or 10 percent of the bail plus a $10 quarter-sessions fee. That was chump change for most people, but it was more than half of Odessa's biweekly welfare check.

Odessa had only a few dollars left in the house. She had spent her check and stamps on bills and on a fresh load of groceries to feed Israel and his boys. Check day was still two days away. She barely had enough quarters for the parking meters outside the Roundhouse, where she was sure to get a parking ticket unless she kept the meter fed.

It was at times like this that Odessa turned to her old friend Warney.

Warney was a Puerto Rican who ran a salvage yard in North Philadelphia. He was also a neighborhood loan shark. Warney always had cash on hand, which he loaned out at interest rates of 25 percent and more. But because Odessa was an old family friend, Warney had a special rate schedule for her. If she needed cash for personal use—say, to buy something for the house—he charged her interest. If she had a family emergency, such as a death or an arrest, he did not, provided she repaid him within a reasonable period. When Odessa asked Warney for $110 to bail out Israel, he gave her the cash straightaway and told her to repay him as soon as she could.

Odessa drove down to the Roundhouse, breathing heavily from the moist summer air as it mixed with traffic fumes in the searing heat. Her chest was tightening and her legs were swelling. She fed her last quarters into a parking meter, bailed out her son, and drove him home. There she set up her nebulizer and sat gasping until she had sucked in enough cleansed air to open her breathing passages. When she could breathe again, she lay back and put her legs up on the sofa until the swelling subsided.

For the rest of the day Israel sat in the living room, sweating in the still, stale air and stewing about the latest twist his life had taken. It was bad enough that the Recreation Department had told him that there would not be enough money in the budget to pay for his part-time position the following summer. Now he had lost his place to live, and his boys were sleeping on their grandmother's floor.

Israel worried about the boys being wrenched from the woman who had been their surrogate mother all these years. They were fond of Anita. Even though one of the boys had told Anita, "We hate you for lying on our dad," and another had assured Israel, "Let her go, Dad, we'll be okay," Israel knew the boys had to be hurting. Even so, he was through with Anita. In fact, he had just met another woman, who was as gentle and understanding as Anita was shrill and demanding. Her name was Monica. They had already dated once, after Anita had thrown Israel out. Now Israel called Monica and told her everything that had happened. They made a date to meet for lunch the next day.

A few minutes after Israel hung up the phone, it rang again. Odessa answered it. It was Anita. Was Israel there? Odessa looked at Israel, who shook his head vigorously. Odessa got back on the phone and lied—Lord forgive me, she said to herself. She told Anita she had not seen Israel.

Anita sounded pitiful. She was crying into the phone. She told Odessa that she was sorry for what had happened to Israel. She said her niece had called the police on him, not her. She wanted him back. Could Odessa persuade Israel and the boys to come back to her? Odessa did not want to put herself in the middle of all this. It was Israel's business, not hers. She told

Anita that Israel was the one to decide whether he went back, not her. Anita tried to say something else but Odessa hung up the phone.

She turned to her son and said, "What I wonder is, where did she get the mouth to call me and beg me to send my son back to her after she got him locked up for no reason?"

The heat broke the next morning. It broke hard, like a dirty carpet snapping on a clothesline. Everything seemed cleansed and refreshed. The grimy yellow haze of late summer was blown away by a soft breeze that delivered a dry, sweet blanket of cooler air. It stirred the prematurely brown leaves of the sycamores along Allegheny Avenue and it blew the litter off Odessa's porch and into the street. The day dawned clear and crisp. The sky was so clear and blue that Odessa could see far beyond the train overpass to the bright silhouettes of the dead and empty factories near Broad Street.

What a day for fishing. That's what Odessa decided to do. She would drop all her troubles and go fishing. She called her mother and told her to get her fishing pole ready. They were going fishing just as soon as Odessa and Israel got the kids out of bed and off to school.

Odessa marched from room to room upstairs, shouting, "Everybody up! Get up or I'll knock the daylights out of you and you'll be dark the rest of your life!" Four of the kids were heaped in the back room. Jim and Kevin slept on one bed, with little Darryl stretched out below them on a comforter spread across the floor. Brian slept in the corner on a portable mattress because he wet the bed and Jim and Kevin refused to let him sleep with them. In the middle room, Delena stretched and yawned on a bed whose sheets had peeled off and dropped to the floor.

Downstairs, Israel was shouting at his four boys to get up off the floor and fold up their sheets and comforters. With the boys sprawled on the floor, Odessa's living room seemed robbed of its usual symmetry. Normally, the sofas and the home entertainment center were set neatly against opposite walls, leaving a cleared path across the carpet to the dining room.

On the coffee table were neatly arranged family photos. There was Darryl standing on the Graterford grounds in his brown prison uniform, looking bullnecked and muscular in his prevegetarian days, when he was pumping iron daily. There was a dated group shot of Jim, Kevin, Delena, and Brian, looking innocent and baby faced. And there were assorted photos of Odessa's relatives in Georgia. Now, with the living room turned into a bedroom, everything was askew. Odessa tried not to let the disorder disturb her, but it did. She felt a powerful need to have everything in its proper place.

Israel turned on the color TV he had salvaged from Anita's, and it emitted the manic shouts and crashes of a Bugs Bunny cartoon. Odessa stepped over her grandsons and turned on her TV because she always watched the local news while she got the kids ready for school. She cranked up the volume in order to hear the newscaster over the cartoon, and her TV spit out a frantic catalogue of the previous night's fires, murders, and car wrecks.

One of the reports caught her attention. There had been a shooting on Diamond Street, on the west side of Broad Street, about three miles from Odessa's place. Four gunmen had burst into a row house and fired at least thirty rounds. Three men were killed and two more were wounded. Odessa sat up straight when she heard the name of one of the dead men. It was Kevin, her cousin by marriage. She shook her head. The news saddened her, but what could she do? She could call the family and offer her condolences, but that was all. She had so many problems of her own that it was difficult to expend emotional energy on distant relatives, even those killed in such a shocking way.

The living room was in shambles. Israel's boys and Odessa's grandsons were tripping over blankets on the floor, falling into one another as they searched for backpacks and homework. Kevin was slouched in the corner, sucking hard at the plastic mouthpiece of Odessa's nebulizer as he struggled to open his clogged airways. Danielle was bawling because Odessa was wiping hard dried mucus from her nose.

Odessa screamed at Jim: "Run next door and wake up Joyce and tell her to get over here right now and take care of these kids!" Joyce appeared minutes later, barefoot, sleepy eyed, her hair wild from sleep. She yawned and poured cereal for the babies while Odessa dressed Danielle. Then Odessa stood up and grabbed Israel by the back of his shirt and dragged him toward the door. His shoes were not yet tied and his hair was uncombed, but his mother pushed him out the door and to the Caprice parked at the curb. She ordered him to drive her to the financial exchange.

A half hour later they were back. There was just enough time for Israel to run to the Chinese store to change one of the $20 bills Odessa had picked up at the exchange, then speed down to the middle school to give the boys the $3 each they needed for lunch on a field trip scheduled for that day. He reached them just as the bus driver was gunning the engine to leave. Relieved that his sons and nephew would not starve during the field trip, Israel drove back to Odessa's in plenty of time to prepare for his lunch date with Monica.

As Israel came through the front door, he saw his mother holding her worm bucket. It was a plastic orange container with a Halloween jack-o'-lantern painted on the side. Odessa kept her fishing worms inside, under a layer of dirt and cornmeal.

"We're going fishing," she told Israel, dangling the bucket under his nose.

"Maybe *you're* going fishing, but I'm not," he said. "I got a date with Monica."

"Not today, you don't," Odessa said. "You've got to go with me and Mom and be our manly protector."

Israel slowly shook his head. "I just been incarcerated for two days, and now you're telling me I've got to go fishing?"

"Yep. Call Monica and tell her," Odessa said.

"I ain't going to call her," Israel said. "I got a lunch date. *You* call her."

"Gimme her number," Odessa said, reaching for the phone. She dialed Monica's number. When Monica answered, Odessa told her, "Listen, dear, I'm canceling your lunch. I need my son to go fishing with me. I'm sorry. You want to talk to him?"

Israel recoiled. He covered his face with his hands. "Noooo," he said.

Odessa hung up and told Israel to get his hunting shotgun out of her car. She did not want to be pulled over by the police and have to explain why she was driving around with a gun in the trunk. Israel zipped the weapon into a leather case and took it upstairs to Odessa's room to hide it under her bed.

"It's safe up there," Odessa said. "My kids won't mess with anything in my room."

"My kids know not to mess with my gun," Israel said. "If they did, they know I'd shoot 'em with it."

Odessa laughed. She was glad to see that Israel's mood was improving. She knew he loved to fish, and he was good at it. Odessa thought a day spent beside a quiet creek in beautiful weather was the perfect antidote for Israel's tortured brooding over Anita. And the fishing wasn't entirely recreational. She needed the food. With Israel's skill and luck, they might bring home enough fish to feed everyone in the house for a long time.

The two of them got into the Caprice and Odessa drove quickly to her mother's house. She parked a block away because Anita's house was directly across the street from Bertha Boone's place. Israel did not want to do anything that might provoke Anita. He stood next to the car while his mother walked down Howard Street to fetch his grandmother.

One of Israel's nieces spotted him and walked over to greet him. Word quickly spread that Israel was back, and several neighbors and relatives walked over to speak with him. They asked him about his arrest and what he planned to do about the charges Anita had sworn out against him.

Mr. Malone, one of the old heads, walked over to make sure Israel wasn't planning to walk past Anita's place. Israel assured him that he was staying on the block only long enough for his grandmother to walk to the car.

"Well, like I tried to tell you the other day," Mr. Malone said, "you've got to keep your cool where women are concerned."

Israel nodded and said, "No disrespect, Mr. Malone. I heard you the other day, but I was out of control. My niece was telling me to keep cool, too, but I wasn't able to listen. That woman got inside my head. I let her take control of me."

"That's it exactly," Mr. Malone said. "A woman will do that to you. But you've got to get past that. You've got to shut her out."

Israel reached out and patted Mr. Malone's shoulder. "That's exactly what I intend to do," he told him.

As he spoke, Odessa and her mother emerged from the narrow doorway of Bertha's row house and made their way down Randolph Street. Bertha got in the Caprice's passenger seat and Israel climbed into the backseat. Odessa sped away, bound for her secret worm site, an empty lot in West Philadelphia. She always dug her own fishing worms; good earthworms cost $3 for a bucket of thirty at most bait shops.

Odessa did not tell anyone outside the family about the lot in West Philadelphia. It was rich with the dark, moist earth that sustained earthworms. When Odessa arrived, she pulled a garden trowel from the trunk and scraped at the litter and refuse that covered the lot. Israel crouched next to her, scratching at the dirt with a twig. He rolled his eyes as his mother explained how to sweep aside layers of trash or dead grass to get at the wet, wriggling worms below.

Odessa and Israel bent low, scraping at the dirt. Within ten minutes, they had filled Odessa's orange bucket and two plastic containers with fat brown bloodworms. They got back in the car and Odessa sped away toward the Ben Franklin Bridge, which would carry them into New Jersey and down to their favorite fishing hole in the muddy, slow-running waters of Woodbury Creek.

At the creek, Israel unloaded the trunk. His boys' encyclopedia set was still inside, and he pawed past the heavy books and a trash-picked VCR to find his tackle box and his two fishing rods. He pulled out his mother's and his grandmother's rods, too, and hauled everything to the bank of the creek. He baited two hooks and flipped two lines where the water gurgled and pitched over a small concrete dam and into a calm pool below. He was sweating in the heat, and dark spots showed where his T-shirt—it bore a map of Africa and the words *Black Power*—clung to his thick biceps and heavy shoulders.

Bertha Boone carried a folding lawn chair, which she set up in the brown mud at the water's edge, where she would not have to stretch to get her baited hook out into the water. She held her rod with one hand, and with the other she gently flipped the line into the still water, where it made a soft splashing sound. She put on a straw hat with plastic pink flowers to shade her tender scalp from the sun, and she leaned back to await her first bite.

Odessa sat down on the concrete buttress of the dam wall where it protruded from the overhanging willow trees. She baited her hook with a short, stubby worm from her bucket and, with a quick flick of her wrist, sent her line sailing out into the dark water. Then she took a plastic spoon and dipped into the small cardboard container of hot pepper soup she had bought at a convenience store along the way. Some of the soup spilled onto the letter *W* on the front of her T-shirt, which bore the message *Williams Family Reunion,* a souvenir of the family gathering Odessa had organized the summer before.

Soon a competition was under way at the water's edge. The Boones took their fishing seriously. The number of fish a family member took in was a measure not only of skill and patience but of character. They chided one another about their fishing abilities. No one was above interfering in someone else's elaborately calculated projections concerning where to cast a line and how fast to reel it in.

Israel caught the first fish, a good-sized yellow perch. Two more quickly followed, one on each line. Odessa and Bertha had not yet felt so much as a nibble.

Israel began to gloat. "I'm fishing. You two old ladies are just playing. I told you two I'd show you how to fish," he said.

Odessa looked up at him and said, "Don't you be catching all the fish, or I'll throw you *and* your fishing pole in the water."

"Dessa, you may be my mom and all," Israel said, "but that doesn't mean I have to *like* you."

From the muddy bank, Bertha shouted: "Son, stop your talking. You're scaring my fish away. Why don't you go over to the other side and leave us in peace?"

Israel reeled in another perch. He pried the hook from the fish's mouth and tossed it in a bucket of river water. Then he advanced toward his grandmother and shook his fist at her.

"Watch out, Mother Boone," he told her. "I got a reputation. I knock people's teeth out. I'll knock your teeth out and it won't even show. No blood, no bruises, no nothing. That's my reputation."

Bertha waved him away, but secretly she was glad Israel had mentioned his troubles with Anita. She had been wanting to raise the issue with him, and now she felt it was proper to do so. But before she could mention Anita, Israel began talking about her.

"That woman," he said. "She hooked me good. She reeled me in and threw me in the pot. She got me locked up good."

Odessa laughed and said, "Looks to me like she took you to the creek and drowned you."

"Mind your own business, Dessa," Israel said.

"She's right," Bertha said. "It's true. That woman took you all the way down to the bottom of the creek and left you there."

"Yep," Odessa said, "you were a fool, Israel. You weren't even a cool fool. You were just an ordinary fool."

Israel tried not to smile. "Hush up, both you old women," he said. "You don't know nothing about me and Anita, and you sure don't know nothing about fishing."

By the end of the afternoon, Israel had easily won the day's fishing competition. He caught nearly thirty perch, and he boasted about it the rest of the evening. Odessa caught fifteen, and Bertha about a dozen. All the fish were destined for Odessa's freezer. But first Odessa would have her four-year-old grandson, whom she had nicknamed Weed, help her clean them. Weed, who was Fred's boy, loved to scrape off fish scales with a teaspoon.

Back home, as Weed flailed away at the perch with his spoon, scattering scales and guts across the dining room table, Odessa figured she had at least $30 worth of fish on hand. That was $30 she could spend on other food. All it had cost her was a few dollars' worth of gasoline. And she had enjoyed a relaxing afternoon in gorgeous weather with her son and her mother. She felt blessed.

Even if she came into some real money one day, she thought, she would still go fishing at every opportunity. But she knew she might not make the effort to clean and freeze the bony perch if she ever reached the point where she did not absolutely have to fish for food as well as for recreation.

As she scaled and gutted the perch, a little rhyme came into her head, and she recited it for Weed.

"When I get off welfare," she told the boy, "I won't hook 'em to cook 'em. I'll buy 'em to fry 'em."

The fresh load of perch did not relieve Odessa of her worries about food. She still had to go shopping, and she still had to make her welfare check and food stamps stretch from one check day to the next. The next morning, she left the babies with Elaine and set out in the Caprice on her regular rounds of thrift stores and food markets, searching for discounts and bargains.

As she left, Odessa told Elaine she was going to Gimbel's and Macy's. That was a little joke among people in North Philadelphia. When someone said they were shopping at Gimbel's and Macy's, it meant they were going to the thrift store or the dollar store. There were no shopping malls in North Philadelphia, much less a high-end department store like Gimbel's or Macy's, or even a Philadelphia institution like John Wanamaker or Strawbridge and Clothier. Those places were in Center City or the suburbs. In the ghetto, there were only thrift stores and dollar stores and discount centers.

Odessa drove first to the Kensington Discount Outlet. A neighbor had told her that eight-packs of chicken backs were on sale for $1 each. Also on sale, she was told, were school composition books at $1 apiece. That was a bargain. The books were $1.89 at Kmart and at the Chinese store.

Odessa had been searching for low-priced composition books. Jim's teacher had told him he would need thirteen of them that semester, six of them by the next day's class. Odessa was determined to get the books that day, even if it meant shortchanging the food budget. She did not want Jim's good grades to suffer because of something as fundamental as a lack of composition books.

At the Kensington Discount Outlet, Odessa bent low to look inside the meat freezer. It was empty. A clerk told her the chicken backs were sold out. She walked to the front of the store to look for composition books. They were gone, too—sold out, the cashier said.

Odessa got back into the Caprice and noticed that the gas gauge was low. The fishing trip had eaten into her gasoline budget. She tried to calculate whether it was worth spending $1.09 a gallon at the Merit discount self-service station in order to drive around trying to save a few pennies on composition books. But she also needed food for dinner, so she decided to invest in some gasoline. She drove to the Merit station and spent $3 of her remaining $25.

Odessa drove down Aramingo Avenue to the Dump, a big warehouse of a store where discounted and damaged household items were sold. The goods were delivered by the trainload and displayed in cardboard cartons arranged on rough wooden tables. Among the items on sale that day were Christmas decorations. Though it was only early October, Odessa was tempted by the low prices. But as important as Christmas was to her family, she considered Jim's notebooks a higher priority. And besides, she had already told her grandchildren that she could not afford a tree that year, much less decorations for it.

She looked down the aisle and saw eight-packs of toilet paper on sale for $2.79. The price elsewhere was $3.99. Odessa put an eight-pack in her shopping basket. She was desperate for toilet paper. Between Israel and his kids and Joyce and her kids, she was going through a roll a day.

Along the back wall she saw a sign for school supplies. She made her way there and found a stack of black composition books. She took off her glasses and squinted at the price tag on the shelf. It was smeared, but it seemed to say $1.09. She counted out thirteen of the books and moved on to the cash register.

The sales clerk ran one of the notebooks through an electronic scanner. On the face of the register the number $1.49 appeared in green computer numerals.

Odessa looked at the number and blinked and said, "I think they're $1.09."

The woman ran another notebook through the scanner. The number $1.49 appeared again. "It's showing $1.49," she said.

"Well," Odessa said, "it said $1.09 on the sign."

The clerk shrugged. "I don't know," she said. "But we have to go by what rings up here."

Odessa sighed and looked down at the notebooks. She counted out six and handed them to the clerk. She would have to come back for the remaining seven notebooks after check day. She paid for six notebooks and the toilet paper. After the clerk said, "Thank you, have a nice day," Odessa muttered under her breath, "That's way too much for composition books."

She drove back to Allegheny Avenue to Cousin's Food Market. She was hoping Cousin's would have meat on sale. She had only $10 left from her welfare check. Inside, she saw that five pounds of chicken legs were selling for $3.49. She picked up a package. She saw oxtails at $2.29 a pound. She loved oxtails, but she would need at least three pounds to make a meal. Chicken wings were out of the question, too. They were priced at five pounds for $4.99.

Odessa ended up buying the chicken legs at $3.49 and a loaf of white bread for $1.69. After she paid, she walked out to the parking lot and said, "That's it. That's just about my last dollar. All I got left now is soda money."

The chicken, mixed with rice and beans and served with corn bread Odessa had on hand, would make one meal. On the following night, she would thaw out some of the perch, bread it and fry it, and serve it on the white bread. With leftover rice and beans and corn bread, that would feed everybody until her monthly SSI check arrived at the end of the week.

As Odessa pulled out of Cousin's parking lot, she saw a familiar woman walking across the pavement. It was Joanne, Israel's first wife and the mother of three of his boys. Odessa wanted to tell her about Israel's fight with Anita.

She called Joanne over to the car and said, "Your kids were thrown out on the street.

"Say what?" Joanne said.

"Anita threw them all out the other night," Odessa said. "She got the police on Israel, got an order out on him, got him locked up. The kids were left out on the street in the middle of the night."

"Where are they?" Joanne asked.

"I got them at my place," Odessa said.

Joanne put her hands on her hips. "I'm gonna smack that woman's face, putting my kids out on the street," she said.

"Don't do that," Odessa said. "We got enough trouble with that woman. But I do want you to come over and see the kids. They're upset. Can you do that for me, baby?"

Joanne squeezed her arm. "Okay, Mama, I'll do it," she said.

Odessa was glad she had run into Joanne, especially with Israel's sons suffering from severe dislocation and anxiety. She was proud of the way Israel took care of his boys, and the way he was always there when they needed him. But they needed a mother's care, too, she thought, and she was stretched too thin by her other grandchildren. She thought Joanne could reassure the boys that everything was going to be just fine.

Odessa drove back home to find both TV sets turned on full blast and the kids running up and down the sidewalk. Israel was watching a cartoon about Elmer Fudd. The classified section of *The Philadelphia Inquirer* was spread before him, with various job opportunities circled in ink. Joyce was home from school, watching Oprah Winfrey on Odessa's TV. Jim was threading his way past both TVs, carrying a plastic laundry tub full of wet clothes.

"Jim!" Odessa said. "You got the wrong clothes! You're supposed to take my clothes out."

Israel looked up and said, "Those are Joyce's clothes, Dessa."

"What are her clothes doing in ahead of mine?" Odessa said. "Mine have priority. It's my house."

Odessa felt overwhelmed by the crush of people in her home. It seemed to her that she had lost control of her life. She was out of money, she had a house full of people to feed, and now she couldn't even get her grandchildren's clothes washed properly.

Israel waved his hand. "Chill out, Dessa," he said. "Everybody's clothes are going to get washed."

Odessa turned and stalked down to the basement to check on the washer. She saw that the dryer was set on cool heat, not full heat. She shouted up the stairs, "Why—is—the—dryer—on cool heat?"

Joyce shouted back that she was drying a pair of jeans that had a design printed on the rear. She didn't want the design to melt. Didn't Odessa remember? They were the jeans they had found while trash picking in Upper Darby.

Odessa muttered to herself and walked back up the stairs and out to the porch. She had to sit down and rest. She hooked up the nebulizer and gave herself a treatment. As she was putting the machine away, she saw Iesha coming out of Elaine's doorway. The sight of the girl reminded Odessa that Danielle needed her medicine. Odessa had taken Danielle to the doctor for her coughing and fever. The doctor had written out a prescription, which Odessa had given to Iesha with orders to fill it.

Now Odessa shouted up the street at Iesha, "Did you get your baby's medicine?"

The blank way that Iesha looked back at her let Odessa know that Iesha had forgotten all about it. That was inexcusable, Odessa thought. The medicine didn't cost a cent. Iesha was covered by Medicaid through welfare. All she had to do was walk to the pharmacy.

"Get your medical card right now and get over to the drugstore!" she screamed at Iesha, who disappeared behind Elaine's front door.

"I don't know what's wrong with young people today," Odessa said, staring at Elaine's door. "Her baby had ringworm and it was two weeks before Iesha got the medicine for it. She wants to be an adult, but she doesn't want to grow up. She's nineteen years old. It's time to stop being a child. And she's skipping school. I'm so mad at her, I want to . . . Oh, I don't even want to talk about it."

As she spoke, a man walked up the steps to number 712 and poked at the furniture Odessa had stacked there. Among the items was a bureau Odessa had retrieved from the porch of a man on Eighth Street, who let her take it after she had stopped and inquired about it. It was for Joyce. There were also two trash-picked TV sets and some end tables. The man started to lift the bureau.

"Ain't nothing up there for you!" Odessa told him.

The man flinched. "Oh, I thought you was throwing it out."

"If I was throwing it out, it would be over there," Odessa said, gesturing toward the curb, "and not up here on the porch. That's how it works around here."

"I understand," the man said, and he walked away.

As the man left, a much younger man turned the corner and approached the house. Odessa recognized him. It was the man she called the Clothes Man. He sold men's and women's clothing door-to-door. He was holding up a flannel jacket that Jim had said he wanted. He was asking $35 for it. Odessa told the man it was a fine-looking jacket, but she was broke. He would have to come back next month.

The Clothes Man was disappearing behind the sign for the Chinese store when someone stepped from the vestibule out onto the porch. Odessa looked up at a thin, haggard woman who was smiling at her. It was her daughter Brenda. She had not seen her for more than a week.

"Hello, baby," Odessa said. "I didn't know you were here."

Brenda leaned down and hugged her mother. Her breath smelled of peanuts; someone had bought a bag from Donald the Peanut Man. "Been in the kitchen," Brenda said.

Odessa laughed. "Never far from food, are you?"

Brenda looked awful. Her eyes were droopy and bloodshot. The skin sagged on her narrow face. Her hair was wild and matted. She wore a dirty black sweatshirt that hung limply from her bony shoulders and across her flaccid breasts. On her feet she wore an old pair of purple sneakers with their laces missing and their backs squashed flat, like slippers. Her speech was slurred, and she rocked back and forth as she spoke.

Odessa knew Brenda had come by either to get food or because she had had a fight with her boyfriend. She lived with a crack addict named Jeff, who worked as a short order cook. Jeff let Brenda live in his stepfather's row house off Frankford Avenue in exchange for a cut of the money she earned as a prostitute. The two of them had a tempestuous relationship. But at least they never got violent, the way Brenda and her previous boyfriend had. Brenda had once poured kerosene on the boyfriend as he slept, then set him afire. Remarkably, the man survived with minor burns. The relationship survived the attack, too. It ended only after Brenda sold all the boyfriend's clothes while he was away one day.

Odessa had long ago resigned herself to Brenda's degeneracy. She allowed her to come and go as she pleased. She fed her when she was hungry and she let her sleep over when she fought with Jeff. But she never gave Brenda money, no matter how often she begged for it. And she never, ever left her alone with her children. They were Odessa's children now. She regarded each child's birth to Brenda as nothing more than a biological accident. It did not matter whose womb had delivered them. What mattered was who cared for them now.

When the children were younger, kids from the neighborhood teased them about their mother. They called Brenda a streetwalker and a crack whore. When the children came crying to Odessa, she would dry their tears and tell them, "You tell them they can say what they want, but you have a grandma who loves you."

Now Brenda rocked on her heels and looked out at Allegheny Avenue through her filmy brown eyes. "Where's my baby?" she asked. She meant Brian.

"Bus is late," Odessa said.

"Number seven-seven-nine," Brenda said. She had memorized the number of Brian's school bus.

Soon the big yellow bus pulled to the curb next to the trash cans.

Brenda staggered down the porch steps and walked over to greet Brian. The boy pushed past his mother without looking at her. The driver leaned down and said something to Brenda, who nodded and thanked him.

Brenda followed Brian to the porch, where she told Odessa: "The driver said Brian was extremely bad on the bus—Geronimo himself!"

Brian's behavior had been deteriorating. He was wetting the bed every night. His teacher had called again to complain about his disruptions in class. The week before, Odessa had caught Brian stealing pennies from her penny jar. She had punished him by telling him he wouldn't be getting any more quarters from his friend, and by squeezing and twisting the fold of skin under his arm—a painful attack she called a "frog." "DHS says you can't beat your kids," Odessa had said at the time, "but they don't say you can't give 'em a frog."

Now Odessa questioned Brian about his conduct on the bus.

"What did you do on the bus, Brian?" she asked.

"Just followed what another boy was doing," he said.

"Don't follow anybody," Odessa said. "Just do what Brian's supposed to do. Now, where's your homework?"

Brian pulled out a folder. Inside were instructions that read: "Write a story using all of your spelling words." Written below were the words "one," "globe," "cooking," "north," "American," "Wednesday," "great," "attack," "chart," "puzzle." Brian had written two sentences: "I am great. Tomorrow is Wednesday."

Odessa told Brian to go inside and finish his homework. She told Brenda to clean up the breakfast room. It was a mess from all the kids who had been eating there all day. Brenda wandered into the room, and Odessa could hear her rummaging around for food and stacking the breakfast dishes.

In the living room, Israel was hanging up the phone. Anita had just called. She told him she would drop the charges if he would come back. Israel refused. He told her that all he wanted was his tools back. Anita still had them. He told her she could keep the refrigerator and washer, even though he had paid for them.

Israel related the conversation to Joyce and Odessa. He knew they would take his side against Anita. He was family. Anita wasn't—not anymore.

"She told me, 'I'm sorry I caused all this mess,' " Israel said. "And I said, 'Don't come saying you're sorry now. It's too late. When you took out a warrant on me, that killed anything we ever had.' "

Odessa told Israel that Anita's mother had called her earlier to inform her that Anita had been to the doctor, who had diagnosed her with a swollen heart.

Israel's mouth dropped open. "A swollen heart?" he said. "She's got a swollen heart? You notice she didn't say anything about a swollen lip or a swollen jaw where supposedly I hit her. And now I gave her a swollen heart. What did I do—reach inside her chest and squeeze her heart?"

Odessa shrugged. "Well, you know Anita is a big storyteller," she said. She wanted to reassure Israel that she believed him. She knew he had a bad temper, but she also knew she had taught all her sons never to strike a woman.

As Odessa spoke, there was a crashing sound from the kitchen loud enough to be heard over the earsplitting volume of the two TV sets. Brenda appeared in the dining room holding something in her hand.

"Your gravy bowl is broke," she told Odessa.

"What?" Odessa asked.

"I broke it," Brenda said, and she held up two pieces of brown china.

Odessa leaned back heavily on the sofa. "Why?" she asked. "What are you doing in there?"

"I was putting stuff away on top of the refrigerator, like you told me," Brenda said.

"Oh, Brenda," Odessa said, "you *know* who gave me that bowl. My white son gave that to me. Michael did. Oh, that just breaks my heart."

Brenda rubbed at the dry white patches on the back of her thin hands. "Sorry," she said in a whisper. "Just trying to help."

Odessa told Brenda to go back in the kitchen and clean up, but carefully. Then she pulled Jim aside and asked him if his mother had been eating the family's food. Jim said he didn't know. He did not pay that much attention to his mother.

Jim followed Brenda into the kitchen. He reached out and tapped her on top of her scruffy head. Brenda whirled around, and there was the sound of scuffling. Brenda's voice said, "Back off, boy! I'm gonna hurt you! I'm gonna knock you out!"

Jim came out of the kitchen, grinning and covering the back of his head with his arms. Brenda was smiling, too, and she pretended to kick her oldest son in the seat of his jeans.

"Don't you hurt my boy," Odessa said. "I'm the only one allowed to hurt him."

Brenda peered through the breakfast room doorway. "He ain't your boy," she said. "He's my boy."

"How'd he get here?" Odessa asked.

"I brought him into this world," Brenda said.

"And I brought *you* into this world," Odessa said. "So if it wasn't for me, there would be no you, and if there was no you, there wouldn't be any of these kids who aggravate me to death in my old age."

Brenda laughed and ducked back into the breakfast room. After a few minutes she emerged carrying a black garbage bag stuffed with kitchen trash. She dragged it into the living room and across Odessa's trash-picked carpet.

"Brenda!" Odessa said. "Don't drag it! It's gonna ruin the carpet. There's garbage in that bag."

Brenda lifted the bag onto her bony shoulders. She pushed her way out the front door and ran into Odessa's nephew Bo, who was walking across the porch. Bo pushed past her and hurried inside.

"Odessa! Come quick!" he said. "They're grabbing stuff out of Joyce's place."

Everybody ran outside and down the street to the remains of Joyce's row house. A car was pulling away and speeding down Franklin Street. One of the neighbors ran up and said, "I tried to get the license number, but he got away too fast."

They looked at the house. Joyce's front door was gone. The window frames had been ripped out, and the rear storm door had been pulled off its hinges. In the basement, the copper pipes had been torn out. Some of the electric outlets were gone, too. The place looked as naked and empty as a crack house.

Odessa didn't know what to say. She knew there was no point now in trying to rebuild. At that moment she decided that there was not going to be any family get-together to fix up Joyce's house. She looked at Joyce and saw that Joyce knew it, too. She had already turned to walk away. She was never going back.

CHAPTER EIGHT

In the House
of the Lord

The burglar alarm was ringing, ringing, ringing. Leonardo, the soft-spoken caretaker of St. Edward the Confessor Church, wished it would stop. It was the third time in the past two days that the alarm had sounded. It was probably pipers again, Leonardo thought. They were always breaking in, looking for a place to smoke crack or scrounging around for something to steal. There wasn't much to take at St. Edward's. The massive old church was abandoned. It was an enormous, empty box of carved stone. And it was Leonardo's job to guard it.

Leonardo stepped out from the rectory next to the church and looked south on Eighth Street toward the stone steps of St. Edward's and its towering red front doors. At the corner of Eighth and York, a few steps from the church, he saw a young woman with flowing brown hair leading a little girl by the hand. The woman was holding a cup of take-out coffee. The girl was carrying a school book bag. Behind them walked a group of about twenty men and women toting blankets and babies and placards. The brown-haired woman directed everyone to the front steps of St. Edward's, where they sat down. The alarm was still wailing, but the people on the steps did not seem concerned. Leonardo walked back inside the rectory to call the police.

In the brilliant morning sunshine, Cheri Honkala stood on the pale gray church steps and addressed the people seated before her. Mariluz and Elba were there with their six children, including Destiny, who held her book bag in her lap even though she was not yet registered in school. J.R. and Tara were there, holding hands. Katie was there, too, smoking a cigarette next to Flaco, the homeless Puerto Rican who had driven the battered red Tent City truck to Independence Hall and who, on this late September morning, had loaded women and children on the back of the truck and driven them to St. Edward's from the Quaker Lace lot.

Cheri stubbed out her Marlboro and told everyone else to put out their cigarettes, too. "The church is a sacred place, so we can't afford to offend anyone by smoking," she told them. Then she laid out her plan for taking over St. Edward's Church.

"Listen up, people," she said. "The police will be here pretty soon. Our message to them is: We are borrowing the church for a while to keep warm and keep all our families together. The cops will ask us to show permission to be here. We will say that God gives us permission to live in his house."

If the police ordered them to leave, Cheri said, mothers should take their children out to the sidewalk. If Cheri and other leaders were arrested, she said, everyone should set up a little Tent City in the small park across the street. She passed around a notebook for people to write down their names. "Real names, not nicknames," she said. "We have to have your real name to get you out of jail."

After everyone had signed, Cheri retrieved the notebook and stepped to the church door. She stood beneath a stone statue that depicted St. Edward the Confessor, the canonized English monarch, wearing a crown and flowing robes. She banged her fist three times against the smooth wood and waited. Then she banged again, harder, so that the thumping could be heard over the screeching of the burglar alarm. There was a scraping noise from inside, then a loud creak as the heavy door swung open and Chicago's bearded face appeared.

Women and children rushed through the opening, ushered in by Cheri, who was shouting, "Hurry! Hurry! Everybody inside!" Their shoes left tracks in the layer of fine gray dust that coated the stone floors. The entryway was blocked by overturned pews. People had to push them aside, raising dust that made the children sneeze and cough.

Just beyond the vestibule, everyone stopped and looked up in awe. The cathedral ceiling soared high above graceful arches that rested on polished black columns. Through tall, arched windows, the yellow sunlight from the street was filtered into pale pinks and blues that bathed the church in soft pastels and faint shadows. Toward the front of the vast space, a majestic marble altar rested atop polished steps. A delicately carved, low altar rail stretched in front of gray statuettes of saints that stood guarding the sanctuary. To the rear of the church, a massive pipe organ rose to the textured ceiling, gleaming like gold in the fractured light.

The English Gothic grandeur of St. Edward's ended abruptly at the church's stone floor, which was smeared with filth. Fast-food wrappers and old newspapers and crack vials littered the surface. Some of the pews had been smashed, and they lay on their backs, splintered. Someone had ripped the marble from the base of the altar and from every column, leaving crushed stone and rubble scattered across the floor. High above, someone had torn out dozens of the church's elaborate stained-glass windows. In each blank frame, all that remained was dull, ordinary glass.

The mottled sunlight through the glass made Mariluz's dark hair shine as she parked her baby stroller next to the altar and unfurled several placards. She taped them to the dark columns, just below the signs for the confessionals. The placards read, *Welfare Cuts = More Poverty and More Problems; No Housing, No Peace; Affordable Housing Now;* and *There by the Grace of God Go I."*

Across the carved stone wall before the altar, Cheri draped a black-and-white banner that read, *Kensington Welfare Rights Union.* She weighted it down with chunks of stone broken off the altar. Across one of the upright pews she laid an American flag.

Seeking sanctuary in a church for the poor and dispossessed was an inspired concept. If any institution could be expected to offer solace and refuge to the downtrodden, it was the church. But St. Edward's was not just any church, and Cheri's selection of the abandoned facility was a shrewd tactical move in her ongoing war with the city. The recent history of St. Edward's was heavily weighted with issues of religious morality and duty and, especially, the church's attitude toward the black and Hispanic underclass of North Philadelphia.

St. Edward's, a church that had served generations of European immigrants for more than a century, had been transformed during the previous two decades into a church of Hispanic and black parishioners. As North Philadelphia's economy deteriorated during that period, white Catholics fled to the suburbs. Hispanics and blacks moved in, but in smaller numbers. Between 1970 and 1990, the number of Catholics in North Philadelphia dropped by half—from fifty-four thousand to twenty-four thousand. The overall population of the North Philadelphia census tracts with Catholic parishes fell from 246,000 in 1980 to 216,000 in 1990. At St. Edward's Parish, which had celebrated its centenary in 1986, the number of registered Catholics had dropped from three thousand in 1970 to one thousand in 1990. Only about 450 of them actually attended Mass on a typical Sunday.

Citing the shrinking congregations at St. Edward's and other Catholic churches in the ghetto, the Philadelphia Archdiocese closed down St. Edward's and eight other North Philadelphia churches in 1993. St. Edward's School, located next door to the church, also was closed. Parishioners and students were transferred to an equally poor parish, Visitation of the Blessed Virgin Mary on Lehigh Avenue, not far from the Quaker Lace lot.

The closings outraged the community. Advocates for the poor accused the archdiocese of race and class bias, pointing out that not a single church in Philadelphia's white, middle-class suburbs had been shut down. Parishioners picketed the archdiocesan offices. They carried placards that read, *The Lord Hears the Cry of the Poor, Why Can't the Archbishop?* and, *The Last Corporation to Leave North Philly.* The second of these scornful placards offered a pointed commentary on the fortunes of North Philadelphia, given its abandonment by commerce and industry. The sentiments inherent in the placard were particularly devastating for the archdiocese. The Catholic church was considered by many residents of North Philadelphia—particularly Hispanic immigrants from Catholic homelands—as the only institution that could be counted on for unswerving support. These Catholic immigrants did not fully trust the city or the police or the business community, but they poured their faith into the church. Now, it seemed, even the church was fleeing the barrio.

If the archdiocese insisted on portraying the closings as purely an economic decision, the protesters decided, then they would challenge the church on economic grounds. They asked fellow Catholics to stop contributing to the archdiocese's $101 million fund-raising campaign— money Cardinal Anthony Bevilacqua himself had recently said was needed to assist the "increasing number of financially struggling parishes." At the same time, a member of the Philadelphia Catholic Worker, a group of laymen who assisted the poor of North Philadelphia, staged a hunger strike outside the archdiocesan offices. And the group revealed that the archdiocese, while complaining of tight budgets, had used a $118,000 donation to refurbish a beach mansion where the cardinal vacationed every summer.

The archdiocese, which chose to call the closings "consolidations," said it could no longer afford to operate the churches at a financial loss. Phrases like "diminishing financial resources" were offered up by church officials. But to those in the ghetto, it seemed that the North Philadelphia parishes were cut down as boldly and swiftly as any marginally performing corporate subsidiary. They were, in effect, downsized.

By that September, St. Edward's Church was as cold and desolate as a tomb. It had been ravaged not only by pipers and vandals, but by the archdiocese itself. The marble and the stained-glass windows had been ripped out not by thieves, it turned out, but by archdiocesan workers. The archdiocese said the valuable items were torn out to prevent their certain looting by street "elements" in North Philadelphia. The marble and glass were sold to other churches, with the proceeds turned over to the newly consolidated Visitation Parish.

Given the extensive and not entirely favorable publicity the church closings had received, Cheri knew that the archdiocese was in no position to evict homeless families from an unused church. It would be difficult, she thought, for the archdiocese to explain why a church it had abandoned in a poor neighborhood could not be used now to shelter the poorest of the poor.

Cheri held no grudge against the archdiocese, despite its actions against its poorest parishes. She merely saw in the empty church an opportunity to confront the city once again with the sight of poor people struggling to survive on welfare and food stamps, with no resources to pay for housing. She considered the Catholic church an ally in the political battle over welfare reform. Just seven months earlier, in fact, Cheri had joined with Catholic clergymen and others to form a coalition called Save Our Safety Net. The group had staged a rally downtown, where Cheri read portions of a public letter from Cardinal Bevilacqua denouncing Republican welfare reform proposals.

Cheri thought about what she would say to archdiocesan officials, particularly concerning the delicate matter of the break-in that morning. Some of the Tent City men had smashed the lock on a rear door of St. Edward's, setting off the alarm. Breaking into a church was a crime not likely to generate public sympathy, even if the perpetrators were desperately homeless families. Cheri decided that the best course was to profess ignorance. If she was asked how her people had gotten into the church, she would simply say she did not know.

Inside, Cheri gathered everyone at the pulpit. Portable cribs were set up for the babies, and blankets were laid on the floor for toddlers. Mariluz found a box of plastic pink flowers and handed them out. Cheri led a brief prayer, and then everyone sat quietly and waited for the police. Cheri took Mariluz's hand and said, "Keep calm."

Within minutes, someone at the front door cried out: "The cops are here!" A police cruiser pulled to the curb. Out stepped Off. Rick Grykin, a beefy, moonfaced man with a faint, blond mustache. Grykin walked the length of the church, his footsteps echoing off the stone floor of the nave. Cheri and her group sat kneeling in silence, watching the officer moving steadily toward them. Suddenly Grykin's handheld radio squawked, and everyone flinched.

Grykin twisted a knob and the sound died. He approached the pulpit and looked down at Destiny and Desiree, Mariluz's baby girl. The children were squatting on the front step.

"Hi, kids," he said, grinning. "How are ya this morning?"

Cheri let out her breath. It did not appear that an arrest was imminent. "What can we do for you?" she asked Grykin.

"Well, we're gonna try to straighten out this little problem, okay?" he said. "I got a supervisor on his way down here, and then we can all discuss the situation."

There was silence. Nobody knew what to say.

Grykin reached into his pocket. Time for handcuffs? Cheri thought.

The officer held up what appeared to be a small deck of playing cards. "Hey kids," he said, "you got my baseball cards yet?"

He handed Destiny a card with a color photo of Grykin smiling as he leaned against a patrol car. It was one of the police trading cards the department had printed up for beat officers as part of a public relations effort. On the back, a message revealed that Officer Grykin had won a commendation for bravery and spent his off-duty hours playing sports and enjoying time with his family.

All the children pushed forward, pawing at Grykin as he struggled to hand out the cards. Cheri laughed and said, "Hey, can I have one, too?"

"Sure," the officer said, giving Cheri a card. "Just don't hold it up on TV."

Cheri looked up and saw TV crews and reporters coming through the doors. They moved quickly to the pulpit and set up their cameras and started asking questions. Cheri tried to pull her thoughts together, so that she would remember to stress the desperation of the Tent City people in the face of the city's housing shortages and the state's welfare cuts.

One of the TV reporters wanted to know how the "protesters" had gained entry into the church. Of all the issues to be raised, Cheri thought, the means of entry into the church did not seem to her the most significant. But newspeople loved drama, and breaking into a church was dramatic stuff, she had to admit.

"The doors were open," Cheri said to the camera.

"Who opened them?"

"They were open," Cheri repeated.

The woman asked her what she would do if her group was charged with trespassing.

"We're counting on a higher law," Cheri told her. She tried to speak in short sound bites. "A law higher than any local statute. A law that says everyone is welcome in the house of the Lord, especially the poor."

The TV crew moved on to Mariluz, who was asked why the group had taken over the church.

"We gotta get warm," Mariluz said. "Winter's coming. The children can't stay out on the lot in the rain and cold."

How long did she expect to stay?

"Till they kick us out," Mariluz said.

Was she on welfare?

"They cut me off," Mariluz said. "I have no idea why. They said I missed an appointment, but I think it's because I'm active with this group. I've got to live off donations now."

The question about welfare reminded Mariluz of her appointment at the welfare office. It had been for eight-thirty that morning. Now it was almost noon. She had been so preoccupied with the move to the church that she had forgotten all about it. She was supposed to register Destiny for school that morning, too. The school year was nearly three weeks old. Mariluz slapped herself on her forehead. Sometimes she hated herself for being so absentminded. Then again, she thought, these things would not be happening if she did not have to worry about where her children would sleep every night.

Mariluz left the TV people and ran over to Elba, who was trying to keep the children from climbing on the overturned pews. Mariluz asked Elba to watch her children while she went to the welfare office. Then she told Cheri she would be back as soon as she could. "Don't get kicked out while I'm gone," she told her.

Mariluz walked to Lehigh Avenue and caught a city bus that took her to the welfare office. She ran inside, past the line that wound out the front door, and past the security guard sitting below the *Don't Stand Here* sign. She tried to peer past the guard to see if she could spot Mrs. Staley, the caseworker, at one of the cubicles in the rear.

The guard looked up from his newspaper and told Mariluz that she was not allowed past the front counter. "Just trying to find somebody," she told him. She looked behind the counter and saw Mrs. Staley, who was holding a stack of folders and shouting out names. Mariluz bolted around the side of the partition that separated the counter from the waiting room. The guard shouted at her back, "Yo! You can't go in there!"

Mariluz grabbed Mrs. Staley by the arm. The woman turned and gave her a blank look. Mariluz smiled and said, "Mariluz Gonzalez."

Mrs. Staley raised her eyebrows. Mariluz tugged again on her arm said, "Remember? I was here yesterday. I got my papers now."

She showed Mrs. Staley a set of forms that Cheri had filled out for her, verifying her status as a homeless single mother bereft of male support.

Mrs. Staley looked at the papers and said, "Oh, yes, I remember you. But weren't you supposed to be here first thing this morning?"

"Had an emergency," Mariluz said. "We got kicked off the lot." While that was not entirely true, it was true that she was caught up in something approaching an emergency situation.

"We had to go find shelter in a church," Mariluz went on.

"A church?" Mrs. Staley asked.

"Yeah, the Lord's house," Mariluz said.

"So you're still homeless?"

"Oh, yeah," Mariluz said. "This is just temporary. They're probably gonna kick us out soon."

Mrs. Staley added Mariluz's forms to the stack of folders in her arms and told her she would receive a letter within three days informing her that her cash assistance had been reinstated. Her food stamp benefits would continue, she said, as would her medical coverage.

"Oh, thank you," Mariluz said, and she patted Mrs. Staley's arm. On her way out, Mariluz smiled at the security guard and held up her hand, palm out. The guard slapped her a high five.

Back at the church, Cheri was still waiting for the police. The camera crews were milling around, filming sleeping babies and taking long shots of the magnificent cathedral ceilings.

Finally Capt. Herb Lottier, of the 26th District, appeared near the steps to the altar. He was a short, compact man who wore a peaked police cap and a starched white shirt with gold bars on the shoulders. He stood with his hands jammed into his rear pockets, gazing around at the sculptures of saints and the intricately carved buttresses beneath the high windows.

He saw Cheri below the pulpit and asked, "Who are you with?"

"The Kensington Welfare Rights Union," Cheri said. "We're seeking shelter in the church. It's abandoned. It's got warmth for the kids."

The captain stroked his chin. He seemed to be a man of few words. He thought for a moment and then told Cheri that someone from his district was trying to contact the archdiocese. He wanted to find out the archdiocese's position on people living in the church.

Cheri asked if the police intended to let the families stay.

"I'm not the ultimate authority," the captain said. He looked up at the vaulted ceiling. "Who's to say who the ultimate authority is?"

As the captain spoke, he stepped aside to allow Flaco and Chicago to move past him. They were carrying a mattress, which they laid across two pews to form a makeshift bed. Other mattresses and blankets were spread before the altar. A new Tent City suddenly was rising up from the church floor.

After the captain left, a man in a dark suit pulled Cheri aside and said, "Don't you remember me? You knew me the other day at the Liberty Bell."

Cheri grimaced. "Oh, no. Civil Affairs," she said. "I knew you'd be here sooner or later."

"How long you gonna be here?" the Civil Affairs officer asked.

"As long as we can," Cheri said.

"You know what's gonna happen, don't you?" the officer said.

"No, tell me," Cheri said.

"The archdiocese won't let you stay. You know that."

"We'll see," Cheri said, and she walked away.

At the offices of the Archdiocese of Philadelphia on Seventeenth Street, the call from the police caught everyone by surprise. There had been break-ins at churches many times, but never had people broken in and then stayed. The police were not certain who the people were or what they wanted. All they were able to tell the archdiocese was that the people inside St. Edward's seemed determined to live there.

Several archdiocesan officials had read a *New York Times* article about Tent City the day before. They had not paid much attention to Cheri's off-hand reference in the article to moving into a church. Even if they had interpreted her remark as a threat to break into a church, they would not have been able to prevent it. The city was full of abandoned churches.

It was late in the afternoon by the time the men from the archdiocese arrived at St. Edward's. There were four of them—a tall monsignor in a white collar, a heavyset Hispanic priest from Visitation, and two men in sport coats who looked like insurance salesmen but who were actually the archdiocese's specialists on social services and the homeless.

The men asked Cheri if they could "have a dialogue" beneath the pulpit, away from the reporters and TV crews. Cheri summoned Mariluz, Elba, Tara, and Katie, and the women sat in a tight circle, facing the men from the archdiocese.

In a firm but polite way, the men told the group that the families were breaking the law. They could not stay. St. Edward's was not designed for habitation, particularly for children. The families would be much more comfortable in church-run hospices. There was St. John's Hospice for men and Mercy Hospice for women and children. There the families would have warm beds and hot food and working toilets. They could put their names on the city's waiting lists for vouchers for transitional housing. Wouldn't that make more sense? the men asked. Couldn't Cheri be reasonable?

Cheri told the men they had missed the point. The point was not the services the archdiocese provided for the poor. The point, she said, was the city's failure to provide affordable housing to poor families at a time when their primary source of income—welfare—was under threat from Washington and Harrisburg. Putting the families in church-run shelters was no better than putting them in city-run shelters, she said. They needed homes, not shelters, particularly not shelters like the hospices, where men were separated from their families.

One of the men from the archdiocese repeated that Cheri was breaking the law.

Cheri raised her voice and said, "There's a higher law involved here."

The monsignor said, "Cheri, you're an educated person. You can't look me in the eye and say our laws aren't just."

"I'm saying our laws are not designed to protect the interests of the poor," she said.

The monsignor shook his head. "You're wrong," he said.

"I thought a man of the cloth would want to discuss spiritual and moral issues, not the law," Cheri said. "You have a very narrow viewpoint."

"You're not leaving, are you?" the monsignor asked abruptly.

Cheri did not respond. Somebody suggested a prayer. Everyone joined hands as the Lord's Prayer was recited in English and in Spanish.

When the prayer had ended, one of the men from the archdiocese suggested that Cheri take some time and reconsider her position. If the archdiocese agreed to let the families stay for two nights, he asked, would Cheri agree to have everyone leave after forty-eight hours?

Cheri wanted to buy some time. She was weary of confrontation—with the police, with Civil Affairs, with the church people. She wanted to start setting up beds for the families to spend the night. She could not think of a counteroffer. So for lack of an alternative, she agreed to the forty-eight-hour limit. But she did not tell the men from the archdiocese that she intended to raise the issue with the war council. If its members voted to stay, the deal was off. If that happened, she would have to try to rationalize breaking her word.

There was one more promise to the clergymen that Cheri knew she might not honor. Pressed by the monsignor to quit smoking, she had told him she would give up the habit. But after everyone shook hands and the men from the archdiocese drove away, Cheri walked outside and lit up a Marlboro. The smoke rose up and drifted like a shadow across the stone face of St. Edward the Confessor.

All that evening and throughout the following day, food and clothing and bedding poured into the church. Les the Pretzel Man brought loads of pretzels and fresh bread. He parked his sedan in front of the church, where cars driving up Eighth Street slowed to read the Best of Philly Awards pasted to the rear window. Other Tent City supporters saw stories about St. Edward's in the papers and on the TV news, and they arrived with canned food and more clothing. The college students from Empty the Shelters showed up en masse, bringing games for the children and offers to take the adults grocery shopping.

On the first night, everyone feasted on platters of baked lasagna provided by Les. The next day, the college students brought lunch—casseroles of scalloped potatoes and bowls of fresh garden salad. Along the rear wall, there was enough donated bread, cereal, peanut butter, lettuce, carrots, tomatoes, and canned fruits and vegetables to serve hundreds of meals. On the second morning, a bakery truck delivered boxes of jelly doughnuts.

Many of the donations had been solicited by a new Tent City patron who had presented herself at St. Edward's the day the group arrived. Joanna L. Sorlien, a thin, pale woman with a long, patrician nose and silver hair, was a Philadelphia heiress. She was drawn to quixotic causes involving the poor, to which she had donated portions of the wealth she had inherited from the J.B. Lippincott publishing fortune. She was so inspired by the church takeover that she had interrupted the negotiations between Cheri and the archdiocese to offer to pay rent for the church. The men from the archdiocese were dumbfounded. Finally one of them told Joanna that the church was not suitable for occupancy, regardless of the rent she was willing to pay.

"It was a stupid thing for me to say, offering rent," Joanna said afterward. "It put the focus on money, rather than on people's needs. They shouldn't have to pay anything to live in the house of the Lord."

Instead of offering rent money, Joanna decided to organize a relief drive. She called dozens of churches and community organizations and asked them to provide donations. At the same time, she asked Cheri to list her group's most pressing need. With the weather turning cooler, especially at night inside the vast church, heat soon would be essential, Cheri told her. Joanna said she would buy two large kerosene heaters.

As the group settled in, Mariluz organized a cleanup crew of men and women. They used donated brooms to sweep the trash from the floors, then wiped them down with mops provided by the college students. The men set up the pews as barriers to create distinct living areas for families, couples, and single adults. In the sacristy, where priests had once prepared for Mass, Chicago managed to get the only toilet in the church to flush, and he coaxed water from the sink. Someone donated a refrigerator, which, to everyone's surprise, actually began to hum when plugged into a wall outlet.

The discovery of working electricity set off a frenzy. People scoured the neighborhood for friends and relatives who might loan them a TV set or toaster or microwave. The first color TV was set up late on the second day. Pews were arranged around the set to provide a community room, complete with a ragged easy chair and sofa from the Quaker Lace lot. That evening, a hot plate was plugged in next to the refrigerator, which by now contained milk for the children and jars of jelly for sandwiches. On the second morning, an electric coffeepot appeared, plugged into an outlet and balanced on the ruins of a marble column.

Mariluz and Elba created a comfortable double bed by laying their king-size mattress from the lot across two long pews. By placing the bed on a raised platform, they kept it off the cold floor and created a secure storage area underneath. They stored the children's clothing and toys in the cavity. In the donation pile that was growing by the hour at the front of the church, the two women found carpet samples that they laid over the stone floor. On top of carpets they set up foam padding and sleeping bags for the older girls, Yazmenelly, seven, and five-year-old Destiny. Elba's daughter Keishla, three, slept with her mother in the big king-size bed, along with Mariluz and her two small children. Elba's fat baby boy, Edgardo, slept in his portable playpen.

Along the wall behind the bed were confessionals, with a sign in Spanish that read, *Confesiones* and the days *Domingo, Sabado.* Mariluz was not Catholic, so she did not consider herself guilty of sacrilege when she used the booths to store the children's medicine and vitamins. On the carved stone ledges outside the confessionals, she carefully laid out everyone's combs and toothbrushes. On the communion rail she set up infant formula and the babies' bottles. If the archdiocese chose not to use the church for worship, Mariluz thought, then she would use it for the necessities of daily existence.

In the dark and moldy church basement, Mariluz found a trove of children's items someone had stored there. She dragged a baby bath and a high chair up the back stairs to her sleeping area. She wiped the dust from them and arranged a small children's bathing and eating area next to the confessionals.

Mariluz and Elba were satisfied with their new home. The church was cold and drafty, but it was also dry and solid. The front door could be locked at night, providing a sense of security that was never present on the open, exposed lot. St. Edward's was almost as close as the lot to both women's welfare office on Lehigh Avenue, as well as to the welfare office on Broad Street used by many other Tent City women.

Other Tent City veterans were settling in, too. Tara and J.R. set up a mattress on the floor of the sacristy, where they were near the bathroom and not far from the makeshift kitchen. To one of the radiators they attached a rope that served as a leash for a small mongrel Tara had rescued from the lot and named Rusty the Homeless Dog.

Chicago claimed the raised area to the side of the altar. He set up a bed and nightstand, complete with a working desk lamp. On the floor he laid down an area rug, upon which he neatly arranged his sneakers when he got into bed. On a donated coatrack he hung his Chicago Bulls jacket, a white shirt, black dress slacks, and a narrow tie. The clothes hung over what

Chicago called his office, which consisted of a bookcase, a small table, and a working typewriter.

Beneath a sculptured Station of the Cross that depicted Simon the Cyrene assisting Jesus with the cross, a homeless man named Luis set up a mattress atop the pews. Luis and his wife, Beatrice, had been singled out by the men from the archdiocese as an example of why the church was an unfit home. Both Luis and Beatrice had AIDS. An abandoned church was not the place for them to try to care for themselves and their three small children, the archdiocese's people said. But Luis and Beatrice were healthy enough to care for themselves and their children, as they had while living in a tent on the lot. The archdiocese's men insisted that they belonged in the church hospices, which they said were were set up to assist homeless people with AIDS. But the day before, the couple had rebuffed offers by the archdiocese's men to take them directly to a hospice. "This church is better than any shelter I've ever been to," Luis said later.

Now, on the third day, the forty-eight-hour extension was about to expire. Cheri called a meeting of the war council on the steps below the altar. She asked for a show of hands from those who wished to remain in the church. There was no discussion. Everyone—Mariluz, Elba, Chicago, Tara, J.R., and the others—put their hands up. It was done. They were staying.

From the balcony that contained the church's ornate pipe organ, Cheri hung a banner made from a white bedsheet. On it she had written in huge letters: *48 Hours. Then Where Next, Lord?* Cheri had other signs made up and hung near the confessionals. They read: *Empty the Shelters, Fill the Homes,* and, *Matt 25, Verse 40: Insomuch as you do unto the one of these, you have done it unto me.*

When the men from the archdiocese saw the new signs upon their arrival that afternoon, it was clear to them that Cheri was reneging on her promise. She told them so when they approached her near the altar. "I'm sorry," she said. "We have no place else to go." She did not know what else to tell them.

One of the archdiocese's men told Cheri that by breaking her word, she had destroyed whatever trust had existed between them. Further negotiations would be difficult, if not impossible, he said. Even so, the archdiocese's position had not changed. The people living in the church were breaking the law. They would be better off in a church hospice. The archdiocese stood ready to transport them there.

For three days, reporters and TV crews had been pestering the archdiocese's men with questions. The news media wanted some sort of position statement from the archdiocese. That afternoon, the archdiocese sent its public relations specialist to St. Edward's. Susan Gibbs, director of the archdiocesan Office for Communications, was a slender young woman who had been on the job for only a few months. This was her first media crisis in Philadelphia; she had been working in Washington during the archdiocese's last difficult media event—the closing of the North Philadelphia churches.

Gibbs knew Cheri by reputation only. She had read local news stories about her exploits at Tent City and Independence Hall. In any case, Gibbs did not anticipate a confrontation with her. Cheri had already negotiated with the archdiocesan officials at the scene. It was not Gibbs's job to debate Cheri. Her job was to present the archdiocese's position to the news media. It was important for Gibbs to counter Cheri's portrayal of the archdiocese as uncaring and unsympathetic to the poor. Through the news media, Cheri had depicted her followers as victims who had enough problems dealing with welfare and poverty without having to live in fear of eviction by the Catholic church. Gibbs had to offer the media a rational and compelling reason for denying homeless people sanctuary in a church the archdiocese had let stand empty for three years.

For one thing, she told the reporters, the archdiocese did not intend to let the church stay vacant forever. Just one week earlier, Gibbs said, the archdiocese had met with city officials and local residents to discuss converting St. Edward's into a low-income housing site or community center. More meetings were scheduled, she said. Asked whether there was a timetable for putting the church to use, Gibbs said it would likely involve a long process.

Several reporters asked Gibbs why the church wanted to "kick out" the homeless people. Gibbs was anxious to draw attention away from evictions. She told the reporters the archdiocese was interested in helping the families, not evicting them.

The archdiocese was offering the families "an opportunity," Gibbs told the reporters. They could stay in church hospices, where their names would be put on a waiting list for transitional housing.

"We are asking their leadership," Gibbs said, meaning Cheri, "to share our concerns about the welfare of the children. We ask them to accept our offer to help them get to permanent, affordable housing. These kids shouldn't be here. They should have warm beds, proper toilets, meals."

Somebody asked about the forty-eight-hour deadline.

"Well," Gibbs said, "they made a good-faith agreement to leave after forty-eight hours."

Were they going to be evicted?

"We're not in the business of throwing people out," Gibbs said.

"What if they stay?" a reporter asked.

"I don't think they'll stay," Gibbs said.

After Gibbs had left, the reporters went to find Cheri. She was inside the church, bent over a placard. She was writing a message with a black marker. The reporters told Cheri that it did not appear that the archdiocese intended to evict the Tent City people anytime soon. Cheri looked up and said, "Well, if they want to find us, they know where we are." Then she put the cap back on the marker and held up the fresh placard. It read: *Welcome to the Struggle for Affordable Housing.*

CHAPTER NINE

Riding with the Devil

O dessa did not know precisely how many steps led to Brian's third-floor classroom at William H. Hunter elementary school, but she knew this much: there were far too many steps for a weary, heavy-set great-grandmother with asthma, high blood pressure, and swollen legs. She stood on the dirty sidewalk outside the redbrick building, watching a cold autumn rain lash the metal cages that protected the smeared windows of Brian's classroom high above. She was wondering whether she could make it up the towering set of steps that led to the main floor, where she had to report to the principal's office in order to get Brian out of school early. As she stood there, the rain began to dampen and flatten the neat cornrows her niece had set her hair into that morning. She knew her new hairdo would be ruined unless she negotiated this obstacle. So she let out a deep breath and began to lift her heavy legs up the steps, one at a time, careful not to slip in the rain.

It had to be done. Today was Brian's therapy day. Once a week, he left school early for a one-hour session with a behavioral therapist. It was Odessa's responsibility to get Brian out of class and drive him to therapy, but the school's steps made each visit an ordeal. It took every bit of strength and will Odessa possessed to climb the steps before collapsing onto a bench outside the principal's office. Hiking all the way up to Brian's classroom was out of the question; indeed, Odessa had never set foot inside the room. To spare herself the impossible trip to the third floor, she always arranged for the school secretary to telephone Brian's teacher, Ms. Chisholm, who would send the boy running down the stairs to greet his grandmother.

Odessa, huffing and wheezing, negotiated the final step and shuffled across the hallway. She fell heavily onto a wooden bench to catch her breath. From inside the principal's office, the secretary saw her and waved. She picked up a phone and called Ms. Chisholm in Room 16 to tell her that Brian's grandma was waiting for him downstairs. Then she grabbed a piece of paper from her desk and walked into the hallway to speak to

Odessa. She read to her from the paper: "Ms. Chisholm would like you to know Brian has homework *every* night, no matter what he tells you, and he hasn't been doing it. Your little boy is falling way behind, Grandma."

Odessa sighed and said, in a voice so strained and small that it sounded like a child's: "I know, I know. Ms. Chisholm called me. We talked all about it—and I talked to Brian, too. That boy knows what he's supposed to do. And I'm gonna make sure he does it, if I have to beat him half to death."

From the stairwell, a sharp, clapping sound reverberated down the hallway. Odessa looked over and saw that Brian had leaped from the last flight of stairs, his sneakers smacking against the hard floor. He ran over and hugged Odessa and asked, "Grandma, can we go to Mickey D's after therapy?"

Odessa shook her head vigorously and told him no. It was difficult to keep Brian focused on the matter at hand. She wanted him to think about his therapy, not McDonald's hamburgers and sodas—which she could not afford anyway, because her snack money was used up for the month.

Odessa realized that Brian was only seven years old and was still affected in countless unknown ways by his mother's cocaine abuse. But still, the child sapped her energy and tore at her heart with his violent mood swings and his mercurial attention span. Just the week before, Brian had tried to punch a boy who pushed him in the lunch line. He missed, but his fist struck the jaw of a teacher. Brian was suspended for a day. When he got home, he was so enraged and humiliated that he bit halfway through his tongue, splattering his bedroom with blood. Odessa had to drive him to the clinic at K and A to have a doctor stitch his tongue back together. Along the way, Brian blurted out that the devil had come into his head and told him in a very clear voice to leap from the moving car. This episode chilled Odessa; she believed Satan did indeed attempt to influence people's actions, particularly children's. Later she questioned Brian intently. He assured her that he would never do what the devil told him because he knew whatever the devil said was wrong. Even so, from that day on Odessa made certain Brian sat within arm's reach of her in the Caprice so that she could grab him if he tried to leap from the car. And when she said her prayers at night, she asked the Lord to keep the devil out of her grandson's tormented mind.

Now Odessa sat outside the principal's office and looked at Brian. She saw that his jeans were ripped on both legs. His dark bony thighs showed beneath the slits. Those jeans were practically new. Odessa had retrieved them from somebody's trash can in Upper Darby. Now they were ruined.

"Brian, how did you tear your pants?" she asked.

Brian smiled and ran his fingers down the long, neat slits along his pant legs. "I tore 'em," he said. "It's the style, Grandma."

Odessa shook her head and grabbed Brian's hand and dragged him down the front stairs and over to the Caprice, which she had parked on Dauphin Street. It was a short drive to Lehigh Avenue, where the therapist's clinic was located in a once-handsome stone building originally designed to house a bank. Now the structure was so dilapidated that it blended in with the shabby walk-ups and abandoned storefronts along Lehigh where the road tumbled toward Broad Street a few blocks west of the Tent City lot. The only thing that distinguished the building from the rest of the desolate urban landscape was a professionally printed sign that read: *Community Mental Retardation and Substance Abuse Center.* Inside, a towering set of stairs confronted Odessa. Still winded from the school steps, she took the clinic's steps one at a time, pausing every few steps to bend over and lean on her knees and suck air into her tight lungs. Brian raced ahead of her and ran into the second-floor clinic, shouting "Rebecca! Rebecca!" for that was the name of his therapist.

Rebecca was a pleasant young white woman whose brown hair fell from her forehead in little wisps that framed her small, oval face. She wore glasses, which gave her a slightly clinical look, and she dressed in casual clothes, which put Odessa at ease. When dealing with professionals, especially white professionals, Odessa sometimes felt self-conscious about her trash-picked wardrobe. But she felt comfortable with Rebecca, who seemed genuinely interested in Brian's welfare. Rebecca was friendly and patient, and it pleased Odessa that the therapist not only questioned Brian about his feelings but also asked his grandmother how his behavior affected her own life. The weekly therapy sessions weren't just for Brian, Odessa thought. They were for her, too.

Odessa, still wheezing from her walk up the stairs, sank into one of the chairs inside tiny, airless Conference Room Number 1. When Rebecca asked her how Brian had been the past week, Odessa struggled to get out the words in her oxygen-starved, high-pitched voice: "Too . . . much . . . energy."

"Good energy or bad energy?" Rebecca asked. She stole a glance at Brian, who was sprawled on the floor, tearing through a box of children's toys and games.

"Bad!" Odessa said. Her voice was a tiny squeak. Then she swallowed hard, caught her breath, and said in a nearly normal tone: "He's driving me bananas. Driving his teacher bananas." Suddenly her round face broke into a smile that lit up her dark eyes behind her spectacles. She finally had caught her breath. "How about I just leave him here with you till next week, Rebecca?" she asked in a light voice.

Rebecca shook her head. "You're really fantasizing now," she said, laughing.

Rebecca began the session by asking Brian what he would say if some-one asked him to write a story about himself. Brian reached into the toy box and pulled out a puppet of a fireman, which he stuffed onto his hand, wiggling his fingers so that the fireman appeared to be dancing madly in the air. Odessa, abruptly reminded of the fire at Joyce's, closed her eyes and breathed deeply.

"You want to be a fireman?" Rebecca asked Brian.

"No," he said. "I'm an artist—no, an illustrator. And I want to grow up to be a lawyer." The O. J. Simpson trial was broadcast live on television that summer, and the coverage blared from Odessa's living room set most afternoons. But it was not the dark-suited lawyers in a Los Angeles court-room who inspired Brian. Instead, he had seen a fast-talking, wisecracking, floridly dressed lawyer on a *Simpsons* cartoon. He loved the way the char-acter was too smart and shifty for everyone else on the show.

"When you're a famous lawyer, will you take care of your grandma?" Rebecca asked.

"Yeah, I'll get her out of jail, too," he said.

"I won't ever go to jail—unless somebody tries to hurt you and I have to beat 'em to death," Odessa said.

"Don't worry, Grandma, I'll get you out."

Rebecca smiled at Brian and said, "Well, you need good grades to be a lawyer." She turned to Odessa and asked, "How are his grades?"

"Just fine," Odessa said. "Grades aren't the problem. He's got too much energy. He starts on something, then he's off to something else before he's through. Then the teacher has to get on him. Then he gets an attitude and talks back—"

Brian interrupted her, shouting, "I gotta go to the bathroom!" He was standing up, grabbing at his groin.

"Then go!" Odessa said. "You know where it is."

Still clutching himself, Brian tore from the conference room and disap-peared down the hallway. But in a matter of seconds, he was back. "It's locked!" he said.

Odessa looked at Brian's pants. A dark, wet circle was forming at his crotch. "Oh, Brian, you're starting to urinate on yourself again. Run to the other bathroom!" she said. She shook her head. Brian was too old to be peeing in his pants, yet he still wet the bed most nights. Odessa blamed Brenda and her cocaine habit.

Brian left again, and Odessa resumed her litany of complaints about his behavior. "He acts up at home. He gets kicked off the school bus. Then he refuses to get on the bus." She went on in this vein for several more minutes.

"Any changes at home?" Rebecca asked finally.

"No—except my little granddaughter Danielle came to live with us about a month ago. She's sickly and she's got seizures and her mother's only eighteen and doesn't really take good care of her. But now Brian gets jealous of Danielle."

Brian walked back into the room, zipping his pants and seemingly oblivious to the damp circle between his legs.

"So, Brian," Rebecca said, "you're not the youngest in the family anymore?"

"No," Brian said. "I got my cousin Danielle."

"How is it, having more people in the house?" Rebecca asked.

"It's fun," Brian said.

"Really?"

"Yeah. I play with them."

"You're not upset, not having your grandma all to yourself?"

"Well," Brian said, "Danielle takes up all the room on Grandma's lap. She's pushy."

"Is that okay with you?"

"Yeah, she's just a baby."

"And you know your grandma loves you and is always gonna be there for you, right?" Rebecca asked.

Brian squirmed and stared at the ceiling. The light fixture reflected in his dark brown eyes. "I guess so," he said.

Odessa reached out and turned Brian's head toward her and asked, "So why do you throw tantrums when Danielle gets on my lap?"

Rebecca cut in and said, "Can Grandma set up a special hour every week at home just for Brian?"

Odessa said, "Well, we really do that already, because the bigger kids don't need as much attention anymore and I have more time for Brian. But he still throws tantrums when he doesn't get his way."

Rebecca looked at Brian and asked him, "Can your grandma be angry at you and say no to you and still love you?"

"Yeah," Brian said.

"If she says no, does that mean you're a bad person?"

"No."

"So why do you think she says no sometimes?"

"Maybe," Brian said, "because I'm always begging."

Odessa decided to change the subject. She wanted Brian to confess his role in Joyce's fire. And she wanted Rebecca to know about the fire so that she would fully appreciate the seriousness of Brian's disruptive behavior.

"Tell Rebecca what you did at Aunt Joyce's that was bad," Odessa said.

Brian looked down at the floor, then up at Rebecca. In a low whisper he said, "I told my cousin Geedy to light the bed on fire and he done it and Aunt Joyce's house burned down."

Rebecca raised her eyebrows. "It burned down? When?"

"Thursday," Odessa said.

Brian shook his head vigorously. "It wasn't me!" he told Rebecca. "It was my cousin!"

"Was anybody hurt?" Rebecca asked. Her fair face was reddening.

"No, thank God," Odessa said.

Rebecca let out her breath. "Oh my gosh," she said. She looked at Brian, who turned away. She was trying to think of what to say to a little boy who had helped burn down a house.

Finally she asked, "Did you want your cousin to do that?"

"No, not really," Brian told her.

"So why did you say it?"

"Dunno."

"What if someone had got hurt?" Rebecca asked.

"I'd feel bad," Brian said.

"Would you do it again?"

Brian squeezed his eyes shut and shook his head. "Nope," he said.

Rebecca turned to Odessa and told her it was time for another psychological evaluation for Brian. She thought he might need to get back on the drug Ritalin, which a psychiatrist had prescribed for a while but then withdrew. She told Odessa that Brian's behavior was getting impulsive and risky—as if his own grandmother didn't know that already.

Odessa knew that getting Brian to take his medication would be difficult, and that it would require more trips to the pharmacy and more Medicaid forms. But she was desperate. She did not believe she could make it another week with Brian so out of control and with so many people living in her home and disrupting her and Brian's life together.

"We got to do something," she told Rebecca. "They're ready to throw him out of school."

Odessa explained how Brian already had been moved from his favorite school, Potter-Thomas—which was close enough that he could walk to class—because the school did not have a program for children with serious behavioral problems. He was transferred to a special program at Hunter, which necessitated the daily bus rides that Brian so despised and where his temper often flared. On some days Brian was so frustrated and angry that he came home crying and begging his grandmother to send him back to Potter-Thomas.

"He gets home some days, he's hurting so bad he gets pains in his chest," Odessa told Rebecca.

Brian heard her, and he added: "Yeah, I get so mad my heart hurts, like a heart attack."

"Maybe we can get you some medicine that can help you," Rebecca said.

"Oh, yeah, I want to take medicine," Brian said.

Rebecca looked surprised. "Why do you say that?"

"Because it'll calm me down and then I can go back to my real school, Potter-Thomas," Brian said. That was where his cousin Geedy went to school.

Odessa explained that the Potter-Thomas school would not take Brian back until his teacher at Hunter verified in writing that he no longer exhibited serious behavioral problems. She turned to Brian and said, "You can go back to Potter-Thomas once you start behaving. Try it right now. Just sit there real still."

Brian froze in his chair, his hands clasped tightly in his lap. He pursed his lips and furrowed his brow.

"How does that make you feel, just sitting there quietly?" Rebecca asked.

"Sad."

"Why?"

"It's boring," Brian said.

"Brian, you're a very bright boy," Rebecca said. "Is class going too slow for you? Do you have to wait for the other kids to catch up?"

"Yeah," Brian said. "It's boring."

"So what can we do?"

"Beat me?" Brian said. He seemed to think that was the expected reply.

"Beat you? Why?" Rebecca asked.

Odessa interrupted and said, "If that's the solution, then give me a stick. I'll beat the problem out of him." She made a face at Brian.

Brian shrugged and said, "Yeah, last time Grandma beat me, I had a real good day."

"But Brian," Odessa said, "I can't beat you every single day."

Rebecca asked if anything else was bothering Brian.

"Nope," he said.

"He's a happy kid," Odessa said. "Only time he's unhappy is when he doesn't get his way."

Rebecca wrote down a few notes and then told Brian to wait outside so that she could speak privately with his grandmother. When he was gone, she told Odessa that she would arrange for another psychological evaluation and for a possible resumption of Brian's medication. Odessa listened to her in silence, her head in her hands, her eyes downcast.

Rebecca reached out and patted Odessa's shoulder. "I know you're having a hard time right now," she said. "I hope we can improve things for you."

Odessa sighed and told Rebecca about Joyce and her kids moving in, about Israel and his boys taking over her living room. She complained that her privacy was gone, that the structure of her life was unraveling. She never had a moment alone. When she slept, there was usually a sick child in bed with her. Even when she went to the bathroom, there was a child pounding on the door, demanding attention. She feared that she was going to burst under the weight of her family's troubles.

"Sometimes," she told Rebecca, "I just feel like giving up and getting in the car and driving away and never coming back."

Rebecca gave her a light hug. "You're caring for your children, your grandchildren, your great-grandchildren. You just took in someone else's child," she told her. "There's something good inside you—a big heart."

A few minutes later, as Odessa clutched at the banister and slowly eased her big body down the steps of the clinic, she felt a new sense of serenity. Rebecca's kind words had warmed her. It occurred to her that what she needed was acknowledgment, from someone in the world beyond Allegheny Avenue, of her deprivations and sacrifices. She did not expect it from her family; she took care of them because she loved them and because it was her duty. But to receive such reassurance from an outsider afforded her a sort of absolution for all her dark thoughts about abandoning her responsibilities. She had felt a deep, pervading guilt for the small but persistent voice inside her that sometimes told her to flee her own life. Now, with Rebecca's soothing words and her promise of help with Brian, she was at peace with herself.

She looked down the long flight of steps at the top of Brian's tightly shaven, oblong head as he swung himself from the metal door handle in the narrow lobby below. She thought he looked so small and helpless. "Hey Brian," she heard herself say, "let's go to McDonald's."

They drove down Allegheny and across Broad Street, taking the long way to McDonald's because Brian loved to drive by the Pep Boys automotive store on the western end of Allegheny. Outside the store stood huge ceramic statues of the Pep Boys, Manny, Moe, and Jack, in their gold shirts and black trousers, with Manny's opaque eyeglasses and Moe's slick black hair. The heads of the figures were out of proportion to their small bodies, and they seemed ready to topple over from their own weight. Brian giggled every time he saw the characters' oversized, grinning faces. "Them big-headed men" he called them, and he would laugh so hard that his own head would wobble on its fragile neck.

At McDonald's, Brian managed to behave himself, though he wolfed down his Big Mac and french fries and got ketchup all over his fingers and the front of his shirt. But Odessa did not reprimand him. And when Brian complained that the free toy he received with his meal was a girl's toy and not the same toy that was advertised in the poster at the front of the restaurant, Odessa demanded to see the manager. The man apologized and sent a worker into the back of the store, where he found the proper toy and handed it ceremoniously to Odessa, who politely thanked him for his trouble. On the way home, Brian sat quietly in the back of the Caprice, playing with his toy, and not once did the devil come into his head.

The next day, Brian left for school in the same light, carefree mood. On the bus, he felt so happy and full of energy that he hoisted himself in the aisle and swung his legs wildly, like a gymnast on parallel bars. Suddenly he felt his leg strike something soft. He turned around to see that he had accidentally kicked the bus attendant in the rear end. The woman was furious. When the bus arrived at school, she told the secretary, who told the principal, who announced that Brian was suspended from the school bus for an entire week. She told him his grandmother would have to drive him to school.

That night, Odessa called the principal at home and spoke sharply to her. It pained her to speak in such a way to a woman she admired and respected. The principal had done a great deal to help Brian, and she had showered him with attention. Odessa knew, too, that the principal struggled mightily to educate the poverty-stricken children at the Hunter school, where 61 percent of the students were from welfare families and where just 11 percent scored above the national average on reading tests. Even so, Odessa felt deep in her heart that Brian had not intentionally done anything wrong.

"Brian will hit a kid in a minute, but he would never hit an adult deliberately," she told the principal over the phone. "This was an accident. Accidents happen. You can't punish him so severely for something as silly as this." She reminded the woman that Brian was seeing a therapist for his behavioral problems, and that he had been making progress.

The principal stood her ground. She had to follow the rules, she said, and the rules clearly stated that students were not allowed to have physical contact with a bus attendant. The suspension was mandatory. There was no appeal.

Odessa hung up the phone and stared at her flickering TV screen. Now she would have to find the time, not to mention the gas money she already had spent at McDonald's, to drive Brian to school and back for the next five days. And the kids on the bus were sure to tease Brian about his misfortune. She feared he would explode again, and punch a child—or worse, a teacher. She worried, too, about subjecting Brian to more rides in the car.

That only gave the devil more opportunities to insinuate himself into the boy's fertile mind. That night, as Odessa read her customary half chapter in the Boone family Bible, she said a small, special prayer for the troubled third-grader who not so long ago had been her little bitty baby.

On the late-night TV news the following week, Odessa saw a report about the Tent City people. They had taken over an abandoned church. The announcer said it was at Eighth and York. Odessa knew exactly where they were talking about. It was the old Catholic church where she used to go years ago to pick up surplus food that was donated to poor folks like herself.

The TV announcer said the Tent City people were facing a long, cold winter in the church. The report showed a video clip of Cheri Honkala talking about threats by the archdiocese and City Hall to kick the families out of St. Edward's. Another clip showed Mariluz Gonzalez talking about people bringing donations of food and clothing, and about the need for heat inside the drafty, stone church.

At that moment Odessa decided she had to get down to the church to help. Just that week, she had plucked an electric heater from a trash pile on Bustleton Avenue. She decided to donate it to the Tent City people. As long as she had $5 to send Israel to the gas station for a container of kerosene to fire up the big, smelly portable heater in her living room, she did not need an electric heater.

Watching Cheri's performance on TV, Odessa began to feel nostalgic. Cheri's outrage at the political power structure and her sense of righteousness in her cause were feelings that had long been dormant in Odessa. Years before, she had marched in the same sort of rallies and protests that Cheri now organized, and for many of the same issues. In the early 1970s, Odessa had marched with other welfare mothers to City Hall and to welfare offices, demanding better housing and medical care. She was a devout follower of a fellow welfare mother named Roxanne Jones, who went on to become the first black woman elected to the state legislature. Odessa thought now that Jones was a 1970s version of Cheri Honkala; she had thrived on public confrontation and audacious stunts on behalf of a group she headed called the Welfare Rights Organization.

Some of Odessa's children's earliest memories were of their mother dragging them along on long marches that bored them and made their legs ache. To this day, Israel complained to Odessa about an incident in which she had made him and his siblings sit down with her in the middle of a busy highway during a protest. Odessa was filled then with a sense of shared mission and an abiding concern for the rights of poor people. She could no longer shoulder those burdens, for her family's needs consumed her now. But the sight of the Tent City protesters in the church near her old home stirred up supressed memories, and once again Odessa heard the call of the dispossessed.

The next morning, she put on Pastor Tony's red Super Snoopy jacket, a pair of trash-picked sweatpants, and two ragged slippers with white socks. She got her nephew Bo to haul the electric heater up from the basement and out to the car. Then I drove her the short distance to St. Edward's, where we pulled up next to the park and Odessa noted with dismay how shabby and dirty it had become. The old church looked worse, too. It was dark and forbidding, looking nothing like what it had been in the old days, when the priests and nuns came every day and the cries of children at St. Edward's School echoed off the stone walls.

On the front steps, a woman was addressing a small group of people. Odessa recognized Cheri right away from her TV interviews, with her flowing brown hair and her intense, driven look. Odessa made her way across the street and sat down heavily on the cold stone steps to listen to Cheri. Apparently, there was a protest rally scheduled for that morning. Cheri was talking about going downtown to the city Office of Housing and Community Development to demand vouchers for subsidized housing. She told the group that she had heard the office was secretly planning to issue 350 emergency vouchers. If people living in the church wanted a voucher, she said, they would have to go downtown and scream at the people at the housing office. The city certainly wasn't going to offer vouchers to people who didn't play by the rules.

Everyone sitting on the steps nodded, including Odessa. Among the listeners were Chicago, Katie, J.R., and Tara. They all knew the drill by now; they were veterans of several confrontations at the housing office. They were practically on a first-name basis with John Kromer, the housing director, who had engaged Cheri in a number of public shouting matches. But this was all new to Odessa, and she listened intently, intrigued by Cheri's sense of command and resolve.

"So we're gonna go down there like some big posse and say, 'John'—no, 'Mr. Kromer—we're here once again to ask for affordable housing—and where the hell is it?' " Cheri said. "Listen, people, you have to understand how city politics works. Politicians get elected by building a machine that guarantees jobs and other goodies to people who can deliver the vote in certain neighborhoods. One of the things they hand out as rewards is housing vouchers. They give them to favored groups, but they don't let anyone else know they're available. And let me tell you, we're not part of anybody's machine, and we're sure as hell not anybody's favored group. So to get what we deserve, we've got to yell louder than anybody else."

People in the group looked at one another and said, "Uh-huh," and,

"That's right." It made sense to Odessa. She knew from her own protest days how things worked. If you didn't have political muscle, at least you could raise a ruckus and force people to pay attention to you. She felt invigorated. Though she had a house, she felt a solidarity with those who did not. And she liked the direct way that Cheri explained things to them, and the way she set up a common enemy in the politicians and bureaucrats downtown. She reminded her of Roxanne Jones in the old days.

When Cheri finished, I introduced her to Odessa. Cheri reached out and hugged her, as if they were old friends, and she thanked her for dropping by the church. She assumed Odessa was there to join in the rally downtown. Odessa smiled and said she had attended a lot of poor people's rallies in her time, and she mentioned Roxanne Jones. Then, trying to make conversation, Cheri asked her: "Not easy being on welfare, is it?"

It was a rhetorical question, but Odessa answered directly. "Well," she said, "I've always found that if you can live off of nothing, you can live off a little bit. But if you live off a lot, you can never get used to living on just a little."

Cheri interpreted this as a comment on impending welfare cuts in Washington and Harrisburg. "It looks like the people in Washington and the people at the state level are competing to see who can cut the most people off welfare, and who can cut benefits the most," she said. "Either way, we're fucked."

Odessa was taken aback by Cheri's profanity, for she did not allow cursing in her home. But she quickly recovered her composure and told Cheri that she had an electric heater to donate. Cheri shook her hand and thanked her and told her to find Mariluz Gonzalez, who was in charge of donations. Then Cheri was pulled aside by Katie and Chicago, who peppered her with questions about the impending protest, and Odessa walked off to find Mariluz.

Inside the church, Mariluz was sitting beneath the confessional, sorting through a pile of donated clothes. Odessa recognized her face from the TV reports, and she walked up to her and announced that she had an electric heater to donate. "Oh, thank you, thank you!" Mariluz said, standing up and shaking Odessa's hand. "We're freezing to death in here."

Odessa tugged at her Snoopy jacket, pulling up the frayed collar around her neck. The autumn cold was seeping up from the floor and through her slippers. "It's awful cold in here, colder than outside," she said. "I can see how bad you need heat."

"Yeah," Mariluz said, "people give us plenty of clothes, but what we really need is a way to stay warm in this place."

Odessa said she would bring the heater from the car. "I don't have much money, but I want to help. When I had a fire at my house, somebody stepped in and helped me. So when the Lord helps me, I want to help Him help others."

Mariluz did not know how to reply; she was not a devout person, and her recent dealings with the archdiocese had not improved her low opinion of organized religion. But Mariluz was accustomed to people walking in with donations—and with all manner of explanations about why they wanted to help. So she said to Odessa what she said to everyone: "Thank you. That's so nice of you to help." She could not help but notice that Odessa had a pleasant, open face and a warm smile. She seemed sincere, and she did not ask for a receipt for tax purposes, as some people did.

Then Odessa said something that Mariluz had not heard from anyone bringing donations. Referring to the heater, Odessa said: "I found it trash picking."

Mariluz looked up from her pile of clothes. "Trash picking? I love to go trash picking. Where do you go?"

The two women soon fell into an animated conversation about trash-picking locations and techniques and bargains. Within minutes, they laid plans to go trash picking together. They were discussing how Odessa might scour Northeast Philadelphia for a trash-picked portable TV for Mariluz's new home next to the confessional when Cheri burst into the church and shouted, "Let's go, people! Get moving! We're going downtown!" Mariluz and Odessa made vague plans to get together again to plan a trash-picking trip. Then Mariluz gathered up her two youngest children and joined the rest of the Tent City residents for a ride on the number 23 bus downtown, and Odessa went back to the car for the drive to Center City.

A half hour later, everyone gathered on Market Street in front of the glass tower that housed the city Office of Housing and Community Development. Cheri gave a quick speech about what they would demand and what they would say to John Kromer once they bullied their way into his office. They wouldn't take no for an answer, she said. They would chant and clap until Kromer heard them out. Cheri told everyone to hide their protest placards in the baby strollers pushed by Mariluz and some of the other Tent City mothers. Then Cheri assembled everyone inside and began trying to squeeze the entire group of twenty men, women, and children into a single, oversized elevator for the ride to the housing offices on the seventeenth floor.

The group had been followed to the elevator by a security guard, who could not help but notice that a loud collection of disheveled and poorly dressed street people were congregating in his office tower. He tried to intercept them as they crowded inside, saying, "You don't need to go up there. There's no reason to go up there."

J.R. and Chicago pushed roughly past the guard, helping the women roll their strollers into the elevator. The guard stood back but repeated, "I'm telling you, you don't need to go up there."

When everyone was inside, the guard slipped into the car as the elevator doors closed. J.R. stared at him and asked in a harsh voice: "You gonna give us a hard time?"

The guard folded his arms and said, "Don't worry about it."

"Whose side are you on, brother?" J.R. asked the guard, who was black. "Why you working for them?"

"Don't worry about me," the guard said. "Better worry about where you're going."

The elevator reached the seventeenth floor, and the doors flew open onto an empty corridor. At one end was a glass office with lettering on the doors that read, *Office of Housing and Community Development*. The doors were locked. The lights were off. There was no one inside.

Cheri and J.R. looked at each other. Mariluz cursed softly as she struggled to get her stroller off the elevator. The security guard cleared his throat.

"As I was trying to tell you," he said in an even voice, "there's no need to come up here, because they're closed. It's Columbus Day. It's a city holiday." He paused for effect, then added in a triumphant voice, "Maybe next time you'll listen to me."

With a flourish, the guard punched the down button. The doors of the elevator flew open with the sound of ringing chimes. The guard swept his arm out grandly and said to Mariluz, "After you, ma'am." Mariluz sang out sarcastically, "Oh, thank you," and rolled the stroller back onto the elevator.

Outside, Cheri cursed her own mismanagement. She should have read the papers. On most days, she was able to find an abandoned copy of the *Inquirer* and skim it for news of welfare cuts, heat assistance programs, or housing issues. But today she had been too busy organizing the demonstration to read about the Columbus Day holiday. "Damn," she said to the Tent City group, which had assembled on the Market Street sidewalk. "Damn, this was an expensive mistake. We wasted a lot of bus tokens."

Suddenly Cheri brightened and said, "Okay, we go to Plan B. The mayor cares a lot about the convention center, so we'll go there."

The city's new convention center was located two blocks away. The mayor had trumpeted the massive facility as a symbol of Center City's rebirth—despite its proximity to abandoned storefronts, a well-stocked corner porno shop, a topless go-go bar, and a soup kitchen where dozens of ragged homeless men lined up every afternoon. The convention center seemed to Cheri as good a place as any to highlight what she regarded as the city's misplaced priorities: $532 million for a gaudy new convention center to entertain out-of-towners, but precious few vouchers for afford-able housing for the city's poor.

When everyone arrived at the glass doors of the entryway to the convention center, it, too, seemed empty inside. Odessa sat down on the wall outside to catch her breath. She had forgotten how much physical exertion public protesting required. She decided to sit out the convention center demonstration and rest herself for the long walk back to the car. She was joined on the wall by Lucy, a plump Hispanic woman who had camped in the sacristy at St. Edward's. Lucy was breathing heavily, too.

At the entryway, Cheri tugged at the door handle. The face of a female security guard appeared inside. "Open up!" Cheri said. The guard opened the door from the inside. Cheri and J.R. pushed past her, followed by the mothers and their strollers. The guard fumbled with her radio, trying to call for backup, and ran after the group, shouting, "May I help you? May I *help you?*"

Cheri stopped abruptly and turned to face the pursuing guard. "Yes," she said. She looked at the Tent City group and shouted: "What do we want?"

Everyone responded: "Affordable housing!"

"When do we want it?"

"Now!"

The guard scratched her head. "Are you sure you got the right place? This is the convention center. It's closed."

Cheri looked around. The center was deserted, except for three more security guards who were jogging down the long corridor toward her, their keys jangling on their belts. Cheri organized another chant: "We need housing now!" Mariluz unfurled a paper placard that read: *Who's Pocketing the Money for Housing?*

The three guards ran up to the group, panting and reaching for their radios. One of them called for police help while another told Cheri that her group had to leave because the center was closed. Cheri ignored the guards and led the protesters, still chanting slogans, toward the escalators. They rode up and marched and chanted through the empty second level. Then they rode back down and marched and chanted through the first-floor corridors, trailed by the security guards chattering into their radios. By the time the city police arrived on their bicycles, Cheri's group was filing out the front door, still chanting, still in search of an audience.

Outside, Odessa and Lucy sat on the wall in the mild sunshine, eating sandwiches. Odessa had bought lunch from a sidewalk cart for Lucy, who was penniless. She felt much better now, from the rest and from the pleasure of providing for someone even more destitute than herself. She was refreshed and ready to protest, eager to hold a placard and to begin chanting slogans. But she realized from looking at the Tent City group that their protesting was done for the day. They looked defeated; everyone plopped down on the wall and waited for Cheri to talk to them. All Cheri could say was, "A mistake. A stupid, stupid mistake."

When Odessa returned home that afternoon, she was confronted by a sea of troubles that made her long for the focused simplicity of the protest march. At least the protest had a clear purpose and a defined goal. But Odessa's life at home seemed one deep, nagging wound that never healed. As soon as she solved one crisis, another one emerged. And it always seemed that it was Odessa—not Israel or Joyce or Elaine or Brenda, who were grown people, after all—who was called upon to attend to each new calamity.

On this afternoon, it was Kevin. He needed money for a school party. It seemed to Odessa there was a party at school every week. When did these kids have time to learn? And the teachers always asked the parents for party money. Why couldn't the schools pay for the parties? It was only the middle of the month, but already Odessa was out of party money. She didn't have $5 to pay for a classful of kids to eat junk food.

"Don't these teachers know most people around here are on fixed incomes?" Odessa said loudly, trying to make herself heard over the racket of the kids coming in from school and the sound of the Oprah Winfrey show on TV. "I can't do it," she said. "I know it's embarrassing for these kids to go empty-handed to school, but you can't expect parents on fixed incomes to come up with money just like that."

Already, Odessa's shortage of ready cash had cost Jim in school. He had brought home an F in science on his latest report card, in part because he did not have the required notebook for the class. The six notebooks Odessa had managed to buy him for $1.49 each at the Dump had been used for other subjects by the time Jim needed one for science class. So Jim did without a notebook, and his grades suffered. Odessa was infuriated. The child had been penalized because he was poor—or more accurately, because his grandmother was poor. Odessa had been meaning to buy more notebooks, but Jim had not reminded her. With everything that was happening in her house, the notebook issue had been superseded by more pressing events. And now Odessa began to regret each little pleasure she had allowed herself or her grandchildren, from Brian's trip to McDonald's to the sixteen-ounce Pepsi from the Chinese store that she permitted herself most afternoons. Later that day she dipped into the small change jar she kept in her bedroom, and she went to the discount store and bought two five-subject binders for $5. That gave Jim ten subjects; he would have to persuade his teachers to let him keep several subjects in a single binder.

As soon as Odessa returned, the children began to pester her about Halloween. They wanted to decorate the front porch. Other people on the street had decorated their porches with synthetic spiderwebs and leering cardboard jack-o'-lanterns and paper skeletons. But instead of making Allegheny Avenue look festive, the decorations only added to the gloom of the dark row houses and the bare sycamores. Odessa certainly wasn't paying for store-bought decorations; it was all she could do to keep up the layaway payments for the children's Christmas gifts. If the kids wanted Halloween decorations, she told them, they would have to make them themselves. The next day, Brian dragged out Odessa's orange worm bucket and arranged it on the porch so that its black jack-o'-lantern face looked out toward the street.

Brian was still erupting into periodic temper tantrums. His latest outburst was over a bicycle Odessa had bought him as an early birthday present. She had intended to save it for Christmas, but she couldn't wait to see the look on Brian's face, for he had been begging her for a bike since summer. She had paid $5.95 for it at the thrift store; it was a fine bike, a bit outdated, but clean and in good working order. Brian loved it at first, and he rode it up and down the sidewalk in front of the porch after school every afternoon. But one day he burst into the house in tears, telling Odessa, "They all bustin' on me about my bike." The other kids on the street were ragging Brian, calling his bike a "banana bike," and worse, a "Pee-Wee bike." Brian was humiliated. He refused to ride the bike in public again. Now Odessa was out $5.95, and stuck with a bike that had been completely and utterly dissed in the 'hood.

She also had other, more pressing problems with other types of vehicles, namely cars. Her mother had called her from Howard Street to tell her that one of her neighbors was upset with Fred because Fred had parked one of his junked cars too close to the neighbor's tiny lot. So Odessa had to drive over to Howard Street, find Fred, and get him to move the car. It peeved her that she had to intervene to solve a neighborhood spat all the way over on Howard Street. She had wanted to ask her mother why she couldn't have rounded up Fred herself. But she knew Bertha was not feeling well, so she took care of it. Then she vented on Fred. "What I should've done," Odessa told her mother later, "was jump on little ol' Fred and whup him good for causing me all these headaches."

At the moment, Odessa was ready to whip Israel, too, for he also had embroiled her in a dispute over a car. To earn money, Israel had been performing minor repairs on cars for people in the neighborhood. He had found a part-time job cutting up old furnaces with an acetylene torch—a burner's job, like his father's—but the work was sporadic. And now Israel's van had broken down. In order to raise the cash to fix the van and get to his occasional burner jobs, he passed the word that he would do minor car repairs. He had repaired the car of a woman who lived across the street from Odessa, but now the woman was not satisfied and wanted part of her $50 back. She did not call Israel. She called Odessa. "She's aggravating me to death for something that's between her and my son," Odessa said when she hung up the phone. She regarded the woman as a congenital busybody. But as always, she intervened. She talked to Israel and then talked to the neighbor lady, and finally she worked out a settlement. Afterward, she told Israel he would have to solve his own car repair problems from then on.

While she was at it, Odessa also felt like telling Israel to make sure his four boys did their chores. They were supposed to clean the upstairs bedrooms every day, but they did not. She could fill an entire trash bag with the junk she found up there after they had supposedly cleaned up. But Odessa chose not to press Israel about his boys, for Israel had enough problems. The welfare people were harassing him about his food stamps, which he received on behalf of his sons. Israel's new address at his mother's house apparently had triggered something in the Department of Public Welfare computers and revealed that more than one person in the home was receiving food stamps. Odessa told Israel not to worry about it. She would call Cheri, who was an expert on straightening out the people down at DPW.

Food stamps were the least of Israel's worries. In addition to his van's breakdown, which prevented him from reaching his burner's job, Israel had lost most of his work tools. According to Fred, who lived near Anita on Howard Street, Anita was telling everybody in the neighborhood that she had sold Israel's tools. She told people she had thrown all his clothes in the trash, too. Israel did not know whether to believe that Anita was capable of such spite, but he was not about to violate his protection order by going to Howard Street and confronting her. Odessa was proud of her son's maturity and restraint. She was proud, too, of his glowing reputation around Howard Street. That very week, Israel's former neighbors had got up a petition to the Recreation Department, demanding that Israel be given his summer job back so that Waterloo Playground would not be reclaimed by the Dauphin Street gang.

Odessa's third car problem involved Iesha—or more specifically, Iesha's boyfriend, Curtis. Curtis was the proud owner of a 1980 Buick Regal, which he had recently bought with his salary from his part-time job as a security guard. On many nights Curtis stayed over at Elaine's house with Iesha, parking his car at the curb in front of the bar on the north side of Allegheny Avenue. One morning that week, Curtis woke up at 6 A.M. to discover that his car was gone.

Like everyone else on Allegheny Avenue—or so it seemed to Odessa—Curtis figured Odessa would know what happened. He walked down the block and banged on Odessa's door as she was getting her children and Israel's children ready for school. Without saying "Good morning" or even "Hello," Curtis stood in the vestibule and announced: "Somebody stole my car." He was a tall young man with a dark, chiseled face, and his lanky form and black leather coat seemed to overwhelm the tiny vestibule.

Israel, rising from the sofa, looked over at Curtis and asked, "You drive a Buick Regal?"

"Yeah," Curtis said.

"Well," Israel said. "Your car hasn't been stolen. The cops took it. Towed it away."

Israel had watched a police tow truck haul the Buick off at dawn. He had had no idea it was Curtis's car. If he had known, he told Curtis, he would have intervened. Now Israel turned to Odessa and asked whether the cops customarily towed people's cars away for no good reason.

"How do I know, Israel?" Odessa said. "Do I look like I work at the police department?"

Both Israel and Curtis were staring at Odessa as if they expected her to get the Buick back. They looked so expectant that Odessa, despite serious misgivings, heard herself say, "Okay, Curtis, I'll try to find out what happened."

For the rest of that day, Odessa was consumed by the missing Buick. She drove Curtis to his mother's house to retrieve his registration and license plate number, listening along the way to Curtis's long, rambling explanation of how he had bought the car for cash from an acquaintance who had assured him that the car was "clean," not stolen. Back home, Odessa telephoned the police impound lot, the Traffic Division, the local police district, and finally the police commissioner's office. No one had any record of Curtis's missing Buick. In exasperation, Odessa told the man at the commissioner's office, "If you can make a car disappear, you shouldn't need any help fighting crime. Just use magic."

The next morning, Odessa walked up the street in the cold to Elaine's row house to find Curtis and resume their search for his car. Curtis needed the Buick to get to work. Odessa knocked loudly and then pushed open Elaine's front door, easing her big body past the heavy door with its missing lock and its small window covered by a magazine ad that had been taped there for privacy. Inside, the living room smelled of kerosene from a portable heater. Fast-food wrappers littered the floor. There were holes in the wall and peeling wallpaper and scraps of food on the orange plaid sofa. Odessa could look down through holes in the floor and see the basement lights. A bitter wind was whistling through cracks in the front door, despite the old newspapers crammed there. Little Darryl was running around the cold room in just his Pampers, which sagged with his latest bowel movement. Iesha was holding little Khalil as she watched Curtis play a video game on the TV set.

Odessa suggested that Iesha move the kerosene heater to a safer location so that Darryl did not burn himself trying to play with it. She also suggested that she change Darryl's diaper. Iesha glared at her but said nothing. Then Odessa mentioned to Curtis that she believed the police still had his car, but for some reason were not admitting it. Suddenly Iesha stood up and began arguing with Odessa, shouting that the car had been stolen, not taken by the police. She stood face-to-face with Odessa, her voice growing louder. Iesha was a stout, big-boned young woman with heavy shoulders and strong legs. But even stretched to her full height, she looked small and insignificant next to Odessa. For an instant Odessa thought about smacking the girl and knocking her down, but she did not. Instead, she drew in a deep breath and told Iesha, "It's best if you stay out of my way and I'll stay out of your way. You've chosen your way. Now you can live with it—and keep me out of it."

Odessa turned and stomped out of the house. She was afraid she would punch Iesha if she stayed any longer. She went back home to have her coffee and prepare to take Danielle to the doctor. The girl was still waking up at night with fevers and seizures. Nothing the doctors tried seemed to help. Neither Danielle nor Odessa had had a proper night's sleep for some time. Rather than wait for Iesha to take Danielle to the doctor, Odessa had been doing it herself. But that morning, she did have Elaine come get Danielle to take the child to Elaine's row house and have Iesha dress her for the doctor's visit.

A few minutes later, Elaine was back at the door, hauling all three of Iesha's children—the twins, Danielle and Darryl, and the baby, Khalil. Elaine was irritated that she had to drag Iesha's kids to their great-grandmother's while Iesha sat around her house with her boyfriend. Inside Odessa's living room, Elaine asked sharply, "Where's Darryl's coat?"

"His new one?" Odessa asked. "Upstairs."

Elaine sighed and hauled herself up the stairs, saying over her shoulder, "The zipper on Danielle's coat is broke."

Odessa reached out for Danielle, saying, "Come here, wormhead. Grandma fix your coat." Danielle toddled over, her nose thick with green mucus. Odessa took a tissue and wiped the girl's nose and asked her, "Why can't your mama keep your nose clean, girl?"

Danielle was wearing the new coat Odessa had trash-picked for her, but not her wool cap. "Where's her hat?" she shouted up the stairs to Elaine.

"I forgot," Elaine said, coming down the stairs with Darryl's coat in her hand.

"Go get it," Odessa said. Elaine tossed down the coat and stomped out the door.

Odessa sniffed the air. "Danielle!" she shouted. "You stink! You smell like a rough road, girlfriend!" She patted the girl's diaper and wrinkled her nose. "Phew-wee, we got to change you."

Odessa had a box of Pampers upstairs that she had bought in bulk at the Lot. But she was not about to use her diapers on Danielle when it was Iesha's responsibility; Odessa had already put a new pair on Danielle when she got her out of bed that morning. She waited until Elaine came back with Danielle's cap, then told her, "Go get some Pampers from Iesha."

"Iesha don't have no Pampers," Elaine said. "She won't buy 'em."

Odessa exploded. "This is Iesha's responsibility! She has got to buy her own Pampers. That what her check is for. You go tell Iesha I want my Pampers replaced!"

Elaine shrugged. "Iesha ain't there. She's gone to Joyce's."

Odessa sank back on the couch and shook her head. Elaine stood with her hands on her hips and said, "I'm tired of taking care of Iesha and her kids. Those aren't my kids. I got my own kids to take care of. Sometimes I wish I could take Iesha and her whole bunch and just leave them at the train station."

Odessa laughed sourly and said, "Yeah, and I'd pay for their tickets, too."

The two of them agreed that something had to be done about Iesha, but they did not know what. She was cutting school, neglecting her children, forgetting Pampers. She had promised Odessa several times that she would call to apply for a job training program. But Iesha never got around to calling. Just about the only thing she could be counted on to do, Odessa thought, was to pick up her welfare check and food stamps every two weeks.

"Iesha needs a life," Odessa told Elaine. "It doesn't look like she's gonna get one. She doesn't do anything . . . Joyce spoiled her. Anything Iesha wanted growing up, she got. Now she gets away with anything."

Odessa stared at the floor and went on: "If push comes to shove, I'm gonna take care of those kids. They're my blood. I'm not gonna leave them hanging. But I don't want Iesha to know that. Sometimes I want to just stay out of it and let them go to pot and show Iesha how her behavior will hurt her kids. But I know my nerves wouldn't ever let me go that far."

Elaine finished dressing Darryl and said: "Iesha needs to do something for herself. She won't even go to school, which ain't all that hard. I can't talk to her anymore. She's too hardheaded. I keep trying to talk to her about all these welfare cuts, but she's got no desire to better herself. Me, I'm calling PIC [Private Industry Council of Philadelphia] every day to see what they've got for a person like me who's already used the program twice. I know what I have to do. I know welfare's gonna be cut off sooner or later, probably sooner. I intend to do something about it. Iesha, she's just gonna sit around till she wakes up one day and her check is gone for good."

Odessa reached out and wiped Danielle's nose again and looked into Darryl's weepy little face. "Iesha needs to take Darryl to the doctor to get his tear ducts fixed," she said in the offhand tone of a mechanic studying someone else's car engine. "They don't work. His eye keeps dripping."

Elaine put Darryl's coat over his narrow shoulders while Odessa changed Danielle's diaper and put an extra undershirt on the girl to keep her warm. Then the two women gathered up Iesha's three children and hauled them to the Caprice for the drive to K and A to see if the doctor could do something about Danielle's seizures.

It seemed to Odessa that she spent half her life at the doctor's. Earlier that month, Delena had come home from school with a report that said her lead levels were dangerously high. That required several doctor's visits, the last of which determined that the school's lead test had been inaccurate and Delena was fine after all. The extra visits to the clinic only added to Odessa's mounting pressures. She had lost count of the number of times she had taken Danielle in for her seizures or her asthma. She had been taking Kevin, too, for on certain days his breathing grew so shallow and faint that not even the nebulizer could clear his passageways fast enough. Odessa had seen a report on the TV news about the severity of asthma in inner-city neighborhoods; it said asthma was aggravated by dust and dirt and even mice droppings. She had plenty of dust and mice at her place, not to mention rats. She tried to keep the place clean, but the kids overwhelmed her. She set out mousetraps in the kitchen and dining room, where rats feasted at night on food crumbs. She had caught several rats, but more soon arrived, and they scratched and scurried at night behind the drywall in the dining room.

And it wasn't just the children's illnesses that kept Odessa at the clinic at K and A. She made regular visits to her own doctor there for her asthma, her high blood pressure, and a condition Odessa described vaguely as "nerves." The doctor gave her Valium, which she took on those nights when she feared she was about to lose control and throttle some misbehaving grandchild. Sometimes she wondered how much all the doctor's visits and medication cost. She never paid a cent. It was all covered by Medicaid under her welfare plan. On many nights, when Danielle or little Mikey lay ill next to her in bed, Odessa gave thanks to God for Medicaid.

She prayed, too, that the state legislature in Harrisburg would not go through with a plan to cut Medicaid benefits to hundreds of thousands of people in the state, most of them in Philadelphia. Odessa had not been able to figure out from TV news reports whether she or anyone else in her family were among those targeted for cuts. But the way her luck had been going, she figured, they probably were.

She was most concerned about her mother, who relied heavily on her doctors at the clinic. Bertha did not drive, and Odessa was not about to let an eighty-one-year-old great-great grandmother take a city bus alone. So Odessa drove her. That week, the doctor had sat both women down and told them that he had something important to tell them: He suspected that Bertha might have colon cancer. Odessa was shocked; her mother had always been so strong and healthy. She could not imagine her falling sick and feeble, even at eighty-one. She prayed hard that the doctor was wrong. The doctors had been wrong before—about her own illnesses, about Delena's lead levels. They were wrong this time, too. She was certain of that. Bertha, on the other hand, accepted the doctor's news with equanimity. Her only complaint was that she was required to take home urine sample bottles and fill them.

"I got to fill up all these jars," she told Odessa when they got back to Bertha's row house on Howard Street. "I'm an old woman. I don't have that much pee in me."

Almost every night on the TV news that autumn, Odessa saw something that made her fear for the future of motherhood and for the safety of children. The things some people did in her own neighborhood tested her faith. In a period of just three weeks, the TV news had revealed one depravity after another in her part of North Philadelphia. On Old York Road, a man who was trying to find out who had broken into a nearby house was shot in the head and killed by a man he had stopped to question. On Lawrence Street, a clerk at a corner store was shot in the back and killed by two men who robbed the place. On Thirteenth Street, a fourteen-year-old girl was shot twice in the leg during a traffic dispute. On Eighth Street, a man who got into an argument on the sidewalk at dinnertime was shot three times and left to die in the street. On Cumberland Street, a man died behind the wheel of his double-parked Chrysler after he was shot four times. On Fifth Street, a man on his way to church noticed the body of a man, dressed only in flowered boxer shorts and wrapped in a carpet. A cross had been sliced into his chest with a knife. Two other incisions were cut between his armpits and stomach. Someone had drained the blood from his body.

One of the TV reports frightened her more than all the others. It was about two schoolgirls who had been raped on their way to school. One of them, a fourteen year old, had been attacked behind a community center on Huntingdon Street, just a few blocks from Odessa's home. The other girl, a thirteen year old, had been dragged into a stairwell at Julia de Burgos Bilingual Magnet School and assaulted. That was Jim's school. Delena walked to her own school near both sites where the girls had been raped. Odessa sat Delena down and carefully instructed her, as she had many times before, on what to do if someone approached her on the street: Run, yell, scream—do anything to get away and summon help. Delena did not seem overly concerned. "I'll be fine, Grandma," she told Odessa. "I know what to do." Even so, Odessa made sure Jim and Kevin accompanied Delena to school and back.

Later that week, Odessa watched a report on the 11 o'clock news that said a batch of bad heroin had been turning up in the Badlands. Five addicts had died, and three dozen more had been sent to hospitals, sick and delirious. They had bought heroin from corner dealers who had stamped the trade names "Polo," "Death Shot," and "Chanel" on their blue glassine packages. Odessa called her mother, looking for Brenda, often dropped in on Bertha, begging for food or money. Bertha's row house was not far from the part of Kensington Avenue where Brenda bought her drugs and performed sex with strangers for cash or drugs. Brenda was not there that night, but Odessa told her mother to call her the next time Brenda came by. She mentioned the heroin deaths, and Bertha agreed that they needed to warn Brenda.

The next afternoon, Bertha called. Brenda was there. Odessa drove over to Howard Street and confronted her daughter. Brenda assured her that she knew all about the bad heroin. She reminded her mother and grandmother that she used cocaine, not heroin.

"But that bad poison could be on the cocaine, same as on the heroin," Odessa said. "You don't know what you're buying out there on the street."

Suddenly it struck Odessa that what she was doing was absurd. She was trying to instruct her crack addict daughter on the art of buying street drugs. What did she know about heroin and crack? This was how low Brenda had brought her.

"Well, if you won't stop doing drugs, at least be careful who you buy it from," she told Brenda. "Don't buy it from anyone you haven't bought it from before. And look at it close. If it looks different or smells different, don't buy it."

Brenda nodded and said, "Don't worry, Mama, I know what I'm doing."

CHAPTER TEN

A Teenaged Prostitute

When Cheri drove to Cheryl's HUD squatter house in Northeast Philadelphia, she saw immediately that her old friend had lost control of her life. The house was a wreck. Cheryl's four daughters were in tears. The youngest child was not wearing diapers, and she wet Cheri when she picked her up. The two oldest girls reached into their school backpacks to show Cheri slips of paper their mother had given them. On each one was written Cheri's name and phone number to call in an emergency. Cheri thought this qualified as an emergency. Cheryl was in a nearly catatonic state. Cheri envisioned her as another Susan Smith—the distraught South Carolina woman who had drowned her two young children. At that moment Cheri knew her worst fears had been realized: Cheryl would have to hand her girls over to DHS.

Arriving at the house with Cheri that day was Willie Baptist, a longtime supporter of KWRU who was perhaps Cheri's most trusted confidant. Willie was a squat, powerfully built man who wore thick eyeglasses and a bushy black beard. Soft-spoken and reflective, he was the one person Cheri turned to in moments of crisis. Now Willie, in his patient, gentle way, helped Cheri try to persuade Cheryl to give up her children. She was in no condition to care for four small children. There was a bench warrant out for her arrest for failing to appear at a hearing on charges stemming from a KWRU demonstration at City Hall the previous summer. Cheryl was already in the process of losing her HUD house after months of harassment from neighbors. Her girls had to go somewhere, but Cheryl was in no condition to find the family a new home. It was up to Cheri and Willie to persuade her to let DHS care for her children while she gradually fought through her despair.

Willie and Cheri put Cheryl and the girls into Cheri's old maroon Renault and drove back to St. Edward's. There they left the girls in Tara's care and drove with Cheryl to a quiet side street for a long talk. Sitting in the car, Cheri and Willie told Cheryl flatly that she was no longer capable of caring for her children. She had made it this far, they said, only because Tara and J.R. and Chicago had been taking care of the girls while Cheryl camped out at Cheri's row house. In fact, Cheri told Cheryl, if it hadn't been for Tara, she would have lost the girls already; Tara had taken the two oldest girls to school after DHS called and threatened to come for the girls if they missed any more school days. Cheryl had not acted. The only decision Cheryl had seemed capable of since the death of her lover, Faith Evans, Cheri told her, was deciding that she didn't care about living any longer.

"You're spaced out," Cheri told her. "As your friend, I can't stand by and let you do this to yourself or your kids. It's like you're disconnected from your body. It's not about loving your kids or not. I know you love them. But you're not able to take care of them right now."

Cheryl was weeping and saying that she could never give up her kids. She had fought too long to keep them. If she couldn't have them, she said, she didn't want to go on living. She was twenty-five and already the mother of four, with another child on the way. She had been kicked off welfare and food stamps for her obstinate refusal to play by the system's rules—and for her militancy as president of KWRU, she believed. She had been beaten and intimidated by her first husband. The one man she cared about had brought down the wrath of her neighbors on her children, and now he was dead. She saw no reason to go on.

Willie offered to take Cheryl to see a psychiatrist. Reluctantly, she agreed. They drove back to the church, where Cheri gathered up the four girls and had them tell their mother good-bye. The girls looked small and lost. The oldest, Crystal, had just turned seven. The others were five, three, and eighteen months. Crystal idolized her mother. When she was asked in school one day who the president was, she had blurted out, "My mom!" She meant president of the KWRU. Unlike most of her classmates, Crystal knew the name of her congressmen and the mayor. Now she kissed her mother good-bye. Everyone inside the church cried, and then Willie took Cheryl away.

Cheri put the girls in her car and drove toward the DHS office. For a brief moment, she considered taking them home with her, but she knew that would prove disastrous. Though she despised the bureaucrats at DHS and had grave doubts about some of the foster parents used by the agency, she knew her little row house on Randolph Street was no place for four distraught girls. They would probably be tossed out on the street with her when she missed her next rent payment. And taking the girls to the church was out of the question. The people living there barely had control of their own lives. Cheri drove on to DHS.

There, she was told to wait. She didn't feel like waiting. She demanded to see a supervisor. Told that she would have to wait for a supervisor, Cheri went into her street activist mode. She began ranting and screaming, terrifying the girls even more but also getting the attention of most of the staff at DHS. Finally Cheri was able to tell her story to a supervisor, who agreed that the girls should be temporarily cared for by DHS until Cheryl could make more formal arrangements. But DHS would need Cheryl's signature before Cheri could leave the girls there. Cheri mentioned, with heavy sarcasm, that Cheryl was somewhat preoccupied at the moment, what with fighting off the urge to kill herself and pouring out her heart to a psychiatrist. The supervisor relented and said the signature could wait. "I'd have gotten the kids in faster if I'd just left them on the front steps," Cheri said acidly.

When Cheri returned to the church, she was trying to hold back her tears. It was the first time in the five months I had known her that Cheri seemed more overcome with sorrow than rage. Her mascara was streaked and her eyes were downcast. "That was the toughest decision I've had to make in a long, long time," she told me. "It's breaking my heart."

Cheri's own son was causing her heartache, too.

Mark was deeply involved in a venture that put him at risk. He was a devoted graffiti artist. On many nights, he and several friends would sneak inside abandoned warehouses and spray the interior walls with florid graffiti. Sometimes they would go into the white enclave of Fishtown and spray abandoned buildings with slogans like "Fuck the Klan" and "Racism Sucks." Cheri rationalized Mark's delinquency on two grounds. First, he tagged only the inside of buildings—and only abandoned ones—so he was not contributing to the blight of graffiti that defaced the exterior walls of homes and shops and office buildings. And second, some of his graffiti were quite artistic and also espoused a progressive agenda. Even so, she worried for his safety and his future. The city had embarked on an antigraffiti crackdown, with the mayor himself issuing stirring condemnations of the practice, calling it a social evil that was destroying the city. Mark had already been caught once by a pair of cops, who'd thrown him against a wall and sprayed his face and sneakers with his own paint. The next time they caught him, they warned, he would be arrested and charged.

One morning that week, after Cheri had tried to talk to Mark about cutting back on his graffiti jaunts, she got into the shower before heading to St. Edward's. Predictably, her beeper went off as soon as she turned on the water. She stepped out, dripping wet, and hit the button on her beeper. The display screen read 911. It was another emergency at the church; when Cheri was needed for a church crisis, someone ran across Eighth Street to a pay phone, dialed Cheri's beeper number, and punched in 911. Cheri got dressed and drove quickly to St. Edward's, where she she saw several municipal cars parked on the sidewalk.

Inside the church, several men in dark business suits were milling around the front vestibule, where J.R. and Chicago and some of the other homeless men were trying to hold them back. Cheri ran up the steps and shouted, "What's going on here?" She looked around and recognized Bill Parshall, whose formal title was deputy city managing director but who was better known as the city's "homeless czar." It was his job to handle the city's burgeoning homeless population and shelter system. Cheri had confronted Parshall many times—more than once by barging into his office building with placards and chanting women and demanding an audience with him. The two of them had a strained, adversarial relationship.

"Hi, Bill," she said to Parshall. "What do you want?"

Parshall smiled wanly and said, "Don't worry, Cheri, we're not here to kick you out, no matter what the people here seem to think." He was a tall, thin man with a pale, narrow face and lank blond hair the color of corn silk. He wore a black suit that made him look like a funeral director. He spoke slowly and patiently, as he always did in Cheri's presence, for it was his intention to avoid provoking her. He explained that he had brought some people from the city health department and from DHS for what he called an assessment visit.

"So what more do you need to assess?" Cheri asked.

"Well, for one thing, does anyone need a doctor?" Parshall said.

As he spoke, two men in dark suits representing the health department began to walk through the living area, bending down to talk to women who sat with their children on mattresses set up on church pews. Cheri turned to Tara and said, "Tara, go follow those two suits who are poking through people's personal belongings and make sure they don't hassle anybody."

As Tara followed the men, a woman from DHS began to question Cheri, asking whether the children in the church had access to a flush toilet, whether they were all attending school, and whether Cheri could provide a list with the names of every child living there.

Without looking at the woman, Cheri spoke to a short, bearded, light-skinned black man named Ronald Casanova, an unpaid organizer with the National Union of the Homeless and a veteran of many years of activism in North Philadelphia. Casanova had won a HUD home through protests, but he spent his days at the church. "Cass, here's a quarter," she told him. "Go to the pay phone and call Debbie Freedman and tell her she needs to get down here right away because DHS is getting ready to harass people." Deborah Freedman was a staff attorney at Community Legal Services. For three years, she had represented Cheri and KWRU at no cost. As an attorney who represented indigent clients against the city or welfare bureaucracies, Freedman admired Cheri's obstinacy and perseverance, and she was always on call to help her deal with city officials.

While she waited for Freedman, Cheri turned to the DHS woman and said, "No, we are not going to do any of these things you're asking. You have no right to ask us. Why don't you go to OSHA [the Office of Services to Homeless Adults, the city agency that certified homelessness] and get a list of the mothers and kids they tell to go sleep in the park when all the shelters are full?"

Then Cheri stalked off to help Tara shadow the health officials, leaving Parshall to answer questions from Luis, the homeless man with AIDS who had been the target of archdiocesan and DHS attempts to persuade him to move his family to a shelter.

"If you're here for an assessment, why don't you assess the city shelter system?" Luis asked Parshall. He had learned in Cheri's leadership classes to confront officials asking questions with questions of his own. He went on, "I was just in the shelter on Fifteenth Street a while back and, man, they got filthy bathrooms and fleas and rats and these nasty old wildcats. My son got infested with fleabites. How do they get around the regulations, having fleas like that?"

Parshall nodded gravely. "We almost shut them down for the fleas," he said. "I didn't know it was still going on. Let me make a note of that." He wrote something down on a legal pad he was carrying.

Casanova, just back from calling the lawyer, walked up to Parshall and said, "Man, they ought to close that shelter system down. The shelters are dirty and dangerous and they don't do anything to help get people housing. You try to go in one with a family, and they won't even let the family stay together in the same shelter."

Parshall shook his head and told Casanova that five city shelters accepted both men and women. "It is not city policy to break up families," he said. "On certain nights, all beds might be full and there would be problems. But there's still forty to fifty two-parent families staying in shelters on any given night."

That was beside the point, Casanova said. "The point is, the government is afraid people will be able to survive without government. They know we can rehab abandoned houses much cheaper than running a big shelter system, but they don't support us because that would break up their big bureaucracy. We don't want shelters. We want affordable houses. We don't want to rely on welfare. We want to rely on ourselves, on each other."

Parshall did not feel like engaging in a philosophical debate, but he did want to stress current political realities to Casanova and the other homeless people who were now gathering in a little cluster around him. He told them that given what was happening in Washington and Harrisburg, poor people would be getting less government aid, not more.

"This is a mean-spirited time," Parshall said. "Things are changing fast. For instance, you have to go through the city shelter system to qualify for

Section Eight. But Congress is going to be cutting money for Section Eight, so the longer you people are living here at the church and not in the shelter system, the farther behind you're going to get. Right now, you'd have a six-to-seven-month wait for Section Eight if you entered the shelter system now. The way things are going, I'd predict the wait is going to be two years pretty soon. So you've all got a big decision to make."

Casanova and Luis and some of the other homeless people murmured among themselves and told Parshall he was probably right. But they believed in Cheri and the KWRU, they told Parshall, and they were certain they would get housing vouchers if they stood their ground and boycotted the shelter system. Even so, Casanova said, he was pleased that someone from the city had actually taken time to listen to the views of homeless people. He was also surprised that someone like Parshall seemed as concerned about federal and state cuts to the poor as the people living in the church.

"Thank you for listening to us," he told Parshall.

Just then Cheri walked up, followed by the health department men, the DHS woman, and Debbie Freedman, who had just arrived. They had all agreed that Cheri would read to the officials from a list she had prepared that outlined the services KWRU was providing people living in the church, largely through the efforts of volunteers who provided expertise and assistance free of charge. Cheri produced a piece of notebook paper and read from it:

> *One*, adult basic education and leadership classes. *Two*, counseling by an Episcopal priest and nun. *Three*, English and Spanish lessons. *Four*, a working toilet and running water hooked up by a professional plumber. *Five*, life skills management lessons. *Six*, food and clothing donations—we distribute leftover food and clothes to the surrounding neighborhood. *Seven*, hot food is brought in. *Eight*, people take showers at the KWRU office or at my house. *Nine*, a doctor visits regularly. *Ten*, nurses from the clinic on Kensington Avenue visit and bring medication, which we keep locked up in our little pharmacy downstairs . . .

When Cheri finished, one of the health department men suggested that people use public health clinics nearby.

"We know all about the long waits there, and how they use information from people's medical cards to report them to DHS," Cheri said. "We have our own doctor who comes here."

The health department official said, "We just want to make sure nobody falls through the cracks who needs medical attention, that's all."

Cheri thanked the man and shook his hand. "Nice meeting everybody," she said, dismissing the group. The officials looked at one another and then each one shook Cheri's hand. They walked toward the front door, thanking Cheri for her time and telling her to call if she needed anything.

Cheri and the war council were convinced that the city and the archdiocese were conspiring to find a way to evict them from the church. She believed the visit was a sort of reconnaissance mission designed to probe her group for vulnerabilities. It was only a matter of time, she feared, before they found a pretext—the children, fire codes, winter weather—to drive them out. Cheri grew even more upset when Luis told her that a man from the archdiocese had approached him and offered to take care of him and his family if he would just leave the church. At the same time, J.R. reported that an archdiocesan official had pulled him aside and told him, "just between you and me," that he could probably help J.R. find a job if he would just leave the church. That convinced Cheri that one archdiocesan strategy was to try to split the group by picking off one member at a time.

At a war council meeting that evening, J.R. swore that he would never allow himself to be co-opted. "They're trying to use us," he told the council. "Let's use them. Let's play along, see what they're offering, then use it against them. They think they're dealing with children here. It's like, give them a piece of candy and they'll stop crying."

Cheri told everyone on the war council that Parshall had arrived at the church with an eviction order but had decided not to enforce it after Cheri called in her lawyer. She warned that Parshall or someone else from the city would be back with another eviction order. She handed out slips of paper with Debbie Freedman's name and phone number.

After the meeting, Cheri decided to put up a new sign at the front of the church, where visitors and volunteers could see it as they approached the building. She wanted people to know that the people living there were an organized, committed group with goals and structure, not a ragged group of homeless people camping out and begging for handouts. The sign read:

WHERE ARE PEOPLE WHEN THEY'RE NOT HERE?
1. Speaking about Tent City
2. Organizing in the welfare offices, OSHA, soup kitchens
3. Distributing food and flyers through the neighborhood
4. Writing letters, returning phone calls
5. Meeting with community leaders and politicians
6. Demonstrating against housing and welfare cuts
7. Learning something or teaching something
8. Taking care of personal life

As I was reading the new sign outside the church later that week, I encountered John Wagner, one of the archdiocesan officials responsible for homeless and housing issues. It was Wagner who had approached Luis and J.R. He had urged both men to leave the church and take up residence in church-run hospices. Wagner was a familiar figure around the church, a thick-set, middle-aged white man with gray-streaked hair who dressed in sport coats and slacks. He seemed a gentle and inoffensive man, but Cheri and J.R. regarded him as an interloper—and an unctuous front man for the arch-diocese in its campaign to get the KWRU people out of the church. I asked Wagner what the archdiocese intended to do about the people living at St. Edward's.

"I think the archdiocese has been wonderful about this whole thing," Wagner said. He spoke in a weary way, tinged with the earnest intensity assumed by church people when speaking to the nondevout. "We want to help these people, not throw them out. Just about everybody in there has some sort of special need—AIDs, mental illness, drug abuse, alcoholism. We want to address each person's needs."

I told him that not everyone inside the church was an addict or alco-holic or mental patient. While many of the hangers-on were indeed former or current drug users, or suffered from mental or emotional problems, I said, the core leadership consisted of sober and competent people.

"Of course, of course," Wagner said. "There are fine people there. J.R., for instance. He's a very solid, very impressive young man. He would be successful in any job. Luis is a very good person as well. But is it fair for the leadership of this group to be the broker for all the others in getting hous-ing vouchers for them? And for a lot of these people, a house isn't going to solve their problems. You think they're capable of handling a house and running a household, some of them? It wouldn't be fair to them. They have serious problems. Giving some of these people vouchers would be like a doctor giving a cancer patient painkillers to make him feel better but not doing anything to treat the cancer."

I asked Wagner about his overtures to J.R. and Luis. J.R. had rebuffed him, but two weeks later Luis and his AIDS-stricken wife Beatrice would be persuaded to leave St. Edward's and take up residence in two church-run hospices—one for Luis and one for Beatrice and her three young boys.

"Oh, I know they think I'm some kind of strikebreaker, that I want to undermine their organization by picking them off one at a time," Wagner said. "They have this solidarity thing going. I'm trying to help them case by case, not as an organization. The problem with Cheri is, she refuses to compromise. She's acting against people's best interests for her own politi-cal reasons. She's not doing them any favors."

After speaking with Wagner, I decided to visit Parshall to hear his views on Cheri and the KWRU. I met him in his office on the fourteenth floor of a drab Center City high-rise filled with second-tier municipal agencies that didn't fit into the main City Hall edifice, just across Market Street. In his white shirt and tie, surrounded by stacks of reference books and boxes of files, Parshall seemed the quintessential bureaucrat. He was pleasant and accommodating, eager to discuss his little niche of city services—the thankless job of dealing with the poor, the miserable, the lost, the homeless.

Parshall stressed what other city officials had been saying in the newspapers. Cheri's days of circumventing the shelter system were over. Her people had to wait in line with everybody else for transitional housing vouchers. (The vouchers committed the city to paying a portion of the rent in a private apartment, usually for twelve to eighteen months, while a recipient waited for subsized HUD housing.) Parshall pointed out that of the roughly thirty-eight KWRU individuals or families who had received transitional housing vouchers in 1993 and 1994, nearly half of them later dropped out of the voucher program. Many did not fulfill requirements that they remain drug free and find jobs or further their education.

"The whole experience left us all with a bad taste in our mouths," Parshall said. "If we did it again, Cheri would be back every year with new people, demanding more and more. We would encourage copycats. Now we have a baseline position. People have to go through the shelter system to get the goodies. If we did things Cheri's way, we wouldn't have a system."

That, of course, was precisely Cheri's intent. She was a revolutionary. She wanted to overthrow the system. The point was not lost on Parshall. If Cheri thought her public outbursts would force the city to relent, he said, she was wrong. This time, he said, the city intended to wait Cheri out. He believed the people living in the church would soon realize that getting into the shelter system was the surest way to getting a housing voucher.

"There aren't enough vouchers or houses for everyone, so we have to have a selection process," Parshall said. "Cheri's people can't jump ahead of people who play by the rules. Cheri seems to think they are somehow more worthy or more needy than everybody else. . . . If Cheri's people went into the shelter system today, we'd have them approved and certified within thirty days for vouchers. Then they'd have a six-month wait to get the actual voucher and use it to find a place to live.

"Cheri is doing them a disservice. The longer they wait, the fewer housing options we can offer them. That's not because we're heartless people and we don't want them to have affordable housing. It's because resources are drying up. Housing in the cities is federally funded, and these funds are being cut in Washington."

As for Cheri's argument that the city should throw open its twenty-seven thousand abandoned properties for poor people to fix up, Parshall said, most of the places were beyond repair. About twenty thousand of them had been abandoned so long that they had been stripped clean; it would cost at least $100,000 each to make them habitable. Another six thousand homes would cost about $45,000 each to rehabilitate. That left only about a thousand homes in good enough condition that as little as $5,000 to $10,000 each in repairs would be needed to make them habitable. But Philadelphia was a city with at least twenty-four thousand homeless people, with a waiting list for Section 8 housing more than fifteen-thousand-people long.

I asked Parshall about Cheri's claim that he had gone to the church intending to evict her group. He let out a dry laugh and said, "If I had an eviction notice, I would have served it. Cheri has a hard time with the truth sometimes. She's always crying 'eviction.' I guess it rallies her people. She said the same thing when her people took over the HUD houses. If I had a dollar for every time Cheri said I was going to evict her, I'd be very well off indeed. If we come to evict her, it'll be with the proper legal paperwork and after serious consultation among all city agencies concerned."

Parshall seemed pleased that he had gotten Cheri's attention. Smiling slightly, he peered through his spectacles down his long nose and said of his trip to the church: "Cheri comes to visit me so often, I decided to go visit her."

He said he wanted to speak to the homeless people at St. Edward's directly, rather than having his information filtered down through Cheri. He said he wanted them to understand the risks they were taking by staying in the church. "Just because they claim to be a political organization doesn't give them the right to endanger the lives and safety of their children. They seem to think they're absolved of all personal responsibility and all they have to do is hang with Cheri and everything's going to be okay."

A hint of color was spreading into Parshall's fair complexion. I asked him if Cheri and her confrontational approach made his job difficult. He thought for a moment and said, very carefully, "Cheri doesn't even make my top five list of worries. I'm worried about welfare cuts. I'm worried about Section Eight cutoffs. I'm worried about all the winter storms ahead of us. And as the mayor says, there's a freight train coming with all these budget cuts, and it's gonna run us over. The question is, what are we going to do about it? That's the question Cheri should be asking."

When Cheri arrived at the church the next morning, she was bombarded with problems and complaints from the people inside. Someone told her that thieves had broken into the empty convent next door and stolen the few remaining stained-glass windows. The cops had shown up and hinted strongly that some of the men living in the church were responsible. But then one of the men, Homeless Mike, pointed to a man lounging on York

Street and said he had seen him and another man hauling the windows away. The cops questioned the man and, to everyone's surprise, they later arrested him—and eventually were led to the stolen windows.

The other problems were more daunting, and they presaged worse crises to follow. According to J.R., there had been a near riot after the donated food ran out. He'd had to break up several fights before someone mercifully showed up with a batch of donated sandwiches. Then someone stole the expensive new kerosene heater that the publishing heiress Joanna Sorlien had donated—the one so big it blew out blasts of orange, fiery-hot air like a jet engine. Now people were shivering in their sleeping bags, feeling grouchy and ill at ease.

That morning, Chicago had nearly coldcocked Homeless Stanley after Stanley accused Chicago of conspiring to get the war council to evict Stanley and his wife. The confrontation escalated with Stanley pulling a knife on Chicago and then Chicago bolting back to his sleeping area to fetch his axe handle, screaming over his shoulder, "Call the ambulance! This motherfucker is *dead!* He's about to get killed with an axe handle!" Chicago reemerged waving the axe handle over his head like a lasso, to which Stanley responded by feverishly tearing apart his living area, trying to free one of the wooden support posts that held up his covered bed, so that he could use it as a club. Finally Tara rounded up some of the homeless men and they grabbed Chicago and Stanley and managed to wrest their cudgels from them. Later on, Chicago and Stanley shook hands, but the sudden emergence of weapons and threats had clearly unsettled everyone.

There were also disturbing rumors about Savoy, the homeless young Jamaican man who had performed minor repairs around the church and who had helped Cheri keep her old Renault in running condition. Savoy had suddenly packed up his meager belongings and disappeared, Cheri was told. It seemed odd to her that Savoy would simply leave without saying anything. She had thought they had a solid, open relationship. But later J.R. was able to fill out the story: He said Savoy was an active crack addict who had stolen a bicycle from one of the church people and had then sold it on the street to raise cash for drugs. It seemed Savoy had also intercepted a load of frozen meat intended as a donation and stashed it in the freezer of his mother's home nearby. When J.R. heard about the thefts, he said, he and other members of the security detail set up by the war council had decided not to let Savoy back into the church. Savoy had left, but not before threatening revenge, especially against Cheri, whom for some reason he blamed for his eviction from the church.

While J.R. was relating the Savoy incident to Cheri, an old Plymouth pulled up to the church. A white man with long, greasy hair leaned out of the driver's side and told Cheri he had just been robbed at Sixth and Lehigh. He was certain his assailants were, as he put it, "some of those homeless people living in the church." Cheri strode to the Plymouth and leaned down and began shouting into the man's face. "Oh, sure, gotta be the homeless people! Like they don't have enough to do, just trying to survive? They gotta go robbing other people, right?" The man seemed shocked. He ducked his head back into the Plymouth, put the car into gear, and drove off. Cheri shouted after him, "That's right! Run away! You can't stand to hear the fucking truth!"

Cheri sat down on the church steps and pulled out a notebook. On a sheet of paper inside she had written two lists: "Things to do Today" and "23 Things Cheri Can't Do Today." As the war council members sat down in a semicircle around her, Cheri began reading from the first list. They had to collect enough donations to get the KWRU office phone on Fifth Street turned back on; it had been cut off for lack of payment. Checks from local churches and colleges and community groups—the Unitarian Church was particularly dependable—arrived from time to time in the KWRU post office box Cheri had set up. But the few hundred dollars those donations provided every week or so was not nearly enough to pay the KWRU office rent and utilities, much less provide kerosene, heaters, and other necessities at St. Edward's. So Cheri had to exhort everyone to solicit donations.

At the same time, the war council had to make sure that leftover donated food was delivered to the neighborhood before it went stale. KWRU followers also had to be kept informed about welfare cuts and Medicaid cuts being proposed in Washington and Harrisburg. Cheri pulled out a stack of *Inquirer* articles on welfare cuts that she had been clipping and handed it to Katie. "Make sure everybody reads these," she told Katie. "We have to keep informed. We can't stop what they're doing to us unless we know exactly what they're trying to do to us."

Cheri pulled out a pile of business cards and scraps of paper with the names of people who had volunteered to help the people living in the church. She gave it to Mariluz and told her to add the names and phone numbers to the list that Mariluz had been keeping of contributors and volunteers. It was difficult to keep up with sympathizers. Every day they left dozens of messages on Cheri's answering machine. She tried to assign someone every evening—usually Mariluz or Tara—to write down the messages and call the people back. But everyone inside the church was too busy dealing with their own problems, from welfare cutoffs to sick children, to keep up contacts with people from what they called "the outside world."

Cheri began to lecture the war council on the group's community relations. "We have to maintain our relationships with people who want to help us, people who give a damn," she told them. "If our only relationship with people like Les the Pretzel Man and Joanna and Jim the Bakery Man is they give us stuff and leave, that's not gonna last. We have to thank them and tell them what they mean to us. We have to tell them what's going on with our struggle, so they get a sense of how they're helping us achieve our goals."

Cheri moved on to speaking engagements. There were regular requests from universities and churches and community groups for speakers from KWRU to address local groups. Some people had been showing up late for their speaking engagements, and others had been squabbling over the speaker's fees. J.R. and Chicago had engaged in a shouting match over how much each speaker was entitled to; it ended amicably, with Chicago brushing off J.R. by saying, "J.R., I been to more speaking engagements than you been to Spanish parties." But Cheri wanted to set the record straight. She reminded everyone that they were entitled to half the speaker's fee—which rarely topped $50—with the other half going into the meager KWRU checking account.

Next, Cheri mentioned the stolen heater. They would have to replace it right away. People were freezing. Someone from Temple University had just donated $100, Cheri said. That was not enough to buy an expensive new heater like the one Joanna had donated. But it was enough to buy a used heater from the drug dealers and junkies who sold heaters on the street. Cheri asked a question: did anyone object to buying a heater off the street, knowing it was probably stolen? Everyone shrugged. No one objected. The motion passed. They would buy a street heater that evening.

Finally, there was the matter of drugs and alcohol, Cheri said. Too many homeless people had been allowed to drift into the church and sleep while drunk or high on crack. The security committee had to do a better job, Cheri said. If anyone smelled of alcohol or looked high, they were not to be allowed inside. The church wasn't a homeless shelter, she said. She would make up more signs saying that no drugs or alcohol were allowed on the premises. And several professional people had offered to set up drug counseling sessions inside the church. Cheri announced that she would have a new sign made up that said: *Free Counseling Services for Drugs and Alcohol.*

Later, after the war council meeting had broken up, Cheri found a piece of folded paper tucked into her notebook. She unfolded it and began to laugh. It was a cartoon Willie Baptist had drawn and given to her. On one side of the paper Willie had drawn a half-naked man with wild hair, running madly down the street, ranting and raving, his eyes wide with fright. On the other side of the paper, he had drawn a picture of a house on fire. He had given the cartoons to Cheri after they had discussed ways to get people to see the whole picture of poor people and people on welfare. "You think a man running down the street is crazy until you realize his house has

burned down," Cheri said, sitting on the church steps and holding the cartoons. "It's the same way with people on welfare. You assume they're lazy
cheats until you see the whole picture of what's happened in their lives."

When Cheri got home that night, she listened to an odd message on her
answering machine. It was from someone named Wally, who said he was
from South Philadelphia. Wally said he had a client who wanted to help
"all the poor people living in that church up there." This wasn't the first
message Cheri had received from this Wally character, but none before had
been this explicit. Now there was a specific mention of help. Maybe she
would call Wally back.

But that evening, with so many things on her mind, Cheri forgot all
about Wally. For one thing, there were nearly forty messages on her tape.
For another, she had to deal with her son, Mark, who was still going out
with his friends and spraying graffiti inside abandoned factories. Cheri was
terrified that he'd be caught and arrested under the new city crackdown on
graffiti. There was also the matter of rent. Cheri was more than a month
behind. The landlady was making noises about having her evicted. Cheri
hadn't mentioned this to Mark, for she did not want to upset him, especially now, when he was doing so well in school, but they would both be out
on the street if she did not come up with some cash quickly.

Cheri had originally rented the row house in which she and her son now
lived under false pretenses. On the lease application, she had written that
she worked as a counselor at Dignity Housing, a nonprofit group. She had
arranged for a friend to take the landlady's verification call. The friend told
the landlady over the phone that Cheri had a full-time job and salary and a
"very solid work history." The landlady, who lived in New Jersey, did not
check further. She signed the lease, and Cheri and Mark moved in. But
Cheri had been receiving welfare and food stamps then. Now she was
entering her third month without benefits. This month she couldn't even
pay her telephone bill, which was $304.90. And that account, too, was a
deception. She had been cut off so many times in the past that she could no
longer get phone service in her own name. With the now-deceased Faith
Evans's permission, she had obtained phone service in his name. Faith
hadn't minded; he lived in Washington. Now there was a notice from the
electric company, too. Cheri owed $143.04. If she did not come up with
$107.25 within ten days, the notice said, her electricity would be cut off.

Cheri tossed the electric company letter on the dining room table. She
was more concerned about her rent than her electricity. "My landlady has
no idea what I really do," she told me that evening. "She has no idea her
nice little working girl is really a subversive activist who drags welfare people and homeless people into her nice little row house."

The row house was sturdy and clean, and Cheri had made a few desultory attempts to decorate it. She had put up a painting of a Spanish woman in the living room, along with a full-length mirror that Mark had tagged with red graffiti. She owned an old color TV and VCR, which was frequently used by war council members who retreated to Cheri's place to sleep and shower. There was a stained beige carpet on the living room floor, and on one wall hung a clock whose hands were stuck at four-thirty. Several colorful South American dolls were arranged on the radiator below a framed photograph of Cheri and Mark at Mark's grade school graduation ceremony, to which Cheri wore a dress and looked almost matronly. The only other photograph downstairs was a black-and-white photo of Cheri being evicted from a takeover house in Minneapolis. It was one of those stark news photos in which everyone seems frozen in shock: Cheri's hair is flying and her mouth is curled in rage. A burly cop is grimacing as he tries to pin Cheri's arm behind her back. And on the roof, a man is intently pouring water down on Cheri's head. There were other totems in the house to Cheri's life of public protest and social commitment. There was a futon for homeless visitors to sleep on, and handwritten signs instructing visitors to turn off the shower and lock the door when they left. Cheri's bookshelf was crammed with socially aware titles like *Women and Self-Esteem, Blue Collar Women, The Cinderella Complex,* and *The Woman Alone,* and a 1967 copy of *The Moynihan Report and the Politics of Controversy,* bought for $1 from the Minneapolis Public Library.

Cheri sat down on the futon and tried to figure how to pay the rent. She did not have much left to pawn. Because she had let her home become a public gathering place, her belongings kept disappearing. Someone had stolen her guitar, small amounts of cash, and worst of all, Mark's cherished baseball card collection. One of Cheri's last remaining possessions of value had been an onyx ring, which she had pawned for $30. She had given the money to Mark so that he would not have to break a dinner date he had made with his girlfriend, Amanda. Mark had not wanted to tell Amanda that his mother was broke. With the ring in hock, about all Cheri had left was her blood plasma. But even selling blood was out of the question now; the last time Cheri had tried, a nurse told her that her blood was unacceptable because a test showed her to be anemic.

Many times over the previous months, I had asked Cheri how she managed to pay her rent and bills under such circumstances. Each time she'd answered vaguely. She mentioned something about cleaning houses or waiting tables. But I knew that from the time she awoke every morning until ten or eleven at night, Cheri was consumed by her work with KWRU and at the church. Unless she worked a midnight shift, there was no time for her to hold down a job, even a part-time job. And when would she sleep? When I raised the subject again on this particular evening, Cheri shrugged and said, "It's late-night work, part-time, when I can get it." When I asked her how she explained her late-night absences to Mark, she said, "I tell him it's late-shift, waitress-type work." Then she changed the subject. Her late-night activity clearly was a sensitive issue, so I dropped it.

We then talked about the effects of her increasingly public life on Mark. Sometimes Cheri felt that she was failing him because of the long hours she spent at the church. She was away from home when Mark left for school each morning, and on most evenings she didn't return until well after dark. On many nights she got back into the car and drove to a gas station to fill kerosene containers because people at the church had run out of kerosene for the heaters. She worried about Mark's diet. Sometimes she would cook a pot of macaroni and cheese or rice and beans, or open a can of spaghetti, and that would last several nights. Many nights she brought home donated food, usually cold cuts or sandwiches, and then made big pitchers of powdered iced tea. Mark did not often complain, but he did draw the line at Oodles of Noodles; he told his mother one day that he couldn't eat another bowl of the stuff. So the previous Saturday, Cheri had bought him a treat: a jumbo box of sweetened Apple Jacks cereal. With the help of Mariluz and her children, they'd eaten the entire box in one sitting. Cheri tried to make sure that Mark ate at least some fruit and vegetables every week and, despite his haphazard diet, he was a healthy boy. He was slender and supple, with bright eyes and blond hair that drooped over his forehead and across his eyes. He was handsome in a River Phoenix way, and in fact wanted to be an actor.

I asked Cheri whether she missed having a normal life with her son. Did she ever long for a traditional nuclear family, a mother and father and son in a tidy little home with a picket fence and a hearty dinner on the table at six-thirty every evening?

Cheri drew hard on a Marlboro and said, "Yeah, sometimes I wonder if Mark's getting cheated out of a normal life. I try to do things with just the two of us, but things are so hectic it's not always possible. And, yeah, I miss doing normal things like going shopping or fixing up the house and going out to a movie or dinner. All that's gone for me, and I miss it."

"The only way I get through it is, I tell myself I'm developing leaders. J.R., Tara, Mariluz, Katie, Chicago, Cheryl—they're all developing into real leaders who can teach people that their survival depends on each other."

Cheri paused and gestured to her bookshelf. "I'm reading up now on how to make something out of nothing. I'm reading about how the North Vietnamese used spoons to dig tunnels. That's what I feel like these days, like I'm digging some huge tunnel with a tiny little spoon."

She stubbed out her cigarette and said she would find a way to pay the rent and utilities. At the moment, she said, she was more concerned with KWRU's finances. There was exactly $16 in the organization's bank account. And the KWRU fund for heat at the church stood at $20. There were dozens of phone calls and letters from people offering money and assistance, but Cheri had not been able to reply to them all. She had arranged for Mariluz to answer some inquiries. The rest she would have to answer herself. Now, as Cheri roused herself from the futon to start returning phone calls, she mentioned something that she feared would complicate—if not poison—her relationship with sponsors and volunteers. The *Inquirer* was preparing a Sunday magazine profile about her. And now she feared she had told the reporter something she probably should not have.

I had sat in on a long interview Cheri had given to the reporter, John Woestendiek. Although I had heard Cheri's life story more than once, I wanted to hear what Cheri would tell the newspaper. I was a friend and coworker of Woestendiek, who had agreed to let me listen in as he interviewed Cheri late one afternoon in the trash-strewn park on Lehigh Avenue across from the old Quaker Lace lot.

Woestendiek gently questioned Cheri and then listened intently as she launched into long, descriptive narratives from her past. She spoke haphazardly, sometimes answering questions directly and other times wandering through episodes in her life many years apart. She spoke in a detached way, as if describing another person's life:

"I was born in Minneapolis. My biological father left a couple of months after I was born. I was raised by my mother and stepfather. I left home at thirteen. I had been sexually abused by my stepfather, who was an alcoholic. Finally I told my mother, who called the police on my stepfather. Rather than removing my stepfather from the home, they removed me. I was sent to various agencies. My stepfather threatened me and I went into police custody. I never went back home. From ages thirteen to sixteen, I lived in foster homes, group homes, 'girls' homes.' I was basically homeless.

"My mother was basically illiterate. She hardly ever worked outside the home. I remember taking a cab one day with my mother to fill out forms to apply for welfare, and a judge declared her unfit because she couldn't read well enough to fill out the forms.

"My stepfather beat my mother for years. She let herself get beaten every day so we could stay together and have food to eat. That was before battered women's shelters and before anyone cared about spousal abuse. One of my first memories is of a dog down the street being abused and taken care of by the SPCA. Yet my mother was abused and nothing was done. My mother was a good mother, just poor. She went to work in three-point-two bars to support herself. She finally went on welfare for a while. There was a stigma about welfare then, as now. My stepfather had a thing about hard work. He'd have G.I. days where we kids would scrub the baseboards and pick up all the cherry apples that fell down from the trees. My stepfather would be drunk and gone at Christmastime and Mom would steal his booze money and buy fifty-cent toys at Woolworth's and go cut down somebody's Christmas tree and bring it home.

"My stepfather sexually abused my three sisters and he beat my brother, Mark, so badly that he had psychological problems long afterward. In nineteen eighty-one, my brother jumped off a railroad bridge and killed himself. He made the front page of the Minneapolis paper, which wrote about these homeless guys who stole his ID and the lucky charms he carried in his pockets. I went to the hospital and he was dead. He was nineteen years old.

"I saw my mother as being in a cage, being choiceless. It was all tied to economics. If my mother had had the economic ability to leave, she'd have been out the door the first time that man laid a hand on her or one of her kids. But she was trapped.

"I sought economic independence for myself. I got pregnant. It got me a home and food. I married the guy after he got me pregnant. I had met my husband at the Last Chance Motel, a place for people kicked out of institutions or who had heavy drug problems. If you had a problem with shame, they'd put a 'shame ball' around your leg, or if you acted like a baby they'd put a diaper on you. My husband left the place just before I did. I convinced a guy at a car lot to 'sell' me a Camaro for no money down. I lived in it for a while when I was pregnant. Then we found a rental house together. My husband was a heroin addict who sold everything in the house. We were married for one month. Then the rental company came and reclaimed all the furniture. I had just turned seventeen when I gave birth to Mark."

During Mark's early childhood, Cheri said, the two of them drifted from apartment to apartment. She got on welfare and managed to finish high school and three years at the University of Minnesota. She got that far only because she defrauded the system. Not only was she on welfare and receiving food stamps, but she was attending college on a student loan. She knew that was illegal, she said, but she justified it by telling herself it was the only way she could educate herself and raise her son. She was caught and charged with welfare fraud, although the charges were later dropped.

"I wanted to plead not guilty on the basis of necessity. I wanted a jury to tell me that they would have done any different under the circumstances. They were charging me with deciding to live—to feed, clothe, and house my kid. If I could just have taken care of child care, I could have graduated and become a teacher and lived happily ever after. Then I saw the welfare file, which my lawyer had demanded. I saw photos they had taken of me on the street, records of people I had met, when I came and went from my house."

Eventually Cheri found a job teaching social studies at an alternative school. Somehow, she said, the local United Way chapter, which helped sponsor the school, heard that she was a single mother working to raise her son. They took her picture with Mark and put it on a billboard with a testimonial about her "reaching self-sufficiency."

"They put me on this 'Pull yourself up by your own bootstraps' type ad, even though I was on welfare at the time. They bought me a dress and gave me a hundred dollars, which helped us stave off eviction from our apartment. Later on we were homeless. I learned a lot of survival skills being homeless in the winter in Minneapolis. I kept skipping out on bills I had incurred at Mark's day care centers and I starting calling all these social welfare agencies and asking if they had any help for poor, single mothers. They all said, 'That's an important issue, blah, blah, blah, but we don't really deal with it.'

"Then I helped form a group called Women, Work and Welfare. As much as I hated it, I was forced to meet with other welfare recipients. I considered other people on welfare lazy, no-good freeloaders. The whole thing turned into a self-help group instead of a group that fought the larger issues. So I split off."

Soon Cheri attracted the attention of Marian Kramer, a leader of the National Welfare Rights Union (NWRU) in Detroit.

"Marian was a feisty woman who could walk into a welfare office and not kiss everybody's ass and not feel obliged to explain herself or apologize for being there. It seemed so sane to me. I had always wanted to do that but never had the courage."

Cheri was so inspired by Kramer that she formed a group in Minneapolis composed of welfare mothers like herself. She called it Up and Out of Poverty Now and affiliated the group with the NWRU. She led welfare protests and takeovers of abandoned houses. In 1989, the NWRU sent Cheri to a convention in Philadelphia, where she met Bob Brown, president of the local electrical workers' union. The two of them hit it off. After Brown flew to Minneapolis a few times to visit Cheri, he proposed and they were married. Cheri and Mark moved to Philadelphia to live with Brown. Within a month, she found a job as counselor at a city-run juvenile justice center, working with delinquents.

"My job was to work with poor youths and their families and figure out how to 'give them life skills' and get them back into high school, but not teach them how to survive so that they had enough to eat. I had the pleasure of watching children being sent off to jail like cattle." When one teenaged boy was shipped to a juvenile center in a suburban county because there was no room for him in the Philadelphia facility, Cheri was so enraged that she drove out in the middle of the night and picked the boy up and brought him home. The next day, she quit her job. She called a press conference to air her grievances with the juvenile justice system. Nobody showed up.

The next year, Cheri formed the KWRU. The year after that, she and Brown separated. "End of story," Cheri said.

Woestendiek listened politely for well over an hour, diligently writing down each detail of Cheri's life story. He was wondering how he was going to ask her a disturbing and difficult question. Like any good reporter, he had saved his most prickly question for the end of the interview. He knew it was prudent practice to extract everything possible from your subject before you shocked him or her into silence—or worse, rage—with an impolitic question. The question John Woestendiek wanted to ask Cheri Honkala that day was this: was it true she had once been a prostitute?

In researching his story about Cheri, Woestendiek had come across newspaper stories in Minneapolis about her protests and takeovers. In one of them, Cheri herself had made a reference to being so poor as a teenager that she had engaged in sex for money.

Now Woestendiek looked at Cheri as she sat smoking on the broken park bench. He cleared his throat and, barely raising his voice, said to Cheri, "Uh, I read somewhere that you said you'd had to turn to prostitution to support yourself."

Cheri blinked and swallowed. She quickly recovered and said, "During my life, I have always been able to find ways to feed and clothe my child. If it means taking over houses, selling myself, or doing whatever else I have to do, I intend to be his care provider. So for a time in my late teens, I was a prostitute." Cheri stopped and puffed on her cigarette. "So, yeah, I've got like nine million skeletons in my closet. Being in the limelight is more scary than exciting, because I'm not exactly Mother Teresa, you know."

Now, several weeks later, Woestendiek's profile was about to appear on the front of the *Inquirer*'s Sunday magazine, and Cheri was anxious about her long-ago brush with prostitution. She was not overly concerned with the impact on her reputation; among local politicians and city officials, she thought, her reputation could hardly sink lower. The person she worried about was Mark. The kids at school already teased him about his mother. What would they do with something like this? She decided she had to tell Mark before he found out another way. One evening, after the war council people had left, she sat Mark down and explained how desperate she had become when he was a baby. She told him explicitly what she had done.

Mark did not have much reaction, except to hug his mother and tell her, "I'll always be proud of you, Mom."

When the article on Cheri was published, the front page photo showed Cheri sitting on the St. Edward's steps with Mariluz, Elba, and Tara. The headline said, THE OUTSIDER. *Activist Cheri Honkala breaks the law, bends the rules and bucks the system. But does she succeed?* Several people around St. Edward's remarked on the article's opening sentence, which they thought captured the essence of Cheri:

> If "the system" assessed grown-ups the way teachers do elementary school students, Cheri Honkala's report card might read a little like that of a troublesome first grader, the one who throws tantrums, fails to join with the group, and refuses to stay inside the lines, who always asks "Why?" and won't accept "Because that's the way it is" for an answer.

Woestendiek mentioned prostitution only in passing, and in a single sentence deep into the story: "As a teenager, she says, she was desperate enough for money to work as a prostitute." No one said anything about it to Cheri, either at the church or in city offices downtown. And if Mark encountered any problems at school because of his mother's past, he never mentioned them.

All that week, there were phone messages from Wally in South Philly. The man was sounding desperate. He kept saying he absolutely had to speak to Cheri about an important offer to help the people living in the church. Cheri was still intending to call him back when Wally showed up at the church one afternoon.

Wally stepped from a late-model black Cadillac. He was a fleshy man of average height, with black hair combed straight back and a smooth, olive complexion. He was dressed almost entirely in black—black slacks, black shoes, black leather jacket. He introduced himself as Wally Lucidi and told Cheri he had a client in South Philadelphia who wished to sponsor a charitable event for the homeless welfare recipients living in the church. His client had seen TV news reports about Tent City and St. Edward's. He had been trying to choose between an orphanage and Cheri's group, Wally said, and ultimately he'd decided the homeless people needed more help.

It did not occur to Cheri to ask who Wally's client was. It was not a matter of great importance to her, as long as he was offering help. Cheri often received anonymous donations. Wally asked if Cheri would be willing to meet with his client at his place of business in South Philadelphia to discuss ways that he might contribute to her group. It was all quite cryptic, but Cheri agreed. What did she have to lose? Wally shook her hand and said he would be in touch. He got back into his Cadillac and drove away.

Back inside the church, Cheri sat down to listen to an update from Tara about her problems with medical coverage. She had been cut off from her $102.50 bimonthly welfare check in September for failing to show up for appointments—appointments Tara said she never knew about because she was homeless and never received letters informing her of the times and dates. Tara managed without the money, for it amounted to only about $7 a day. And she still received $93 in food stamps every two weeks. She and her boyfriend, J.R., survived nicely. They had built a private bedroom from mattresses and pews set up in the loft that held the church organ, high above the main floor. They lived off donated food and clothing, and they spent their days attending war council meetings and helping Cheri attend to donations and the day-to-day affairs of KWRU.

Tara's only problem now was medical coverage. It was scheduled to run out one year after her welfare cutoff date, or the following September. Tara figured it would probably run out well before then because the state legislature was considering a bill that would cut off medical benefits to tens of thousands of poor, single, childless adults unless they worked one hundred hours a month. The bill also would require anyone covered by medical insurance to pay a $150 deductible. For those reasons, Tara was eager to have her hearing checked. She was nearly deaf in one ear and suffered from hearing loss in the other. She wanted to have the hearing corrected or at least get fitted with a hearing aid—and have it paid for by medical insurance—so that she could find a job. She had worked as a secretary, a lifeguard, and a waitress, but her hearing loss made it difficult to speak on the phone or deal with impatient customers. Under her medical coverage, a doctor had to test her hearing and verify her hearing loss before she could receive treatment. She had missed one appointment while caring for Cheryl's children at the Northeast house. Now she was worried that she would be denied a second appointment. Cheri told her that Debbie Freedman, the lawyer, would write a letter for her if she encountered any problems.

Cheri had been impressed with Tara's leadership and organizational skills. She was a determined and forthright young woman who did not shrink from a challenge. More than once, Tara had confronted a drugged or drunken panhandler trying to sneak into the church. More and more, she was speaking her mind in war council meetings. A high school graduate, she was an articulate speaker and a clear, concise writer. Tara had come a long way from the plump, frightened, disheveled girl who had arrived at Tent City the previous summer after sleeping in the park. She spoke now of studying to become a physical therapist. She was also becoming more outspoken in her political views—particularly on the issue of single mothers and welfare.

"Newt Gingrich has the nerve to say a young girl is going to deliberately get pregnant so she can get a bigger welfare check," Tara told Cheri. "Puleeze. He thinks I'm gonna have a kid just for the lousy extra hundred dollars every two weeks, or whatever it is? I hate to burst Newt's bubble, but people don't think that way. Does he really think a young girl is going to say: I'm gonna have a baby and put myself deeper into poverty for the next eighteen years? And Congress—it doesn't want to pay for welfare, but it won't pay for abortions either. So what they're saying is: If you get pregnant, you better have that baby—and raise it in poverty because we won't pay to help it."

As Tara spoke, Katie sat down with Cheri to bring her up-to-date on her latest problems with her daughter Nancy's housing voucher. Katie had just come inside from talking to Nancy on the pay phone across the street. Nancy had told her flatly: "Bad news. The landlord wants us out by Sunday."

Katie, her daughter Nancy, and Nancy's children—Gina, nine, and Billy, seven—were still living in the same row house in Northeast Philadelphia they had obtained through one of the housing vouchers reluctantly awarded to KWRU by the city. But after many threats from the landlord, they were finally being kicked out. Katie, with Cheri's help, had managed to extend the voucher. But now the landlord said he wanted the family out, voucher or no voucher. She believed the man feared the housing voucher would run out and he would be stuck with a welfare family unable to pay the full $625-a-month rent.

With Cheri's help, Katie had managed to locate another row house, for $550 a month. But it was in Fishtown, a trashy, run-down neighborhood dominated by blue-collar whites well known for their hatred of blacks and Hispanics. That meant it would be risky for KWRU people like Chicago or J.R. to visit, but Katie felt that she had no choice but to take the place. While she could always sleep at St. Edward's, she refused to have her daughter and grandchildren live there. They needed a traditional home. The landlord—Katie called him "the slumlord," for the row house was shabby and dirty—had agreed to rent her the place if her housing voucher was extended for another six months. The voucher would pay for the bulk of the rent, leaving Nancy enough money from her welfare check and Katie's SSI check to feed and clothe the kids.

When Katie asked Cheri for help getting an extension on the voucher, she did a surprising thing. She told her Cheryl would take care of it. Katie knew of Cheryl's depression, and she was not sure of her present condition. But when she found Cheryl at the church and spoke with her about the voucher, Cheryl seemed her old, confident, aggressive self. Cheryl made several phone calls to the housing offices on Katie's behalf. In each one, she pleaded and cajoled and threatened the housing officials. Miraculously, Nancy's voucher was extended for six months. It meant she would be responsible for just $91 of the $550 monthly rent. Now all she and her mother had to do was come up with a $163 deposit and another $150 to hire a truck to move their belongings.

Katie thanked Cheryl profusely, but she was stricken by the thought of once again uprooting her grandchildren from school. This would be their ninth school since Nancy had moved them to Philadelphia six years earlier.

When Katie broke the news to Billy, the boy began to cry. He said he loved his teacher and did not want to leave her. When he told his teacher he was moving again, she asked him, "Can't you get your mommy to stay?" Billy made a card that said, "To the greatest teacher in the world," and gave it, along with an apple, to his teacher. She gave him a single red rose to remember her by.

Moving her daughter and grandchildren once again left Katie feeling helpless and defeated. Later that day I saw her crouched on her mattress inside the church, crying into her hands. Katie was also facing two court hearings—one for criminal trespass for taking over a HUD house in 1994, and another for blocking the highway when she was arrested along with Cheri, Mariluz, Tara, and others during a housing protest outside City Hall. Katie was not worried about going to jail or paying a fine if convicted. In fact, she took a certain perverse pride in thumbing her nose at the system. "What we do is legally illegal," Katie explained one day.

Still, Katie was worried about Nancy, who also had been arrested at the City Hall protest. She knew Nancy could not afford to take precious time away from the children—not to mention the bus fare downtown—waiting around for court hearings. Nor could Nancy afford a fine, much less jail time. Katie wished she had never brought Nancy to the protest, and she promised herself she would never again involve her daughter in KWRU demonstrations. It was not fair to her grandchildren. When Katie and Nancy's court date arrived, the judge offered to clear each woman's case in return for guilty pleas and $30 fines. Katie refused on principle, and her case was continued. But she urged her daughter to pay the fine. Between the two of them, they managed to come up with $30 in cash, and Nancy's charge was cleared.

As dejected as Katie felt, her struggle for the voucher extension seemed to energize Cheryl. Between her psychiatrist and the support of the people on the war council, Cheryl had made a remarkable recovery from the depression triggered by her lover's death. She began appearing daily at the church, sleeping on a mattress there on some nights and staying at Cheri's place on others. She was dressing in neat, crisp clothes and wearing makeup, and her hair was brushed and clean. She began wearing a watch imprinted with the logo of the National Organization for Women and taking an active role in KWRU affairs. She spoke vaguely of writing two books, one a murder mystery about a middle-aged woman running for mayor of a major city, and the other a biography of her dead lover, Faith Evans.

One afternoon, I watched Cheryl lead one of the daily KWRU classes designed to indoctrinate newcomers into the group's philosophy. Cheryl stood next to the church altar, writing with a felt-tip pen on an easel. She had written, *What is an organization?* and she was asking for replies from a group of bedraggled homeless people who had expressed a vague interest in joining KWRU. They offered answers: "A bunch of people," and "People getting together to get something done." Cheryl nodded and said, "Good, good," but she did not write down their answers. Instead, she wrote:

1. People all together for one cause
2. People who stick together
3. Helping others
4. Common good
5. A base to operate from
6. A core of strategic leaders, like our War Council
7. Protest/Rallies to force change

Some of the homeless people actually pulled out spiral composition books and began writing down what Cheryl had written. Others leaned back in the moth-eaten Tent City sofas and craned their necks to catch a glimpse of a Montel Williams talk show blaring from the color TV hooked up near the sanctuary.

When the lesson was over, Cheryl sat down on the church steps in the brittle autumn sunshine and told me about her recovery: "I was so depressed, so far down, that the first day I met with my psychiatrist, she took one look at me and said, 'I don't know where to begin with you.' The other day, when Willie was driving me to see the psychiatrist, we ran out of gas. Willie got all upset that we were going to be late, but then he looked over at me and I was just sitting there. He said, 'You're so calm.' And I said, 'After what I've been through, this is nothing.' "

Cheryl seemed to have accepted the loss of her children to DHS. She considered it a temporary arrangement until she could pull herself together and care for them again. She spoke of applying for a job at a nursing home. She had worked off and on for several years—as a waitress, house maid, receptionist, lottery machine operator, insurance saleswoman—and she longed to work again, especially now that her welfare checks had been cut off. At the same time, she had rededicated herself to KWRU and the war council.

Cheryl did not tell anyone at the church where her children were living. She was concerned that their father might try to find them. She was worried, too, that her mother and sister would try to get custody of them, for they had threatened many times to take the girls away from Cheryl. But for all her anxiety over her children, she still managed to laugh about her circumstances.

"I remember one day when I was still living in the house and Tara and J.R. were staying over and helping with the kids. Tara was watching a soap opera where somebody was having just an awful time in their life. I told Tara, 'That's nothing. My whole life is just a bad soap opera.'"

Cheryl laughed bitterly and lit a cigarette. She tried to sum up all the calamities that seemed to dictate the course of her life. "Let's see," she said, "I had my fiancé die, I lost my house, I got mugged, my sister tried to steal my kids out of school, my mom threatened to take my kids to their abusive father, my kids got sent to DHS, and I brought shame to my family by getting pregnant by a black man."

It was not widely known around St. Edward's that Cheryl was pregnant. But Cheryl glossed over this detail, as if it were just another routine entry in the long and complex catalogue of her life. She did not dwell on the subject. Instead, she joked about being mugged at gunpoint a few days earlier at Sixth and Lehigh, a few blocks from the church, by two men who stole the last few dollars she had in her pockets. It was the second robbery that week of someone living in the church.

The crimes set people at St. Edward's on edge. There had already been petty thefts from within the church, despite Cheri's efforts to set up a security force of trusted war council men. Now people were afraid to walk the streets around the church. They felt trapped—their valuables at risk even when they were inside the church, their lives at risk if they left the building. Mothers, in particular, needed to go out every day to buy baby food and diapers, or to visit health clinics or pick up their welfare checks and stamps. They felt compromised and exposed, inside and outside their makeshift home. Based on a church history assembled for St. Edward's centenary celebration, in 1986, it seemed that little had changed in the neighborhood over the past century. A description from the 1870s noted that the area around St. Edward's "contained a few good, but many more careless, neglectful and bad Catholics. . . . Intemperance, especially among the women, was one of the worst features. . . . Two priests in succession resigned the charge of the parish, dismayed and discouraged by the condition of things."

Inside the church, Mariluz was trying to build barriers around her living area to discourage thieves. She'd stacked pews and timbers so that the only way into the living area was through a narrow passageway. She and Elba agreed that at least one of them would remain inside the living area at all times, to watch the children and to protect their growing collection of belongings.

For all her worries about security, Mariluz at least had attended to the two primary concerns that had dominated her life since moving into St. Edward's—her welfare check and Destiny's schooling. Just as Mrs. Staley from the welfare office had promised, a letter from the Department of Public Assistance had arrived at the KWRU office on Fifth Street, informing Mariluz that her welfare payments had been reinstated. She was now receiving $299.50 every two weeks to support herself and three children. Her food stamps had been reduced, without explanation, from $342 a month to $277. But neither that reduction nor the fact that the first welfare payment came in the form of a check and thus required her to pay a $8.65 check-cashing fee seemed to upset Mariluz. Feeling flush after a period in which she had received nothing, she returned from the corner check-cashing store in good spirits. "I'm back in the system," she said with a smile, "and that's what counts."

That same week, Mariluz finally got around to enrolling Destiny in school. But because of her KWRU duties of returning phone calls and organizing donations, she had not had time to actually take her to the new school. The school had tried to track Destiny down through the only home address Mariluz had left on the enrollment form: St. Edward's Church. One morning Leonardo, the caretaker at the rectory, got a phone call from the school. Where was Destiny? Leonardo found Mariluz in the church and told her that the truancy people were going to come for Destiny if she was not in school the next day.

The next morning, Mariluz asked Tara to handle donations and left her two youngest children with Elba. Then she walked the half dozen blocks to the William McKinley school on Diamond Street. She passed two active drug corners along the way, one featuring a lavish memorial to a dead corner boss. To Mariluz, the presence of the dealers meant that she could never let Destiny walk back and forth to school unescorted.

McKinley school was a low, one-story building wedged so tightly into the neighborhood that the row houses surrounding it seemed to rise up out of the classrooms. The school had contracted the same wild contagion of graffiti that afflicted the row houses; almost every outside surface of McKinley school was smeared with painted scrawls. But inside, Mariluz was pleased to see that the hallways were clean and tidy. The school had a warm and cozy feel. The walls were decorated with children's art and handmade signs said, *Welcome to McKinley School*—although the bulletin board featured a police poster warning of a rape suspect who had been active in the neighborhood.

Mariluz introduced herself to Destiny's new first-grade teacher, Ms. Carrigan, a slender, fair-skinned woman with high cheekbones who wore her hair pulled straight back. She seemed, to Mariluz, high-strung but also unflappable, talking calmly as children chattered all around her. Ms. Carrigan had taught at McKinley for eight years. Mariluz told her briefly about Tent City and living in the church, and the reasons for Destiny's delay in attending school. She mentioned that Destiny knew her shapes and colors, and her letters from A to P. Ms. Carrigan assured Mariluz that Destiny could catch up with the class by doing makeup homework.

Ms. Carrigan also told Mariluz about the $6 fee for a Halloween field trip and the $2 registration fee for school. Destiny would also need notebooks, pencils, glue, erasers, and a book bag, she said. Mariluz reacted to this bit of news casually, as if she had all the money in the world to spend on school expenses. "Okay, no problem," she told Ms. Carrigan.

Back at the church, Mariluz poked through the donation pile and found a nearly new pink-and-yellow school backpack emblazoned with the words *Official Barney Item*. Later she walked to the dollar store and bought notebooks, pencils, and glue. She took a city bus to the Rainbow discount store on Front Street, where she bought new clothes for school; she did not want Destiny wearing donated clothes with worn spots and stains. Then she set up a rotating schedule for people at Tent City to walk Destiny to school each morning. On most days, as it turned out, Elba took Destiny along with her own daughter Yazmenelly, who already was enrolled in third grade at McKinley. On other mornings, Mariluz broke away from her donation collection duties to walk both girls. On one morning, when both Mariluz and Elba were busy, I ended up walking Destiny and Yazmenelly to McKinley. There I asked Ms. Carrigan how Destiny had fared during her first week of classes.

"Oh, Destiny has done just fine," Ms. Carrigan said. "She's a very outgoing child. She talks about her mother and the welfare union all the time. I know Destiny's mom is very articulate and very committed and active in the organization. Destiny seems to get a lot of support from the people in the group there. She showed everybody a newspaper picture of her mom. They did a story about people living in the church. Destiny was so proud, and the kids were excited, too. They thought she was famous."

I asked if the other children had teased Destiny about being homeless. Ms. Carrigan looked perplexed. "Teasing? About being homeless?" she said finally. "They're not really aware of it. And even if they were, it wouldn't be a big deal to them. You have to remember, these kids all come from some pretty tough family situations." Sixty-four percent of McKinley's students came from welfare families, and only 6 percent of the school's pupils scored above the national average on reading tests. The surrounding neighborhood was among the poorest and most crime ridden in the entire state.

Back at the church, Mariluz had been confronted by a fire marshal, who informed her that he would have to order the church shut down if fire extinguishers were not in place by the following day, now that people were living in the church. Mariluz called Cheri, who contacted the student group Empty the Shelters. In a matter of hours, the students had raised enough money by going from dormitory to dormitory on campus to buy two new fire extinguishers.

At the church the next morning, Mariluz saw that people were unloading donated clothes in plastic garbage bags. She hauled the bags back to her living area to sort them by size, gender, and condition. As she sat on her bed, the clothes scattered around her, a homeless man named Ernest poked his head through the privacy sheet. "You got clothes?" he asked, stepping into the living area. Mariluz resented the man's impudence. She liked Ernest just fine; in fact, he had watched her children a few times while she sorted donated clothes. But he had no right, she thought, to interfere with her sorting now. That was her job, assigned by the war council. And Ernest certainly had no right to barge into her personal living area.

"You got no right to come in my house!" she shouted at Ernest. "Get out!"

Ernest's mouth dropped open. He was a tall, loose-limbed man prone to confrontation. Some people at St. Edward's were afraid of him. "What you say to me, woman?" he asked.

"I said: Get the fuck out of my house!" Mariluz said, her voice even louder than before.

"You don't talk to me like that," Ernest said. "You tell me to get the fuck out, and I say to you: Fuck you!"

Mariluz stood up and screamed into Ernest's face: "Get out! Out! Get the fuck out!"

Ernest looked down at her and said, "You talk to me like that when I'm the guy who fed your fucking kids and watched over your fucking kids so you could take in all your fucking donations? Well, fuck you!"

As Mariluz turned her back and went back to sorting clothes, Ernest reached out and smacked her in the back of her neck. Mariluz whirled, cursing and sputtering, and tried to punch him back. Suddenly Cheryl ran over, screaming, "Stop it, Ernest!" She grabbed him with both arms and shoved him out of the sleeping area, keeping her body between Ernest and Mariluz, who was still flailing at him. Cheryl was a solidly built woman, and she was able to maneuver Ernest away from Mariluz. She quickly forced him to the other side of the church, and Mariluz watched him go, cursing him and rubbing the back of her neck.

Mariluz sat down on the heap of clothes. She didn't feel like sorting them anymore. She sat there for a long while, until the stinging in her neck went away, wondering whether to call the cops on Ernest or to just forget about the entire incident.

Later that afternoon, Mariluz went to the welfare office on Lehigh Avenue to pick up her latest welfare payment, remembering to remove her rhinestone earrings so that a caseworker didn't mistake them for diamond earrings and ask her about her sources of income. This time the payment was routine, which meant it was issued in cash. Leaving the office, Mariluz saw a street vendor selling cheap framed prints of paintings. Among them were the vivid seascapes and sad-eyed clowns and mournful children commonly seen in the narrow living rooms in North Philadelphia row houses. For $5 Mariluz bought a framed print of an Indian princess. It reminded her of Cheri, who was part Indian. Mariluz felt an ethnic kinship with Cheri, for she, too, had some Indian blood.

Later Mariluz found Cheri standing on the church steps, where she presented the painting to her. Cheri's face grew soft and her eyes moistened. She studied the painting closely, then reached out and hugged Mariluz and kissed her cheek.

"Must be check day," Cheri said, laughing.

Mariluz blushed. Cheri kissed her again and said, "Thank God for check day."

Mariluz tried to think of something to say. She looked around at the trash blowing across the sidewalk and at the winos slumped near the corner of Eighth Street. She blurted out, "Don't leave this anywhere around here, Cheri. It gets ripped off, I'll kill you."

CHAPTER ELEVEN

A Necessary
Butt Whipping

Graterford prison is a gray fortress that rises like a massive boulder from the rolling farm fields and gentle hillocks of eastern Pennsylvania. That autumn, as dead cornstalks lay flattened against the damp ground and cutting winds tore at the last remaining leaves on the oaks along the ridgeline, the prison had a spectral, forbidding look. The only hint of color amid the grays and rusts of the fields and forest was the pale green fall cabbage that had thrust itself up through the dying earth. Odessa noticed the cabbage immediately as she drove down the winding one-lane road to the prison, past the sagging Graterford Inn with its orange neon beer signs and past the faded sign that read, *State Correctional Institution Graterford*. The cabbage reminded her that she had to pick the cabbage and collards from her mother's tiny urban garden on Randolph Street before the first hard freeze killed them. That was the first chore she wanted to tend to when she returned from her visit with Darryl.

Odessa drove up to the prison grounds, the car tires bumping over the carcass of a stray cat flattened on the roadway. Along the horizon, in the same sight line the prison guards saw from their high towers, Odessa watched crows flap and soar from the stark tree branches. Beyond them, across the rolling fields, she saw dirty white steam billow up from the cooling towers of a power plant in the distance. She parked in the sloping prison lot, where the pavement was streaked with black mud, which smeared the bottoms of Odessa's sneakers as she slowly made her way to the prison entrance. It was early afternoon, but already a thick cover of gray clouds had settled on the high prison walls and smothered the daylight. The security lamps atop the thirty-foot walls gave off a sickly yellow glow that washed over the pale green doorways and latches. A cold, steady drizzle had begun to stain the walls the color of ink. The utter bleakness of the day left Odessa feeling sad and empty, and she had to remind herself that it was Darryl's birthday—and that by the time his next birthday rolled around, Darryl would be a free man with only vague and fleeting memories of the five years he had spent in prison.

Inside the Graterford waiting room, Odessa went through the routine she had come to know quite well from her many visits to her son. She signed in, wrote down his prison number from memory, and wrote down her own name, address, and phone number. She walked over to a bank of lockers against the south wall and opened one. Inside she placed some of the most valuable possessions she owned: her asthma inhaler, her house keys, her car keys, and her welfare ID card. She held on to a $10 bill to cover the security deposit for the locker key. Visitors were not permitted to carry any personal items into the inmate visiting area. Visitors were permitted to take money inside to make purchases from the soda and snack machines. Odessa always brought coins, for signs were posted throughout the visiting room that read: *No Asking Guards for Change.* She intended to buy Darryl his favorite snack—microwaved popcorn—and a Pepsi for herself.

Odessa sat down on a plastic chair to wait for Darryl's name to be called. Sometimes she waited for an hour or more, depending on the daily schedule inside Darryl's cell block. There were other relatives waiting, too. All but a few of them were black or Hispanic, for the inmates of Graterford were overwhelmingly men of color. Most of the visitors were women—wives, girlfriends, and mothers. Most, like Odessa, were poor, on welfare, and from North Philadelphia. Prison, along with welfare, was one of the institutions that intruded on their lives, and the main reason was drugs. The focus of the nation's War on Drugs was on poor, minority neighborhoods like North Philadelphia, where drugs were sold openly and arrests were easy to make—at least of low-level street dealers and addicted drug buyers. As a result, state prisons like Graterford were filled with young black men like Darryl. Largely because of drug prosecutions, nearly one of every three black men age twenty to twenty-nine was either in prison, on probation, or on parole. At Graterford, few of the inmates were big-time drug kingpins. Most were, like Darryl, petty addicts and users caught up in police dragnets that regularly swept through the ghetto and the barrio but rarely intruded on the white suburbs, where young white men certainly used and sold drugs, but discreetly, and not in open-air street markets. Whites tended to use powdered cocaine, the penalties for which were one-tenth as severe as for an equal amount of crack cocaine. In and around Philadelphia, whites who did smoke crack tended to drive into North Philadelphia to buy the drug, but in swift drive-up sales that reduced their exposure to arrest. They usually smoked the stuff far from North Philadelphia, in the relative safety of their white suburbs in Pennsylvania, New Jersey, Delaware, or Maryland.

Odessa did not concern herself with issues of race, crime, and prosecution. She accepted the fact that Darryl had broken the law. She had urged him to turn himself in so that he could serve his time, break his addiction, and move on with his life. Now his time was nearly up, and Darryl was about to emerge into the world at large as a reformed man who had given his soul over to God in a gesture that Odessa considered the most significant he had made in his thirty-three years. She longed to look into his eyes, and wrap him in her arms, and wish him a happy birthday face-to-face. It had been many weeks since she had visited.

At last, after an hour of waiting, one of the officers called out, "D. Williams!" and Odessa moved as quickly as her heavy body and weary legs would allow. She let herself be patted down by a female warder, who checked her pockets and peeked inside her socks and sneakers. The woman put Odessa's change purse through a metal detector and then permitted her to walk unescorted down a dark flight of stairs to the basement visiting room. It was painted institutional green, a color made even more impersonal by the metallic glare of fluorescent lights. There were green bars on the windows, and a raised security station, where guards looked down on inmates and their loved ones as they sat on cheap furniture arranged around a bank of vending machines.

Odessa walked into the room and Darryl rushed over from the security station and embraced her. He was grinning as he held tight to his mother's thick neck, murmuring into her ear. Odessa smiled broadly and said, "Happy birthday, son." Darryl looked fit and trim. He was wearing a green prison uniform and brown brogans. He had his brother Israel's powerful build, but he was shorter, with sharper features. He had his mother's strong jaw and straight white teeth, and his dark brown eyes behind his gold-framed spectacles were alert and expressive, like Odessa's. Holding hands, Darryl and Odessa walked over to the vending machines, where Odessa emptied the coin purse into his hands. He bought two bags of popcorn, two bags of chips, and two cans of Pepsi. They took the food to a sofa and sat down to talk.

Darryl wanted to know all about the family. Odessa told him about Israel's fixing up the row house next door and moving in, about Israel's boys still living at home with her, about Israel's getting $97 a month in emergency food stamps to tide him over until he could find a full-time job. She told him about Joyce's move to West Philadelphia. She filled him in on Elaine, and on Iesha's irresponsibility toward her children, and on the episode with the towed car belonging to Iesha's boyfriend. Then she mentioned the fire that Brian and Geedy had set at Joyce's place. Darryl had heard about the fire from his grandmother, but he did not know the details. Odessa told him the whole sad story, knowing the resonance it held for Darryl, who had burned down three houses of his own as a child.

Darryl asked about Brenda. Odessa shook her head and pursed her lips. "Still out on them drugs," she told him. Even so, she said, Brenda had said something to her the other day that gave her a faint sense of hope. Darryl leaned forward to hear her, for he had beaten his own addiction and was eager to advise his wayward sister. Odessa told him that Brenda had turned to her one day in Odessa's living room and suddenly blurted out: "I'm tired, Mama." When Odessa asked why, Brenda had told her, "I'm tired of what I'm doing. I hate it. It's no good. It's wearing me out."

"You know, I think that's the first time Brenda ever said anything like that," Odessa told Darryl. "Before, she'd always say, 'I like what I'm doing, I ain't hurting anybody, so I'm gonna keep on doing it.' "

Darryl nodded. "If you like it, you'll keep on doing it. I know *that*," he said. "You've got to *want* to stop, else you're never gonna quit and it'll just eat you up."

"Well," Odessa said, "I got a little bit of hope for Brenda. Not much, just a tiny bit."

Darryl asked about Joyce, who had defeated her own drug addiction. Odessa told him that Joyce had continued her job training and computer classes, despite the fire and despite the difficult move to West Philadelphia. Somehow, that got them to talking about the time Joyce made a call to a 900-number phone sex line and ended up making a date to meet a man with a sexy voice on the other end of the line. When the man showed up, Joyce was horrified to see that he was short, ugly, bony, and—as Odessa put it—"He had a head the size of a peanut." It was calls to 900 numbers, in fact, that had gotten Odessa's long-distance service terminated for failure to pay $400 in overdue charges. No one in her house ever confessed to having made the calls, but the cutoff meant that Darryl could no longer call his mother collect. Odessa regretted it, but she was not about to pay for some-one else's 900 calls.

Odessa told Darryl, too, about her plans for a Boone and Williams fam-ily reunion in Georgia. She was putting aside a few dollars from each wel-fare check and SSI check to pay for gas to drive there the following August. She asked Darryl if he thought he would be out of prison by then. "Oh, yeah, Mama, I'll be out by June," he told her. He would be eligible for parole on June 15, he said, and his perfect prison record—aside from punching the white prisoner who had called him a nigger—meant that he was sure to be quickly approved for parole. Odessa squeezed Darryl's hand and began outlining her plans for the car trip to Georgia. She told him about the fried chicken she would put in a cooler to eat on the way, and thus save money on restaurants. She talked about the propane stove and frying pan she would take to cook the perch she had caught and frozen, and about the discount-store-brand sodas she would buy to keep the kids happy—and to avoid paying for overpriced vending machine sodas. And if she saved enough money by August, she told Darryl, she planned to take her grandchildren from Georgia on down to Walt Disney World, sleeping in the car along the way.

Darryl listened and smiled, and he told his mother that he might even be paroled to a halfway house in time for the annual Boone and Williams Easter family picnic. "Oh, I hope so," she said. "It would be a special Easter with you there." She thought for a moment, then added, "But I hope they don't send you to a halfway house in North Philly. That's a rough area, with too many crazy people."

They began to talk about Darryl's future. Odessa had already arranged for her son Fred to hire Darryl part-time at his auto repair shop near Randolph Street, and for her son Willie to find part-time work for Darryl in his contracting business in New Jersey. Darryl said he hoped, at some point, to open an air conditioner and refrigerator business. He was on the waiting list to take prison classes in refrigerator and air conditioner repair.

Odessa asked Darryl if he needed any clothes. He told her he had used the money she had sent him over the years to order clothes from catalogues over the prison phone. In a footlocker in his cell, he had slowly built up a postprison wardrobe of new, never-worn clothing: four pairs of sneakers, eleven pairs of undershorts and socks, one pair of Timberland boots, one pair of felt boots, and one set of pajamas. He also told his mother that he had bought a gold crucifix on a chain, which hung now from his neck under his prison uniform.

Odessa was not one for spending money on jewelry, but she approved of this purchase because of the crucifix and what it represented for Darryl's conversion from crack addict and petty criminal to devout Christian. She reached out and touched the cross and told Darryl it was beautiful. Then she looked at him closely and said, "You got so big, I don't know if all those clothes I been saving are gonna fit you." She had been saving trash-picked clothes in Darryl's size, filling up her hall closet with slacks, shirts, and sport coats.

Darryl had entered prison at 167 pounds, lean and somewhat malnourished from his crack habit. He had pumped himself up to 220 pounds, which he realized was too much weight on a man who stood well under six feet tall. "I'm too short to carry two twenty," he said. "I was so bulky it was hard to move." By becoming a vegetarian and by modifying his workouts, he was now down to 196. He was still thickset and muscular, but he was not the bullnecked, overmuscled man in the framed photo in Odessa's living room.

Darryl told his mother he would continue to work out once he left prison, but he intended to maintain his vegetarian diet and pursue a Christian lifestyle.

"I'm going to work hard and save my money," he told her. "I'm not going to spend it on fancy clothes or on a woman, like these guys I see coming out of here. I've seen so many guys get out, and then before you know it, they're right back in. They say, 'Well, I was desperate for cash for my woman or for some new clothes, and I didn't have no job, no other way to get money except to stick somebody up.' Not me. I'm never coming back here. I got straightened out. I don't need this place anymore. I got my Bible. That's all I need."

At the mention of the Bible, Odessa reached out and hugged her son. "I'm so proud of you," she told him. The two of them sat there for a while, eating their popcorn and sipping their Pepsis, watching the other inmates neck with their girlfriends and play with their children, until visiting hours ended and Odessa walked wearily up the darkened stairwell for the long drive home in the rain.

The next morning, Odessa awoke early. She had to take Danielle to the doctor's for a follow-up visit. She had insisted that Iesha accompany her; she was Danielle's mother, after all. And beyond that, Danielle was covered by her mother's medical plan as part of Iesha's welfare benefits. As she made her grandchildren's breakfasts, Odessa sent Kevin to walk Danielle up the street to Elaine's row house so that Iesha could clean her up, change her diaper, and dress her for the trip to the doctor's. When Kevin and Danielle returned ten minutes later, slick green mucus was running down Danielle's lip and dripping onto the collar of a thin jacket Odessa had trash-picked for her that fall. Odessa looked at her and shouted, "Girl! Your mama doesn't know how to dress you for the cold! It's getting to be wintertime out there, and she's got you in that little ol' jacket." Odessa pulled out a blue plastic tub full of trash-picked clothes and pawed through it until she found a heavy winter coat for Danielle. Then she wiped her nose with a tissue.

The door opened and Iesha appeared, ushered in by a blast of cold air. "Ready," she said. She was wearing a sweatshirt but no coat, and she hugged herself to keep warm.

"You're late. Where you been?" Odessa asked.

"I had things to do," Iesha said.

"What things are more important than your baby's health?" Odessa said, her voice rising. "Your baby is sick, just out of the hospital, and you don't even dress her in a warm jacket."

Iesha shrugged but said nothing. Her broad face had an empty, bored expression.

"You call that number I gave you?" Odessa asked her. She meant the number for the job training center. Odessa had been badgering Iesha to find out about entering a program there for unwed welfare mothers.

"Lost the paper the day you gave it to me," Iesha said.

"Girl, you can't hold on to nothing," Odessa said. Her voice was high-pitched now, and she was gasping for air from the effort of scolding her granddaughter. "You better find that number and call that place and get yourself in a program. They are fixing to cut off all this welfare and you'll be out in the cold with nothing. You can do what you want to yourself, but I'm not gonna let you leave your children out in the cold."

She paused to catch her breath. Iesha stared at the floor, stomping her feet to stay warm. "Do something for your children, if not for yourself," Odessa went on. "Do it *now*, not later, because later is gonna be too late. There's no more room for excuses, because you have been warned. It won't be no surprise when they cut off your check, so don't come crying to me when they do."

"Uh-huh," Iesha said, and she walked back out the door and up the street to fetch her baby's heavy coat—and her own winter coat, too. There, she told me that she didn't want to call the job training center because she preferred to stay at home with her children. She said she had tried working—six weeks at a Wendy's in suburban Horsham for $4.75 an hour—but by the time she paid for bus and train fare, she didn't have much money left over. And she had to leave her children with her aunt Elaine, which caused stress at home. In any case, she said, the income from Wendy's did not begin to match what welfare paid her to stay home: $248 in cash every two weeks, plus $288 in food stamps every month. "So it's better to be home with my kids," she said.

Iesha said she had tried to get into an advanced career training course, but she had tested at 98, or far below the 125 score needed for admission. ("I think she's retarded," Odessa had said bitterly at the time.) Iesha dropped out of high school, she said, because "I just didn't like it—or the people there. The kids there talk too much trash. They act out in class and the teacher stops teaching and you can't learn anything, so what's the point? I'd rather be at home."

I asked Iesha why she did not seek financial help from the fathers of her children. She shrugged and said, "They ain't worth chasing after. They don't have any money anyway." Besides, she said, her current boyfriend,

Curtis, helped out with his income from his part-time security job. And Curtis cared for her, she said, unlike the previous men in her life.

Iesha's previous boyfriends had been a source of persistent tension between her and her grandmother. Odessa had known that Iesha was having unprotected sex with her boyfriend of the moment when she was in her early teens. She tried to persuade the girl to go the clinic and get a prescription for birth control pills. "I told her if she absolutely had to have sex, then there's a right way and a wrong way," Odessa told me one day. "The wrong way was having sex without protection. The right way was birth control. She told me she'd get some pills, but she never did. She's hardheaded. I guess that's why she got pregnant when she was only sixteen."

Odessa also tried to counsel Iesha on her choice of boyfriends. "One look at that boy who's the father of her first baby and you could see he wasn't about to support Iesha," she said. "I don't know if Iesha even believed it. She just wanted a baby to make herself feel grown-up. She was determined to have a child. And she knew welfare would take care of the baby—or Grandma would. So it didn't matter to her that the father wasn't going to be around to help."

All that week, Odessa prepared her annual Thanksgiving Day feast. She cooked two types of greens with onions and froze them. She made macaroni and cheese and froze that, too Thanksgiving party. She cooked chitlins, smelling up the house so badly that she had to retreat to the front porch, gasping in the frigid air. She refused to eat chitlins, having been made severely ill by them in her youth, but she knew others in the family loved them. She hating cleaning them, too. She persuaded a niece and a sister-in-law to help her strip the top layer of fiber from the intestines, scrape them clean, pick the inner lining clean, soak them in water, boil them with salt and vinegar and bay leaves, then boil the whole mess with salt for two hours. Odessa preferred hog maws, which she intended to buy the day before Thanksgiving with the final $20 that remained from family contributions to the dinner.

Israel helped Odessa, for he was an accomplished cook. He baked a vanilla cake, cooked thirty pounds of turkey wings and baked one of the hams. Day after day, Israel and his mother argued and fussed about the food—who would cook what and when, what got frozen and what didn't, who had to chop the onions for the potato salad. Several times, Israel raised a serving fork at Odessa and threatened to stab her in the throat if she didn't stop carping at him. Odessa punched her son on the arm several times, and once she shoved him into the freezer, laughing at him when he slipped and lost his balance. The Boones were a physical family, Odessa admitted, but she figured it was better to get out your frustrations by push-ing and shoving and threatening, rather than have them build up and erupt in actual violence. "People in this neighborhood kill each other all the time over stupid little arguments," Odessa said one day. "We have our little arguments, and they're loud and rough, but then they're over and nobody gets hurt."

"Yeah," Israel said, stirring a pot on the stove beneath a wrinkled strip of flypaper dangling from the ceiling, "nobody gets hurt. But I guarantee you if somebody does get hurt, it's gonna be you, Dessa, and not me."

Odessa swung her heavy arm at her son's midsection, but he backed away and she missed. Israel would never tell Odessa so, but he treasured the hours they spent in the kitchen, cooking and arguing. It reminded him of all the times he had spent as a boy with his mother in the kitchen of their home.

"My mom made sure everybody in the family could cook, in case we got up with a woman who couldn't cook," Israel said. "Now Anita, the rela-tionship I just got out of, she couldn't cook when I met her. I had worked two and a half years at an Italian restaurant, so I taught her. But that didn't mean I didn't cook for my boys. I still do, mainly when Dessa doesn't feel like it."

Odessa, sitting in the living room as Israel's boys watched *I Love Lucy* on her TV and *The Flintstones* on their father's TV, overheard him and shouted toward the kitchen: " 'When Dessa doesn't feel like it' is getting to be just about every day, as much as you all aggravate me."

Israel and his boys were indeed wearing her out. It was all she could do to keep up with the four grandchildren who lived with her, plus Danielle and little Darryl. The week before, she had blown up at Israel's boys after warning them that she would whip them if they didn't do their share of cleaning. She had just cleaned the house and gone to check on her mother, on Randolph Street. When she returned, Israel's boys were playing karate in the living room and had tossed Odessa's papers and trash-picked clothes everywhere. They had left dirty underwear and potato chip wrappers in the upstairs hallway, where one of them had spilled a Pepsi bottle, which was being attacked by flies even in thirty-degree weather.

Odessa got out her belt and told Israel's boys, "I've been warning you and warning you, and you didn't listen. Now I'm going to whip you—not because I don't love you, but because you don't listen to me." She whipped each one on his butt and the back of his legs, starting with Steven, the old-est, and working her way down through Ray-Ray and Anthony to David, the youngest. The older boys bit their lips and tried not to cry, but the younger ones bawled in agony.

Israel heard them and came into the room and said, "Mother, you can't be whippin' my kids. My kids get whipped, it'll be me doing the whipping."

Odessa stared hard at him. "No, Israel, you're in *my* house, so I'll whip them," she said. "I haven't whipped them before because I warned them and warned them instead. But now I'm through warning. I'm ready to do some serious butt whipping because it's necessary."

Now, a week later, the spankings seemed to have broken some of the tension between Israel's family and Odessa. Israel's boys had begun keeping the house clean, even folding up their blankets and bedclothes every morning. Odessa felt even more charitable than ever toward Israel. She called Cheri Honkala, who explained to her how to get Israel back on emergency food stamps; he had been cut off after Anita called the welfare people and told them that Israel was not homeless, as he had reported, but had merely lost his previous home and moved in with his mother. With Cheri's guidance, Odessa managed to make the phone calls necessary to have Israel's $97-a-month emergency stamps reinstated. Soon after that Odessa went trash picking in Upper Darby and found a nearly new king-size mattress and box spring, which she gave to Israel. When he saw it, Israel hugged his mother, and Odessa knew that all was well between them.

On the Tuesday before Thanksgiving, Odessa took out a macaroni-and-cheese casserole she had made for Brian's school party. She had promised Brian she would go, though she dreaded the ordeal of walking up the three flights of steps to his classroom. Beyond that, she was not certain Brian deserved to go to the party. Earlier that week, it had snowed just enough for Brian to make a tiny snowball and throw it at a woman getting off a bus on Allegheny Avenue. The woman confronted Brian and demanded to know where he lived. "Any other kid would've said, 'Timbuktu,' " Odessa said later, "but Brian was honest." He not only told the woman where he lived, but also brought her home. The woman told Odessa what had happened, and Brian was put on punishment. But because he had confessed to his crime, Odessa decided that Brian could attend his class party after all—with his grandmother, too.

Odessa left early for Brian's school in order to afford herself plenty of time to negotiate the stairs. Balancing the casserole in one hand, she walked slowly up the outside stairs, rested on the bench in the vestibule, then began the long journey up to Brian's classroom. It took nearly five minutes, with Odessa stopping on each narrow landing to catch her breath. She made her way into Ms. Chisholm's classroom. She handed the casserole to Ms. Chisholm, then collapsed into a child's chair, saying breathlessly, "This is the first time I've been up here. It's such a *long* climb."

Looking around, Odessa noticed that only two other parents had come to the party. There were two dozen children in the class. She looked out the window and noticed how different North Philadelphia looked from three stories up. She could not see the trash and the drug dealing and the graffiti. There were only black rooftops and the dark outlines of abandoned factories and warehouses, and tiny back lots with withered trees and stunted weeds. And stretching to the horizon, as far as she could see, were more rooftops and brick and tar and electric poles. It was hard to believe anyone lived there.

Suddenly Brian came running over to her, holding a pair of scissors he had been using to cut out a cardboard Pilgrim.

Ms. Chisholm intercepted him. "Brian!" she said, grabbing his hand. "What's the rule about scissors?"

Brian grinned sheepishly and said, "Don't run."

"Why?"

" 'Cause you could stab yourself or put out your eye."

"Right," Ms. Chisholm said and took the scissors from him.

She sat down in a child's chair next to Odessa. She knew Odessa wanted to discuss Brian's behavior.

"Brian was a big problem when he got here, as you know," Ms. Chisholm said. "He caused a lot of trouble. He was a very angry little boy who couldn't say what he was angry about. He didn't pay attention. He didn't follow instructions. He disrupted the entire class. He wet himself. He got out of his seat constantly. There wasn't a rule he didn't break. He talked back. Whatever I'd say to him, he'd say, 'No, no, no,' or, 'Why?' or, 'I *won't* do it.' "

She paused here to allow Odessa an opening for explanation or contradiction. Odessa merely nodded and said, "I know, I know."

"I think we're getting a handle on it now," the teacher went on. "He hasn't wet himself in a few days. We've been trying to give him a lot of attention. He needs attention. He's crying out for it."

Odessa thought she knew what part of the problem was. "He's always telling me he wants to see his dad," she said. "He wants to know who his dad is. You see, the other three kids have the same dad, and he calls them once in a blue moon. At least they know who he is. They can picture him. But Brian, he doesn't know anything about his dad. He feels so left out."

She did not mention that Brian's father was a crack addict and career criminal. The last Odessa had heard of the man, he was locked up in a prison down South, charged with murder.

"A male role model is crucial for little boys," Ms. Chisholm said. "I try to fill in part of the void. I hug Brian no matter what he does. I force him to get close to me. I tell him Ms. Chisholm loves him no matter what. I try to get him to tell me what's bothering him. He's frustrated and angry and he can't articulate it. But he's doing better. He listens to me, like with the scissors thing just now. I think his therapy is helping. He needs to know somebody cares about him—and I sure do."

Into the room walked the school principal, Ms. Gilbert, the same woman who had insisted that Brian be suspended for kicking the bus attendant. Ms. Gilbert smiled and greeted Odessa, who smiled back and wished her a happy Thanksgiving. Ms. Gilbert said she had come to hand out Perfect Attendance Awards. She presented them to most of the students in the class, including Brian, despite the days he had missed while on suspension.

Brian took his Perfect Attendance certificate and sat down. The principal called four more names, including that of Brian's deskmate, Omar Mateo. Brian looked up to see that Omar and the others were being awarded more substantial certificates—for the Good Student Award. He put his head down on his turkey plate and began sobbing. Odessa pulled him toward her and tried to console him. "Brian, you know you have to be good the whole month to get the Good Student Award," she told him. "You're just getting started on being good."

Ms. Chisholm walked over and asked Brian why he was crying. Brian looked up through his tears and said, "I'm gonna get in trouble."

"Why?"

"I was bad."

"Why do you think you were bad?"

"I didn't get the Good Student Award," Brian said.

Ms. Chisholm put her hands on her hips. "Brian, Brian, Brian," she said, "you want to know why they got those awards?"

Brian put his head back down and mumbled something.

Ms. Chisholm whispered to him: "Brian, you have to talk to me. Remember? You have to tell me what's bothering you."

"I'm sad," Brian said. He was fighting back tears; one droplet, crystalline and pure, formed on his thick eyelashes and spilled onto his cheek.

"Listen to me," Ms. Chisholm said. "They got those awards because they *didn't* get Perfect Attendance Awards. I had to give them something, or else *they'd* be hurt. You understand?"

Brian wiped his eyes. "Yeah," he said softly.

"So be proud," Ms. Chisholm said. "You earned your award."

Brian looked at Odessa and held up his certificate. "Grandma, can we put it up in the living room where everybody can see it?"

Odessa promised him she would make a space right next to the photo of Brian when he was a baby.

She hugged Brian and told him to behave. She took his certificate and thanked Ms. Chisholm for paying so much attention to her troubled grandson. Then she made her way slowly downstairs, past the construction-paper turkeys pasted to the walls, down all three flights of stairs, and out to her old Caprice. It was a short drive through the late afternoon shadows to Cousin's, which looked as grim and forbidding in the twilight as Graterford prison. The store had metal grates protecting the windows, and walking through the front door was like entering a bunker. But once inside, Odessa felt the pleasant urgency of the last-minute Thanksgiving shoppers pulling the last few frozen turkeys from the freezers. It was truly beginning to feel like the holidays.

Odessa made her way to the meat counter and found the hog maws. She selected nearly $20 worth, which was enough for everyone in the Boone and Williams families to have at least one small portion each. The maws were the most tender portion of a hog's stomach, and Odessa loved their strong, meaty taste. She lugged them to the checkout line, thinking hard about how she would prepare the meat. She would clean them and boil them until they were soft and pliable. Then she would slice them and soak them in vinegar. She would sprinkle them with salt and black pepper and simmer them until they were cooked through and tender. Knowing the Boones, she thought, she would have to fight them all just to get a plateful.

At the checkout line, the cashier rang up the hog maws. They came to just under $20. Odessa reached into the pocket of her old denim coat for the $20 bill she had tucked there that morning; it was all that remained from family Thanksgiving donations. Now there was nothing. She reached into the other pocket. Nothing. The bill was gone. It must have fallen out of her pocket—most likely, she thought, in her haste to get to Brian's party. Odessa apologized to the cashier and walked away, leaving the hog maws on the counter. She went out into the remains of the gray afternoon and drove slowly home to tell Israel he could forget about cooking hog maws this Thanksgiving.

The next day, as Odessa and Israel spent the afternoon and evening cooking in her cramped kitchen, Brian and his cousin Geedy got to go to Burger King. Brian had just turned eight years old. For his birthday present, I had offered to take him and his cousin to the Burger King at K and A. Brian had been complaining that his grandmother had not allowed him to have a birthday party; she did not have enough money for cake and ice cream and decorations.

On the drive up Allegheny Avenue, Brian mentioned that his mother had not given him a birthday present. He said it in a matter-of-fact way, as if relating a known truth, with no more emotion or regret than if he had said, "Thanksgiving is always on a Thursday." I asked him if it upset him that his mother had forgotten his birthday.

"Nope," he said. "She never remembers."

"She doesn't even call you?" I asked.

"Naw, she never calls anyways, even if it's not my birthday," Brian said.

"Why not?"

" 'Cause she don't care."

"Why do you think she doesn't care?" I asked.

" 'Cause she on drugs," Brian said flatly. He thought for a moment, then added, "But she can't help herself. Those drugs take over your mind. They make you do stuff you wouldn't do otherwise. Like, you don't take care of your kids and you don't eat right and you wear dirty old clothes. Pretty soon you get real sick and then you can't take care of yourself, and you do more drugs."

I was not certain whether that description of drug addiction had come from the drug awareness sessions at Brian's school or merely from observations in his own home and neighborhood. From the backseat, Geedy added: "If you on drugs and you have a baby, it'll be a crack baby." Geedy did not seem to be making a reference to Brian; he seemed merely to be expressing a statement of fact. In any case, Brian seemed thoroughly unoffended by the reference, and the conversation shifted to the relative merits of McDonald's versus Burger King.

At Burger King, Brian and Geedy ran to the front of the line and tried to push their way to the counter. I pulled them back to the rear, where they stood on their tiptoes and read loudly from the overhead menu. By the time they reached the counter, they were able to recite the descriptions, weight, and price of each item of food they ordered. They heaped their trays with Kids Club cheeseburgers and french fries and drinks and desserts, and selected a table at the rear, away from the noisy packs of teenagers and the elderly people hunched in silence over their meals.

I pulled out Brian's gift, a set of toy motorcycles I had wrapped in cheap paper from B.J.'s. Brian threw down his hamburger and tore at the wrapping paper. When he saw the motorcycles, he let out a whoop and shouted, "Decent! Oh, man, they so shiny! Oh, man, oh man! Happy birthday for Brian today!"

He ripped one of the cycles from its moorings and held it up to the harsh fluorescent light of the Burger King. "Ain't nobody gonna play with these but me!" he told Geedy.

"Can I have one? Gimme the white one," Geedy said.

Brian reached into the box and tore out a white motorcycle. "This one's yours," he told Geedy. "The rest belongs to the birthday boy. Oh, man, what a birthday!"

The two boys began running the motorcycles up and down the table, crashing them into each other while carrying on a free-form conversation that touched at one point on who was responsible for the fire that burned down Joyce's house. They quickly fell into an argument. Geedy said Brian had urged him to "stick it to the bed" as they sat lighting matches. Brian said it was Geedy's idea to begin scratching matches in the first place. I tried to intercede, asking them what they had learned from the episode.

"We learned our lesson," Geedy said. "People could have died if we didn't run out and tell Grandma." He paused and looked at Brian. "But Brian *did* tell me to do it," he said.

Brian looked up from his motorcycle set. "Would you jump off a building if I told you to?" he asked.

"Shut up, Brian," Geedy said. "I don't listen to you no more."

"I don't listen to you, neither," Brian said quietly.

That seemed to end the dispute, and the two cousins finished their hamburgers. They walked outside to the parking lot, Brian clutching his torn box full of motorcycles, and Geedy making motorcycle noises as he waved his white cycle through the air. At the car, Geedy stopped abruptly and pulled a wad of Burger King napkins from his pocket. Slowly, as if he were sitting on a park bench killing time, Geedy began to rip each napkin into tiny pieces. He let the scraps of paper flutter to the pavement.

Brian reached out and grabbed his cousin's hand. "Quit it, Geedy. That's littering," he said, and he gestured to the trash that blew through the lot and the clumps of stale garbage that sat festering in the side streets behind the Burger King. "Don't you know Philly is the dirtiest city in the world?"

The night before Thanksgiving, Odessa stayed up until 2 A.M., finishing up the food and putting up a set of pale green curtains she had trash-picked in the Northeast. She vacuumed the rug and floor, moved the sofas against the wall, and rearranged her home entertainment center in such a way that guests could pile onto the sofas and watch the football games on either TV, Odessa's or Israel's. As she worked, Israel and Elaine got into a mock fight over Israel's car keys. Elaine raised her fist at her brother, who adopted a boxer's defensive pose and said to her, "Go ahead, fatso, take your best shot." Odessa stepped in front of Israel and put up her own fists, giggling at the sight of her son and daughter squaring off. "Israel, the two of us is bigger than you," she said. "We could take you out, so you better back off." Israel laughed and said, "I don't have time to waste on you two, I got all this food to cook."

One of the first guests to arrive on Thanksgiving morning was Brenda. She wore a dirty sweatshirt that bore a message that read, *Hug Me, It's Christmas*. With her was her live-in boyfriend, Jeff, a thin, wiry, unkempt little man who wore a greasy overcoat. His hair was matted and his fingernails were stained black with grime. Jeff sat down and stared at the two TVs while Brenda, on Odessa's orders, began bringing serving plates of food from the kitchen to the dining room table.

Soon other family members began to arrive, greeting Odessa and Israel and Elaine with elaborate hugs and kisses. They studiously avoided any contact with Jeff or Brenda, stepping around them as if they were furniture; they did not hate Brenda and Jeff, and they sympathized with their addiction, but they deeply resented what Brenda's depravities had done to her children—who were their own flesh and blood, after all. Brian, Kevin, and Jim ignored their mother and her boyfriend, too, reaching around them to load their plates with food as the house began to fill with the raucous sounds of people laughing and joking and shouting to be heard over the roar of two competing football games on the TV sets. Only Delena spoke to her mother, and the two of them huddled and whispered next to the freezer in the cramped anteroom off the kitchen.

Willie arrived from New Jersey with a case of Budweiser and a bottle of wine—the first time I had seen alcohol in Odessa's house. Willie was smoking a foul-smelling South American cigar, which aggravated Odessa's asthma and got Kevin to coughing. Odessa ordered him outside to the porch. Joyce arrived, looking rested and fit. She told her mother that she had already begun looking for jobs in anticipation of graduating from the job training school. Elaine rushed back and forth between her house and Odessa's, hauling last-minute supplies of napkins and plastic silverware. On one trip, Iesha emerged in Odessa's doorway behind Elaine. She made her way quietly to the table, paused as Odessa made all the children stop and say a Thanksgiving prayer, then piled a paper plate with food and retreated back out the front door to eat at Elaine's.

In Iesha's wake came Bertha, Odessa's second-oldest daughter. She had her mother's thickset frame, wide hips, and broad face. She was well dressed and loaded down with a platter of food, and her mother and sisters swarmed over her to greet her and fuss over her new hairdo. Behind Bertha came Jeanette, a tall, heavyset woman with light brown hair, whom Odessa called "my white sister-in-law," for Jeanette had married the brother of Odessa's ex-husband. She was the best-dressed person in the house, walking through the vestibule in a long black dress and black high heels. Arriving just behind Jeanette was another white face. It was Phil, whom Odessa called her "adopted white son." She had raised Phil from the time he was a toddler, back in the days when Odessa served as a certified foster parent for DHS. Now Phil was a grown man and lived across the river in Camden. He was outgoing and effusive, a stout and barrel-chested man with wavy dark hair and a full face. He wore a black jacket with a message across the back that read, *Funky White Boy*. Phil's arrival seemed to further energize the gathering, and the joking and laughter and storytelling grew louder.

Odessa presided from a dining room chair, issuing orders to Israel and Elaine and Bertha for food to be brought out, uncovered, and then arranged on the table. Soon every inch of surface on the old table was covered with platters wedged against one another: carved turkey, pork ribs, pork skins in cabbage, chitlins, macaroni and cheese, turnip greens and collard greens, green beans with ham, stuffing, banana pudding, apple and pumpkin pies, vanilla cake, and plastic pitchers of iced tea and freshly squeezed lemonade. Odessa got up from her chair only once, to intercept someone carrying a tray of ice from the freezer. Stuck to the bottom of the tray was a frozen perch Odessa had caught that summer. She peeled the stiff fish off the tray and put it back into the freezer, announcing to everyone, "That's not for Thanksgiving. That's my winter food."

It took more than two hours for everyone to eat. Most people stood shoulder to shoulder and balanced their plates on one hand and stabbed their food with plastic forks. A few sat wedged together on the couches, eating from paper plates in their laps. The children ate on the run, grabbing food from the table, their thin arms reaching from behind the adults packed around the table. Odessa found small areas in the corners of the dining room for the babies to sit on newspapers as their mothers bent down to cut up bits of turkey and dressing. Several times Flower, Odessa's new puppy, snatched the meat from their plates.

Later, Jim and Kevin led all the boys, and some of the girls, in a football game out on the frozen sidewalk. Some of the men joined in, bumping and shoving and tackling on the hard, cold pavement. Then everyone came back inside to stand over the kerosene heater and warm their hands in its hot, filmy haze. Some of Odessa's grown sons and nephews started wrestling on the living room floor, rolling around and bellowing. Odessa stood over them, playing referee and whipping the losers with a broken car antenna.

Delena went upstairs to her room to get away from the ruckus. Her mother came up later. Together, they arranged a lamp on the old color TV set Odessa had trash-picked for Delena. Under the glare of the fixture that hung by a bare wire, they straightened the covers of Delena's bed and set up her dolls on her bureau. They talked about Christmas, though Delena did not ask about a gift from her mother, because she knew Brenda would not be able to provide one. She spoke instead of wanting a Walkman, which she knew her grandma could not afford, and of expecting a Secret Diary computer journal, which she hoped her Grandma would buy for her. She mentioned, too, that Jeff had promised each of Brenda's four kids an envelope with $10 inside, to be presented by Jeff himself on Christmas Day. Delena told her mother she wanted her to spend the night with her in her room, but Brenda said Odessa would not allow it. They decided to take a nap instead. The room was warm, having absorbed the heat of the kerosene burner, situated directly below them, through the thin floorboards. They felt listless, but somehow contented, for Christmas was coming and they were together as mother and child. The two of them lay down on the mattress, with Delena's back arched into the curve formed by her mother's bent midsection as she lay curled behind her. Brenda stretched her arms out and enclosed Delena's face in a gentle embrace, and together mother and daughter drifted off to sleep.

CHAPTER TWELVE

Skinny Joey

When Cheri awoke the next morning, she looked out her front window and saw two familiar men sitting in a car parked on narrow Randolph Street. They wore sport coats and slacks. They were inside a nondescript white, late-model sedan. To Cheri, all Civil Affairs cops looked alike, dressed alike, even drove the same kind of city cars. Did they teach them that at the police academy? She had seen these two before—one of them at the Independence Mall protest and the other at the church the day Cheri's people had moved in. Now Cheri dressed quickly and locked the house. She had to get to St. Edward's to organize a protest she had scheduled for that afternoon at the city housing office downtown. This was the same protest that had collapsed out of sheer ineptitude at John Kromer's office on Columbus Day.

As Cheri walked to her car, she stared at the two Civil Affairs men. They stared back at her. She smiled and waved. They waved back. One of them said, "Hi, Cheri." Their shadowing of her seemed harmless, almost playful, but it was beginning to weigh on Cheri. She could not figure out whether it was pure harassment or something more. They knew she had bench warrants out for missing court appearances for her arrest at the City Hall demonstration. Why didn't they just lock her up? In fact, one Civil Affairs officer had showed up at the church at 10 P.M. a few nights earlier, asking for Cheri. He left after Katie told him Cheri wasn't there, but Katie feared for a moment that she was about to be arrested. And just the night before, when Cheri convened a war council meeting at a late-night diner on Girard Avenue, two Civil Affairs cops walked in and sat in the booth behind them, effectively ending the meeting just as it was beginning.

At the church, Cheri decided to press ahead with the housing office demonstration, regardless of what Civil Affairs might be planning. They couldn't stop her and her people from expressing their views to Kromer, as long as they remained nonviolent. And if they intended to arrest her on the bench warrants, they could have done so that morning or the night before.

Cheri quickly organized about twenty KWRU members. She handed out bus tokens for the ride downtown and sent everyone on their way.

At the Office of Housing and Community Development, on Market Street, everyone knew the way to John Kromer's office. This time, the heavy glass doors to the housing office were unlocked and the lights shone brightly inside. A man in a business suit saw Cheri and her troupe get off the elevator, carrying signs and pushing baby strollers. He walked quickly to the doors, trying to lock them before the horde of homeless people could reach them. But Cheri and Chicago slipped through before the man could block their way. He backed off, and the rest of the protesters streamed through the doorway. They had already begun their standard chant:

"Whadda we want?"

"Affordable housing!"

"When do we want it?"

"Now!"

The receptionists and secretaries rolled their eyes. They had endured these protests before. One of them made a hushed phone call, whispering into the receiver, "The homeless protesters are here again." The call was to Kromer's office, down a corridor behind the reception area. Cheri and Kromer had a long, contentious history. Kromer was one of the city officials, along with Bill Parshall, who had given in to Cheri's public protests two years earlier and awarded housing vouchers to KWRU members who had refused to go through the shelter system. The strained relationship between Kromer and KWRU was documented in an exchange of curt letters over the years. In a 1994 letter to the group, Kromer had written:

> KWRU's actions last year and during recent weeks are designed to convince the public that homeless people are pathetic creatures and that no one is doing anything worthwhile to address the problem of homelessness in Philadelphia. Why else would KWRU parade young children in front of television cameras while ignoring offers of direct assistance from responsible organizations?

In the same letter, Kromer called KWRU "the only organization I know of that has actually prevented poor people from obtaining access to affordable housing and services. . . . As I did last year, I must again question the motives of your organization." In a 1993 letter, Kromer complained bitterly about Cheri's ambushes: "You have never requested a meeting with me, but have instead made unscheduled visits to my office and home, preceded by advance publicity made available to the media, and have delivered a series of demands to me."

Now Cheri was once again launching a guerrilla attack on Kromer. She had most of her protesters sit down in chairs inside the housing office waiting room, while Mariluz and Laverne, another woman from St. Edward's, circled the room, pushing baby carriages and chanting. Laverne inadvertently brushed her stroller against the leg of a woman sitting nearby. The woman snapped at Laverne, demanding an apology. Laverne refused. "I'll whip your ass and teach you some manners," the woman said. Laverne cursed and moved toward the woman, spitting out, "I don't *think* so! Maybe I'll whip your ass and teach you something . . ." Cheri grabbed Laverne and pulled her away, saying, "We're here to fight for affordable housing, not fight other people." The woman glared at Laverne, who sat muttering in her chair.

To refocus her protest, Cheri led the group to the set of doors at the entrance to the corridor that led to Kromer's office. A security guard appeared. The protesters crowded around the doorway, blocking access to the corridor and to a women's restroom next to the doorway.

They chanted, "What do we want?"

"John Kromer!"

"When do we want him?"

"Now!"

A woman appeared at the rear of the little scrum, trying to force her way through. When the protesters ignored her and continued to chant, the woman began a chant of her own: "What do I want?" she yelled, trying to make herself heard over the protesters. "The *bathroom!* . . . When do I want it? . . . *Now!*"

The crowd parted. "Thank you," the woman said, and she slipped into the ladies' room.

Everyone was laughing now, including the receptionists. Cheri gave up trying to force her way into the corridor to reach Kromer's office. She turned to the receptionists. "We'll give Mr. Kromer ten more minutes," she said. "Then we go find him."

A receptionist made another call. Then she told Cheri: "He'll see you in the boardroom."

Cheri gathered up the protesters and seated them around an enormous conference table in the boardroom, located just outside the waiting room. She warned everyone that Kromer might bring the police with him, so anyone with any outstanding bench warrants might want to consider leaving. Mariluz, Tara, and Katie all had warrants for missing hearings on the arrests from the City Hall protest. All three decided to stay.

"Well, okay," Cheri told them. "But watch out for this Kromer guy. He's one of those people who smiles all the time, no matter what's going on. He's got this little Hitler mustache, and he's always smiling underneath it. He'd smile even if he were saying to you, 'I'm gonna toss your ass in jail.' "

At that moment, Kromer walked into the boardroom. He was a tall, middle-aged man in a dark suit. There was a thin dark mustache on his boyish face, and a shock of straight brown hair that flopped over his forehead. He was tanned and smiling. Trailing Kromer were two plainclothes police officers. Cheri recognized one of them as the Civil Affairs officer she had seen at the diner the night before and outside her row house that morning. She expected them to ask her about her bench warrants, but they stood silently, their arms folded in front of them.

Cheri looked at Kromer and announced, "I think you know who these people are, Mr. Kromer. They're the families who have been trying for months now to find affordable housing. We're here today to have a discussion about what emergency housing vouchers are available."

Kromer sat down, flanked by the Civil Affairs officers. "Oh, yes," he said, still smiling. "You came here on Columbus Day, which we all know is a city holiday. We'll be glad to give you a schedule of city holidays. Now you've come without an appointment. Why is that, Cheri?"

"Well, John," Cheri said, "we've been trying for months for affordable housing—"

"Answer my question!" Kromer snapped. He was still smiling.

"We're here, John. We've been here before," Cheri said.

Kromer stabbed at the table with his forefinger. "Answer my question!" he said, his voice rising. "And tell the truth! Why didn't you schedule an appointment?"

Cheri raised her voice, too. "We will *not* be ignored!" she said. "Let's get beyond this, Mr. Kromer. These people want to get on the list for emergency housing vouchers. They need to get out of the church and into proper houses."

Kromer waved his hand dismissively. His face was reddening beneath his tan. "I don't think you're really interested in poor people," he said. "I have serious questions about you and your motives."

Cheri stared hard at him. "You are *not* some god in this process!" she said, her face flushing beneath her makeup. "We want answers to our questions *now!*"

Katie, sitting across from Kromer, interrupted. "No disrespect," she said to Kromer, "but how much do *you* really care about poor people and housing?"

Kromer smiled. "My record is public record," he said.

Cheri demanded again to be given information about emergency housing vouchers, and she accused Kromer of conspiring to keep the vouchers out of the hands of KWRU members. Kromer shook his head, exasperated, and said wearily, "That information is publicly available. You know that."

"Well, can we get it?" Cheri asked.

"I'll have it written up—again—and get it to you," Kromer said.

"Great. Excellent," Cheri said. She was smiling at him, but in a mocking way.

"And write down your questions," Kromer said, "so there's no misunderstanding." He got up and left the room, giving Cheri time to write down her requests.

Cheri tore a page from her *Things to Do Today* notebook and began writing. How many emergency vouchers were available? When would they be available? What were the criteria for getting them?

A few minutes later, Kromer was back. He took the paper from Cheri and asked for her fax number.

"A fax? We don't have a fax, John," Cheri said. "Things are rough, you know."

"Well," Kromer said, "I did notice that the poster you slipped under my door the other day was of the highest art-store quality."

Cheri did not respond. Kromer asked her: "And what are *you* doing to provide information on what's available to these families?"

"These families are probably the city's leading experts on affordable housing," Cheri said.

"What about AIDS, job training, drug and alcohol prevention?"

"They're getting help," Cheri said.

The discussion turned to the city shelter system. Despite Cheri's earlier success in circumventing the shelter system, Kromer told her, her people now had to enter the shelter system before becoming eligible for housing vouchers. There would be no more exceptions.

"If these families had gone into the shelter system in July, they would be in transitional housing or permanent housing by now," Kromer said. "Our system is not perfect, and its resources are going to be reduced by budget cuts, but it's still not too late for you to take advantage of the shelter system."

Cheri let out a harsh laugh. "Would you want *your* family to have to live in a city shelter?" she asked.

"Is it any better to be living in an abandoned church?" Kromer shot back.

Suddenly Tara leaped up from her chair and screamed, "Hell, yes!" She began shouting at Kromer about the filth and danger in the city shelters, about her welfare payment cutoffs, about people pulling together at the church to live as a cohesive community. She said she had tried to apply for a housing voucher but had been turned away.

Kromer listened in silence to Tara's tirade, then asked quietly, "Give me your name and I'll check on your application."

"No way!" Tara said. "No way I'm gonna have repercussions behind this. They see I'm with KWRU and that's it."

"If you don't give me your name, how can I verify what you're telling me?" Kromer asked.

"Believe me, the shelters are unsafe," Tara told him. "I've stayed in them. As a young woman, you're always in danger of being violated in there. There's drug abuse. And if you miss their curfew, you get kicked out—"

Cheri cut in and said, "You're falling into his trap, Tara," she said. "The shelter system is not the main point. The point is, everyone is entitled to affordable housing, not a cot in a homeless shelter. Mr. Kromer, you're just a city servant. You can't hold affordable housing as a threat over the heads of poor people."

Kromer sighed and stood up. He and Cheri had reached the same impasse that always stymied them. There was no point in arguing further. The meeting was over.

"This is all a smoke screen," he said. "You'll get your response this afternoon."

Cheri stood up and walked over to Kromer as everyone filed out of the room. She offered her hand, and Kromer shook it. Cheri thanked him for seeing her, and he smiled. As she walked away, she said to him over her shoulder, "Nice tan, John."

In the doorway, Cheri spoke to one of the Civil Affairs officers. "Hey, didn't you have dinner right behind us at the diner last night?" she said. The officer blushed and shrugged, but said nothing. Cheri smiled at him and said, "Yep, I thought I recognized you. See you again soon."

Inside the boardroom, Kromer sat at the table and explained to me, somewhat wearily, that the housing vouchers were available only to people who entered the shelter system and became certified as homeless. "We made an exception once for Cheri and her people, and it didn't work," he said. "We gave them vouchers. Some of the people didn't show up, some weren't eligible, some didn't meet their responsibilities. And KWRU didn't assist them or follow up. And now here's Cheri trying the same tactic. She wants special consideration again. Last time, they camped out on my lawn while I was away on vacation. Now they're coming to my office without an appointment, making the same old demands."

Kromer shook his head and smiled thinly. "Cheri is up to her old tricks," he said. "I guess she likes to stay in the limelight."

Cheri was indeed concerned that the families living in the church were fading from public consciousness. The media attention at St. Edward's had dried up, and no reporters or camera crews had responded to her press release advising them of the demonstration at Kromer's office. The week before, Cheri had managed to attract two local TV crews to a protest stunt held first at City Hall and later at the offices of the archdiocese. At City Hall, the protesters made it all the way to the door of the mayor's office before the police cut them off. Cheri had everyone take off their shoes and leave them on the mayor's doorstep, along with leaflets inviting the mayor to *Walk in Our Shoes* by attending a special KWRU dinner at St. Edward's. The police ordered the shoes removed, but the protesters persuaded them to set aside one pair of sneakers and a leaflet for the mayor.

Later, at the archdiocese's office downtown, Cheri led the protesters into the ornate lobby, trailed by two local TV crews. But before they could reach the elevators to ride up to the main archdiocesan offices, they were cut off by security guards. Cheri demanded to see someone from the archdiocese, and within a few minutes a woman came down to the lobby. As the woman stepped off the elevator, several pairs of shoes were tossed at her feet. Recalling the scene later, Mariluz said, "That poor lady. She looked like she was gonna throw up, those shoes stunk so bad."

The woman refused to take the shoes. As the TV cameras focused in on her, Mariluz bent down and laid her shoes carefully on the floor. She was able to leave a *Walk in Our Shoes* leaflet and dinner invitation, too, before the city police arrived and threatened to arrest anyone who did not leave the building. Everybody, including Mariluz, put their shoes back on and walked outside to catch the bus back to St. Edward's. A few days later, when KWRU held its first Walk in Our Shoes dinner, a number of people from local community groups and public service agencies attended. No one from the archdiocese or the mayor's office showed up.

Following the dinner, Cheri decided to take a dozen people from the church to join with other community groups protesting impending welfare cuts at the state Capitol in Harrisburg. Cheri was leery of entering the city limits of the state capital; a bench warrant had been issued for her in Harrisburg for failing to appear in court on criminal trespass charges. A year earlier, she had been evicted bodily from the balcony of the state House of Representatives and arrested after she had led a protest against proposed welfare cuts. The cuts passed, dropping from the state welfare rolls an estimated fourteen thousand people forty-five and over who could not document physical or medical reasons for being unable to work. Now Cheri, considered a fugitive by the authorities in Harrisburg, was going back to the scene of her arrest.

As soon as Cheri and her group walked inside the Capitol, she was approached by a Capitol policeman. The officer uttered a single word: "Cheri?" Cheri looked at him and answered, "Yeah." The officer said, "Come with me." Two other officers appeared, and the three of them led Cheri down a hallway to the Capitol police booking unit. There, one of the officers told her, "You're under arrest." A moment later, he added: "We *told* you never to come back." While the Capitol police argued with the city police over who should have the privilege of arresting Cheri, she asked and received permission to make a phone call. She called the office of state senator Roxanne Jones. An aide to Jones answered, and Cheri told him she was about to be locked up.

Meanwhile, the city police apparently had won claim to Cheri. They told her she would be taken to the city jail, where she would have to post bail in order to be released. That meant she would be spending the night, for she had spent almost all of her pocket money on the $22 round-trip bus ticket from Philadelphia. Two city officers escorted Cheri outside to a waiting police car. As she was getting into the car, she saw Roxanne Jones running down the Capitol steps, shouting, "Stop! Stop!" Jones huddled with the officers and worked out a deal. She would pay Cheri's $100 bail—and guarantee that Cheri showed up for her court hearing on the year-old criminal trespass charges. Jones pulled out her checkbook and wrote the check on the spot. Cheri caught the next bus out of town.

After Cheri returned from her arrest in Harrisburg, she organized yet another protest. Welfare recipients at the church had been complaining to her that they were required to wait hours in the welfare office to have their photos taken for new welfare ID cards. Cheri decided she would lead a few members of the war council to the Public Assistance office on Lehigh Avenue, just down from the old Tent City site, and straighten out the situation.

On the morning of the planned protest, Cheri gathered everyone on the front steps of the church. She wanted to instruct them carefully on what to tell welfare recipients at the welfare office. She gave them a brief summary of the latest attempts in Washington and Harrisburg to cut welfare benefits. She mentioned that state legislators had just voted themselves an 18 percent salary increase and implied that welfare cuts would pay for it. She also mentioned Republican proposals to lump welfare programs into block grants for the states to administer.

"You know what block grants mean, right?" Cheri said. "They mean they've picked their target and it's us—single women with children on welfare, the most hated people in America. This means the state's gonna be able to cut you off, and you won't have that federal entitlement anymore."

Katie, listening on the steps, cut in and said, "Yeah, it means all the poverty pimps will have a much smaller pile of goodies on the table and you're gonna have to jump in there and fight for your little share of it."

Cheri laughed and said, "Katie doesn't mince words, does she?"

Then Cheri turned to specifics, telling her followers to instruct welfare recipients that they were entitled to help in locating Social Security cards, birth certificates, and other documents constantly demanded of them by caseworkers. "They can't deny you benefits if you can show you made a good-faith effort to obtain the documents," Cheri said.

Welfare recipients were also entitled to subway tokens to travel back and forth to appointments at the welfare office, she said. "They have subway tokens," Cheri said. "But whether they give you one depends on how they're feeling, whether it's time for their lunch break, or whether they like your looks."

Katie interrupted again to say, "Everybody should know they're trying to put a five-year lifetime cap on welfare." She had been reading welfare reform updates in copies of the *Inquirer* Cheri had given her. "So if any of youse have been on for more than five years, like me, you're gonna be out of luck. Sorry, no check. And they'll decide who's gonna get welfare among everybody who's left. If they decide only people with green teeth will get welfare, you better have green teeth, by God."

Some of the mothers sitting on the steps seemed stunned. It was the first they had heard of a five-year cap. They were new to St. Edward's and KWRU. They did not watch TV or read the newspapers. They regarded welfare as an institution, as solid and enduring as Independence Hall. One of them raised her hand and asked Cheri, "What if you was on welfare, then got off, then got back on—and it adds up to five years?"

Cheri waved a hand at the woman and said, "Hey, let's not sweat the details till it actually happens. If we get off our butts and yell loud enough, maybe we can keep it from happening." She ordered everyone to make their way to the welfare office for the protest.

The Lehigh Avenue welfare office was a depressing place, a gray, squat building set behind a chain-link fence. It had tiny slits for windows, which gave the building the appearance of a bunker. Inside, black and Hispanic women—and a handful of pale, stringy-haired white women—sat dejectedly in plastic chairs, waiting for their cases to be called. The workers inside had attempted to create a festive look by festooning the drab surroundings with orange cardboard pumpkins and *Happy Halloween* banners decorated with cats and ghosts. The decorations only made the dirty linoleum floor and drab beige walls seem more dismal than ever. Nor did the Halloween trimmings alter the mocking effect of the limp American flag that stood before a color photograph of a smiling Gov. Tom Ridge, the most prominent promoter of the latest plan in Harrisburg to cut welfare payments and medical coverage to the state's poor.

Cheri brushed past a set of cardboard pumpkins and began questioning people waiting for their cases to be called. She explained to each one what

KWRU was trying to achieve, and she asked each recipient what had prompted her visit to the welfare office. Two women mentioned that they had been waiting for hours for ID photos. Several others responded, in staggering detail, with wretched accounts of being somehow mistreated by the welfare system. To each tale, Cheri responded, "That's bullshit. They can't do that." But she also told the women, "You have rights, but they don't do you any good unless you demand them." The women nodded listlessly and leaned forward in their chairs, straining for the sound of their names being called by the reception clerk.

While Cheri interviewed welfare recipients, Mariluz and Katie worked the room. They handed out leaflets promoting KWRU and announcing an upcoming demonstration at the local HUD office. Most of the recipients glanced at the leaflets and then stuffed them into their pockets. But one man sitting with five young children read the leaflet and called Mariluz over. He told her he was homeless but had been denied public assistance for his five children because he was unable to provide a fixed address. He showed her the landlord verification form he had been asked to fill out— the same form Mariluz had been required to provide months earlier. Mariluz called out to Cheri, who snatched the form from the man and signed her own name under *Landlord*. She wrote that she rented a residence on North Fifth Street to the man for $75 a month, and she filled in the address of the KWRU office. Then Cheri gave the man the address of St. Edward's and told him he and his children could live there as long as he wanted.

Then Cheri walked briskly to the reception counter, cutting in front of two dozen people waiting in line to check in. She told the intake receptionist that people were complaining of waiting hours for their ID photos. "This is ridiculous," Cheri said. "Let me see a supervisor—now." The receptionist blinked in surprise. Cheri stared at her. The woman picked up a phone and said, "I'll let the supervisor know you're here."

Cheri whirled around, her hands on her hips, and looked at the people in line. They shifted and stared at the worn floor. "Anybody here need to see the supervisor?" Cheri asked them. "If you do, don't just stand there. Demand to see the supervisor."

Two women slowly raised their hands. A man looked at Cheri and said, "Hey, I seen you on TV."

Others in the line began to mutter and crane their necks to look at Cheri. Suddenly Cheri seemed transformed. She paced up and down the line, her eyes flashing, her hair flying across her back. Her face was contorted and she shouted out: "What do we want?"

Katie and Mariluz, standing at the rear of the line, answered, "We want the supervisor!"

A security guard, slouched in a chair beneath a sign that read, *Don't Stand Here*, looked up from his newspaper, startled. The receptionist stood on her chair and stretched to reach a microphone attached to the public address system.

"What do we want?" Cheri shouted again.

Several people in line shouted back: "We want the supervisor!" Within seconds, everyone in line was clapping and stomping and chanting, "We want the supervisor!" The chant spread to the people sitting behind them, who slammed their plastic chairs against the floor as they screamed for the supervisor. The receptionist finally reached the microphone and her high-pitched voice carried across the room: "We need a supervisor out here *now!*"

Cheri and Mariluz and Katie were clapping and chanting and stomping their feet. The security guard scrambled to his feet and stood, his arms crossed, staring at the sudden eruption. He seemed agitated, but also fascinated by the swift release of energy from such a normally placid group. Cheri raised her arms, and in unison people in the chairs stood up and chanted for the supervisor. Cheri screamed at them: "Let's go, people! Let's all stand together—all of us who are being messed over by the system! We're gonna march back there and find that supervisor!"

As Cheri turned to lead the chanting crowd beyond the partition to the rear offices, a balding man in gray slacks and a green tie emerged. This, apparently, was the supervisor. The crowd stopped short at the sight of him, and everyone broke into applause and cheers. "It's the supervisor!" someone at the front of the throng shouted to those in the back. The man looked surprised, like someone shaken awake from a nap. Cheri grabbed his hand and told him, "People are waiting all day just to get a photo taken. That's ridiculous. You gotta do something." The man scratched his head and said quietly, "I'll try to get somebody out here to deal with it."

He retreated to the rear offices. Cheri stood directly beneath the *Don't Stand Here* sign and watched him go. The security guard started to say something to her, but he drew back when Cheri turned to face him, arching her eyebrows. He sat back down and looked at his newspaper.

A minute later the phone rang at the front desk. The receptionist answered it and then stood on her chair and reached for the microphone. "Listen up," she said. "Anybody waiting for photo IDs line up over here." Several people burst from the crowd and began forming a line. The guard walked over to the gathering group and spoke for the first time. "Form a *neat* line," he ordered.

With the photo problem solved, Cheri turned to Paula, a thin, haggard woman with dirty blond hair who was one of the women Cheri had approached in the waiting room; she had told Cheri that her benefits had been cut off after a caseworker claimed she'd said her sister was giving her money to live on. She said her $230 welfare check every two weeks had been her only source of income since her separation from her abusive husband.

When Paula was called to see her caseworker, Cheri accompanied her to the tiny cubicle in a rear office. The caseworker explained that Paula had been denied benefits for missing an earlier appointment and because she had reported receiving cash support from her sister. Cheri demanded an appeal. The caseworker said he had to interview Paula first.

He began by asking for information about her husband. Cheri cut in and said, "She's concerned about physical threats from her husband, who she has left. So in that case, she does not have to provide any information about him."

"I disagree," the caseworker said.

"No, I know the rules—probably better than you," Cheri said.

The caseworker smiled pleasantly. He was a small Asian-American man with a crisp, reserved manner. "I don't think so," he said. But he moved on to a question about Paula's seventeen-year-old son. He wanted to know if the boy was working or otherwise providing his mother with money. Paula looked confused.

Cheri touched Paula on her arm. "You have to report his income, even if he only made fifty cents all year," she told her. "Even though it's really none of their business to go poking into your son's life."

"That's right," the caseworker said. "You have to report his income."

"He doesn't work," Paula said. "Didn't work all year."

"No one in the family has income?" the caseworker asked.

"Nope," Paula said.

The caseworker punched several keys on his computer keyboard and squinted at the screen. "You reported before that your sister was giving you income," he said.

Paula looked over at Cheri, who leaned forward to read the information on the computer screen. "It doesn't matter what you say now," Cheri told her. "It's what's written down here that counts. I know it sucks, but that's the system."

Paula thought for a moment, then said her sister had been unemployed for the past year. The caseworker sat silently, staring at the computer screen. Paula looked at Cheri expectantly. Cheri sighed heavily, then leaned toward the caseworker and said in a low voice, "She's really in need of money. Her husband is threatening her. Can't you give her a standby appointment so she can appeal the cutoff?"

The caseworker drummed his fingers on the desk. He pursed his lips and said to Paula, "You'd have to come in early and wait. And you'll need documentation." He rattled off a list of required documents, from a birth certificate to a rental lease to a marriage license.

"You ever dream there were this many pieces of documentation in your life?" Cheri asked Paula.

"I don't have half that stuff," she said.

"Don't worry," Cheri said. "We'll get it."

The caseworker told Paula to come in first thing the next morning and be prepared to wait several hours for an appointment. Cheri thanked him and asked for two bus tokens for Paula to get to the welfare office and back home the next day.

The caseworker looked as if no one had ever made such a request of him. "You know you have to supply tokens if they're requested," Cheri said.

"You'll have to ask the manager about that," the man said.

Cheri gave him a skeptical look, then smiled sweetly. "You can take care of that for her, can't you?" she said.

The caseworker smiled back. "Yeah, okay," he said.

"Thank you so much," Cheri said, and patted his arm.

Cheri stood up abruptly and walked deeper into the maze of rear offices. Having worked her way past the security guard into the inner workings of the welfare office, she wanted to take advantage of the opportunity to find Arthur Sokolove, the director of the Lehigh Avenue office. She had built a tense but reasonably cordial relationship with Sokolove, who did not appreciate Cheri's confrontational tactics but nonetheless had allowed the KWRU table in the waiting room.

Cheri wandered the back hallways until someone alerted Sokolove, who bounded out of an office and greeted Cheri with a handshake. He was a short, bearded man who spoke quickly and pointedly.

"So, Cheri, other than upsetting my staff, what are you up to?" he asked.

Cheri laughed and mentioned the problem with long waits for new photo IDs. She also chided Sokolove about bus tokens. Sokolove, speaking rapidly as he gently escorted Cheri back toward the front waiting room, assured her that he would make sure tokens were available. And he told her that he had already taken steps to make sure that people did not have to wait inordinately for new ID photos, even though he was now processing forty-five a day with no increase in staff or resources.

Sokolove continued talking until he had escorted Cheri all the way back to the front room. When people waiting in line saw Cheri with Sokolove, they raised their fists in triumph and muttered, "All right," and "Go, Cheri."

Sokolove ignored them and said to Cheri, "So, why did you *really* come in today. What's your *real* agenda?"

Cheri turned to leave and said over her shoulder, "To make your life miserable."

Sokolove stood next to the line of welfare recipients and watched her go. "I thought so," he said.

Mariluz was determined to make sleeping on top of pews in a drafty church seem normal to her children. If her family were living in an actual home, she thought, they would do all the ordinary things that families with small children do. For one thing, they would decorate their house for all holidays. Halloween was upon them now, so Mariluz set about finding decorations that would please the children. She wanted them to forget, at least for the moment, about the hurried meals they ate from plastic milk crates, about the hand-me-down clothes they wore, about brushing their teeth from a bottle of water, about going to the bathroom in a filthy toilet that reeked so badly that Destiny held her breath every time she entered the sacristy. She wanted them to stop feeling the damp cold that penetrated their little bodies and left them curled up tightly at night, sleeping in their overcoats beneath layer after layer of donated blankets. If Halloween decorations could divert the children's attention from living in this haphazard way, then they would have the best decorations Mariluz's welfare check could buy.

After check day, Mariluz went to the dollar store and loaded two shopping bags with orange streamers and flags that said, *Happy Halloween*, and also with silky spider's webs and plastic jack-o'-lanterns. By the time she included household items such as paper towels, cleaning supplies, and Pampers, she had spent $48. But she considered the money well spent; it went to improve her living conditions, and by extension the well-being of her three children. Mariluz draped the spider's webs across the front of her enclosure, where she had created walls out of donated sheets. She taped the streamers and flags to the sheets so that they framed the doorway, and anyone entering would have to duck to avoid the leering plastic jack-o'-lanterns and the wispy spider's webs. Mariluz pawed through the donation pile and found more cardboard decorations of black cats and owls, and she set them up along the stone floor at the border of her enclosure.

On Halloween night, Destiny emerged from her mother's enclosure wearing a red fright wig, an oversized woman's skirt, and red, knee-high, plastic boots. "I'm a princess!" she announced. All the homeless people huddled around the communal kerosene heater clapped and whistled as Destiny paraded in front of them. One of the homeless women asked where she had found the outfit. Destiny stopped, put her hands on her hips, and looked at the woman in mock surprise. "Where did I get it?" she said. "From donation, of course!" Everyone around the heater chimed in and said, in unison, "Donation! Of course!"

The adults were dressing in costume, too. The war council had organized a Halloween party, which was to take place after adult volunteers had escorted the children on a trick-or-treat excursion through the neighborhood. The trick-or-treating went off without incident, for the drug dealers and pipers and drunks seemed to honor the presence of children in costume. On each block, they shrank into the shadows as the children knocked on doors and people's arms reached out to fill bags with candy. There was an unspoken code for holidays in North Philadelphia; it was understood that on Halloween and Easter and Christmas, children on the street had the right-of-way, and the denizens of the rowdy corners where drugs were sold and ingested and alcohol was swilled moved out of sight until each child had safely passed.

When the Tent City children returned to St. Edward's, their plastic shopping bags stretched taut with candy, they were permitted to gorge themselves and watch the adults carry on. It had been decided that the war council members would dress in costumes that offered a commentary on their circumstances as poor people at war with the system. The Empty the Shelters college students showed up, providing an eager audience and passing out white bags of candy marked *Boo!* Everyone bobbed for donated apples in a donated plastic tub—eating every last apple, a pointed reference to scavenging for food. Mariluz dressed as a baby, symbolizing the innocence of those in need. Chicago dressed as a clown, apparently to underscore the absurdity of living in abject poverty in the world's richest nation. Tara dressed as Mayor Ed Rendell; she greased back her hair with mousse, put on a donated white dinner jacket, applied a mascara mustache, and stuffed donated clothes beneath the jacket to approximate the mayor's substantial midsection. To hoots and boos, Tara ordered one of the Empty the Shelters students—he wore a security guard's uniform—to arrest everyone in sight for committing the crime of being poor.

Cheri dressed as a bag of donations. She tied a donated bagel to her ankle, a donated shoe to her knee, and wore a black plastic garbage bag as a cloak. In one hand she carried an empty ice tray—an inside joke that referred to the mayor's comment the previous summer that the city had done its part to help Tent City at the Quaker Lace lot by providing shipments of ice. The ice tray got the biggest laugh of the evening. Then the parody ended and J.R. cranked up his portable cassette player, and everyone sang and danced as hard as they could through the night, trying to forget where they were.

On the drive down to the courthouse the next morning for their 8 A.M. hearing, Cheri stressed to Tara and Mariluz the importance of showing up in court on time. She had spoken to a public defender, who had told her that the bench warrants issued for them would almost certainly be withdrawn if the three of them merely appeared in court. The case was almost certain to be postponed to a later date, which meant that a few hours spent in court would be sufficient to put off their legal problems for several more weeks. Tara and Mariluz listened intently, chewing on candy from the students' Halloween *Boo!* bags. They were anxious to end their status as fugitives from justice.

At the courthouse, the three women were met by Chicago and Katie, who wanted to provide moral support. Chicago was holding a Halloween fright mask from the night before. Katie was eating candy from her own white *Boo!* bag. When Katie passed through the courthouse metal detector, the alarm sounded. A guard asked her to empty her pockets. Katie reached into her jeans and produced a spoon. "What's that for?" the guard asked. Katie blushed and said, "It's my spoon. I always carry my spoon."

Outside the courtroom, an impromptu war council meeting evolved as everyone sat on a bench, waiting for court to be called. Cheri brought up the rent for the KWRU offices, and the rent and utility bills at her row house. It was all coming due.

"Any ideas on how to pay for all this?" she asked.

Chicago raised his hand. "Yeah, we could rob a 7-Eleven. We got the masks," he said.

"Right," Cheri said. "I think I'd rather find a loan shark."

"Loan shark?" Tara said. "J.R. knows a good loan shark."

"No, I don't think so," Cheri said. "The last thing I need is some North Philly loan shark hunting me down for repayment."

Cheri was desperate. She had had to borrow $10 from her ex-husband for gas money and cigarettes. She didn't even have enough cash to retrieve the gold-and-onyx ring she had pawned for her son's date. She was running out of options.

Tara reached out and hugged Cheri. "I wish I could just dig in my pocket and hand you a thousand dollars," she said.

"I know, Tara, thanks," Cheri said. "I'm not telling you all this to beg for money. I'm just fishing for some creative ways to raise cash."

"I have a color TV I found at the church," Tara said.

"That's maybe thirty-five dollars," Cheri said.

Mariluz thought for a moment and said, "I keep a toaster in the church basement I found trash picking."

"Five bucks, tops," Cheri said, staring at the floor.

Tara said, "I've got jewelry back at the church that might be worth something."

Inside the courtroom, Cheri, Tara, and Mariluz took a seat on a bench that reminded Mariluz of the polished wooden pews back at the church. The three of them looked around at the scruffy collection of petty drug dealers, prostitutes, and subway fare beaters and decided that they did not look so bad by comparison, despite their post-Halloween outfits. They felt vaguely superior, having committed their crimes for what they regarded as a higher purpose—that is, civil disobedience in the service of public protest. At least, they thought, they weren't in court for something as common and utterly mundane as drug dealing or streetwalking.

After a long wait, the bail commissioner emerged through a door in the rear and took his seat. He was an overweight, balding man in a suit and tie. Cheri looked up at him and whispered to Mariluz, "Dammit, they tell us to be here on time, like we got nothing else to do but sit around and wait all day. Then this fat bastard waddles in an hour late, like some kind of fucking royalty."

The commissioner worked his way through several cases before reaching Cheri's. He called out her name, then Mariluz's and Tara's, mispronouncing all three. He rattled off a long string of FTAs—failures to appear—for each woman. He noted that all three had been approved for ARD, or Accelerated Rehabilitative Disposition, a routine bit of paperwork designed to clear the docket of petty cases. But Cheri told the public defender that they did not want ARD, even though it would clear their cases, because ARD implied a guilty plea.

The public defender spoke up: "They don't want ARD. They want to go to trial on this." The commissioner looked puzzled. It was not often that somebody demanded a jury trial on a failure-to-disperse charge. Then he shrugged. "Okay," he said, "bench warrants withdrawn." There would be no cash bail; the three defendants could sign their own bail, he said. He set a new court date and sent Cheri, Mariluz, and Tara on their way. Cheri stood up and shouted up at the commissioner: "Thank you, Commissioner!" The commissioner peered down at Cheri, who was dressed in tight jeans and a baggy white sweater, which gave her a haphazardly stylish look. He seemed perplexed. Not many defendants thanked him so effusively. "Well," he said finally, "you're welcome."

Outside the courtroom, Cheri slapped palms with Tara and Mariluz. She loved working the system. By demanding a trial, she could play the game forever. She knew the courts would continue the three cases in perpetuity in order to avoid the costs of a trial. She knew nobody went to trial these days. Everything was plea-bargained. But if you refused to bargain, Cheri thought, you could paralyze the system. There were no bail costs and no legal fees. All it cost her was time, and time was just about the only thing she had not run out of.

When Cheri walked through the rear door of the majestic, wood-paneled courtroom inside the federal building nine days later, she was dressed in a way that no one from Tent City had ever seen. She wore a cream-colored blouse, crisply pressed black wool slacks, black pumps with tiny, under-stated bows, and an elegant black wool topcoat. Her long hair was clean and shiny and neatly brushed in place. She wore lipstick and rouge, and her dark brown eyes were clear and luminous.

Several members of the war council were in federal court that day to watch Cheri's hearing on the charges from the Independence Mall rally. Odessa was there, too, for she wanted to show her support. She sat in her Snoopy jacket and sweatpants next to Cheri and Mariluz on a hard oak bench, one row behind Jeff Lindy, the same lawyer who had represented Cheri the day of the Liberty Bell confrontation. Lindy sat facing the judge's raised bench, set above a deep blue carpet and beneath a gold Seal of the United States mounted on dark paneling. To his right, in the jury box, sat several Park Service police, dressed in green-and-gray uniforms, their gold badges pinned to their chests and their broad-brimmed hats in their laps.

Lindy showed Cheri the evidence the park police had assembled against her to prove their charge, which court documents listed as "Residing in a park area—Independence National Park." He handed her several Polaroids showing Cheri, Katie, and others, framed by KWRU banners, helping to raise the tent on the mall. Written below the Polaroid of Cheri in her brown T-shirt were the words *Organizer in T-shirt*. Lindy explained that the maximum fine under the residing-in-a-park charge was $500 and/or six months in jail. He said a $100 fine was more likely, with the opportunity to pay in installments, "given your current, uh, status as unemployed."

Cheri smiled at Lindy and held out her wrists. "Or they can take it out in blood," she said.

"It's not quite *that* serious yet," Lindy said. Lindy warned her that the court would not permit any political demonstrations by her followers, or any political oration by Cheri herself. Cheri nodded and wrote something down in a notebook she had brought with her. She passed it to Mariluz and told her to make sure everyone from St. Edward's sitting in the gallery read it. The note said: "The judge is warning us that there will be no political statements made in the courtroom of any kind. They pleaded with me to plead no contest. I said NO."

On another sheet of paper, Cheri wrote:

The "law" has nothing to do with justice—or what's "right." This is a room of politics, opinions and cattle—people with no money, therefore no power. I didn't do anything wrong but stay in a federal park asking for housing for homeless people. Pleading no contest means that I'm not arguing what the government is saying.

She handed the note to Mariluz for distribution to her supporters seated behind her.

The courtroom was nearly filled now with defendants and lawyers and investigators. They were not the sort of people seen in most federal courtrooms, where major narcotics and racketeering and fraud cases were heard. This was the federal courtroom set aside for petty offenders. It was called the Central Violations Bureau, and it provided swift adjudication before a federal magistrate judge of cases considered too minor for U.S. District Court.

A half hour later, Magistrate Arnold C. Rappoport appeared in court, pulling his robe over his shirt and tie. He quickly worked his way through a case involving a young man charged with shooting up heroin in Independence Park while on his way to a drug therapy session. Then he called Cheri's case and read the charge. "Residing in a park area?" he said. "What do we have here—a homesteader?" He looked down at Cheri. "You want a trial?"

"Yes, Your Honor," Cheri said firmly. She sat down and squeezed Odessa's hand for good luck.

The first witness was Maj. Calvin Farmer, the National Park Service officer who had been assigned to monitor the protesters' every move. Farmer was a short, compact man with curly black hair, a trim mustache, and spectacles. In a clipped monotone, he described how the Tent City people put stakes in the ground, raised a makeshift tent, and hauled in ice chests, sleeping bags, and "lots of children."

Then Senior Investigator Levi Rivers took the stand. It was Rivers who had taken charge of the investigation, ordering photographic and video surveillance. Now, in a smooth, unhurried tone, he recited crucial events from the videotape taken at the crime scene.

"One-twenty-eight P.M.," he testified. "Shows Miss Honkala putting a metal pole in the ground and carrying a bed onto the grass . . . One-thirty P.M.—a tent went up without a permit . . . One-thirty-two P.M.—a stove and grill . . . One-thirty-nine P.M.—wooden poles hammered into the ground . . . One-forty-seven P.M.—Miss Honkala directing the group. . . ."

Rivers described how rangers had given Cheri a list of park regulations she was violating and had told her that she would be able to get a permit to demonstrate on the Judge Lewis Quadrangle. He mentioned the Park Service's concern about having to arrest mothers of small children.

After Lindy had cross-examined Rivers on the matter of the Park Service's explanation to Cheri of the Judge Lewis Quadrangle option, Lindy asked the magistrate to dismiss the case.

The prosecutor, Asst. U.S. Atty. Kristen Hayes, a slender, light-haired, unsmiling woman, argued that the government had chosen to negotiate in order to "resolve a difficult situation . . . a peaceful group protesting in favor of a legitimate cause." But, she added, "the fact that we didn't cite them at ground zero does not constitute a waiver."

The magistrate denied Lindy's motion, and Lindy called Cheri to testify.

Cheri spoke in a clear voice, but with a tinge of nervousness that gave her comments a strained, nasal pitch. She told the magistrate that she was unemployed, but that she worked every day of the week to assist the poor, the homeless, and people on welfare. She described the distribution of donated food to the neighborhood twice a week, the help KWRU provided to families seeking afforable housing, the intervention by the union in disputes with the authorities over welfare, food stamps, utilities, and health care.

The magistrate cut her off. "The issue here is residing at Independence Park," he said.

Quickly, Lindy asked Cheri about her living expenses. She said they amounted to more than $1,000 a month. "I'm greatly in debt," she said. She said she had been cut off from welfare. She described living conditions at Tent City on the Quaker Lace lot, including a heat-and-humidity factor she put at 129 degrees, and the forty-seven people in the city who had collapsed and died during the summer heat wave.

"Why did you move to Independence Park?" Lindy asked.

"Desperation," Cheri said. "We found out the city was going to demolish our tents . . ."

"But why Independence Park?" Lindy asked again.

"All the city shelters were full," Cheri said. "There was no place for homeless children. We decided to seek refuge on federal land because we weren't betting on help on the city level."

"Were you aware that other homeless people were sleeping in Independence Park?"

"Yes," Cheri said. "And there were several families sleeping on benches in the park the night we were there."

Lindy paused and asked the magistrate to dismiss the case because of selective prosecution. He quickly denied the motion.

Prosecutor Hayes rose to cross-examine Cheri. She asked curtly whether she had sought a job.

"I'm always seeking employment," Cheri told her.

"Anything now?"

"Not at this moment," Cheri said.

"How do you support yourself?"

"I've been borrowing money from friends."

"How often do you go out on job interviews?"

"Résumés are sent out every month," Cheri said. "Most recently, I've applied as a field organizer for NOW."

Hayes asked why Cheri's welfare payments had been cut off.

"Failure to provide information they needed from my child's birth certificate," Cheri said.

The cross-examination ended without any specific questions that might have forced Cheri to testify about her part-time, late-night jobs.

Hayes ended by saying that "notwithstanding the undisputed righteousness of the Kensington Welfare Rights Union and the terrible problems of the homeless," the Park Service had no choice except to issue the citation against Cheri. Hayes told the magistrate that the government did not seek to incarcerate Cheri, but she did recommend the maximum, $500 fine. She said the fine was justified because Cheri had created "a huge problem for the Park Service."

The magistrate listened, then asked Cheri, "Why did you leave your last job?"

"It's a long story," Cheri said wearily.

"I don't want to hear a long story," the magistrate said.

He asked a few more questions, then told Cheri, "You're involved in a public war versus homelessness and it's catching up to you in your personal life." He offered to delay judgment to give Cheri time to find a full-time job. Cheri and Lindy huddled for a moment. Then Lindy said, "She'll accept a four-month suspension of sentence and get a job."

Hayes cut in to say that she wanted probation, contingent on Cheri's getting a job. She said it had cost the federal government "tens of thousands of dollars in law enforcement costs" for the investigation, negotiation, and prosecution of Cheri Honkala.

Cheri stood up and looked at the magistrate. "For what it's worth," she said, "I was just trying to help some families and children get a house to live in."

"I understand," the magistrate said. "But a more immediate concern is to get yourself a job. You can't take on the problems of the world without taking care of yourself first."

As Cheri stood staring at the magistrate, he suddenly looked down at some paperwork on the bench and said: "Guilty." He gave her six months' probation and said he would ask the U.S. Probation Service to help her "find a job she's comfortable with." He set Cheri's fine at $250—payable in installments if the Probation Service agreed.

Cheri was stunned. She had hoped the magistrate would be moved by her commitment and dismiss the charges. Now she had to pay money she didn't have and report to authorities she despised. Rappoport saw her dejected look and told her, "Miss Honkala, they will lend their assistance. It's not their job to hassle you—and they won't." As the judge spoke, Mariluz and Odessa walked up to Cheri and threw their arms around her.

Cheri had no intention of getting a job, or at least not the kind of job the U.S. Probation Service seemed to envision. Her job was leading the Kensington Welfare Rights Union. If the federal government, in all its wisdom, did not consider that a certifiable job, then she would find a way to string them along for six months. She had managed to outwit the city of Philadelphia's justice system so far. Slipping through the nets of the federal system should not be too taxing, Cheri thought. If she couldn't outfox government bureaucrats, then perhaps she wasn't the right person to lead the city's dispossessed against the system.

The week before Thanksgiving, on the very day Cheri was scheduled to meet with her federal probation officer to begin her six months' probation, the federal government seemed to provide her with a stroke of good fortune. The government was shutting down. Because of an ongoing budget dispute between the White House and Congress, the federal bureaucracy had ground to a halt. Federal workers across the country were being sent home. Surely, Cheri thought, the federal building in downtown Philadelphia would be shut down tight, including the U.S. Probation Service offices. But when Cheri called to ask about rescheduling her appointment, she discovered that the office was open despite the general shutdown. The probation office, she was told, was considered "essential."

Cheri was in a foul mood as she made her way downtown in a cold, soaking autumn rain. She walked through the lobby, which was deserted except for the security people, who were as gruff and officious as they ordered her to empty her pockets and pass through a metal detector. Up on the second floor, most of the offices were dark. But the lights were on in the probation office. Inside sat a small, bearded man dressed in a blue shirt and tie. His spectacles dangled from an elastic string around his neck.

"Good morning," the man said, standing up to shake Cheri's hand. "My name is Ray Hall and I got a feeling this case is gonna be a pain in the ass."

Cheri sat down in a chair across from Hall's desk and said, "Well, I guess you're just in a bad mood because you got declared essential and had to come to work while everybody else got paid vacation."

She was in no mood to suffer any smart remarks from some federal bureaucrat. But then Hall laughed at her crack about being essential, which put her at ease. And as soon as Hall began telling her, in a casual and lighthearted way, about what she could expect while on probation, she began to think that the next six months might not be as onerous as she had anticipated.

For one thing, Hall told her that giving someone six months' probation was a waste of their time and his: "Give 'em a year or else put 'em out to pasture and don't bother me with this six months nonsense." For another, Hall seemed willing to accommodate Cheri when she told him that, despite limitations on her travel imposed by her probation, she intended to attend a welfare rights convention in California the first week of December and to fly to visit her mother in Minneapolis at Christmas. He advised her to write a letter to the judge explaining that both trips had been planned prior to her sentencing.

Then Hall told Cheri to prepare for a long interview. He was about to ask her an endless series of questions. He showed her a set of detailed forms he was required to fill out.

"Let's get started. What do you do for a living?" he asked.

"It's more than a living," Cheri said. "I'm a volunteer for poor people's issues—welfare, health care, housing, homelessness."

Hall put down his pen in a way that suggested mild annoyance. "That doesn't sound like a job to me," he said.

"Well, it's not exactly a job," Cheri said.

Hall muttered to himself, "I knew this case was gonna be a pain in the ass."

He told Cheri she could terminate her probation simply by finding a paying job. "If I were you, I'd run out today and find some kind of little 'ol job, I don't give a shit what, just something that pays. You could save you *and* me a whole lot of paperwork."

Hall looked down at some papers on his desk. "What did you get convicted of, anyway? It says here you were . . . what? Residing at Independence Park?" He stared at the paper, rubbing his eyes wearily. "What for?"

"I was taking part in a protest," Cheri said.

"Well, if this was the sixties, you wouldn't be sitting here with me today," Hall said. "But that kind of stuff doesn't go down in the nineties."

"Yeah," Cheri said, "my timing is awful."

Hall stroked his beard and thought for a moment. "I'm gonna tell you something I tell everybody who comes in here, so don't be offended," he said. "I just need to tell you that you are subject to being tested for drugs, and that includes marijuana."

Cheri shrugged and said, "Fine." She didn't use drugs—except for caffeine and nicotine.

Hall read from probation regulations that prohibited people on probation from associating with lawbreakers or felons.

"This means that for six months, your activist days are over," Hall said. "If you associate with people who protest and break the law, you violate the terms of your probation. So I'd advise you to stay away from any demonstration because if you get arrested, you got big problems with us. The best thing for you to do is get a j-o-b and lay low."

Cheri nodded, but she had no intention of changing her lifestyle. Just about everybody on the war council had a bench warrant outstanding or had recently been arrested for refusing to disperse or trespassing during a protest. She intended to "associate"—as Hall put it—with them every single day, just as she always did. Hall seemed to sense her defiance.

"I *told* you this case would be a pain in the ass," he said. "I gotta do all this paperwork for somebody sleeping in the park? Puleeze."

He told Cheri that a probation officer might show up at her home unannounced from time to time.

"Now *that* would piss me off, if he came without warning," Cheri said.

"Hey, that's what we do here," Hall said. "But let me be honest with you. I ain't coming by anybody's house at ten P.M. I've been here twenty-two years and I never heard of *anybody* going out at ten P.M. unless it's for some big-time coke dealer, which I don't think you are. So it's not likely somebody's gonna knock on your door for sleeping in the park. But the point is, we *can*. And you gotta let us in. If I knock and you're in there and don't answer, I'm gonna be pissed off. And you don't want that."

"What if I'm having a meeting?" Cheri asked. She envisioned everyone on the war council diving out her row house windows to escape a probation officer pounding on her door.

"Fine," Hall said. "The polite—and smart—thing to do is to say you're in a meeting, and we'll say this will only take a minute, and then you can go on with your little meeting."

There was also the small matter of Cheri's $250 fine, Hall said.

"You gotta pay that," he said. "If I was you, I'd beg, borrow or steal two hundred and fifty dollars and be paid up by Thanksgiving. If not, how much can you pay monthly?"

"A dollar," Cheri said.

Hall put down his pen again and rubbed his moist eyes. "Well," he said slowly, "you're gonna be on probation a long, long time."

"Okay, twenty-five dollars a month," Cheri said, "but that's stretching it."

Pulling out more forms from his desk, Hall began the arduous process of taking Cheri's personal history.

For the next thirty minutes, Hall elicited from Cheri the following information: She was five foot five and weighed 115 pounds. She had brown eyes, brown hair, and a light complexion. She was born on January 12, 1963. She had had fifty-four arrests, most of them for trespassing, but no convictions aside from residing in Independence Park. She was the oldest of four daughters and a son born to her mother, Geraldine Okkelberg. She had married the father of her only son, Mark, on Valentine's Day 1981 and divorced him in January 1990 in order to marry her second husband, Robert Brown, the following month. She was one credit shy of a bachelor's degree. She did not use alcohol or illegal drugs. She was not taking medication.

When Hall asked Cheri for her ethnic category, she asked him to read through all the choices. When he read out, "American Indian," Cheri told him she was half Indian, half white.

"There's no category for that," Hall said. "You gotta be American Indian or Other."

Cheri leaned over and read the form. "Hey," she said. "There's biracial!"

"Fine," Hall said, marking the category with his pen. "You're biracial. See how easy I am to get along with?"

Hall was equally accommodating when Cheri answered his question about income by saying, "I borrow money. And I get additional funds from my mother." He nodded and wrote something on the form.

Then he groaned and read from the form: "Mental problems? Oh, I know. You've probably got tons."

"Millions of them," Cheri said.

Hall frowned. "I'll put down 'none.' "

"Assets?" he asked.

"None," Cheri said.

"Liabilities?" Hall winced as he said the word.

"Oh, God," Cheri said. "I owe money to half the people in America. I owe JCPenney seven hundred dollars. I owe friends two thousand dollars . . ."

"I'll just put down that you're in debt," Hall said.

Then he asked for Cheri's version of the events that had led to her arrest, careful to add that he would appreciate "the condensed version."

"Well," Cheri said, "to put it simply, I was demonstrating for affordable housing for homeless families and their children."

Hall wrote something down. "And I just filled out my United Way donor card for the homeless," he said.

Then it was over. Hall stacked the forms neatly on his desk and thanked

Cheri for her time. He reminded her again that finding a paying job and coming up with the $250 fine would end her probation.

Hall gave her his business card, which was embossed with the gold-colored seal of the U.S. Probation Service. "Don't try selling it," he said. "One of my clients grabbed a bunch of them off my desk and was selling 'em on the street, telling people they could melt them down for the gold."

Cheri laughed and took the card. She shook Hall's hand and left his office. At the end of the hallway, as she was reaching to open the security door while the receptionist buzzed her through, Cheri felt a light tap on her shoulder. She turned and saw that it was Hall. He leaned forward and whispered, "Good luck—and, privately, keep up your good work."

At the church the next day, Cheri was confronted with the customary set of emergencies that had been swelling and festering in her absence. Casanova, the leader of the homeless rights group, lay on a mattress spread across two pews, his clothes soaked through with sweat despite the frigid autumn winds that whistled through the church. Cass had AIDS, and now his fevers had overwhelmed him. He looked shrunken and drawn. He could barely raise himself up on his elbow to talk to Cheri. Cheri pleaded with him to go to a hospital, but Cass refused. Finally, Cheri found one of the college students, who persuaded Cass to let himself be driven to a hospital for treatment. He spent the next week there, regaining his strength.

After Cass had been evacuated, J.R. told Cheri that Savoy, the young man who had been evicted by the war council, had been seen in the neighborhood, threatening to get revenge for being thrown out. Mariluz told her that Savoy had tried to get into the church, demanding to see Cheri, before Mariluz told him, "Fuck off," and the security team had chased him away. Cheri felt cold inside. Several times in recent weeks, someone had left threatening messages on her answering machine. One said, "Don't go to that march on City Hall." Another said, "You're gonna get shot and killed someday." She was certain it was Savoy. Even before Savoy was kicked out of the church, he had been acting irrationally. One night, as Cheri was driving Savoy to buy kerosene, he had suddenly grabbed her keys and turned off the ignition. He demanded that Cheri drive him to the Ben Franklin Bridge so that he could commit suicide by jumping off. Cheri bolted from the car and left Savoy sitting there. Later, when she and Willie Baptist retrieved the car, Savoy was gone. Since then, one of her tires had been slashed while the car was parked outside her row house. Now Cheri had to park several blocks away from home to hide the car from Savoy. She feared he would try to hurt Mark, so she asked some of the men from the neighborhood who had befriended the war council to send a message to

Savoy's mother on Sixth Street: if he bothered Cheri again, they would hunt him down and punish him. Cheri did not hear from Savoy again.

As Cheri walked through St. Edward's, she noticed that Luis and Beatrice, the AIDS-infected couple, had moved back in. Cheri was not entirely comfortable having Luis and Beatrice living in the church again. They had left twice and had twice been allowed back in. First they had accepted the overtures of John Wagner, the archdiocese's man, and went to live in two church hospices. But Luis soon complained that the curfew at the men's hospice prevented him from spending any significant time with his wife and children at their hospice. "I had to play by their silly hospice rules, so I told John Wagner he was okay and all, but we had to get out of the hospice system," Luis told me one day. The war council voted to let the family return, despite what many regarded as Luis's treachery in the face of the archdiocese's blandishments.

Luis and Beatrice had left the church a second time after they were accused of robbery. A homeless woman known as Crippled Cheryl, who shuffled around the church with the aid of an aluminum walker, told the war council that she had been robbed by the couple. Luis had held her by her hair, she said, while Beatrice ripped from her hand a tiny leather purse that contained $200 from Cheryl's SSI check. The war council held an emergency meeting in the church and decided to expel the couple for a final time. When Luis and Beatrice cleaned out their tent, Mariluz found empty beer bottles there.

But shortly after being evicted, Luis and Beatrice had returned and pleaded with the war council for a reprieve. Beatrice confessed to the theft, apologized, and offered to pay the money back out of her next welfare check. Luis still denied any role in the robbery, saying, "That's all between the crippled lady and my wife." Over Mariluz's protests, the war council voted to once again let the couple return to live at St. Edward's. Later, Mariluz complained to Cheri, "I can't believe we'd let back anybody who would jump a poor crippled lady."

Mariluz was beginning to wonder how long she could survive at the church. The dampness and the cold and the steady flow of disturbed and irrational people in and out of St. Edward's were wearing her down. There seemed to be so many strange new people—many of them grasping, vindictive types who sought only to feed off KWRU's hard work. The sense of sharing and conviction she had felt at Tent City and in the early days at St. Edward's was eroding. Almost every night, there were squabbles over donated food—who was supposed to bring in the donations, who was supposed to prepare and cook, who was supposed to clean up. Nobody washed out the toilet anymore, and the whole rear of the church reeked of sewage.

For the past week, Elba had been breaking down in tears almost every night. She was desperate for what she called "a real home." She was threatening to take her kids and leave, even though she had no place to go.

Sometimes Mariluz felt like leaving, too. But she believed Cheri's strategy to pressure and shame city agencies into providing houses or vouchers would produce results before the year was out. In her diary, she wrote, "My plan is to stay here til I get a house, though I hear the archdiocese is planning to throw us out by Thanksgiving."

Mariluz had by now trash-picked a TV set, which allowed her to keep abreast of news reports on welfare reform. Based on what she had heard, she was concerned that President Clinton might sign a welfare bill that would allow the states to cut benefits and impose time limits. If that happened, Mariluz told me one evening, "I'd try to get a job somehow, rather than starve my kids. I'd try waitressing, baby-sitting, and try to get someone from Tent City to watch the kids while I work. Or maybe I'd work out something with Elba. That would mean I wouldn't be able to go to school and learn to be a pediatric nurse, but you do what you gotta do. But if they took away my medical coverage, I don't know what I'd do. Something desperate, probably."

For now, she thought, the church was as good a place to live as anywhere else, certainly preferable to a city shelter. It was a refuge away from the rain and snow, though it was hardly warm or dry. Demitre spent his days huddled in his playpen, dressed in a sweater and overcoat and gloves and ski cap, his frosty breath forming runny little icicles around his pacifier. But Mariluz did have two electric heaters—one from Odessa and one she had trash-picked herself. Odessa had given her a long extension cord, which meant she could run both heaters simultaneously from the outlet in the confessional wall. A man from the suburbs who appeared at the church one day had given her a thick new wool comforter. It was so big that she could fit herself and all three kids beneath it, and on some nights they stayed so warm that they sweated through their clothes.

After many attempts, Wally Lucidi finally reached Cheri Honkala by phone at her row house on Randolph Street. He said he was calling to arrange a time for Cheri to meet his client. The man wanted to do something for the homeless and welfare people living at the church. Wally was thinking about a big Thanksgiving dinner down at his client's place in South Philly, Wally said. Cheri was already planning a Thanksgiving Day meal at the church, so she told Wally it couldn't happen on Thanksgiving Day itself. No problem, Wally said. His client would be with his family that day, anyway.

Somewhat tentatively, Wally mentioned to Cheri that she might have heard of his client. He uttered the man's name very softly, almost reverently:

"Joey Merlino?" It meant nothing to Cheri. "Nope, never heard of him," she said. She wrote the name down in her *Things to Do Today* notebook.

Well, Wally said, Mr. Merlino owned a certain establishment in South Philly called the Avenue Cafe, a cappuccino bar just off Passyunk Avenue. Maybe Cheri could come down, meet Wally at his jewelry shop just down the block on Passyunk, and the two of them would walk over and chat with Mr. Merlino at his place. Wally suggested the following Saturday. Cheri said she would be there, but actually she wondered whether it would be a waste of time. She suspected this was some sort of come-on that would provide this Mr. Merlino with free publicity for his café and a few miserly scraps of food for the Tent City people.

The next day, Cheri had a question for some of the homeless men and women she saw crowded around the TV set at the makeshift dayroom inside St. Edward's. "Hey," she said, "anybody ever heard of Joey Merlino?" Everybody looked up. "Yeah," somebody said, "Skinny Joey Merlino. He's a fucking mobster."

Cheri laughed. "Right," she said, "like you guys really know what you're talking about." Just because Merlino's name was Italian, she thought, that did not mean he was a mobster. And why would a mobster bother with Tent City?

Later, Cheri thumbed through several recent copies of the *Inquirer* and the *Daily News,* looking for Merlino's name. If he was as well known as Wally seemed to think, his name should be in the newspaper. And it was. She found it under a front-page *Inquirer* headline that read, *Hit Man's Violent View of Mob Life.* The story was about a mob assassin's testimony in the trial of mob boss John Stanfa in federal court in downtown Philadelphia. The testimony was, the story said, "a gritty tale of underworld chaos, most of it stemming from the bloody war that raged in 1993 and pitted those loyal to Stanfa against a rival mob faction reputedly headed by Joseph 'Skinny Joey' Merlino." The hit man testified that he had tried to kill Skinny Joey but his aim was off. He shot Merlino "in the buttocks," as the story put it.

"Well, damn," Cheri said to herself, "we're in with the mafia."

After she thought about it for a while, going along with Joey Merlino's Thanksgiving plan did not seem like such a bad idea. It would certainly produce plenty of publicity for KWRU and Tent City at a time when the news media seemed to have lost interest in the scene at St. Edward's. And if the mob was putting on a meal, Cheri figured, it was sure to be one hell of a nutritious and satisfying dinner. It was bound to be a vast improvement on the donated sandwiches and canned goods at the church. And beyond that, Cheri had never met a mobster before.

Later, when I spoke with Wally Lucidi at the Avenue Cafe, he insisted that Merlino's offer was "strictly legitimate." Wally said Merlino had approached him the previous summer, saying he wanted to "clear the family" name after an article about him had appeared in the *Daily News*. The story had ridiculed Merlino's efforts to open his café, which had been delayed by complaints from the city department of Licenses and Inspections regarding plumbing problems and the sale of water ice without a permit. The headline—always a work of art at the *Daily News*—was freighted with what Wally regarded as snide puns: CAPO CINO—*Legit Business? You Bet—And Merlino's New Place Is Mobbed, Too.* The story described Merlino as a "reputed mob underboss," the term "reputed" having been elevated to a sort of honorific in any media mention of Joseph Merlino.

At age thirty-two, Merlino was a legendary figure in South Philadelphia. He had survived at least a dozen attempts on his life, according to testimony by the mob hit men in the Stanfa trial. On the day in August 1993 when Merlino was shot in the butt near Sixth and Catharine Streets, not far from the Avenue Cafe, he was with his top associate, Michael Ciancaglini, who was not so fortunate. Ciancaglini was shot dead. On other occasions, according to the testimony, hit men working for Stanfa or for another mob boss, Nicodemo "Little Nicky" Scarfo, bungled attempts to kill Merlino. Once, while Merlino was doing stretching exercises outside his apartment building, he happened to be leaning over a pipe bomb planted under a trash pile. A hit man named Philip Colletti, hiding nearby, pushed a button on a detonator to trigger the bomb. It failed to detonate. On at least six other occasions, pipe bombs were planted under or near cars believed to belong to Merlino. Each time, a remote control detonator malfunctioned. During part of the period when various killers were pursuing Merlino, he happened to be safely in prison. He served two years for a 1989 armored truck robbery in which $352,000 was stolen, and another year for a parole violation. The robbery money was never recovered; that further embellished Merlino's reputation as a man blessed with good fortune.

Now a free man and the proprieter of the Avenue Cafe, Merlino was portraying himself as a local businessman with an abiding concern for the poor. Federal investigators were calling him the mob underboss for Philadelphia, and they worked steadily to build a racketeering case against him. Merlino professed unconcern. That autumn, he had told *The Philadelphia Inquirer*'s organized crime reporter, George Anastasia: "They've been investigating me for fifteen years. If they got something, let them indict me." In the meantime, Wally Lucidi said, Merlino had other concerns, chiefly his reputation—which would only be enhanced by a dramatic gesture designed to display his community spirit.

According to Wally, Merlino had approached him because of Wally's promotional work for the merchants of Passyunk Avenue. "He knew I was the man to see in that regard," Wally said. "He said he needed my help to put on a little charitable event because his family was always involved in charity. And like I said, he wanted to clear the family name after that article" about the Avenue Cafe.

The first charity Wally called was an orphanage. Officials there did not seem overwhelmed by the offer. "They weren't too receptive to the cameras, Joey being who he is, bringing in the press and all," Wally said. "Joey was still pressing me to find a charity, and I knew I needed a group that wouldn't be upset with who Joey is, who would be okay with him—not his reputation."

While Wally tried to figure out what charity might be deserving of Merlino's largesse, he said, he saw a TV news report on the Tent City people living on the Quaker Lace lot. He considered driving to the lot, he said, "but, frankly, I didn't want to go out to that dirty field with all the garbage and the heat." Instead, he called the TV station and got Cheri's phone number—"and I must have left a million messages on her machine before I finally got through to her."

"I didn't mention Joey's name the first couple of times I talked to her," Wally said. "Then I mentioned Joey and the Avenue Cafe, figuring if she was gonna freak out, she'd do it then. But she didn't have a problem with it that I could tell. She said she was on board."

Now, even with Cheri willing to go to the Avenue Cafe, she had decided that she was not about to meet Skinny Joey Merlino alone. She called her estranged husband, Bob Brown, and begged him to accompany her. Bob agreed, and the two of them drove down to Lucidi Jewelers that Saturday morning to find Wally Lucidi.

As Cheri described it later, the visit was pleasant, even cordial. She and Bob walked from Wally's jewelry store to the Avenue Cafe, where they were introduced to Joey Merlino. He was smaller than she had imagined; she assumed all mobsters were musclebound men with overdeveloped necks. Merlino was trim and small boned, and handsome in a street-corner kind of way, with brown eyes, wavy black hair brushed straight back, and a smooth, clean-shaven olive complexion.

"Joey was just sitting there with his friends in the café," Cheri said. "He was wearing one of those expensive Champion sweatshirts, designer jeans, a gold watch with diamonds I could've paid five years' rent with. He introduced me to his little group there—he called it the Passyunk Business Association. Then Joey said he was real glad I came after the article. He said he was afraid it would scare me off. I didn't know what article he was talking about. There were lots of mob articles about him. He said something about having a rough time in the press lately.

"I asked him why he wanted to help us and he said helping people was in his family's tradition. And he said people called him a gangster but the real gangsters were down in City Hall. He said the people from City Hall were all calling him, saying: 'Don't help these people,' meaning our union. But he said he ignored them. He said he liked our fighting spirit. He said: 'You like to fight against the system, just like us.' "

Merlino offered to send a bus to pick up the families from the church and bring them to the café on the Tuesday before Thanksgiving. He asked Cheri to send him a list of all the children's names and ages, and what each one wanted for Christmas. He said Santa Claus would be at the café to hand out presents. And he mentioned one more thing: His people—meaning Wally—would be putting out a press release. Could Cheri have her people issue one, too?

The best part of her visit, Cheri told me later, was the cadre of police across Passyunk Avenue who took photographs of her entering and leaving the café. They had Skinny Joey's place under surveillance. Cheri wondered whether the cops would compare notes with the Civil Affairs officers she had seen parked outside her row house over the past few weeks.

"I can't wait till my little visit to Skinny Joey's gets reported to all my friends in Civil Affairs," Cheri said. "They're gonna say: 'Whoa! Now Cheri's got the mob on her side!' "

CHAPTER THIRTEEN

A Home
for the Holidays

With less than a week remaining before Skinny Joey's Thanksgiving dinner for Tent City, Cheri was beginning to wonder if the promised meal and gifts were worth the effort they demanded of her. Wally Lucidi was leaving more messages on her answering machine, reminding her to put out a press release, to give him the exact spellings of the names of all the children living at St. Edward's, to make sure everyone was lined up and waiting at the church for Skinny Joey's chartered bus at precisely 2:45 P.M. on the Tuesday before Thanksgiving. Cheri was preoccupied with other, more pressing problems, among them the possibility that the city was going to evict everyone from the church before Thanksgiving, and her campaign to find everyone at St. Edward's a home for the holidays. "This guy Wally seems to forget I don't work for Skinny Joey," she said one evening, playing a message from Wally on her tape machine at home.

Before Cheri had a chance to return the call, Wally dropped by the church to donate more clothes. Mariluz sent him to talk to Cheryl, who was only vaguely aware of Joey Merlino's holiday dinner plans. "Are you gonna put out a press release?" Wally asked her. "We want full press on this thing. My people want to make a splash. We're putting out our own press release, but Cheri said she'd do one, too, only I can't reach her."

Cheryl shrugged and said, "Well, if Cheri said she'd do it, then she'll do it."

Wally gave Cheryl a copy of his press release, which was neatly typed in italic script on the letterhead of *Lucidi Jewelers, Importers of 18 KT. Gold, Fine Jewelry*:

> Dear Merchants and Neighbors . . . The Avenue Cafe will be hosting and sponsoring a Thanksgiving Dinner for the children and families of the homeless "Tent City" organization. Mr. Joseph Merlino will provide a full-course Thanksgiving dinner for approximately 45 people in this group.

Afterwards, Santa will distribute toys and gifts to all the children. The
Hedgeman String Band will provide music and entertainment. All local TV
and Newspaper media will be on Passyunk Avenue to cover this event.

   As fellow neighbors and merchants, it should be our duty to stand united
as a business community and show support of this good gesture. It is necessary that we, as business people, give back to our community when called
upon. Your small contribution for this charitable event will show the media
that Passyunk Avenue is a united front, and that we care and support our
less fortunate neighbors.

At precisely 2:45 P.M., just as Joey Merlino had promised, a long silver
bus from the Golden Charter Service pulled up in front of the church. At
least forty-five people filed aboard, the largest group at the church in some
time. It was a twenty-five-minute ride to the Avenue Cafe, and along the
way the passengers could look down from their soft raised seats at the drug
dealers in their heavy black jackets, at the battered row houses with their
yawning, glassless windows, and at the vast empty expanses where structures had toppled, leaving nothing to block the winter winds that cut
through the narrow streets and blasted the surviving row houses with grit
and debris that slowly wore away the graffiti that streaked every wall. They
could pass through the hollow core of the city, past the wrecked cars and
the trash fires sending up black smoke from rusted barrels, past the slump-
ing pipers and the tight metal grates of the bodegas, past the check-cashing
houses and cheap discount stores, and into the sudden brightness of Center City. There the bus passengers could see the designer shops with their
delicate sprays of tinsel and holly, the rows of trees strung with pale white
Christmas lights, the holiday shoppers with their sleek department store
bags from John Wanamaker and Strawbridge and Clothier. They could
lean over and stare up at the polished blue shimmer of the downtown sky-
scrapers, or look down through the spotless glass fronts of restaurants,
where men in dark suits and women heavy with makeup sipped white wine
behind lush ferns.

   Then they were out of Center City and into South Philadelphia, where
the horizon seemed to shrink, and where everything seemed small and
tight and close to the ground. The streets narrowed, and cars were parked
on sidewalks and at crazy angles along the curb. The row houses seemed
more compact than those in North Philadelphia, but they were solid and
well kept. Almost every doorway was decorated with a plastic Santa Claus
or an arc of brilliant Christmas lights or artificial snow sprayed on the windows. The tiny shops squeezed between the row houses did not have metal
security cages or graffiti as in North Philadelphia, and they displayed a rich

assortment of sausages and cheeses and exquisitely decorated cakes and cookies. The sidewalks were thick with people, and big, dark, American-made cars inched down the constricted roadways in the fading afternoon light. Along Passyunk Avenue, the bus had to slow and push its way slowly to the front of the Avenue Cafe, where a crowd of onlookers had gathered to watch Skinny Joey Merlino feed the homeless. And watching the crowd as it watched the café were plainclothes police officers with their cameras trained on the narrow doorway of the Avenue Cafe.

Inside, looking out the café's plate-glass window, was Joey Merlino. He had just finished arranging children's Christmas gifts at the foot of a small Christmas tree, and now he was watching some of the bullnecked men he called "associates" clear a path through the TV crews and onlookers who were blocking the sidewalk between the bus and the café. The Tent City people filed off the bus, looking small and startled in the swell of the parting crowd.

Merlino stood back from the door and watched the homeless people come up the steps, children first, with Cheri and J.R. bringing up the rear. Some of the war council members remarked later that they were surprised at how mild and inconspicuous Skinny Joey appeared, like some prosperous shop merchant instead of a reputed mob underboss. He was dressed in a perfectly tailored, double-breasted glen plaid suit worn over a collarless shirt the color of pearls. He had wavy black hair and pale brown eyes and a complexion as smooth as a child's. He was fine boned, with small, delicate hands. He had once been a jockey. He seemed relaxed and utterly calm, and he issued orders in a voice that did not rise above a whisper. His face carried a deadpan expression, the sort of blank yet focused look that athletes adopt in competiton. His outward appearance gave no indication that the day was a momentous one for Merlino—not because of the dinner, but because a federal jury downtown was at that moment in its final stages of deliberation in the trial of his rival John Stanfa, the mob boss accused of trying and failing to murder Joey Merlino.

As the Tent City people took their seats, they were watched over by a circle of people ringing the table. There was a small, elderly woman, said to be Skinny Joey's mother, who was dressed entirely in black and darted between the table and the kitchen, and a tall, elegantly dressed young woman said to be Skinny Joey's girlfriend, who sat at the bar. There were hovering waiters and a burly cook in a white chef's jacket. And there were several heavily muscled men dressed in bulky overcoats who wore gold chains on their thick necks and stood near the door, humming along with the Christmas carols playing softly over the café's speaker system. They had names like Sal and Sonny and Angelo. These were Skinny Joey's associates. From behind them emerged a young, dark-haired priest wearing a black suit and white collar. He said a brief prayer and blessed the dinner.

"Everybody eat," Skinny Joey said softly.

The waiters brought out Caesar salad, escarole soup with meatballs, rigatoni, peas and carrots, candied sweet potatoes, and turkey with dressing. The Tent City people ate quickly, with an intensity of purpose, and the waiters removed each emptied plate and replaced it with another. Each waiter wore plastic gloves, but this was interpreted by the war council not as a slur against the hygienic conditions of the homeless but as an assurance that they were receiving food prepared and served under the highest sanitary standards.

Mariluz was trying to eat and wipe Destiny's chin and keep Demitre from scattering his turkey across the table. One of the associates suddenly hoisted Demitre from his chair and held him high in the air, making faces and blubbering noises at the child, who giggled and squirmed. Another associate tried to shovel more turkey onto the plate of Elba's daughter Yazmenelly, who said she was full. Suddenly a man wearing a white apron and a black porkpie hat pushed through the gathering and eased a distressed-looking man into a chair. "Yo, Carmine!" the man in the hat said to someone behind the bar. "Here's the bus driver. Get him some food. Guy's gotta eat."

Soon Cheri and Mariluz had finished their meals, and Mark and J.R. had consumed two helpings each. Everyone leaned back and tried to ward off the attempts of the waiters and the associates to load more food onto their plates. When they could eat no more, the cook ordered the waiters to put all the leftover food into Styrofoam containers for the Tent City people to take back to the church. From the kitchen a waiter emerged bearing an enormous cake with candles. It was Yazmenelly's eighth birthday, a fact that had been noted on the fax Cheri sent to Wally. "Yo! Listen up!" said one of the associates. "Got a birthday girl here. We're gonna sing 'Happy Birthday.' "

As everyone sang in unison, Yazmenelly blushed deeply and blew out the candles. Skinny Joey stepped forward with a knife and cut the cake into thick portions that the waiters served to the children and then to the adults. Someone handed Merlino a napkin, and he delicately wiped cake frosting from his hands. Then he gently tousled Demitre's hair. An associate leaned toward him and whispered, "Santa's here. Want him to come in?" Skinny Joey glanced toward the door. "Not yet. Too early," he said. "Everybody's gotta eat the cake."

Three gift-wrapped boxes appeared before Yazmenelly as she ate her cake. "Open 'em!" the cook said. "They're from Santa." Yazmenelly put down her fork and unwrapped the gifts, careful not to tear the paper. In the boxes were a pink cassette tape player, a radio, and an elaborate Barbie doll set. Yazmenelly looked up at the crowd of strangers gathered around her and said softly, "Thank you." Cheri gestured to a tall, silver-haired man named Winfield, a Tent City supporter who also was an accomplished gospel singer. To the tune of "We Shall Overcome," Winfield stood up and led the Tent City people in a rendition of "We Shall All Have Homes . . . Someday." Some of the associates tried to sing along, but they struggled with the unfamiliar lyrics. They gave up entirely once Winfield began singing "Precious Lord, Take My Hand."

When Winfield finished, the cook hollered toward the bar, "Yo! Carmine! Go play some of those happy 'Jingle Bells' kinda songs!" Over the café's sound system came the sound of Bing Crosby's "I'm Dreaming of a White Christmas."

Now there was a commotion at the front door, where a massive Santa Claus was trying to manuever his belly through the narrow doorway. Two elves—a young man and woman dressed in green suits and stocking caps—were easing Santa toward a chair.

Cheri and Mariluz persuaded the children to sit along one wall while Santa presided from a chair next to the Christmas tree. Skinny Joey and his associates began building a pile of gifts at Santa's feet. Through the doorway came a young man with a Polaroid camera who had been hired to take each child's picture with Santa. Merlino told him to get started right away, and Santa reached out and pulled Demitre onto his lap. He managed to coax a smile from the child as the Polaroid flashed. Skinny Joey stood behind Santa, urging him to speed up the process; the café was filling with press photographers and a camera crew, who had been allowed inside after waiting in the throng on the sidewalk for dinner to end. Among the reporters left outside in the rain, specifically banned from entering, was the woman from the *Daily News* who had written the impertinent article about Skinny Joey's problems at the Avenue Cafe.

After each child had sat with Santa and posed for the photographer (including Mark, who hammed for the camera despite feeling foolish for sitting on Santa's lap at his age), they opened their gifts. Mark got a white skateboard, and when he hugged his mother she told him he could one day tell his grandchildren about the time he had Thanksgiving dinner with a reputed mobster. Destiny got a Barbie doll and a Barbie makeup kit. Desiree got an animal farm set. Demitre got a toy car garage set. Skinny Joey inserted the Polaroids of the children into white paper frames and handed them to Cheri to be distributed later. Then he retreated to the bar as the homeless people and the associates and the photographers stood shoulder to shoulder in the crowded room.

One of the associates took off his black leather coat and gave it to a homeless young man named Kenny. Later the cook offered a dishwasher's job to Kenny, who accepted on the spot and was told to report to work the day after Thanksgiving. Another one of Merlino's men took Mark aside and told him he had seen him interviewed during one of the Tent City protests and had been impressed by Mark's maturity. He slipped Mark a $20 bill.

J.R. made his way to the bar, where he managed to engage Skinny Joey in conversation. "This was the first decent meal I've had in seven months," he told him. Merlino smiled thinly and said, "Glad to help. This is what it's all about." J.R. mentioned that the group was trying to find homes for the holidays. If he were living in an actual house next Thanksgiving, J.R. told him, he would invite him over for Thanksgiving dinner. Merlino nodded and said, "I'd like that."

Ralph Cipriano, a reporter for *The Philadelphia Inquirer*, approached Skinny Joey for a brief interview. He was trying to think of a subtle way to ask him what he was hoping to accomplish with the dinner. Like any good reporter, he first asked an innocuous question about Merlino's connection to the Tent City people. Skinny Joey, standing behind the bar next to a well-tailored, silver-haired man he introduced as his lawyer, did not appear eager to be interviewed. But he acknowledged the reporter's question with a slight nod, and he replied, "I heard about these people from Wally. Then I saw them on TV." Cipriano remarked that the Tent City people seemed to be appreciative. Merlino maintained his blank expression and said he hoped to make it an annual event. "Hopefully, next year it'll be bigger." He paused and said in a flat voice, "Hopefully, next year there won't be any homeless."

Then Cipriano asked his delicate question: "Why are you doing this?"

There was a faint spark in Skinny Joey's eyes. He raised his voice ever so slightly. "That's a stupid question," he said, looking directly at the reporter for the first time. "You shouldn't be asking a question like that. If the governor were throwing a party, would you ask him that question?"

"Yeah, I would, actually," Cipriano said. Skinny Joey's lawyer gave him a baleful look.

"No, you wouldn't," Skinny Joey said quietly and without malice. His mild manner was returning, and quickly the deadpan expression was back on his smooth face. He looked away, past the children and Santa, and through the front window.

A moment later, someone turned on the television set mounted on a wall behind the bar. It hung directly over Skinny Joey and his lawyer, who were counting out a pile of cash and checks donated to the Tent City Thanksgiving fund. Some of the donations came from a tip jar on the bar—"Donations For Homeless At Tent City," a sign said—that customers had been filling during the holidays. The rest had been dumped onto the bar from a large envelope. As Merlino counted out a wad of $10 and $20 bills, the craggy, heavy-featured face of John Stanfa suddenly filled the TV screen. Across Stanfa's face was the word "GUILTY." Merlino's lawyer, Joseph Santaguida, grabbed a remote and turned on the sound. A newscaster's voice said Stanfa and seven "associates" had been convicted of multiple accounts of racketeering, among them attempts to kill one Joseph "Skinny Joey" Merlino. Skinny Joey, still holding the envelope, glanced up at the screen, then turned back to the bar. His expression did not change. He finished counting the cash and checks and tucked them back into the envelope. There was $3,500 in all, he said. The TV newscaster began describing an overturned truck on the interstate. Skinny Joey punched the remote and turned off the TV.

"Dessert," Joey said. "We got dessert here. Cake and coffee."

As dessert and coffee were served, everyone looked expectantly at Merlino as he faced Cheri from across the bar, holding the envelope stuffed with cash and check donations. Someone asked if he was going to make a presentation. Skinny Joey turned to Santaguida and said, "No, my lawyer is."

Santaguida cleared his throat. He was a dapperly dressed man with a long, sad face. "I'm sure I speak for Joseph when I say he does this from the bottom of his heart," Santaguida said. "I know he hopes all of you will be at home with your families next year."

There was a burst of applause. The lawyer passed the envelope to Cheri, who shook his hand and then Merlino's. She knew people expected her to give a little speech. She had already thought about what to say. "We want to thank the Merlino family and all the other businesspeople who took part in this special occasion," she said. "We have never received this kind of hospitality. We thank you from the bottom of our hearts."

From the gathering came more applause and cheers. J.R. shouted at Cheri, "Tell 'em what we're gonna do with the money!"

"Oh, yeah," Cheri said. "Perhaps now we can keep warm inside a church that's very cold. This money will go for kerosene to heat the church so we can have a warm Thanksgiving and Christmas."

On the bus, Cheri and Mariluz found that the entire rear section had been filled with baskets of fresh bread and boxes of clothes. Several men's suits hung on hangers, and J.R. tried them on until he found one that fit. There were bags of toys for the children, to be saved until Christmas, and containers of leftover food in addition to the individual meals in the Styrofoam. There were baskets full of flowers from the table settings. Everyone felt warm inside, and blessed. All the way back to North Philadelphia, the children played with new toys spread on their laps. Everyone sang Christmas carols and gospel songs until the stone spires of St. Edward's rose up from the dark and the wind kicked hard at the church door, and suddenly they were home.

When Cheri got back to Randolph Street, she pulled out the envelope and counted the cash and checks again. She would have to fill out a deposit ticket at the bank the next morning to deposit the whole load into the meager KWRU account. She intended to propose to the war council that the money go for kerosene and new heaters, and for the expenses that would be required by her plan to get everyone a true home for the holidays. As she flipped through the checks, she stopped suddenly when she saw the amount of one of them. It was for $2,000, by far the largest contribution in the pile. The check was drawn on the personal account of Joseph Merlino, whose signature was written across the bottom. The next morning, on her way to the bank, Cheri stopped and photocopied the check so that she would have a souvenir of the night she and Mark shared Thanksgiving dinner with a reputed mobster.

The following week, Cheri organized several secret meetings of the war council to lay plans for the union's A Home for the Holidays campaign. She did not want the rest of the people living at the church to know that the war council was planning to abandon St. Edward's. She feared they would panic and undermine the operation before it had fully developed. People were already on edge, for the weather had turned unbearably cold. It was the coldest and stormiest November and December in decades. High winds had dropped the windchill temperature to nineteen degrees below zero. The city had issued a Code Blue alert, giving city workers permission to force homeless people into shelters. Already, two homeless people in the city had died of exposure, and the TV news reports describing their frozen bodies terrified the families huddled under blankets at St. Edward's. Every morning people shook one another awake to make sure that no one had frozen to death overnight.

The war council had a plan. For weeks, Katie and others had been scouting out HUD houses across North Philadelphia. From HUD offices downtown, they had obtained the addresses of HUD properties listed for sale or rent. These were prime row houses—taken over by HUD, typically for foreclosure on an FHA loan or failure to pay taxes, and considered in sufficiently good condition to be repaired and put on the market. HUD owned 260 of these homes, all of them unoccupied and under the management of private real estate agents. Katie had scouted out the most promising locations, carefully noting whether they had active gas and electric hookups. She and Cheri prepared a list of nineteen houses that they believed were ready for instant occupancy—and most important, could be broken into with little effort. The war council assigned each of the nineteen addresses to KWRU members who had been with the group the longest and who had displayed loyalty and commitment to the struggle. The first names on the list were Mariluz and Elba, who were assigned to a prime location, a brown brick row house on Fairhill Street in the Olney section of Philadelphia, a few miles due north of St. Edward's. Also on the list were Tara and J.R. and Chicago.

Cheri set moving day for two weeks before Christmas. She knew that several factors were in her favor. For one thing, the savagely cold weather and the Code Blue alert made it unlikely that HUD or the city would try to evict people from the takeover houses, with homeless people dying in the streets and the shelters full. For another, bureaucrats were not inclined to forcibly remove destitute families from otherwise unoccupied homes just before Christmas. Cheri imagined the newspaper headlines: *Officials Play Grinch, Evict Homeless Families at Christmas.* And there was one more consideration that strengthened Cheri's hand. Because the homes belonged to the federal government, U.S. marshals would be enlisted to evict the families. But the federal government was still shut down, thanks to the bickering between Congress and the White House over the federal budget. So Cheri used some of the donated money from Skinny Joey's party to rent two Ryder trucks and to buy several kerosene heaters at deep discounts from local drug dealers.

The day before the move, Cheri held a war council meeting at her house on Randolph Street to make final plans for the operation. She held the meeting away from the church, for many of the homeless residents of St. Edward's still had not been told of the impending move. Cheri wanted the move to be a covert operation—carried out quickly and efficiently, without complaints from disgruntled homeless people or interference from the city or HUD.

Inside her living room that morning, war council members sat on Cheri's old sofa and on pillows scattered across the floor. Cheri served iced tea in cartons and two bags of pretzels she had bought with Skinny Joey's donations. On her living room wall she had posted signs with slogans that said, *Build Community Support,* and, *Build Our Own Leadership.* A banner read, *The Underground Railroad Project*—Cheri's new name for the operation to move the Tent City people into HUD takeover homes.

Like a college professor teaching a seminar, Cheri pointed to the posters and began a presentation to the war council on the takeover effort and the underlying philosophy of moving into empty but federally owned houses. Tara took notes while J.R. translated into Spanish for Elba.

"Now, people, we're gonna call this the Underground Railroad Project,"

Cheri said. "There was something that happened in history called the Underground Railroad, run by Harriet Tubman during slavery. It wasn't literally a railroad, but she took slaves from the South to freedom, from near-death situations to a new life. Today, with homelessness and welfare, it's not much different than slavery. We're trying to bring people from slavery to self-sufficiency, starting with this move into affordable housing."

"Yeah," said Katie, who was squatting on the floor, smoking a cigarette. "That's why we're all gonna start calling Cheri Harriet Tubman the Second."

Everybody laughed, but Cheri hushed them and resumed her presentation. She stood up, displaying a sheet of paper. It was a contract to be signed by anyone accepting KWRU's help in taking over a HUD house:

1. No drinking or any drugs are allowed in the house at ANY time. People in recovery must attend AA or NA.
2. No fighting is allowed at any time with anyone.
3. The house is to be kept clean at all times. Garbage taken out daily.
4. Everyone must attend weekly house meetings held at 5 p.m. on Wed. nights.
   · Failure to comply with ANY of the above will terminate membership within KWRU.

Cheryl passed out copies of the form. "I'm gonna sign this myself," she said. "Cheri is gonna sign it. It's crucial that you get everyone in the church to sign it."

Cheri explained that Community Legal Services had agreed to set up rent escrow accounts into which the Tent City people would deposit 30 percent of their income from welfare checks; Cheri had been told that low-income people should expect to spend roughly 30 percent of their income for affordable housing. But federal budget cuts had forced layoffs at Community Legal Services, so people would have to go to banks on their own and finish setting up the escrow accounts. Cheri said it was important that people establish the accounts, with the money eventually to be paid to HUD as rent, so that HUD could not accuse them of taking over the houses for free. She passed out affidavits she had prepared, which stated:

I am a resident of the property located at————Philadelphia, PA. I do not have a lease, nor do I have rent receipts. The source of my income is DPA. My rent is being paid into an escrow account until such time when the payments will be forwarded to HUD. My rent is————.

As an example, Cheri cited Elba. She received $497 a month in welfare payments, Cheri told the group, so she should deposit $149 a month into an escrow account. Everyone nodded, including Elba after J.R. had translated for her.

"This affidavit needs to be notarized and then kept in a safe place," Cheri said. "This is what you'll show to police, HUD, neighbors, everybody. So don't let your kids spill Kool-Aid on it. It's your most important document right now, next to your welfare ID card."

People were to show the affidavit to any police who might come to their door, Cheri said. They should say that the house is owned by the federal government, so the police would have to find a federal marshal, who, Cheri pointed out, was not likely to be available, given the government shutdown. "You basically want to swamp the police with paperwork, give them bureaucratic nightmares, make 'em have to call their supervisors," Cheri said.

Cheri turned to Cheryl. "Cheryl, if the cops come, you fade away," she said. "You've got too many bench warrants."

Cheri held up another sheet of paper. It was a petition of support to be signed by neighbors. It read: "I, the undersigned, hereby support my neighbor who lives at————in their current efforts to secure affordable housing."

"Get to know your neighbors," Cheri said. "Keep this petition by the door so they can sign it when they come over to check you out. You want to meet everybody, make them think you're the greatest thing that ever hit their block. Invite them to KWRU meetings if they have housing or welfare problems. Be the best asset on the block. Introduce yourself. Make sure your house is beautiful. Bake some cookies, take them to your neighbors. Act like you belong there. Start cleaning up right away. And on the first Wednesday, Truck Boy will deliver donated food to your house. You should go to your neighbors and offer food to them."

Cheri turned to Mariluz and Elba. She told them that their house would be considered KWRU's "public house." It would be the only house the press would be told about. Mariluz and Elba, with Cheri's assistance, would give the only media interviews.

"It's going to be stressful for you two," Cheri said. "Everything you do will be watched closely, right down to what you put in your trash. Just remember it's important to let the public know there are thousands of empty houses going to waste in this city and you are willing to pay for the right to live in one of them and fix it up. Let people know that just because you're on public assistance doesn't mean you're lazy. You have to dispel all the stereotypes of poor people on welfare. Let them know you want to contribute to the community and build better lives for you and your children."

"Oh, and speaking of the press, the first thing they'll call you is 'squatters.' That has negative connotations because it's associated with people who squat just for fun, or to use drugs. It's not squatters moving into the neighborhood. It's Mariluz and her babies, Elba and her kids. Stress that.

And stress that we are an organization, not just individuals. This is a collective effort. We want all poor people to identify with us."

Cheri reached down and lifted a stack of posters. On each one was written, in large black letters: *This House Has Been Reclaimed As Part of the Underground Railroad Project of KWRU.* People were to put them in the front windows of their takeover houses.

"These are for your protection," Cheri said. "They will let the cops know this is not a burglary or a drug thing. And if you do get some cowboy cops busting in on you, sit down and be still. Don't move! Don't give them an excuse to shoot you. And don't run! You haven't done anything wrong."

Cheri paused and thought for a moment. Actually, she said, they were breaking the law. "You *do* all clearly understand that this is illegal," she said. "I don't want them saying later, 'Cheri misleads poor people.' And I don't want any of you saying later, 'Cheri didn't warn me.' You have been warned."

Everyone nodded somberly. Then Cheri handed out blank posters and felt-tip markers. She told everyone to write, "This is a drug-free and alcohol-free house," and hang the posters in their new homes.

The war council members carefully wrote the message on the posters and then rolled them up. The meeting was ending. People lit cigarettes and put on their overcoats for the long, cold walk back to the church. As they moved toward the front door, Cheri shouted, "Hold up! There's one more thing!" She reached into a shopping bag and withdrew several rolls of toilet paper.

"You each get a roll," she said. "I've always told you I'm here to watch your ass."

All the next day and into the evening, people tore down the partitioned living areas they had built from lumber and plywood and donated sheets inside St. Edward's. Their possessions were stacked in haphazard piles of shopping bags and black trash bags, each one defined by the narrow passageways left for people to pass by as they carried items to the trucks outside.

The first items loaded onto the first truck belonged to Mariluz and Elba, who had torn down their enclosure and loaded their families' belongings into boxes and shopping bags. The two women hauled their mattresses to the truck as Yazmenelly and Destiny trailed behind them, dragging boxes loaded with baby clothes and food. It took less than an hour to load everything the two families owned, including a kerosene heater and a plastic cooler full of donated cheese and lunch meat. Elba lingered behind, sweeping the dirty stone floor where the makeshift bed had stood and recovering a 1995 calendar from Bob's Crab House. She decided to roll up the carpet remnant that served as their living room rug and take it to the truck.

Even though the truck was loaded with other people's possessions, Cheri decided to have it driven to the house assigned to Mariluz and Elba so that they could set up a makeshift household before dark. Quickly, so that people inside the church would not realize that Mariluz and Elba were leaving so soon, the two women and their six children split up between the truck and Cheri's Renault. The truck and car pulled away so swiftly that the bare trees in the park across Eighth Street were a blur, and no one had time to look back to say a proper good-bye to the old church, where the statue of St. Edward the Confessor seemed to raise a hand in farewell.

On Fairhill Street, a narrow, tree-lined street where squat duplexes were set high above the sidewalk, the two-vehicle caravan pulled up to a brick home the color of muddy water, with white paint peeling from the porch windows. Mariluz noticed that there was a corner grocery and a laundry on the next block. She noticed, too, that some of the neighbors had pulled back their curtains to peer out at the strange truck and car on the street.

When Mariluz and Elba walked up the concrete steps, each with a baby in her arms, they found that someone from KWRU had already used bolt cutters to slice open the HUD lock on the front door. Chicago appeared from inside and threw open the door and said, "Welcome to your new house." Mariluz and Elba walked inside and saw a bare living room and dusty hardwood floors that stretched back through a well-lighted dining room, and stopped at the doorway of a tiny kitchen with a dark linoleum floor. It was cold inside, but not as cold as St. Edward's, because the walls were made of plaster, not stone, and the windows were tightly sealed.

Mariluz looked up the stairway and saw doorways that opened into three upstairs bedrooms. Yazmenelly and Destiny burst past her and ran up the stairs to claim their bedrooms. Mariluz went up the stairs behind them and found a large master bedroom with roomy closets and, next door, a tiled bathroom with a sink, mirror, toilet, and old-fashioned tub. She walked back downstairs, where Cheri and Katie were hauling in boxes, and announced, "It's okay. Not bad."

On the sidewalk, as Katie unloaded the truck, an Hispanic woman who lived next door leaned out her front door and asked if she was moving in.

"Nope," Katie said. "Just helping. But you got yourself two nice new families."

"Well, somebody broke in there last week," the woman said. "I called the cops."

Inside, Chicago tore down a sign that read, *Danger—This House Has Been Winterized. The Water Heater Has Been Drained. Do Not Turn On Utilities.* Then he went upstairs and tore down a HUD inspection form that had been signed and dated in two-week intervals, verifying that the house was secure and had not been vandalized. He leaned over the staircase and yelled down into the living room to Cheri, "They'll be back to inspect in a few days, based on the pattern on this paper."

In the basement, Chicago found the water heater, the boiler, and the fuse box. From what he could determine, they were all in good working order. All Mariluz had to do was go to the gas company and the electric company and get them to turn on the utilities. As Chicago walked back upstairs, he stumbled over a sign that read, *A HUD Home for Sale. Ask a Real Estate Agent*.

In the living room, Elba was sweeping dust from the floor and cobwebs from the corners before she set up the baby's playpen. The sofa and chair from their enclosure at St. Edward's had been set up, and someone had filled the heater with kerosene and lit it. The room was thick with the oily scent of kerosene. Mariluz put one Underground Railroad notice in the porch window and another in the kitchen window in the rear. As soon as the small dining room table was brought in, she reached into a box and pulled out a plastic vase filled with plastic pink roses and set it down. "The homey touch," she said.

Well before dark, the mattresses had been set up and covered with sheets and blankets from St. Edward's. Compared to the cold vastness of the church, the house felt snug and comfortable, despite the bare walls and nearly empty rooms. Mariluz opened a black garbage bag to unload the children's clothes, then suddenly recoiled. "Garbage!" she said. "We packed up the garbage!" But then she saw Elba laughing, and she hauled the bag of church garbage out to the curb.

Later there was a knock at the door, and everyone jumped. Mariluz opened the door and saw that it was the Hispanic woman from next door. She introduced herself and asked Mariluz if she was from "the shelter." Mariluz tried to explain KWRU to the woman, but it turned out that the main purpose of her visit was to ask Mariluz to get her black cat out of her house. Mariluz told the woman that she didn't have a cat. The woman said she was superstitious and was afraid to touch the cat. "So am I," Mariluz said, and shut the door.

Just before dark, there was another knock at the door. It was a man from across the street, who introduced himself and asked if there was anything Mariluz needed. Mariluz recognized him as an acquaintance from one of her previous neigborhoods, and he seemed to remember her, too. When she told him she needed water, he rushed back home and returned not only with bottled water, but also with crackers, cheese, and a pot for boiling the water.

They made a meal of cheese and crackers, sandwiches brought from the church, and beans and rice cooked on the kerosene stove. The children were so tired that they did not complain when told to lie down and try to sleep. Mariluz and Elba were exhausted, too, and when darkness fell they knew they would be asleep before long. Lying on the mattress, looking up at the dark patterns made on the ceiling by the candlelight and the waves of warmth rising from the heater, Elba seemed resigned but content. She tried to practice her English, and the words that she spoke in soft, measured tones were, "Home—Sweet—Home." Next to her, Mariluz cuddled with Desiree and whispered into the girl's ear, "We got a home, baby. We got a home."

For the next two days, Cheri barely slept. She was at the church at dawn, supervising each truckload and making sure that the right people were moved into the HUD house selected for them. At night, she drove to the gas station at Fifth and Lehigh to fill plastic jugs with kerosene to replenish the heaters she had bought with the donations from Skinny Joey. She had set up a rotating system of volunteers to deliver the kerosene to the newly occupied HUD houses, where she had assigned one heater per household. There were enough heaters to go around now that the Main Line lady had delivered her contribution of thirteen heaters.

Cheri still had to deal with her regular daily chores, which included talking with reporters, who had found out about the HUD takeovers and now were asking her if she thought the people would be able to stay in the houses until Christmas before they were evicted. She had to drive from one house to the next, solving problems and breaking up disputes, while also making sure the last handful of homeless people packed up and moved out of St. Edward's. She had to care for Mark, too, who was feeding himself junk food for dinner every night.

In the middle of all this, Cheri received a set of what she considered remarkable posters, mailed to her by the National Welfare Rights Union in Michigan. The posters, produced in conjunction with the Women's International League for Peace and Freedom, in Philadelphia, focused on corporate welfare. Below a headline that asked, *Who Gets Welfare?* each poster featured a photograph of a well-to-do, middle-aged white man in a business suit. There was Michael Eisner of Disney, which received $300,000 in taxpayer money to put on a fireworks show. There was Ed Rensi of McDonald's, which received $466,000 from the U.S. Agriculture Department to subsidize costs for advertising Chicken McNuggets in Turkey. There was Daniel Tellep of Lockheed Martin, which received $850 million in "consolidation costs" from the Pentagon. And there was Sam Donaldson, the ABC correspondent, who received $97,000 in federal subsidies for his sheep and angora ranch in New Mexico.

Below each man's photo were two paragraphs pointing out that AFDC accounted for less than 1 percent of the federal budget. The $14.4 billion spent on all social welfare programs in 1994, the message said, was dwarfed by the $104.3 billion spent on corporate welfare. One of the posters contained a message that Cheri thought crystallized her beliefs about welfare:

> Everyone who drives on a toll-free highway, attends a public school or university, deducts mortgage interest payments from their income tax, or enjoys a national park is getting the equivalent of welfare from the federal government. In one way or another, we are all welfare recipients.

Cheri wished she could have thousands of the posters and hang them in corporate and government offices around the country. She wished the same groups would print posters on military spending, on the $265 billion Pentagon budget she had been reading about, with its $2.2 billion Stealth bombers and its $3.4 billion for four new Aegis destroyers. Somehow, thinking of these huge dollar amounts made each $5 bill that Cheri spent to fill up a kerosene container seem significant and vital. In light of the billions spent by the government and the military, she believed she was getting a far greater return on the minuscule amounts that people donated to KWRU. That week, despite the pressures of moving from the church, she took the time to make sure that the posters she had been sent were taped to the walls of several welfare offices and public health centers in North Philadelphia.

At the church on the third and final day of the move, Cheri found that Chicago's enclave was the only one remaining. He had been assigned to stay behind to guard the church, along with Tara and J.R., whose living area had been reduced to a queen-size mattress. Chicago reported to Cheri that the last of the church's former residents had been packed and were waiting to be trucked to their new houses. But this process, predictably, had not been a smooth one. Chicago showed Cheri his hand, which was swollen and wrapped in a gauze bandage.

"What happened?" Cheri asked, though she was not sure she really wanted to know.

"I had to punch out the Jamaican dude," Chicago explained.

According to Chicago, the Jamaican had twice tried to steal his heater and coffeemaker.

"I would've given the hot plate to the mothefucker if he'd just asked for it the right way," Chicago said now. "I got *four* coffeemakers."

That was not the only fight. Chicago pointed to a homeless man named Jesse, who was hobbling on crutches, his right ankle taped and swollen. Jesse had been slammed to the ground by his nephew and bunkmate, Dave, after

Jesse had tried to hit Dave with an iron pipe for the offense of passing gas while the two men were sleeping. Chicago sympathized with Jesse's injury, but he believed that Jesse had brought his misfortune upon himself.

"Jesse was out of line," Chicago told Cheri. "He had no right to go after Dave in those circumstances. It'd be different if Dave was in control of himself, but he wasn't. He was asleep. The rule around here is, if you pass gas in your sleep, that's permissible."

Cheri did not care to hear any more. She didn't have time to hear about fistfights. Her main concern was getting people out of the church and into the HUD houses. And now she was relieved to find that nearly everyone had been packed up and settled in a HUD home without interference from the police or federal marshals. The only problem had come the night before, when a homeless family left their HUD house to buy food and returned to find their belongings tossed onto the sidewalk and a new lock on the door. It seemed to be the work of angry neighbors. Cheri, with Mariluz's help, loaded up the family's belongings into Cheri's car and moved them to a different HUD house.

There had been a few milder complaints from neighbors at other HUD houses, and even a couple of visits from police officers who made perfunctory inquiries and left, but no serious confrontations and certainly no evictions. There was plenty of food; in fact, the war council had put up a sign on the front of the church: *Wait! Before you bring in any donations, please see J.R., Tara, or Chicago. We're overloaded.* There was enough money left for kerosene, too. But there were constant shortages of volunteers and working cars to deliver the food and fuel every day to the HUD houses scattered across North Philadelphia.

Remarkably, there had been no word from HUD. The newspapers and TV stations had by now run reports on the takeover of the houses. But each report said attempts to reach HUD officials for comment had been unsuccessful because of the federal government shutdown following yet another showdown between the White House and Republicans in Congress. For the first time that year, Cheri felt indebted to the very Republicans who were pushing so hard for welfare cuts.

Cheri was convinced that the authorities would not tolerate the takeovers forever. She was planning to leave for a trip home to visit her mother in Minneapolis at Christmas. She feared HUD might move to evict the KWRU people in her absence. She thought it far more likely that the food and kerosene supply network she had set up would collapse without her, and people would begin to bicker and leave the houses in search of warmth and food. Just before she left for Minneapolis, she called a final war council meeting at her house.

There, Cheri stressed the need for leadership in her absence. She praised Mariluz for her role in moving the evicted couple the night before. "Instead of just going back to her own house and abdicating her responsibility, Mariluz stayed and saw the crisis through," she said. She gave her cellular phone to Mariluz and her beeper to Tara, warning both of them not to let the devices be stolen. She left her car keys with the war council, with instructions that it be used nightly to deliver food and kerosene.

Cheri said she was naming the nightly deliveries Project Survival, and the war council decided to put Mariluz in charge. Cheri gave her a typed list of dates and times, with the name of each person—students, volunteers, and KWRU members—assigned to each delivery shift. The war council voted to make Tara administrative assistant, with responsibility for running day-to-day KWRU affairs in Cheri's absence.

Then someone brought up the subject of the security team, which had been charged with intercepting all strangers entering the church and now was required to deal with any trespassers at the takeover houses. Several people expressed concern about a homeless man named Ernest, who was on the KWRU security team but was also abusive, threatening, and unpredictable. Some of the war council members were afraid he was going to seriously hurt someone. Not everyone knew it, but Ernest had also briefly been Cheryl's lover. Even so, it was Cheryl who spoke first to suggest that Ernest be removed from the security team.

"Ernest smokes weed from the time he gets up till he goes to bed," Cheryl said. "He steals. He hates women. He's hit women before. He pulled a gun on a woman's head in the church. He threatened to pull a gun on me. And he's organizing on the race issue. He's dividing people, blacks and whites."

Cheryl's comments triggered a long discussion of Ernest's merits and weaknesses. Cheri and Tara argued that Ernest had leadership potential that needed to be nurtured and developed. They contended, too, that removing Ernest would only create a hostile and alienated force outside the union—and one determined to damage KWRU. It was decided that Ernest would remain on the security team, but under the close supervision of Chicago and J.R., Ernest would be required, like all members of the security team, to attend the union's regular conflict resolution sessions.

Cheryl, sitting on a cushion, slammed her fist against the floor. "You can't do that!" she shouted. "If he's part of the security team, I'll resign. I won't be part of an organization with him in it!"

In an instant Cheri's face was red and contorted. She pointed her forefinger at Cheryl's face as if it were a gun and screamed out: "Quit? You can't just fucking quit the movement because you don't get your way!" I had never seen Cheri fly into a rage so suddenly; it was an astonishing sight. She towered over Cheryl, screaming down at her as Cheryl lowered her head and stared at the floor.

"You've done some pretty fucked-up shit yourself, Cheryl, just like Ernest!" Cheri yelled. "And now you just want to fucking quit on us? Don't quit! Let's struggle through this thing."

Cheryl was on the verge of tears. "He's threatened to kill war council members," she said meekly.

"Bullshit, Cheryl!" Cheri said. "I've been threatened a hundred times! So fucking what? You want me to just give up and quit?"

Everyone sat in silence, stunned by the outburst. Cheri took a deep breath and lowered her voice. "Ernest is from the streets. He deals with problems with violence. But he's a leader. We need to keep him in the organization and change his fucked-up attitude. We'll all be there to watch this cat. But we can't just get rid of him right at the start, and we can't put ourselves in a situation of choosing between Ernest and Cheryl."

She reached down and patted Cheryl's arm. Without looking up, Cheryl said quietly, "Ernest has grabbed me several times and threatened to hit me. If he does, I *will* defend myself. I swore a long time ago that I'd never let a man hit me again. I just want to go on record as saying I hope this decision doesn't lead to people going to prison or people ending up dead."

Cheri bent down and told Cheryl, "It's not gonna happen. I promise." She hugged Cheryl, who hugged her back but did not smile.

"Is there anything else to report from overnight?" Cheri asked.

"Yeah," Chicago said. "A guy last night in one of the HUD houses smoked crack and got kicked out by the other residents and tried to start a fight, but they got rid of him."

Cheri shook her head. "With that bit of pleasant news, let's adjourn," she said.

The next day, Cheri left for Minneapolis. At the church, where Chicago and J.R. and Tara watched over the few remaining homeless men who had taken refuge there, Chicago decided to test Ernest. He gave him money to buy kerosene for the two heaters left behind after the moves to the HUD houses. It was a long time before Ernest returned. And when he did, he had no kerosene and no cash. Chicago questioned him about it, and Ernest challenged him to a fight. Chicago did not fight him, but he did manage to kick Ernest out of the church and into the cold.

Three days after she and Elba moved into their takeover house, Mariluz went to the electric company office at K and A to see about having her electricity turned on. Just outside the office, located between the health clinic and the Burger King, she ran into Odessa Williams. When Odessa found out what Mariluz was up to, she quickly informed her that she was an expert at getting utilities turned on, based on her protest years with Roxanne Jones. Mariluz showed Odessa the affidavit provided by KWRU, and Odessa assured her it would be enough to get the power turned on. "Getting your electricity turned on, that's no problem," Odessa told her as they walked inside the cavernous electric company office. "Paying for it, that's the problem."

Inside, Mariluz handed her welfare ID card and the KWRU affidavit to a woman at the customer service desk. The woman glanced at the affidavit and copied down the address of Mariluz's takeover home. For all the surprise or concern that registered on her face, she could have been copying from a rental lease or home owner's deed. She asked Mariluz for her previous address.

"Church at Eighth and York," Mariluz said.

This information, too, did not seem out of the ordinary to the woman. She punched the address into her computer. Then she asked whether Mariluz was employed.

"No ma'am," Mariluz said. "I'm on DPA."

The woman nodded and asked Mariluz whom she was renting from at her new address.

Mariluz stared down at the affidavit. Odessa leaned over and gently tapped at the raised seal of the notary public Mariluz had paid to notarize the document. Mariluz looked closer and saw that the notary had signed her name: Jacqueline Brown.

"Oh, yeah," Mariluz said brightly. "Jacqueline Brown."

The woman typed the name into her computer. The computer screen flashed and a series of coded letters and numbers appeared. The woman studied it for a moment and then asked, "Is tomorrow okay?"

Mariluz was stunned. "You mean to turn it on?" she asked.

"That's right."

"Sure!" Mariluz said. "Tomorrow is great." She couldn't wait to get back home to tell Elba.

There was one more thing, the woman said. Mariluz's face fell. She was certain a hitch was coming—some required document she didn't have, or some huge cash fee.

"There's a transfer fee of six dollars—it'll be included in your first bill."

Mariluz let out her breath. "No problem," she said.

Outside, Mariluz and Odessa slapped palms. "I never thought it would be so easy—and so fast," Mariluz said.

Odessa looked at Mariluz's smooth young face through her spectacles. "God's on your side, dear," she said.

"I guess so," Mariluz said.

The two of them walked next door to the Burger King, where they treated themselves to lunch. As they ate, Mariluz showed Odessa the cheap ring she had fished out of the donation pile and joked that she was married to Tent City. Odessa showed Mariluz how to repair her torn cigarette—it was her last one—by rewrapping the damaged paper around the remaining tobacco, and then she told the younger woman that even an old great-grandmother knew a little bit about certain things.

Mariluz felt so invigorated by her success at the electric company that she decided to try the phone company, too. Using the same affidavit and welfare ID card, she managed to set up a phone account and arrange for a technician to activate the line in two days. But when she visited the gas company, her luck ran out. After waiting two hours to be seen, she was told that she had to provide a letter from the owner of the house authorizing gas service. And even then, she was told, it would cost $101 to turn on the gas.

Mariluz took a bus home and told Elba the good news about the phone and electricity and the bad news about the gas. The prospect of electricity pleased Elba, for some of the Tent City people had brought in an old refrigerator from the church. She was anxious to have cold milk and fresh meat on hand. Elba had good news for Mariluz, too: Eric, the son of the Main Line heiress Joanna, was supposed to come by and try to turn on the water. And, she said, one of the volunteers from Tent City had promised them a Christmas tree.

Mariluz felt her spirits lift at the mention of a tree, for the children had been begging for one. But while she liked Eric, she did not have much faith in his plumbing abilities. He had spent weeks trying to install two huge, molded shower stalls in the tiny bathroom at St. Edward's. The stalls blocked access to the sacristy all winter long, and they became more streaked with dirt and grime with each passing day. As far as Mariluz knew, they were still standing there.

That evening, a volunteer named Steve arrived with a freshly cut Christmas tree. The children ran over and sniffed at the needles, which smelled deeply of pine. Mariluz ran her hands over the branches and noted with satisfaction that the needles were supple and did not fall off. They put it in the corner next to the porch window, where people could see it from the street. The tree reminded Mariluz that there was only a week remaining before Christmas. She had not yet bought her children's gifts, and she would not be able to buy them until the twenty-first, when Number Five recipients received their second December welfare check.

Mariluz also had to deal with Christmas gifts for what seemed like the entire war council. The day Cheri left, she handed Mariluz, as the war council's new administrative assistant, a package of papers. Among them was a written request from one of the Main Line ladies for a list of Christmas wishes for the KWRU leadership. She wanted to buy gifts for everyone—"anything you want," the note said. It was now Mariluz's responsibility to fill out the list. Since Cheri had not told her what she wanted, Mariluz wrote under her name, "New car." For herself and Elba, she wrote, "VCR, color TV." Under Katie's name someone had already written, "Gold chain," and for Cheryl, "Gold chain—and stuff for the kids." Mariluz sent the list to the woman's address, but she doubted that she would go to the expense and effort of responding with actual gifts.

Another paper Cheri had left Mariluz was a schedule for the week before Christmas. It had been neatly typed, at Cheri's request, by one of the Empty the Shelters students. Under *Things to Do* (how typically Cheri, Mariluz thought) were listed "(1) Money and receipts for kerosene and food, (2) Materials donated, (3) Media, (4) Dealing with the media, (5) Channel 17 wants to interview Mariluz." There was also a calendar of events, which included a listing of volunteers to man the "house relief teams" that supplied kerosene and food to the takeover houses every night. Also listed was a Christmas Eve party at St. Edward's, hosted by Joanna the heiress, a Christmas Day breakfast at a local restaurant, and a Christmas Day dinner at the church.

Mariluz felt overwhelmed. She had her own family to worry about at Christmas. She didn't have water or electricity, much less Christmas presents. She would do the best she could in her new position at KWRU, but she expected help from other people on the war council. And she wouldn't be able to get much done until after the following day, when she and Elba had to take the bus all the way down to McKinley school for prevacation conferences with Yazmenelly's and Destiny's teachers.

The next morning, they boarded the bus for the long trip and transfer to McKinley school. Elba took the children on the bus every morning, so she was accustomed to the trip. But to Mariluz it seemed endless, with a stop at every other street corner. She hated the fact that her children were subjected to this daily ordeal (not to mention the cost of tokens and transfers) but she and Elba were determined that Destiny and Yazmenelly maintain continuity in school, if not in their home lives. Mariluz had heard from Katie of the devastating impact that changing schools had had on Katie's grandchildren. Both Destiny and Yazmenelly felt secure and welcomed at McKinley, and their mothers made sure they were able to stay there even though they now lived several miles away.

At the school, they passed through the chain-link fence that protected McKinley from the neighborhood, which looked less sinister than usual because the bitter cold had driven some of the drug dealers indoors and because some residents had put up Christmas decorations. These garnishings did not obscure the graffiti or the garish mural titled *The Streets Will Always Tell Your Story*, but they did provide a veneer of normalcy. There were blinking yellow lights strung on withered trees, gold ribbons in windows, a cardboard Santa Claus strung to a door, and a paper banner across one stoop that read, *May All Your Xmas Memories Be Bright*.

Inside, Mariluz met with Ms. Carrigan, Destiny's teacher, who was struggling to repair the girl's plastic belt, which had split along the seams. "Oh, don't worry about that," Mariluz told Ms. Carrigan. "That's just a cheap donation belt. We can get another one."

Ms. Carrigan let the belt drop and picked up Destiny's report card to show to her mother. Destiny had earned a C (for "Competent") in language arts, math, science, physical development, work habits, and social studies. She had an M (for "Making progress") in spelling, fine motor skills, and in the subcategories "Knows age and birth date," "Prints letters," "Writes numerals," "Knows full address," and "Knows full telephone number." She received no I's (for "Improvement needed"). She had no late days, but eight absences.

Mariluz explained that the absences had been caused by various crises at the church or by the move. And Destiny had not memorized her new address because she had just moved, and of course the family did not yet have a telephone. Mariluz sounded vaguely apologetic.

"Oh, I know, I know," Ms. Carrigan said. "Destiny has told me all about her new house. She's so excited. I wouldn't worry about her. She's come such a long way. She's a doll to have in class. She's learning a lot about herself. She started real slowly, but she's real quick and knows her alphabet. She needs to work on her numbers, but it's only kindergarten. And Destiny is friendly. You can sit her anywhere and she gets along."

Mariluz tried again to explain how difficult life had been at the church, and how trying it had been to move into an unfurnished house without electricity or heat or running water. She did not mention that the union had broken into the house, or that the family was in danger of being evicted at any moment.

Ms. Carrigan tried to reassure her that Destiny was thriving, despite the upheaval in her life. "Destiny is a very intelligent child," she said. "She's smart enough not to be discouraged by her circumstances. The other kids all know about her being homeless, but they think she's special. They're fascinated with her. And I really think she doesn't realize how difficult her mother has it, and I credit her mother for that."

Mariluz blushed and tried to change the subject. She mentioned a dentist appointment the teacher had scheduled for Destiny through the school. It would be the first time Destiny, who was five, had ever been to a dentist.

Ms. Carrigan asked if the move would make it difficult for Destiny to attend school the next semester. "Oh, no," Mariluz said. "I got plenty of tokens, and my friend Elba takes her every day. She'll be here in class, don't worry. I want her on the honor roll."

From Destiny's classroom, Mariluz walked down the hallway to find Elba, who was meeting Yazmenelly's teacher. She found the two of them in the third-grade classroom, chatting in Spanish and English. It was a bilingual class, and Elba was pleased to see that the report card was in Spanish. Yazmenelly had earned an A in *música* and a B in *arte*, but she had a D in *literatura*. She had C's in *matemáticas, comunicación escrita,* and *estudios sociales.* She had no tardy days and, her mother was proud to note, no days absent, despite the upheavals at St. Edward's and the move to Fairhill Street.

"Her effort and behavior are great," the teacher, Ms. Fox, said to Elba in English, with Mariluz translating. "She gets along with everybody and tries very hard. But she's still below grade level in reading. She needs to read at least fifteen minutes a day. And money—she can identify coins but she has trouble counting money. She needs a lot of help at home with quarters, dimes, and nickels lined up on a table where she can count them. And use her flash cards for math so she stops using her fingers to count."

Elba nodded and folded Yazmenelly's yellow report card and put it in her bag. Then she and Mariluz said good-bye and walked around the corner to the row house of Elba's aunt, where they retrieved the younger children, used the toilet, and washed everyone's face and hands.

When they returned home, they found Joanna's son Eric in the kitchen, ripping out pipes from beneath the sink. With some effort, Eric had managed to install new copper pipes between the sink and the main water pipe in the basement. But he had not been able to connect the new pipes with the water pipe that ran to the street. After a while, he gave up and left, promising to return in a few days and figure out a way to get the water running. The best Mariluz and Elba could do for now, he said, was to fill buckets from the main water valve in the basement and haul them upstairs.

Mariluz was not overly concerned with the water. She could cook and wash from the buckets, and produce hot water by heating a pan on top of the kerosene heater. Without gas, they would not have hot water for showers anyway. Besides, the house now had electricity; a man from the electric company had shown up, as promised, and turned it on. And the phone company had turned on the phone line, so the house now had a working telephone.

Mail was being delivered, too, but this was not an entirely welcome development. That very afternoon, a letter arrived with the return address of the HUD office in Philadelphia and the ominous phrase "Official Business." The letter, addressed to the "Occupant" of the Fairhill Street property, read:

> You are hereby notified that the subject property belongs to the United States Department of Housing and Urban Development (HUD). You are illegally occupying this home and must vacate it immediately. This property is not habitable in its current condition. There are various code violations present, all utilities are inactive and have not been tested for safety, a lead-based paint hazard exists, and the overall disrepair of the home presents a danger. Therefore, your occupancy presents a health, safety and fire hazard to you and the adjoining property owners.
>
> Failure to leave the premises will result in legal action against you which could include a criminal complaint for trespass as well as a civil action in ejectment.
>
> Please be advised that the Department has not granted authorization nor signed any agreements with the Kensington Welfare Rights Union to enter into or lease HUD owned properties to you or any other individual or family. I strongly suggest that you do not pay any rent money to them as they have no right to accept it from you.
>
> If you need emergency shelter, the City of Philadelphia Office of Homeless and Adult Services may be able to assist you.

Mariluz was shaken by the letter and its threats. She was terrified that she would be evicted before Christmas and that her children would spend the holiday back at St. Edward's, but without the comforts of the raised bed and living area, which was now torn down. But as soon as she checked with people on the war council, she found out that others had received the same letter. Cheri knew all about it, she was told, and had talked to the HUD people. Cheri had assured everyone that HUD was paralyzed by the federal shutdown and, in any case, the agency didn't have the guts to evict homeless people over the holidays.

That made sense to Mariluz. Who would put women and children on the street at Christmas? "Thank God for that stupid Congress," she said to Elba. Then she told the children that Christmas would be at home—meaning the Fairhill Street house—and that they would decorate the tree and open presents in front of the fireplace. On the twenty-first, after she picked up her welfare check, the entire family went shopping at the Caldor discount store on Aramingo Avenue, where all items were 30 percent off for Christmas. Mariluz bought a Pocahontas doll for Destiny, a toy radio microphone set and baby doll for Desiree, and a toy train and a blowup chair for Demitre. She gave Destiny a dollar to buy herself a gift; the girl selected a white Christmas ornament in the shape of a dove.

Later, Mariluz went to the dollar store and bought red ribbons to decorate the living room and tinsel for the tree. She bought a huge paper Santa Claus to hang on the front door and a *Happy New Year* sign to hang from the porch. She bought six angels for the tree, one for each child in the house. She bought a gold chain and cross for Cheri and three condoms for Katie, who had told her that what she wanted for Christmas was "to get laid, just once more, before I turn fifty."

When Mariluz got home, she hung a silver cross from a nail in the dining room. She found the six Polaroids of the children sitting with Santa at Skinny Joey's and hung them from the tree. Her friend Cass from the homeless organization came by to drop off a housewarming gift—a watercolor painted by Cass himself, of bright orange macaws resting on a green tree limb. Cass also brought over his color TV—a loan, he said. They set it up on a white TV stand that Mariluz had trash-picked from somebody's garbage pile on Fairhill Street, and the children sat down to watch *Sesame Street.*

The house was feeling more and more like a home. The war council had provided two electric heaters, which, combined with the kerosene heater, spread heat into the upstairs bedrooms. Someone had donated a huge red foldout futon, which was big enough to accommodate Mariluz, Elba, and the six children. The Empty the Shelters students had dropped off Christmas cards, which Mariluz and Elba had taped to the living room wall. Also attached to the wall were two homemade Christmas cards from Cass.

To Elba, Cass had written a verse:

> Though times are ruff and you think they will never get better,
> Pray to God no matter the weather,
> In Christ, through Christ, things will get better,
> You're a strong woman and you must hold on,
> Enjoy Christmas and the Holidays to come
> You and your children are all number ones.

To Mariluz, Cass had written:

> You guys are special to me,
> You bring joy into my heart
> Though times is ruff and hard
> Yet fight you must

You know that from the start
You have a home today
I'm happy and proud of all of you
Enjoy your home and coming holidays
Just remember
I'm with you in every way.

Cass was almost a regular member of the household. His health seemed good now, despite his AIDS, and he often dropped by to check on Mariluz and Elba. Sometimes he moved a heavy easy chair next to the door, blocking it for security, and slept there through the night.

There were other occasional guests, among them a homeless couple from the church whom Mariluz allowed to sleep over, against her better judgment. She kicked them out after one of them snuck upstairs while she was out Christmas shopping and stole $20 Elba had set aside for the escrow account.

"I must be losing my mind, letting those thieves in my house," Mariluz said later. "Maybe it's the Christmas spirit, I don't know, but fuck it. I'm not trusting anybody anymore, not Tent City people, not church people, nobody. I'm watching out for me and my kids, that's it."

Even so, Mariluz later allowed a different homeless couple to camp out in the house. She required them to help clean and watch the children, and she and Elba kept their money with them at all times.

In the final days before Christmas, Mariluz made sure that kerosene and food was delivered to the various takeover houses, and through J.R. and Tara, she kept abreast of developments at St. Edward's, where a handful of homeless men were still living. There were several disturbing visits to her new home by strangers. One man, claiming to be first on a waiting list to be awarded the house by HUD, knocked on the door and told Mariluz that she had to leave because he was due to move in. Another man came by, claiming to be the real estate agent in charge of listing the house; he told Mariluz she had to get out. A woman from DHS dropped by, asking questions about the children and craning her neck to look past Mariluz and into the living room. Mariluz managed to ward off all of them. She remembered what Cheri had said at the war council meeting. No one had a right to come into her house. She didn't have to answer anybody's questions. She was firm and polite, but she shut the door in her visitors' faces and went on with her life.

Two days before Christmas, one of the neighbors left a bag of Christmas toys on the porch. Mariluz was not certain which neighbor had left the gifts, but she was pleased to see that the KWRU letters she had distributed through the neighborhood had produced results. None of the toys seemed

appropriate for her children, so Mariluz took them to the church to be distributed to neighborhood children. There, she found J.R. and Tara asleep
on their mattress in Mariluz's former living area. They had been up until 4
A.M. delivering kerosene and food.

Mariluz shook them awake and asked them for an update on events
inside the church. She saw that some scruffy homeless men were sleeping
next to the altar and that Chicago had made a tent out of old sheets, which
retained so much heat from the blast of kerosene heater inside that
Chicago was wearing a T-shirt. She saw, too, that the old refrigerator was
still plugged in and still plastered with stickers advertising Les the Pretzel
Man's Best of Philly Awards. On the walls were two new signs:

*We are not a charity. If you to want help here, you must join the fight to end
poverty.*

The Meek Are Getting Ready.

When J.R. awoke, the first thing he uttered was a caustic reference to
the archdiocese.

"Did you hear?" he asked Mariluz. "The archdiocese came by and
wanted to give us two-point-five million dollars to build new houses for
everybody."

"Yeah, right," Mariluz said.

Actually, J.R. told her, two men from the archdiocese had come by to
ask when the rest of the homeless people intended to vacate the church.
The archdiocese was eager to reclaim the property, they said.

"They told me they were between a rock and a hard place, that they did-
n't want to evict anybody when it was so cold but that the archdiocese
wanted the church back now that most of the people were gone," J.R. said.
"They said they'd been buying time for us. They said it had been three
months since Cheri told them she'd be out in forty-eight hours, and they
had been so patient and understanding. They said they were the ones who
had kept the archdiocese from kicking us all out. They said please don't let
in any more homeless people, but I said, 'Hey, it's cold out there, what do
you want us to do, let them freeze to death?' They said there was room at
the shelters and the hospice, but I didn't want to have that old argument
again. So they just said, well, please tell the media how good the archdiocese has been about letting everybody stay in the church. And I'm thinking, Oh yeah, that's really what I'm gonna tell the world.

"Then they left. You know, they didn't even say Merry Christmas. They
didn't bring any food or Christmas presents. They just said, 'We'll be seeing
you.' And I said, 'Yeah, to throw us out on the street.' "

J.R. and Tara said they planned to stay at the church through Christmas
and possibly New Year's before moving into the HUD house assigned to

them. Chicago was planning to stay, too. "Why not? We got a tree," he said, emerging from his tent, where a talk show was airing a rowdy debate on overweight women and their husbands.

In the middle of the nearly deserted church, next to the overturned pews and Chicago's smoky little encampment, stood an eight-foot Christmas tree provided by the same volunteer who had donated the tree at Mariluz's new house. Somebody had decorated it with a few donated Christmas bulbs and plastic garlands. And at the foot of the tree was a sign that said, *A Home for the Holidays*.

Back home, Mariluz and Elba made plans for Christmas Eve. They put the children's presents under the tree and plugged in the tree lights. Elba cooked rice and beans on the kerosene heater, and Mariluz brought out salami and cheese and bread. Destiny came downstairs and complained that it was too cold in her room. Mariluz reminded her that she had worn her overcoat and boots inside the church. Now she walked around the house in her pajamas and slippers.

"If you want to go back and live in the church, we can take you and leave you there with J.R. and Tara," Mariluz told her.

"No, no, no!" Destiny screamed. "No—I want my own room. And I want to be where it's warm." She ran back upstairs to her room, where she flopped on her mattress and stared up at a photo of herself with some of the Empty the Shelters students, slowly reading the words the students had written on the border: WE LOVE YOU.

Mariluz swore to herself that she would never go back to the church, even if she got kicked out of her HUD house. She would get the union to find her another HUD house. Her children needed a proper home, with bedrooms and a kitchen and a front porch.

"I got a taste now of living on my own, so, really, I can't ever go back to the church," she told me. "I think we can stay here for a while. Katie told me she stayed seven months in a HUD house. That would be paradise to me. The kids would really feel like they had a home."

As long as the government did not cut her off from welfare, she said, she could survive. Once the children were older and did not need day care, she intended to go to school and become a pediatric nurse.

"Right now, welfare is what's saving me, saving the kids," she said. "It pays for the food and the clothes and a bunch of other little stuff. It won't pay for rent, so I don't see how people make it. Lucky for me, I got this house, which only costs me the thirty percent. But I can't even think about getting off welfare and getting a job till I get these kids taken care of."

She sat in the gloom of the living room for a long while, thinking about how young she still was—just twenty-nine—and how she had never imagined herself in such dismal circumstances. As a young woman, she never pictured herself homeless or on welfare. That was for poor people who couldn't take care of themselves.

"I never, ever thought I'd be homeless. I never thought I'd be living this way," she said. "I don't know what happened. I don't blame the kids. I don't even blame their fathers. They were no damn good anyway. I just wanted to have kids and raise them and love them. I guess that's what did it. But now they're my joy. I'm living for them now."

Mariluz looked at the tree and the gifts and the smiling photos of her children on Santa's lap.

"This is where I want to be," she said. "I'm gonna have Christmas Eve right here with my kids in my new home. That's what I've been working for all this time, ever since we set up Tent City and it was so hot and miserable. This is gonna be the best day of the year. We'll be the perfect little American family, at home, all warm and fat, singing Christmas carols and opening the presents under the tree."

On Christmas Eve, with flecks of wet snow staining the Underground Railroad sign in the window, Mariluz and Elba gathered their children next to the tree. They lit candles, which filled the room with a golden glow. They turned on the tree lights, which flickered like little stars. The children opened one gift each, and they shrieked with joy and surprise. Everyone sang carols until they got sleepy from the heat of the kerosene burner, which warmed them to their bones. Mariluz and Elba lay down on the futon, and all six children curled up around them, warm and safe for Christmas.

Cheri got back to Philadelphia just before New Year's. She looked thin and tired. She had developed an ear infection and strep throat on Christmas Eve. She had spent all of Christmas Eve and most of Christmas Day lying in misery on the sofa at her mother's house in Minneapolis. Cheri and Mark and her mother tried to have Christmas anyway, exchanging gifts and trying to get into the holiday spirit. Cheri gave her mother beans and rice. She gave Mark a book called *Believing in Myself.* On the title page she wrote what she called "a sappy little note," which said, "The most important thing you need to learn is to believe in yourself. I'm very proud to have a son like you. I hope you invest a lot of energy in your life believing in yourself, because that's all you've got." Inside the book was $100 in cash. Mark hugged his mother and cried a little bit and handed her a gift—a bottle of White Shoulders perfume.

"I was touched," Cheri said. "Usually all I get is a homemade card. Mark actually saved up some money for this."

Cheri was reviewing her Minnesota holiday for me as we sat inside a small diner on Girard Avenue, not far from her house on Randolph Street.

We met there often to discuss events at Tent City and, later, at the church and in the HUD houses. Cheri often retreated to the diner to get away from the constant demands of the union and the war council. But now, as she tried to catch up on everything that had happened during her few days out of town, she felt pressured and overwhelmed.

For one thing, there had been several fistfights among the homeless men camped out at the church. For another, the bags of Christmas gifts for KWRU members from the Main Line lady, which she had left at the church for safekeeping, had been stolen. And HUD was making more threats to evict people from the takeover houses. I had spoken on the phone to Karen Miller, the HUD representative in Philadelphia. She told me that while eviction efforts were "on hold" because of the government shut-down, HUD fully intended to remove the KWRU people in the near future.

"We don't intend to let them remain," Miller said. "They have illegally broken in and we can't allow them to continue to break the law. They are illegal."

Miller said Cheri was wrong to call the houses "abandoned." They were homes taken over by HUD, usually following foreclosure on an FHA loan, and offered for sale. The first opportunity to buy the homes was normally provided to nonprofit groups serving low-income people. In fact, Miller said, HUD had offered KWRU more than a year earlier an opportunity to lease the homes for $1 a year for use as transitional housing for the homeless. But KWRU would have to register as a nonprofit agency and meet other requirements, she said.

"They have shown no interest in working within the system," Miller said. "They were not interested in our offer. The rest of us live by the rules. They choose not to—for their own reasons."

Cheri was irritated by Miller's comments about HUD's offer of the $1-a-year program. She had read similar statements by Miller in the newspaper. What Miller did not mention, Cheri said, was the considerable adminstrative cost required to set up a certified nonprofit, and the money needed to run a program providing transitional housing. Even with donations from Skinny Joey and the Main Line ladies, KWRU didn't have that kind of money. "And even if we did, I'm not interested in becoming part of the HUD bureaucracy," Cheri said. "I'm fighting to tear down the bureaucracy, not join it."

In any case, Cheri did not believe Miller's threats to evict people from the takeover houses. She was certain that HUD would find ways to avoid confrontation—and the unsettling sight of TV footage showing federal marshals hauling homeless women and children out of government-owned homes.

As Cheri spoke, she seemed fatigued. She had lost weight, and her hips and legs were slimmer than before. When I asked her why she was so weary and drawn, she told me she was only sleeping two or three hours a night. And when she told me the reason, her explanation not only stunned me but also answered questions that had been nagging at me for months. It explained so much—how Cheri paid her rent and utilities, how she afforded flights to Minneapolis for her and Mark, why she disappeared on so many late nights. What Cheri told me was that she had been working for many months at what she called "dancing," but which she quickly made clear was topless dancing at strip bars. Cheri was a secret stripper.

"Oh, it's sick, I know," she said. "I'm taking money to exhibit my body. I feel like such a little hypocrite. I'm so conflicted by all this, I gotta tell somebody. I mean, I spoke at the NOW convention about sexual exploitation of women. I was invited to the Beijing women's conference to speak on women's rights. It's really hard to live with myself right now.

"I've always said, and always believed, that you do what you have to do to survive," she said. "If I took a nine-to-five job, the union would collapse. That's a fact. I'm not saying that because I think I'm so great, or whatever. But people rely on me twenty-four hours a day. If I had a nine-to-five job, the first crisis that came up, I have to take off and get there. And I'd be fired in a week. I belong right where I am—fighting for poor people's rights. If I have to dance up on a bar with a bunch of scummy guys watching me, I'll do it."

One of the most demeaning aspects of the profession, she said, was the job interview. She had been through several, for she had been fired from more than one club for failing to show for work due to some crisis on the lot or at the church. Basically, she said, the audition boiled down to stripping off her blouse and displaying herself to "some grubby guy in a cruddy bar."

"I tell myself to stay strong, because sometimes I feel like breaking down and sobbing," she said.

But she stuck with it, she said, because she could not earn so much money so quickly by any other legal means. Even though she had to split her tips fifty-fifty with management, she said, she sometimes came home with as much as $500 a night. On her worst nights, she cleared $200.

On many nights, Cheri recognized the faces of certain men at the bar. Some were people she had encountered in her ongoing battle with city authorities—Civil Affairs cops, Licenses and Inspection officials, firemen, City Hall bureaucrats. They recognized her, too, but everyone pretended to be strangers.

"I'm not really worried about these guys telling the world about me," Cheri said. "They're all married, and I don't think they want to have to explain to their wives what they were doing at a strip bar. And I guess they figure I won't rat on them because I need to keep things quiet, too. So I guess you would say we have an understanding. But I have had the Civil Affairs cops yell out my stage name when they see me on the street."

Cheri seemed ambivalent about being found out. Several people on the war council knew what she did late at night, and she had described her dancing to a local, independent film producer who was filming a half-hour documentary on KWRU. And, after some hestitation, she had decided that it was dishonest—and perhaps insulting—to keep her secret from Mark.

"Mark's a smart kid," she said. "He sees me leaving the house late at night, my nails done, my hair all fixed up, and I come sneaking back in at five A.M. He can figure out what's up. So I finally just told him. It was better coming from me rather than someone else. I discussed it with him and told him a lot of poor people got help from the money I made there. I said it was the only way I could think of to earn the money I need to support the two of us and still do the work that really matters to me. He said he understood. He said he was proud of me, and inspired that I cared enough about him to tell him the truth. Since then, we've pretty much left it unspoken between us. He knows I love him and I know he loves me. We'll be together always, and he knows that."

I asked Cheri what she thought the reaction might be once her nightly occupation became widely known, as she knew it ultimately would be.

"Oh, I guess people will say this is some deep dark psychological defect, a secret need to exploit myself or some other psychobullshit," she said. "I doubt whether they'll see it for what it is—economic necessity."

She lit a cigarette and blew gray smoke into the moist, greasy air of the diner. A smile played on her lips. "And anyway," she said, "who says welfare mothers won't find work, huh?"

CHAPTER FOURTEEN

Money Williams

D ecember arrived bitter and harsh, with some of the earliest and heaviest snows in the recorded history of Philadelphia. In the weeks leading up to Christmas, the city was deluged with snow and ice and freezing rain. The snow hid the gulleys and cracks in the sidewalks along Allegheny Avenue, and people tripped and fell as they struggled up the hill toward the Chinese store. For a while, the snow also obscured the trash and garbage that collected in the gutters, briefly providing the street with a fresh and virgin appearance. But the white patina was quickly covered with a black layer of soot and street grime, and Allegheny Avenue looked forlorn and vaguely menacing under the bare sycamores.

Odessa made her way out into the bleak landscape every morning. It was cold and miserable outside, but still she had to forage for food bargains, pick up her welfare check, take Danielle to the doctor's, visit her own doctor, or check on her mother, and make sure the eight grandchildren now living with her got to school and back. There was also the matter of Christmas gifts. After a process that had begun the previous summer, she had paid for and retrieved from layaway most of the presents she had set aside for Jim, Kevin, Delena, and Brian. She had sold the $50 used stereo cassette player she had bought for Jim; it fetched $75, which she used to help finance a new, $129.95 CD stereo player from B.J.'s Wholesale Club. Jim had asked her for a certain expensive brand of sneakers, but Odessa had seen the same brand on the feet of the drug dealers on Wendle Street, so she told Jim he would be getting no sneakers. She would find him some no-brand sneakers in the after-Christmas sales at the discount store.

From the welfare check she had received on the first of December, Odessa paid the balance on Kevin's $90 worth of football gear, along with Delena's $29.99 Secret Diary at Kmart. From her October and November checks, she had paid the $79 for a stereo she had put on layaway for Delena. Her second October check had paid for Brian's $109.99 pinball game. She still had to find a way to pay for the $19.99 remote control cars she intended to buy for Brian and Geedy, along with a walkie-talkie set for

Brian. To prevent the grandchildren from snooping in her closets, Odessa hid some gifts at her mother's house and others at Israel's temporary quarters in the ramshackle row house next door at 712 Allegheny.

Now the time had come to get a Christmas tree, and the children nagged at Odessa to buy one. A small forest of trees had sprung up at K and A, where a shabby side lot had sprouted six-foot firs and balsams. Every time Odessa passed the lot on her way to the clinic or meat market, one of the children would rise up from the backseat and cry out, "Stop! We need to get a Christmas tree!" But by the second week of December, Odessa was down to her last $4, with several days to go before her next welfare check was due to arrive. She told the children, softly but forcefully, that they had to choose: presents or a tree. Glumly, each one chose gifts in lieu of a tree.

To raise money, Odessa turned to hacking. She still had half a tank of gas in the Caprice, so she took up a position in the parking lot of Cousin's Food Market. She had obtained the permission of the store manager to solicit departing customers, offering them rides home for a few dollars. Odessa knew all too well from her days as a carless food shopper that getting to the food store was one thing but getting home with a load of food was quite another. She knew that people lugging bags of groceries were in no mood to wait in the cold and snow to take a crowded city bus. She stood at the door of Cousin's and said softly to each departing customer: "Hacking." There were competing offers from other hackers, but Odessa planted her big body in the doorway so that she was the first person a departing customer encountered. Of the several dozen people she offered rides, seven accepted. Her fares were higher than the bus, but lower than a taxi. She negotiated a fare for each shopper—$5 to $10—based on the distance to their home and the route Odessa would have to take to get there. She offered a slightly lower fee for the elderly. In seven trips, she earned $62, plus $5 in food stamps from one welfare mother. She spent $20 on a huge Christmas turkey and another $30 on a ham massive enough to feed her family for days. She gave $10 to Israel to buy kerosene, for the living room heater was empty and the house was cold and damp. The remaining $2 was for incidentals—a Pepsi or a bag of roasted peanuts from Donald the Peanut Man—until check day.

The next afternoon, Odessa drove Elaine to the thrift store to price suitcases. Elaine was sending her fifteen-year-old son, Raysonno, to a Job Corps program in Pittsburgh. She wanted him out of North Philadelphia, where a boy his age was just as likely as not to get into trouble. The Jobs Corps tour was for two years, and it included a GED program, which meant that Raysonno would have his high school diploma before he was eighteen. Elaine picked through the suitcases at the thrift store until she found a sturdy one for $3. Then she and Odessa went to the discount store, where Elaine used portions of her welfare check to buy Raysonno deodorant, toothpaste, underwear, and socks.

That evening, next to the glowing kerosene heater in Odessa's living room, Raysonno sat down next to his grandmother to tell her good-bye. Odessa reached into her pocketbook and took out a handful of telephone calling cards she had bought for $10 each with her November SSI check. Each one was good for a ten-minute call from Pittsburgh to Philadelphia. Odessa hugged Raysonno and told him, "Now you make sure you call your mom and your grandma." Raysonno took the cards and mumbled his thanks. He was a tall, lanky boy with long arms and a narrow face, though Odessa still called him "Pie," short for his childhood nickname "Pie Face." He was different from Elaine's other five children, not only because he was the oldest but because he was born of a different father than the others. Now Raysonno was the first to leave home. He seemed eager to get to Pittsburgh, and he stood up awkwardly and moved toward the door.

"Just a minute," Odessa said, grabbing the boy's arm. "Go up to my bedroom and get my blue suitcase." That was Odessa's special suitcase; she had owned it for years, and she saved it for important trips, such as visiting her relatives in Georgia. Now she wanted Raysonno to have it, for she believed the thrift shop suitcase Elaine had bought was not sufficient for a young man about to embark on adulthood in faraway Pittsburgh.

Raysonno bounded up the stairs and returned with a blue suitcase. He opened it and held it above his head and watched lint and dust fall softly onto his grandmother's trash-picked living room carpet. Odessa ignored the mess. "You take care of that suitcase," she said. "It's the love of my life. Anything happens to that suitcase, I'll *walk* to Pittsburgh and hunt you down. You understand me?"

Raysonno bit his lip to keep from laughing. "Yes'm," he said, and he ducked through the vestibule and out the door, the suitcase under his arm, as his grandmother sang out, "I'm waking you up to go to the bus station at six o'clock sharp!"

Odessa was up at five-thirty the next morning. She walked up to Elaine's, wearing only a sweater and sweatpants in the bitter morning cold, and woke up Raysonno. She looked around and was dismayed to see her blue suitcase lying empty on the floor. Raysonno had not yet packed for his trip. Odessa rousted the boy out of bed and helped him pack his things while Elaine made him a quick breakfast. As Raysonno ate, Odessa rushed back home to dress and feed Danielle. Then she put Israel in charge of her grandchildren, pulled on her heavy denim coat, and made her way slowly across the icy, rutted sidewalk to make sure her Caprice started in the frigid morning air. It took several grinding turns of the ignition key to bring the engine to life, and it was several more minutes before the heat cut through the frost inside the windows.

At the bus station, there were half a dozen more teenaged boys embarking on the same Job Corps trip. They were all trying to look languid and unconcerned, but Odessa could sense their uncertainty in the way their eyes studied the floor and the way they shifted their thin bodies in the hard plastic seats. Raysonno was anxious, too, though he tried to hide it. This would be his first extended trip away from home. Odessa did not fuss over him in front of the other boys. She just hugged him and reminded him to call home when he arrived. She left him standing there, clutching his blue suitcase and telephone calling cards, waiting for the bus to Pittsburgh.

The sight of the boys leaving home had a powerful effect on Odessa. As she drove home through the icy streets, she was drawn back to her own childhood years, when she had traveled back and forth from Georgia to Philadelphia. Events from her youth rushed back at her, and suddenly North Philadelphia seemed cold and hostile. She longed for the warmth and red dirt and lush trees of her youth in the Georgia countryside. She recalled with stunning clarity episodes from decades earlier. She remembered the day she stole toys from a white lady's house when she was nine years old. She remembered that her mother spanked her all the way from the ditch where Odessa had hidden the toys to the front porch of the white lady's house, where Bertha made Odessa return the toys and apologize. To this day Odessa was thankful that her mother had punished her so severely, for she never again had the desire to take what was not hers. Odessa remembered, too, the day she watched the Ku Klux Klan march around the county courthouse after beating a black man to death. She was seven years old, and she had remarked to her mother that the men were wearing such beautiful Catholic robes. And now she recalled what Bertha had said to her: "Catholic? Honey, that's the Klan. Those people will come burn your house down and kill you."

Now Odessa remembered the desperation she had felt as a teenager to leave Georgia to escape the Klan and the fierce hatred of some white people in the hard countryside. She recalled the relief that had washed over her when she arrived in North Philadelphia, where no one could recall ever having seen a KKK march. She remembered how comforted she had felt when her mother took her at age nine to work the farms of southern New Jersey, and she recalled very clearly the Italian man she had met there who treated her with such kindness that she never forgot him or his name: Jim. He was a deeply tanned, middle-aged man with crow's-feet around his eyes and a drooping walrus mustache. He was a lifelong farmworker and the most adroit and productive picker Odessa ever saw. Jim used to challenge her to picking contests, letting her win. On most days he brought his own lunch, and he included in it a hot Italian sandwich for Odessa. She still remembered the hot sting of the peppers on her tongue. She could still hear Jim's soft voice and his deep soothing tones. Odessa always told herself, even as a child, that other girls had dolls and toys and security blankets, but she had Jim. He was her best friend. Even now, as a great-grandmother, she sometimes included Jim in the prayers she said every night.

When Odessa arrived home, she tried to shake her melancholy mood. Thinking of Jim and her days in Georgia had left her feeling homesick and vaguely adrift. She felt a strong urge to gather up her grandchildren and load the Caprice and move everybody down to Georgia. Sometimes, she thought, her grown children demanded too much from her; just that week, five boxes of ground pepper she bought had disappeared, taken by Elaine and Joyce and Israel, who did not replace what they had used. Odessa tried to hold off these unpleasant and selfish thoughts by forcing herself to think about Christmas and cooking and gifts for the children. And she decided to turn on the television to catch the morning news programs. After the usual recitation of fires and car wrecks and murders, the announcer began talking about school lunches. Odessa turned up the volume. She heard the man say that Republicans in Congress wanted to cut school lunches and medical assistance to the poor. Odessa felt her temper rise. Where did they get the nerve to mess with poor kids' lunches? If her grandchildren didn't have free lunches and breakfasts at school, she would have to buy food with the money she now spent on their school supplies and snacks. She was dumbfounded that people in Congress would deny food to poor children. And she refused to believe they would go so far as to take away medical assistance to the poor. If Odessa had to pay for the dozens of trips to the clinic she made every year for herself and her grandchildren and great-grandchildren, she would be thousands of dollars in debt. If she was a cursing person, she would have cursed those congressmen.

"I don't know what else to think about them except that they're selfish people who don't have any idea what it's like to be on DPA and have to wonder where your next meal is coming from," she told me later. "It seems like they don't care about nobody but themselves. But they'll have to account for themselves someday. I believe everyone has to face God someday, and so will they. A day of reckoning is coming."

As she spoke, someone slid a piece of paper through the mail chute in the vestibule door. Odessa walked over and picked it up. It was a flyer advertising *Job Opportunities*. She unfolded it and read: "Would you stuff

300 envelopes every week for $600? Two dollars for each envelope you stuff! Simple, pleasant work you can do at home!" Odessa tossed the flyer on the sofa. Did they really expect people to believe somebody would actually pay anyone $2 to stuff an envelope? "This has got to be one of those scams, like on 20/20, where they take money first from old people as a down payment on the 'job,' and then they run off with the money, and the money-earning program never happens," Odessa said.

Also in the vestibule was a copy of the *Philadelphia Daily News* someone had tossed inside. Odessa stared at the paper. She didn't take the *Daily News*. Nobody did. You had to buy it at the newsstand. Then she remembered. A woman from the paper had called her and interviewed her for a story she was writing about IMPACT, the program on Indiana Avenue for low-income residents where Odessa had bought low-cost home repair materials. The reporter had interviewed her about the paint, plywood, and kitchen cabinets she had bought from IMPACT and had Willie install.

Now the story was in the *Daily News*, a copy of which apparently had been left inside Odessa's vestibule by someone who had seen her name. Odessa read the article and was surprised to see that it referred to her at one point as "Money Williams." It was right there in a little box tucked within the body of the story: " 'If it wasn't for this place, my money just wouldn't reach. I certainly would not have been this far along on the house.'—Homeowner Money Williams." Odessa read the story again and realized that a careless editor had lifted the quote from a section of the story that read, "Money Williams didn't have." The reporter meant that Odessa Williams didn't have money. And now Odessa was known to readers of the *Daily News* as Money Williams.

All that afternoon and into the evening, friends and relatives called Odessa's house and asked to speak to Money Williams. They teased her about her new nickname and asked to borrow money now that she was apparently so well-to-do. A few relatives asked for a refund on their contributions to her Thanksgiving dinner. Odessa told each one: "I wish there was a reason to call me Money. I wouldn't be sitting here talking to you. I'd be living with all my children in a great big house in the Northeast."

The stream of calls and the gentle ribbing helped to shake Odessa out of her malaise. She felt refreshed and full of purpose again. She decided she would not let a lack of money dampen her grandchildren's Christmas. She went to see Warney, the Puerto Rican man who had loaned her the money to get Israel out of jail. Warney was willing to loan Odessa $200, but he told her he was obliged to charge her his customary 25 percent interest fee because he did not consider Christmas expenses a true emergency. Posting bail, paying emergency medical bills—that was an emergency, he said. Odessa agreed, and they arranged for her to repay the loan, with the $50 interest, after New Year's. Odessa would get not only her welfare check by then, but her SSI check and Brian's, too.

With the money in hand, Odessa gathered her grandchildren at home and told them that it was now possible for the family to have a Christmas tree. But, she told them, they had to agree that Odessa would spend $5 less for each of them on their incidental Christmas gifts in order to cover the cost of the tree. Odessa did not truly intend to cut back on their gifts, but she wanted to instill in them a sense of common sacrifice. The children eagerly agreed, and they begged her to drive them to K and A to pick out a tree.

Odessa asked Israel to go with them to help get the tree home, but Israel was busy trying to repair his van so that he would be able to get to work if a burner's job turned up. Odessa walked next door to ask Elaine to help, for Elaine was nearly as strong as Israel. Odessa pushed open Elaine's heavy front door and yelled up the steps: "Elaine! Let's go! You got to help me get the kids' Christmas tree!" Elaine's voice drifted down from her upstairs bedroom: "Go away, Mama, I'm tired." She was still in bed, though it was nearly noon. Odessa yelled back: "It's almost lunchtime and you're not out of bed? What's wrong with you? You sick?" Elaine's voice was louder this time: "*No!* I'm just worn out. Leave me alone!"

Odessa shook her head and walked back out the front door, slamming it and scattering McDonald's wrappers in the drifts of snow on Elaine's porch. She would haul the tree home herself. She hurried back home and piled her grandchildren into the car and drove to the tree lot at K and A, where trees had been unloaded from a truck, their branches still folded against one another. Brian and Kevin insisted on a fat six-foot tree listed at $25. Odessa told them her limit was $20, but the boys begged and pleaded for the tree. Odessa pulled out a $20 bill and told the tree man it was all she had. The man could see how much the tree meant to Brian and Kevin, and he relented and sold it for $20, telling Odessa, "Merry Christmas, Grandma."

Back home, Odessa and the children decorated the tree with bulbs and lights Odessa had trash-picked and stored in the basement. The tree seemed to give the house a warm and festive glow. It blocked the dreary view of Allegheny Avenue out the front window. The plastic blue-and-red garlands reflected the bright lights and pierced the gloom of the gray winter days. Odessa clipped a few branches from the bottom of the tree to make tiny wreaths, which she attached to the banister leading to the second floor. She took some of the plastic garlands and draped them across the fireplace mantel, where she had already begun to arrange Christmas cards, and where she had attached thrift store stockings for each grandchild. Finally, she thought, the house looked like Christmas.

*   *   *

One afternoon less than three weeks before Christmas, Odessa got a phone call from Brenda. She was locked up again, this time for soliciting for prostitution. She needed money to pay the fine.

"Mama," she said, "can you come get me out?"

"No, I can't," Odessa said. "You got yourself in there. You can get yourself out. If you have to pay a fine, figure out a way to pay it yourself, because you're not getting a nickel from me. I'm not going to take money from your kids at Christmastime and throw good money after bad just because you got yourself locked up. You are not going to ruin Christmas for your kids."

When Odessa told her grandchildren that their mother was locked up again, they said a surprising thing: they preferred to have their mother in jail rather than out on the streets, where she might be stabbed, robbed, or murdered by a john. In jail, they reasoned, Brenda was at least in a place where she would not have easy access to drugs—and where she would not be able to raise money by prostituting herself. They even held out hope that she would stay locked up long enough to get into a drug rehab program, like their uncle Darryl.

But Brenda was quickly released under the city's jail cap, which routinely freed defendants charged with nonviolent or petty crimes. Odessa found out this bit of news from her mother, who told her that Brenda had dropped by her house, offering to do chores for money and asking for food. With Brenda back on the streets again, Odessa had one more thing to worry about as she prepared for Christmas. There were already plenty of troubles weighing on her, most of them involving money or lack of it. Joyce had come to her complaining that her welfare check was not enough to pay her rent and food and utilities, and also pay for Christmas gifts for Geedy and Curtis. She asked if Odessa could help pay for them. Israel, too, had asked his mother to contribute to the purchase of gifts for his four boys. Israel's work as a burner was still spotty, and his occasional jobs did not provide enough cash for anything beyond essentials such as food and kerosene. His boys needed hats and gloves for winter; so, too, did Odessa's four grandchildren.

One cold afternoon less than two weeks before Christmas, Odessa and I were warming ourselves next to her kerosene heater when she detailed for me her money problems. She was worried that she would run out of money for kerosene; already, the kids had to wear their overcoats in the house on days when she had trouble scraping together $5 to send Israel to the gas station for kerosene. She told me she was determined to have a proper Christmas for her grandchildren, even if that meant asking for money. And that was what she was about to do, she said. She was going to ask me for a loan. It was plain from the tight, strained look on her face that it pained her to ask me such a question. She quickly explained that this was to be a loan that she would repay once her January checks arrived. And she made a point of saying she intended to pick up a few more dollars by hacking at Cousin's, by driving elderly neighbors to the welfare office, and by driving her crippled brother, Charles, on his errands. She seemed to feel a need to prove to me that she was a woman determined to provide for herself without handouts, as if I had just met her—and had not witnessed her resourcefulness and resiliency all these months. I tried to put her at ease, telling her that of course I would loan her money, which she could repay when her finances were well in order, whether in January or beyond. "Is a hundred dollars enough?" I asked. Odessa's face relaxed and she let herself smile. The bright new lights on the Christmas tree reflected in her spectacles like stars in her eyes. "Sounds like a winner," she said.

The next afternoon, we drove to the Valu-Plus store on Kensington Avenue. It was the sort of cheap discount outlet where items made in Malaysia and Mexico were tossed into huge metal bins, with cardboard signs advertising low, low prices. The store was tucked beneath the superstructure of the El, where the street was so dark in winter that even the harsh fluorescent lights that stayed on all day could not cut through the damp gloom. That dim stretch of asphalt under the El, in fact, was one of the areas Brenda often trolled when attempting to entice men who drove slowly past in the perpetually stalled traffic under the El.

It was cold and bare inside the Valu-Plus, where welfare women trailed by children were poking through the bins, screaming at the children to be quiet. Odessa was pleased to discover discount faux ski gloves on sale in one bin and polyester knit caps in another. With the $100 I had given her, she was able to buy four sets of gloves for Israel's boys at $4.99 each, plus a set of thermal underwear for Israel in case he found an outdoor job. To help her stretch the money, I bought three more pairs for Jim, Kevin, and Brian, plus a matching pink glove, cap, and scarf set for Delena. I also included a pair of gloves for Israel, whose own work gloves were badly worn. Odessa found knit caps on sale for $2.99, and she swiftly scooped up the last eight for the eight grandchildren under her roof. Before she could get to the checkout counter, I took the caps from her shopping basket and paid for them, over Odessa's protests. I told her to save her money for last-minute Christmas emergencies. She spotted a small heaping of boxed candy canes on sale, three for $1. She quickly bought three boxes—one to decorate the Christmas tree and two to fill her grandchildren's stockings.

Though it was only midafternoon, darkness was falling by the time Odessa hauled her bags of gloves and hats to the Caprice parked beneath the El. She needed to be at home to greet the children when they returned from school, but she still needed to buy gifts for Brian and Geedy. She knew that Jim would take charge if she was not home, so she decided to finish her Christmas shopping while she still had cash in her hands. She drove through the slanting shadows beneath the El and made her way to a Radio Shack outlet on Aramingo Avenue. There she found, to her relief, that the remote-controlled Flame Thrower III race car sets were still on sale for $19.99 and still in plentiful supply. She had feared that last-minute Christmas shoppers would have snapped them up by now. Odessa took the first two sets from the top of the pile and paid for them with two $20 bills. She knew it was extravagant to be spending so much money on toys, but they were for Brian and Geedy, the youngest kids, and Odessa believed strongly that Christmas was for the smallest and most needy of God's children.

There was just enough time, and just enough cash, for Odessa to drop by Cousin's on the way home. She needed food for dinner, and she knew Cousin's had pig's feet for sale. All of her grandchildren loved pig's feet, and so did Israel. It would be a pre-Christmas treat. She selected a good-sized package of pig's feet, and she used her change to pay for a bag of pink beans to go with them. She hurried home and put water on to boil the pig's feet and the beans, but when she told everyone about the dinner surprise, the children paid no attention to her. They were preoccupied with the candy canes. They had hung them from every tree branch, and now they watched intently as the plastic covers of the candy canes fractured the tree lights into sprays of red and green that seemed to paint everything and everyone in the little room with the colors of Christmas.

That weekend, which was the last weekend before Christmas, almost everyone in the house fell ill. Odessa was awakened early on Saturday morning by a pressure on her chest so heavy and insistent that she thought for a moment that Danielle was sleeping on top of her. Her lungs were tight and congested, and her throat burned. She sensed that her blood pressure was elevated, and she feared she was having another stroke. But as she stirred awake and her head cleared, she realized that it was only a cold, or perhaps the flu. She had had a flu shot earlier that week, and the doctor had warned her that she might feel poor as a result. And it had turned so cold—the temperatures were in the teens, with winds that rattled the windows and ice that formed a hard, treacherous veneer across the sidewalks—that she knew it would take a miracle to keep everyone in the family healthy until Christmas.

From the boys' bedroom, Odessa heard coughing and gasping. She made her way down the hallway and looked into the cramped room to see Jim and Kevin lying facedown on their mattress, sniffling and hacking. Brian was on the new foldout mattress that Odessa had just trash-picked for him. His underwear was soaked through with urine that had spread into a dark circle beneath his thin hips. He was coughing and rubbing his eyes. In the next bedroom, Delena was still asleep, her breath squeezing out in sharp rasps. Odessa walked back into her own bedroom, where Danielle was feverish, as usual, with her nose clogged with dried mucus. Downstairs, two of Israel's boys, Steven and Ray-Ray, were sick, too.

Odessa found her medical assistance card and told each one of her sick grandchildren to get dressed and washed up and get ready to pile into the Caprice for the trip to the clinic at K and A. There, after a long wait, the doctor gave Odessa a huge bottle of cough syrup and several packages of Tylenol and told her to send everyone back to bed. On the way home, Kevin leaned out the back window and vomited down the side of the car. The whole mess quickly froze and adhered to the side of the door, where it remained, brittle and hard, until well into the new year.

When Odessa got back home, the front door was wide open, despite the bitter cold. What was Israel doing—trying to heat all of Allegeny Avenue? As she pulled the Caprice into the space at the curb, Odessa looked up and saw gray smoke filling the vestibule and seeping out onto the porch. No— not again, she thought. She refused to consider the possibility that her home was on fire—not at Christmas. She screamed at the kids to get out of the car and she threw open the driver's door and tried to make her heavy legs hurry across the icy, rutted sidewalk and up her front steps. As she reached the vestibule, she smelled something greasy and oily in the smoke that was billowing up inside. The heater! She rushed into the living room, her eyes burning from the smoke. She found the heater next to the stairway and fumbled to turn it off. She was surprised to feel that it was cold. It wasn't turned on.

She looked toward the kitchen, where the smoke was thicker and darker. She hurried inside and saw smoke rising up from the stove. One of the burners was lit, and above it lay a smoking skillet. Odessa grabbed the pan and shoved it into the sink and turned on the water. When the smoke had died down, she saw several black shapes in the skillet. She looked closer and saw they were sausages. Israel! He had left his breakfast sausages burning.

Odessa felt like strangling her son. He had nearly burned down her house—and maybe his own temporary quarters next door, too. The entire house smelled of smoke, the skillet was ruined, the kitchen would have to be cleaned up before Christmas, and the trash-picked green curtains Odessa had put up for Thanksgiving would have to be taken down and cleaned. As Odessa stood in kitchen, waving her arms to clear the smoke, Israel emerged, looking sheepish. He said he had gone to his place next door for a just a minute to check on something, and had forgotten about the sausages. Odessa glared at him and thought for a moment about smacking him with her ruined skillet, but instead she simply said, "You can't keep two things in your head at the same time, can you?" But she felt herself smiling as she said it, and Israel grinned, too, as he set about cleaning up the kitchen.

Later that day, one of Odessa's nieces from the neighborhood told her something that left her feeling as exposed and as threatened as the stove fire. Somebody had broken into the Chinese store. They had climbed onto the roof, cut all the way down through the ceiling, and dropped down inside. They cleaned out the petty cash drawer and stole loads of food, sodas, batteries, and beepers. Odessa made her way up the slick sidewalk to the Chinese store to see for herself, and sure enough, there was a hole in the roof and a sign on the door that read, *Close*.

Odessa felt bad for the Korean couple who ran the place—the Lees— but she felt pain for her block, too. She was considered the unofficial block captain, and she prided herself on keeping the block safe from the violence and mayhem that emanated from the drug corners at either end. Now she felt violated by the brazen robbery at Lees'. And the temporary closing of the store also meant that her older grandchildren would have to venture into the other corner store—the one where the Eighth Street drug dealers congregated—every time she sent them to fetch a Pepsi or a can of tuna. The break-in had direct consequences for Brian, too. He had just persuaded Mrs. Lee to pay him $1 every day after school to sweep out the store and straighten up the shelves.

That evening, Odessa got her pliers and screwdriver and tried to fix the broken latch on her vestibule door. Her nephew Bo had promised to repair it, but he had not. So now Odessa struggled with the screwdriver to make certain that the latch closed securely, or at least tightly enough to deter thieves so cunning that they cut through rooftops. She also opened her bedroom safe and checked the clip of derringer-sized bullets in her tiny, white-handled .22-caliber Colt pistol. If anyone tried to break in, she would not hesitate to shoot them.

A few days before Christmas, Odessa realized that she had not heard from Brenda since the day she had been set free from jail following the prostitution arrest. It wasn't like Brenda to stay away so long, especially in winter, when she often came by in search of food and warmth. Odessa called her mother, who said she, too, was concerned, for Brenda had not been by her place either. That was truly out of character. Because Bertha lived closer to Kensington Avenue than Odessa did, it was a short walk from the alleys where Brenda bought her drugs to her grandmother's row house on Randolph Street. And Bertha was more tolerant of Brenda than Odessa was; Brenda knew she could eat and rest at her grandmother's without being put to hard labor, as she often was at Odessa's.

With her Christmas shopping finished, Odessa had planned to spend the remaining days before Christmas safe and warm in her house, wrapping presents and cooking for the holidays. She had enough money from her December SSI check to send Israel out for kerosene every other day, and to stretch her food budget until Christmas, when there would be enough leftovers to last through New Year's. But now she knew she had to go out into the cold to check on Brenda. Her daughter was the type of hardheaded person who would stand out in the wind and snow until she had turned enough tricks to buy a few vials of crack. She imagined one of the city crews finding Brenda dead and stiff in some doorway, a crack pipe frozen to her lips.

The first place Odessa drove to was Sergeant Street in Kensington, where Brenda spent most nights in the company of her boyfriend, Jeff, in a rotting two-story brick row house. Jeff's father in New Jersey owned the house, according to Brenda, and he allowed Jeff to live there in return for Jeff's staying out of New Jersey. Though Jeff was a crackhead, he was a functioning crackhead, and he managed to show up most days for his four-to-midnight shift as a fry cook. Jeff was already at work by the time Odessa made her way through the snow to the row house stoop and banged her gloved fist on the rickety door. There was no answer, but Odessa heard muffled voices inside. Jeff operated the row house as a combination crack house and flophouse; addicts and hookers drifted off the streets and paid him a few dollars to sleep or smoke there. Now they were rustling around at the sound of someone at the door. Odessa knew what they were up to in there, and it repulsed her. But she pounded again and again until the worn, sunken face of a woman appeared through a crack in the door frame.

"Brenda here?" Odessa asked.

"Nope," the woman said. She had an attitude of vague boredom, but she stood patiently and awaited more questions.

"Have you seen her?" Odessa asked.

"Maybe she on Front Street," the woman said. Brenda sometimes pulled tricks on Front Street.

"I know where to look," Odessa said.

"Or maybe at the mission," the woman added, trying to be helpful. "She always go to the mission."

Brenda often went to the St. Francis Inn, a mission on Kensington Avenue that provided hot meals for the homeless. Odessa thanked the woman for her help and drove toward Kensington Avenue, past the Chinese stores with the Asian faces peering behind metal safety bars, past the bodegas with loitering young men looking huge and clumsy in their oversized black Starter coats, and past curbside posters advertising an appearance that very week by boxer Mike Tyson at a gym on Howard Street not far from Bertha Boone's row house. Odessa parked under the El and made her way on foot through the carloads of men honking at the prostitutes on the sidewalk, who were struggling to keep warm in their short skirts. Odessa glanced to make sure Brenda was not among them. She walked on, holding down her wool hat against the fierce December wind, until she reached a group of ragged, freezing men who stood outside the crumbling walls of the St. Francis Inn, stomping their feet as they waited to be fed. On the wall above their heads, where the steam from their bodies hovered like a tiny rain cloud, someone had written, *All Witches Shall Fall by the Sword—Rev. 19.*

In the line, Odessa recognized an old friend from Howard Street—a tall, shambling man in a worn overcoat who went by the nickname of Cincinnati. Cincinnati was a neighbor of Bertha Boone's who had grown up with Brenda. Odessa knew him as a good and generous man, but he was also a sniffer—he sniffed embalming fluid from a rag to get high. Odessa greeted him stiffly and asked if he had seen Brenda.

"No, Mom, I ain't seen her in days," Cincinnati said. He turned and addressed some of the men in line and asked if any among them had seen Brenda. They removed their stocking caps and shook their heads somberly, as if paying respects to the dead. "Nope," they all said.

"You ought to look up in the alley," Cincinnati said, gesturing up Kensington Avenue. "She hangs there when it gets real cold like this."

Odessa drove up and down Kensington Avenue and over to Front Street, pulling to the curb at each block and peering through the gloom at the narrow alleys filled with garbage and black snow, the remote sort of places where Brenda sometimes huddled to escape the wind. In some of the alleys and door wells Odessa saw glassy-eyed women and a few bedraggled men, but not Brenda. She decided to drive down to the Kensington Bible Church, where on most Sundays Brenda and Jeff endured an hourlong sermon in exchange for a hot breakfast and a cold lunch to go. ("They sit there real quiet and listen to the sermon, but it don't take," Odessa said.) Sometimes Brenda wandered into the church on weekdays, hoping for a free meal. But when Odessa stopped and looked inside, the place was empty.

She drove on to a community resource center in a shabby storefront under the El, where the staff sometimes let prostitutes stand inside to get warm. There were indeed a few prostitutes inside, smoking cigarettes and blowing the warm smoke on their shriveled fingers. But Brenda was not among them, and none of the staff people could recall seeing her in many days.

Odessa got back in the Caprice and tried to warm her hands in the sputtering air of the defroster at the base of the windshield. Her hands were starting to go numb. Her toes burned from the cold, and her legs ached from climbing in and out of the car. She decided to make one more swing through Brenda's customary zone of operation, from Kensington Avenue to Front Street and across to Howard Street. Then she would have to get home before she collapsed from cold and exhaustion.

"I have to admit to myself she's as low as you can go," Odessa said bitterly, staring through the windshield at the gray landscape of junked cars and abandoned factories and collapsing row houses near Front Street. "She's out there selling her body for a few pennies, and she's probably holed up in one of her little hiding spots, not even caring that somebody cares about her. I've tried talking to her. Her sisters have all talked to her, telling her how wrong it is to have sex with all those men, and dangerous, too. I can't imagine myself getting that low. How does she live with herself? I don't know, I guess she's so used to it now she doesn't feel anything anymore. It's nothing to her. She doesn't have any shame anymore."

Odessa was starting to cry now, and she dabbed at her eyes with her thick gloves. She always cried during the holidays, she said. Her tears made it difficult for her to see the street, which was streaked with dirty snow and ice, so she slowed the car and drove slowly toward Howard Street. She had to see her mother. Bertha always knew what to say about Brenda.

Bertha was huddled in her living room, wrapped in a blanket as she sat in her easy chair watching *One Life to Live* on TV. Her two crippled sons sat in silence, staring in the dark room at the soft glow of the TV. On the dining room table, next to the kerosene heater, Bertha's son-in-law Ollie sat boning a chicken. Odessa walked in without knocking, leaned down to kiss her mother, and asked, "You seen Brenda yet?"

"Still hasn't showed," Bertha said.

The two of them sat in silence for a few minutes, watching the soap opera. Then they tried to recall precisely how many days it had been since Brenda was last seen on Howard Street. With the Christmas rush, they had lost track.

"Been four, five days now," Bertha said, bringing her long forefinger to her chin as she counted the days. "It was the day when I told her to clean out that back bedroom. What day was that, Ollie?"

"Sunday," Ollie said without looking up from the chicken.

"Sunday," Bertha repeated. "All she did in that bedroom was fold up a few clothes. When I told her she had to do a lot more than that, she walked out and she hasn't come back. But that's Brenda. She'll be back when she's cold or hungry."

Odessa told her mother that she believed Brenda's disappearance was more serious this time. She usually did not stay gone for more than a day or two. She mentioned the four homeless people who had frozen to death.

"You out on those drugs, and you don't know if you're cold or not," Odessa said.

"And you don't care," Bertha said.

"Right," Odessa said. "So she could be out there laying in the snow, freezing to death. Ain't a one of her so-called friends who'd lift a finger to help her, either."

"Those people don't care nothing about nothing, except where they're gonna get their drugs next," Bertha said, staring at the soap opera.

Odessa told her mother about her fruitless search and mentioned that she planned to look for Brenda again the next day. Bertha offered to help, but Odessa told her it wasn't necessary. All she asked was that Bertha call her if Brenda showed up on Howard Street.

"She does, and I'll hear about it, don't worry," Bertha said.

Before Odessa left, she asked Ollie to go upstairs and fetch Brian's Christmas present, which she had stored there for safekeeping. She wanted to hide it at home now that Christmas was so near. Ollie disappeared up the dark stairs and returned with a box taller than he was. It was long and heavy, and he struggled with it. Odessa took the box from him and made her way down the steps and across the icy sidewalk to her car. She put the box in the trunk, but it was so long it stuck out the rear, where anybody on the street could see that Odessa Williams had bought her grandson a Thunder Rally Electric Pinball Game. Odessa drove quickly up Howard Street, hoping that none of Brian's cousins would see the gift and tell him about it. She wanted to get back home before Brian's bus arrived. Just to be sure, she drove past Brian's school to make sure the bus had not yet left. Then she raced home in the twilight. She hauled the big box up her front stairs to its new hiding place in the closet behind the rows of suits and slacks waiting for Darryl.

"Geedy," Odessa said, "go get my machine and let me have a treatment, then we'll go." She'd nearly forgotten about the special Christmas party the Red Cross was throwing that night. She sat back on the sofa and raised her legs for a few minutes while she inhaled deeply from the nebulizer, breathing slowly to open the passageways left tight by worry and exhaustion.

After the Red Cross party, Odessa was worn out but glad nonetheless that she had gone. Geedy got a hot dog, a hoagie, and a toy fire truck. Odessa got to see her favorite TV newsman from Channel 3 in person, and she encountered professional people from the news media and the city bureaucracy and the Red Cross—the sort of people she did not often have contact with. She felt like a part of the city, and not just a welfare mother from North Philadelphia. It was not until she got ready for bed that she realized she had not thought about Brenda once during the entire affair.

By the next morning, Brenda again weighed heavily on her mind. A soft, wet snow was falling, and Odessa could not shake the image of Brenda's emaciated body sprawled on a vacant lot, the snow slowly burying her. Odessa knew she would have to go out again and search for her. Once again, she pulled on layer after layer of clothes and negotiated the slippery sidewalk outside on her way to firing up the Caprice.

She made the same stops as the day before. She knocked on Jeff's door, where the same wizened woman told her that Brenda had not come home that night. Jeff was gone, too, she told Odessa.

"Now I *am* worried," Odessa said, dropping heavily back into the front seat. "With Jeff and her both not coming home, something's wrong."

Back on Kensington Avenue, the snow was obscuring the faces of the pipers and the hookers in the doorways along the sidewalk. They wore knit caps and bulky overcoats, which made it difficult to discern a distinct shape or form. They all seemed too substantial in size to be Brenda. Odessa pulled the car to the curb and peered through her spectacles at their faces. They looked back at her with blank and hollow expressions.

"She's probably with a man," Odessa said, pulling away on the snow-bound street. "If she's desperate, she do it for them for five dollars. That's enough to buy her a little bit of crack."

Odessa tried the St. Francis Inn again, but none of the men or women waiting in the soup line had seen Brenda. No one at the Kensington Bible Church or the community resources center had seen her, either. She did not know where else to look.

Odessa wondered if Brenda had gloves or a hat. She had always told Brenda that it was essential to keep her head covered in cold weather, but Brenda did as she pleased. If somebody gave her a hat, she wore it. If she didn't have one, she made no attempt to find one. Odessa decided that if she did locate Brenda, she would buy her, as her Christmas gift, one of the knit-cap-and-gloves sets on sale at the Valu-Plus. But she would cut small slices into them, as she always did, to prevent Brenda from selling them to buy crack.

Odessa guided the Caprice down Kensington Avenue, the fat snowflakes clogging the windshield when she passed openings in the El overhead, then melting and cleansing the glass when the car remained under the tracks. She looked again at the haunted faces of the pipers and junkies wandering aimlessly in the snow.

"Look at these addicts," Odessa said. "They look like they're half dead. I don't care if you're black or white, those drugs change your skin color. You go gray. You look so bad, like you're on your way to your own funeral—and I guess you are. I guess Brenda is dying, really. That's the way I have to look at it. She's killing herself and she don't care. Every time I look at her, she's gone more gray."

The sight of the walking dead brought tears to Odessa's eyes. She pulled the car to the curb and sat watching the snowflakes slide down the windshield like butter in a skillet.

"I'm just worried somebody's got Brenda," she said, pulling off her spectacles to dab at her moist eyes. "You would think that after Gary Heidnik, they'd learn not to go off with strange men." Gary Michael Heidnik was a psychopath who had lured mentally retarded women to his row house on Marshall Street, where he beheaded and dissected two of them, and where three more women were found chained to his basement walls the day he was arrested in 1987. Heidnik was a legendary figure in North Philadelphia, a bogeyman whom parents cited when warning their children about talking to strangers.

"Brenda could get stabbed or shot or cut to pieces by some crazy fiend," Odessa said. "Or she could get AIDS and bring it home to the rest of us. Oh, it just hurts me so much to see her out here selling herself. She was such a sweet little girl when I had her with me. I never imagined a child of mine would be out here like this. But I guess what really hurts is thinking about what could happen to her. I keep thinking about her being laid up and knocked in the head and bleeding to death in a dirty alley somewhere."

The snow was falling more heavily now, coating the crack vials and used syringes littering the curb so that they looked like confectionary decorations on a cake. Odessa gunned the engine and pulled out into the storm. There was nothing else to be done. Brenda was either dead or alive.

Only two days remained before Christmas. Odessa had all her gifts paid for and gift-wrapped, but Israel still needed $30 for a Game Boy he had promised to his son Steven. His boss still owed him money for some boilers Israel had burned for him, but it was not likely that he would be paid until after Christmas. Israel turned to Odessa; he knew she had just collected her second and final welfare check for December. He hated having to ask his mother for money, but he had been paying her regularly for his boys' food and expenses, and he had salary due to him. He would pay her back before New Year's. Odessa could not refuse her son. She agreed to cut back on the huge New Year's dinner she was planning and split the cost of the Game Boy with Israel. I loaned Israel $30 to see him through Christmas, and he spent half to buy Steven his Game Boy and the other half on food for the rest of the week.

Inside Odessa's row house that afternoon, her grandchildren were home from school and lounging around the living room, bored and impatient for Christmas to arrive. They hounded their grandmother about Christmas gifts. Jim begged for sneakers. Anthony wanted an electronic game. Brian suddenly decided he needed a pair of expensive winter boots he had seen in a catalogue.

"I'm your grandma, not your mom," Odessa said finally. "I'm doing the best I can, but I ain't Santa Claus. So if you kids want yourself a big Christmas, you better go out there and find Santa Claus and tell him."

From the kitchen, Israel shouted, "Tell Santa Claus I want a job for Christmas!"

Odessa shouted back at him, "I wish you would hurry up and get a job so you can get out from under my roof and stop eating me out of house and home!"

"I'm trying, believe me," Israel said. "I'd rather be out working and getting a nice paycheck instead of sitting around here with all these rowdy kids and their grandma."

"Well," Odessa said, "nobody's forcing you to live here. You can go get a job just as soon as you want."

Israel walked into the living room, drying his hands on a kitchen towel. "That's the trouble with black people," he said, winking. "They won't get a job—and they always want money."

The rest of that day was spent cooking Christmas dinner as a snowstorm howled outside. Israel and Odessa moved back and forth between the living room and kitchen, stirring pots and cutting vegetables while also trying to watch a provocative episode of a TV talk show. The subject on this particular afternoon was "the KKK versus Universal Zulu Women." Israel and Odessa watched with fascination as white racists traded insults with militant black women while the studio audience screamed.

Odessa was appalled that a TV show would provide a setting for the spewing of racial hatred. "This kind of stuff is what's gonna cause this country to blow up one day," she said. "You got hate coming from people of all colors. People of all colors have to stop the ones who hate, or else we're gonna have a big race war in this country."

Israel sensed an opportunity to torment his mother. "You weren't saying that when you were with the Zulu Nation," he told her, mentioning a North Philadelphia black street gang. He winked and looked at me and said, "Did you know Odessa was a den mother for the Zulu Nation when they were fighting over on Diamond Street? She was a regular hoodlum, my mom was!"

"I wasn't no hoodlum, Israel," Odessa said gently. "But it's true, I was their den mother, I guess you could say. I was just a young girl with three little babies and I didn't know any better. I used to hide their weapons. That was my only job—keep their weapons for them."

"My mama the hoodlum," Israel said. "Hey, Dessa, tell about taking all us kids to the protests and sitting us down on the trolley tracks."

"That's right," Odessa said. "We were having a big protest with Roxanne Jones. We took all the families and kids and blocked the trolley line till we got what we wanted. Israel was ten years old then. You remember that, Israel?"

Israel raised his eyebrows. "Do I remember?" he said. "I was scared to death, sitting in the middle of the street, cars speeding past me, and here's Mama saying, 'Now, don't move, they won't hurt you!' "

"Well, it worked," Odessa said. "We always got our way when Roxanne Jones was involved. She taught me how to get things done."

She looked back at the TV screen, where the Klansmen were screaming beneath their hoods, shaking their fists at the Zulu Women.

"My Lord," Odessa said. "If they'd stop worrying about what happened a hundred years ago and start worrying about what's going on right now, they wouldn't be so hateful to each other. Sometimes you've got to bury the past, white people and black people, too. You've got to live for now."

Israel pointed to the TV. "I don't know about all that, but I *do* know those Klan folks better take off those white sheets when they leave there," he said. "And they better let the Klan dudes leave first and hold the brothers back, else they won't make it to the street alive."

They watched the show until it was over and the Klansmen had survived. Then Israel looked out the window at the falling snow and noticed a Parking Authority vehicle blocking the street. He went outside and saw that his broken-down van had been ticketed. That part of Allegheny Avenue was a snow emergency route; it said so on all the street signs. The city had declared a snow emergency, which meant that all cars had to be moved off the street. Now a $35 ticket was under the windshield of Israel's van.

Odessa looked at the ticket and said, "I guess it doesn't matter that it's almost Christmas."

In any event, she said, she had no intention of paying the ticket until after the holidays. No Parking Authority functionary was going to ruin her Christmas. She would take up a collection from family members as part of their contribution to the New Year's family dinner. She intended to spend her welfare check on holiday food and kerosene. Nobody was going to be cold or hungry in Odessa's house at Christmas.

That evening, the phone rang. It was Bertha. "Brenda came by," she told Odessa. She was cold and hungry, as usual, but otherwise she was fine. Brenda did not explain where she had been, Bertha said, though Odessa had not asked. She didn't care. Christmas was coming and her daughter was safe.

On Christmas morning, Brian awoke early. It was 5:30 A.M. when he shook Odessa and Danielle awake, shouting, "Get up! Get up! It's Christmas!"

Brian ran down the hallway to wake up his sister and his brothers and cousins. They all raced down the stairs, whooping and scrambling to reach the tree, where Odessa had laid out their gifts the night before and filled their stockings with candy and fruit. Odessa had just put on her red Bertha Boone family tree T-shirt and was carrying Danielle down the stairs as her grandchildren tore open their gifts.

Kevin opened the box containing his red-and-gold San Francisco 49ers jersey. He quickly slipped the jersey over his head and pulled on the padded white football pants. He stood up and turned around to show everyone the back of the jersey, which said, *Young,* for quarterback Steve Young, and 8—Young's number. He picked up a new football Odessa had given him and stuck a protective mouthpiece between his teeth. The base of the mouthpiece dangled from his lips like a pacifier, undermining the fierce pose he had struck. Suddenly Kevin yanked the mouthpiece out and said, "Grandma, when can you buy the helmet?"

Brian ripped open his pinball game and shouted, "Decent!" at the sight of the flashing lights in the photo of the game on the box cover. Then he shoved it aside and opened up his Flame Thrower III race car set. Within minutes he had the batteries installed and was directing the car around the living room with the remote control, crashing it into Odessa's furniture. He begged Odessa to let him drive the car out on the sidewalk but Odessa looked at him crossly and said, "Brian, what do you think will happen to your new race car if you try to run it through all that snow and ice?"

"It'll get ruined," Brian said, but he seemed intrigued by the prospect.

Jim quietly sat down and opened up his new CD player, which he immediately took up to the bedroom he shared with his brothers. There he set up the speakers on the bureau his grandmother had trash-picked for him and slipped in a CD called "Naughty by Nature." He flopped on his bed and pointed his new remote at the CD. Pressing the buttons and giggling, he cranked up the sound until Odessa hollered up at him to turn it down or she would take it away.

Delena opened her computer diary and withdrew to her bedroom, where she shut the door and lay down on her bed.

Steven tore open the package containing his Game Boy and plopped down on the sofa, punching at the buttons.

David and Anthony, Israel's other boys, ran through the house with their new battery-operated walkie-talkies, trying to see how far their communications would stretch. They pressed the talk buttons and screamed, "Come in, come in! Do you read me? Over! Over!"

One by one, the grandchildren walked over to Odessa, who sat wearily on the sofa, and they hugged her and thanked her for giving them Christmas.

From behind his back, Brian produced a wooden orange crate stuffed with something wrapped in red paper and taped with silver duct tape. It was his Christmas gift to his grandmother. Odessa peeled off the duct tape and red wrapping to find something inside wrapped in newspaper and sealed with more duct tape. When she opened this package, she found that it was a flower vase and a children's Bible.

"Oh, Brian," she said, thumbing through the book. "A Bible! You *know* how much I love the Bible. Where in the world did you get a Bible?"

Brian shrugged and let his dark eyes drift up toward the ceiling. "I asked for it, and it just came. It's the magic of Christmas!" he said.

As Odessa bent down to hug Brian, the other children pestered her about a bulky gift-wrapped box in the corner. She called it the "family present." After first telling them they had to wait until after dinner, she relented under pressure and let them open it. Inside was a set of audiotapes called Hooked on Phonics, an educational series that promised to "increase your reading power." Odessa had bought the set from Ollie the previous spring and taken over the payments, putting aside a few dollars from each welfare and SSI check through the summer and fall.

"I got it because all of us can benefit—including me," she told her grandchildren. "We're all gonna learn to read better, because reading is the key to success."

The children groaned and turned away to play with their individual gifts. Odessa carefully replaced the Hooked on Phonics tapes in their plastic case and put the whole set aside. Her grandkids were right: Christmas was no time for educational aids.

Later that day, Brenda arrived, bearing no gifts. She was thin and haggard. Her eyes were glazed, and she wobbled as she walked. Her boyfriend, Jeff, was not with her, despite his promise to Delena to give each grandchild a $10 bill in an envelope. Jim and Kevin and Brian, intent on their new gifts, ignored their mother, showing no more reaction at her sudden arrival than if the postman had dropped in with the mail. But Delena greeted Brenda with a hug, and she took her by the hand to her room to show her mother her new computer diary. They sat on the bed and talked in low whispers.

When Brenda came back downstairs, she and Odessa talked quietly for a long while. Brenda was hurt and depressed, and that was one reason for her mysterious disappearance; another reason was that she had been busy turning tricks and getting high. But now Brenda was distressed about a spat she had had with Jeff. He had asked her to get out of the house the previous weekend because his stepfather was coming from New Jersey for a visit, and he did not approve of Brenda. It had little to do with Brenda's addiction or prostitution, for Jeff was also an addict, and prostitutes were in and out of his house. The problem was Brenda's race. Though Jeff was black, his stepfather was a white man and, apparently, a bigoted one.

Odessa tried to console Brenda, but she did not have much sympathy for her. Jeff's racist stepfather was Brenda's problem, not hers. Odessa told Brenda, as she had countless times before, that she could solve all her troubles by going back to drug rehab and giving up her street life. Brenda nodded and said she intended to change her life soon, but the way her voice trailed off and her eyes remained unfocused told Odessa the truth behind her daughter's practiced lies. She fed Brenda a hot Christmas dinner and sent her back home to Jeff and his flophouse.

The week between Christmas and New Year's brought Odessa the one Christmas gift she had been praying for but had not yet been granted. She took her mother to the doctor's to get the results of her lab tests for colon cancer. They came back clean. Bertha Boone did not have cancer. The doctors did not know why she had fallen sick, but they did know that it had nothing to do with cancer. They pronounced her a healthy woman, or as healthy as a woman could be who had lived a hard eighty-one years in rural Georgia and inner-city Philadelphia.

"I guess," Odessa told her mother after she drove her back home, "you're too ornery to get cancer."

"And you better let me be or you'll be going right back to the hospital," Bertha said, settling into her easy chair in front of the stories—the soaps on TV.

Odessa left her there and went back home and prayed to God, thanking him for her mother's deliverance.

That same day, Odessa got more good news. Her favorite newscaster on Channel 3 read a report that said the city was forgiving people who had received tickets for blocking emergency snow routes during the most recent snowstorm. It had been decided that the storm had struck so suddenly and so fiercely that people could not reasonably be expected to move their cars. "That's right," Odessa said to the TV. "If people can't park in front of their own homes, where can they park? I don't care if it's snowing or not, I got no place else to park except on the street." The news meant that the family would have extra cash to spend on New Year's dinner, for she had already collected money from family members to pay for the ticket.

Other money was coming in, too. Brian's SSI check arrived early, which meant that Odessa would not have to cut back on kerosene until her first welfare check arrived in January. More people from the neighborhood were asking if they could pay her to drive them to pick up their checks. And she had hit the jackpot at the Salvation Army, where she had stood in the parking lot asking people if she could have whatever they were dropping off as donations. She came home with a load of nearly new sweatshirts in sizes that fit all her grandchildren, a windfall that saved her money on winter school clothes.

"These kids say they're tired of hand-me-downs, but if you're on fixed income, you better get used to them," Odessa said. "And they're not really hand-me-downs anyway, if it comes from a stranger instead of your family. I'm just grateful the Lord gave me the strength not to be ashamed to ask people for things. I'm way beyond being embarrassed asking for help. If you need something, ask for it. Nobody thinks bad of anybody who does for themselves."

Odessa came home with something else, from Goodwill: a framed painting of a pagoda. It had been marked down from $1.50 to seventy-five cents during Goodwill's half-price red tag day, and it was so delicate and graceful that Odessa could not resist. She hung it in a place of honor on the living room wall, between the painting of a big-eyed girl with a puppy and a velvet bullfighter Darryl had given her. She called the new addition "my Chinese house painting."

Israel was having his own run of good fortune. Although the welfare people were still dropping by to question Odessa about his living circumstances—"They don't have any money to give relief to poor people, but they got enough money to send all these people over here to torment me," Odessa said—he was still receiving his $97 in emergency food stamps. He also had a line on two jobs—one at a car wash and the other at a small factory that installed computer chips. He had located both jobs through the newspaper want ads.

Odessa did not want Israel to take the car wash job. She worried that the cold and dampness would make him sick, and he would spread the sickness to the entire family. But she was intrigued by the computer factory job. It was indoors, and it was a semiskilled job that might lead to something better. And it couldn't be as hard as cutting up old boilers with an acetylene torch.

Whatever Israel did, Odessa did not want him going back to the summer recreation job at Waterloo Playground. She knew from her visits to her mother's house that drug dealers had crept back into the playground in Israel's absence. They were a hard bunch—killers, really. Bertha had told her that it was not uncommon to hear gunshots from the direction of the park.

"Those drug people only left because they respected Israel," Odessa said. "They gave in once, but they're not the kind of people to give in again, especially now that they've taken over again. I don't want any son of mine getting involved with them again. Israel is tough, and he can get mean, but he's only one man against that whole bunch. Those are dangerous people. Israel did what he could. It's somebody else's turn to step up now."

There was one bit of good news from Howard Street. Anita had decided to drop charges against Israel. He did not, however, get his tools back—not even his valuable hydraulic jack. But now he was free to visit his grandmother and his relatives on Howard Street without risking arrest for violating a protection order for a woman he never, ever had any intention of going near again. Israel had, in fact, decided to marry his new girlfriend, Monica. They planned to have the wedding the following summer in Fairmount Park, assuming Israel had a job by then. When Israel broke the news to his mother, she was overjoyed. She was still smiling when Israel and Monica told her that Monica's mother did not approve of their getting married. Odessa shrugged and told them, "I guess this means it's gonna fall on me to cook all the food for the wedding."

Odessa felt blessed all week. Brian's teacher called to read her his report card; Odessa had been unable to get to the school in the snow to pick it up. Brian's grades were far better than she had any right to expect, given his mercurial mood swings and pants wetting and disruptive behavior. He got two A's, two B's, and two C's. There were no D's or F's. That same week, Willie showed up with several rolls of new, maroon wall-to-wall carpet. Israel and Odessa installed it in the living room and dining room, giving the downstairs a fresh, modern appearance for the New Year's Day dinner.

Things seemed to be going so well that Odessa was not overly concerned when rats invaded her row house. She knew she had rats because she could hear them rustling in the floorboards that had rotted out along the back wall in the kitchen. She was convinced that the creatures had been attracted to the block by the rice and beans the Puerto Ricans tossed out behind their row houses on Franklin Street.

Now Odessa set about making her house rat free in time for the family New Year's dinner. She put out rat poison at strategic points—under the kitchen cabinets, behind the freezer, underneath the stove. The next day, Flower, the puppy, pulled a dead rat out from under the refrigerator. Odessa found another one laid out beneath the kitchen cabinets. It was a monster—eighteen inches, counting the tail. Later an awful smell permeated the kitchen, threatening preparations for the holiday feast. Odessa's nose told her it was a dead rat under the upright freezer, and she made Israel move the appliance. She put the carcass in a plastic bag and dumped it in one of the trash cans at the curb, knowing the freezing cold would kill the stench.

With the rats exterminated, just about the only unsettling event that entire week involved Elaine's branch of the family. Raysonno was in trouble. Elaine walked down from her row house to tell Odessa that Raysonno had been kicked out of the Job Corps for fighting. He had barely been in Pittsburgh long enough to use his phone-home card. But there was more, Elaine said. As soon as Raysonno got back home, he got locked up for stealing a car in the 35th Police District.

Odessa was shocked but not necessarily surprised. This kind of thing happened when kids in her neighborhood did not get a strict upbringing. Elaine was lucky Raysonno hadn't been shot—or shot someone. As it was, she had to drive up to the 35th District to sign his bail and get him released into her custody. He had a hearing in juvenile court in January.

"If it was me, I'd have left him in jail to learn to deal with life," Odessa said later. "Then I'd send him to the reform school where my son-in-law is a counselor, and let him get straightened out while there's still hope for him. He may be my grandson, but if he stays out there on the street he's either gonna be locked up or dead."

On the afternoon of New Year's Eve, Brenda arrived, unannounced and hungry. Odessa was relieved to see that Brenda was wearing a heavy winter coat, which, it turned out, her boyfriend, Jeff, had given her for Christmas. But while Brenda said she was able to stay warm enough, she complained that her feet hurt. Odessa told her to sit down and take off her ragged old shoes so that she could have a look at her feet. In the years since Brenda had been cut off welfare, after Odessa took custody of her children, she never bothered to reapply for medical assistance. Her health was poor. She was malnourished and her teeth were rotting. When she took off her overcoat, she was wearing only a soiled, striped T-shirt and a pair of baggy black slacks that drooped from her bony hips. Brenda did not bathe regularly; her hair was matted and her skin was gray and brittle, like the ghostly complexions Odessa had seen on the addicts along Kensington Avenue. When Odessa looked at Brenda's bare feet, she saw rows of tough, scaly corns and bunions. She got out her razor blade and, as Brenda squirmed and protested, sliced away at the rough outer layers of dead skin and callus. "Stop complaining," she told Brenda. "I'm the only doctor you got."

As Brenda put her shoes back on, Odessa told her she was going to put her to work instead of letting her sit around and watch TV. She ordered Brenda to watch Danielle, who was whining and sniffling as she lay sprawled on a black plastic bag filled with trash-picked children's clothes. Brenda picked the girl up, limped into the kitchen, and confiscated an opened box of cookies. Then she took Danielle upstairs to try to get her to take a nap. She put her down on Delena's bed, where Delena sat watching an *I Love Lucy* rerun. Soon Danielle was asleep, and the sound of her labored breathing made Brenda sleepy. She reached across the bed for a teddy bear Delena had given her for Christmas, then lay down next to Danielle and curled up with her arms around the bear. Delena moved to the edge of the bed to give her mother more room, never looking up from the TV screen. In a few minutes, Brenda was sound asleep, and the sharp rasp of her snoring, along with Danielle's wheezing, nearly drowned out the sound from Delena's TV.

As darkness fell, more family members arrived to spend the last day of the year with Odessa and to help her prepare the food for the New Year's Day feast the following afternoon. Bowls and platters and saucepans were scattered around the kitchen, spread out below a framed sign that someone had given Odessa for Christmas. It read: *Kitchen Closed Because of Illness—I Am Sick of Cooking!*

Elaine came into the kitchen wearing a T-shirt that showed a cartoon of a naked man inside a barrel, superimposed over an IRS 1040 form, with the message *After Taxes*. As she sat down and began to help Odessa cut collards, the conversation turned to assessments of the outgoing year and the prospects for the new year.

"I got to get my life straightened out in ninety-six, after the year I had in ninety-five," Elaine said. There was a wistful look on her broad, fleshy face. She mentioned Raysonno and his court date for car theft, and the difficulties involved in either obtaining a public defender or hiring a private attorney. She mentioned Iesha, who had just announced that she was pregnant again, this time by Curtis, who had his own car-theft problems now that the police were questioning him about the legal ownership of the Buick they had towed away. Iesha was Joyce's child, but somehow Elaine had become responsible for her and her children, with Joyce living in West Philadelphia and pouring her energies into finishing her courses at the job training school.

Now Iesha's immediate future had become even more attenuated. She had found a phone bill in Curtis's duffel bag that showed a series of calls to an unfamiliar number. Iesha dialed the number and a woman answered. Iesha interrogated the woman and realized that Curtis was having an affair. She kicked him out of Elaine's house, cutting herself off from the limited income Curtis had provided from his security guard job.

"Iesha was already driving me crazy," Elaine said. "She won't go to school, she won't get in a program. She won't go anywhere except to the maternity ward. Here she is pregnant again, so there goes nine more months for me to have to take care of her, and no man to help, either."

Odessa told Elaine that Iesha was a "don't-care person," and Elaine nodded in agreement. "I don't know where she gets it, but she didn't get it from me, I'll tell you that," Odessa said.

Israel, slicing a fresh pan of corn bread, said, "Iesha needs another child about as much as you do, Elaine."

"Oh, no," Elaine said. "I've had all the kids I'm gonna have. My life's messed up enough without another child to raise. I got ten years to go as it is, with my youngest still only six. Really, I've got to get my life straightened out in ninety-six. That's my New Year's resolution. I'm gonna get off welfare and find me a job and make me some real money. I'm tired of my old life. I'm ready for a new one."

In the living room, the door opened and Joyce walked in. She was wearing a new blue sweatshirt Odessa had given her, the one with the message that said: *World's Greatest Grandma.* Joyce was only thirty-nine, but Iesha had made her a grandmother not long after she turned thirty-five.

Elaine saw the sweatshirt and said, "Hey, I need me a shirt like that."

"Why?" Joyce said. "You're not a grandmother."

"I might as well be, as many kids as I've got to take care of," Elaine said.

"Don't push it," Joyce said cheerfully. "You'll be a grandma soon enough."

Under his breath, Israel muttered, "Got that right."

Elaine ignored him and told Joyce: "I'm glad you're in a better mood. You were a grinch at Christmas, Joyce."

"Yeah," Joyce said. "I was really down after the year I had."

"You shouldn't be down," Elaine said. "You got kids who love you, a mother who loves you, and you sure have a sister who loves you. You don't appreciate your blessings."

"I do now," Joyce said. "It's a whole new year."

Joyce had good news. She had gone to a job fair in West Philadelphia, where representatives from Jefferson University Hospital told her they liked her résumé. They said they might well have a job for her after she graduated in the spring. They asked her to apply for a job as a medical secretary. With the updated medical computer skills Joyce was learning, combined with her past experience as a nursing assistant, the representives said she had a good chance of landing the job. The position started at $7 an hour, with benefits, and it would rise to more than $8 an hour after a six-month probation period. That would put Joyce at the same salary level she had reached when she quit her nursing assistant job several years earlier.

"I'm ready to make some real money," she said. "I'm tired of counting pennies. I want to get my own place. I'm tired of sharing an apartment with other people. I'm the kind of person who needs to run her own household."

Joyce looked up on the dining room wall at a 1996 calendar Odessa had already put up. It featured a photograph of the Million Man March on Washington. The photo had been taken by Joyce's former boyfriend, the father of Iesha and the grandfather-to-be of the baby growing in Iesha's belly. He had used a computer program to produce a set of Million Man March calendars, which he emblazoned with the message *Black Men Celebrate Themes of Solidarity, Strength* and a pledge: "I (state your name) PLEDGE that from this day forward, I will strive to love my brother as I love myself. I will strive to improve myself spiritually, morally, mentally, socially, politically and economically for the benefit of myself, my family and my people."

Joyce stared hard at the calendar and said, "Yeah, ninety-six is gonna be the start of a whole new life for this girl."

She reached out across the table and scooped up a handful of peas from a pile Odessa was sorting. She slipped them into her purse. "For good luck in the new year," she said.

"I don't believe in luck," Odessa told her quietly. "I believe in God."

As she spoke, Kevin burst in from the street and announced that someone had stolen his new Christmas football. Odessa scolded him for leaving it in the street, but Kevin begged her for a new one. "I'm not buying you another one," she told him. "Grandma's money is all gone. And when I say gone, I mean *gone*."

From the kitchen, Israel's voice boomed out: "You didn't put the water on for the beans, Dessa!"

Odessa rose wearily from her chair and made her way into the kitchen, where Israel blocked her way with his big body. "Stay out of my kitchen," he told her.

"*Your* kitchen?" Odessa said, pushing her heavy shoulder past her son. "If you want your own kitchen, you better go to your own house."

Israel turned to let his mother pass. "I don't have my own house. But trust me, I'll be out of here big time when I do."

"Go on," Odessa said. "You're nothing but a pain anyway."

"You're the pain," Israel said. "You jump on me when I'm not helping and you jump on me when I do."

Odessa laughed and punched her son lightly in the belly. "I got my New Year's resolution: get Israel a home," she said. "But for now, it looks like we're stuck with each other, don't it?"

For the next hour, they worked busily in the kitchen, boiling hog maws, cooking pork ribs and chicken wings, and slicing bananas for banana cream pie. Elaine helped until she sliced her hand cutting collards, and she went home to treat the wound. Israel's boys stood on call for runs to the Chinese store for last-minute ingredients; the Lees had reopened following the robbery, a development that eased Odessa's worries about her grandchildren's exposure to the drug dealers at the competing corner store.

One of the trips Israel's son Anthony made to the Chinese store that day was to buy vanilla wafers for the banana pudding and Newport cigarettes for Brenda. Reluctantly, Odessa paid for the cigarettes because she was tired of Brenda begging her for them. When Anthony returned with the cigarettes, she told him to go upstairs and wake up Brenda. The least she could do, Odessa thought, was to help clean up the kitchen.

Anthony ran upstairs to Delena's bedroom and tapped Brenda roughly on the arm as she slept. "Brenda, wake up! Cigarettes!" he said. Brenda grunted and rolled over to face the wall, her eyes shut tightly. Anthony shrugged and tossed the cigarettes on the bed. Delena, still watching TV, touched her mother lightly on her shoulder and said, "Mama, your cigarettes are here." Brenda did not move. Delena picked up the pack and placed it gently in her mother's palm as she slept.

By evening, Brenda was awake and roaming the kitchen in search of food, listening to the New Year's Eve conversations about resolutions and the prospects for the coming year. Odessa tasted the hog maws she was preparing, and pushed Brenda's hand away when she tried to pinch off a chunk of meat. "You're not eating anything till you do some work around here," Odessa told her.

Brenda turned and walked into the living room, and Brian rushed past her into the kitchen. He had just watched a TV commercial for a miniature pool table. "Can you buy me one, Grandma?" he asked Odessa. "I promise I'll stay in my room all day and play pool."

Brenda heard him and yelled over her shoulder, "Boy, you better get you a job. Don't ask for anything till you get a job and earn your own keep. You get a job, then you can have anything you want."

Brian looked over at his mother and said, without sarcasm, "Will you get a job? Then you can buy me a pool table."

Odessa rolled her eyes and tried not to laugh.

"I got to get myself together first, Brian," Brenda said. She was leaning against the door frame for support. She was having difficulty holding her head up. "Once I get myself together, I'll be in shape to go out and look for a job and make some money."

Odessa shook her head and told Brian to get out of the dining room so she could prepare the New Year's food. Brian ran across the worn floor, pushed his arm against his mother's bony thigh to move her out of his way, and rushed upstairs to make sure that no one was playing with his new race car set.

Brenda, watching him go, said she ought to come up with a New Year's resolution. She thought for a moment and said, "No resolution for this girl, I guess. My resolution is to stay alive." Odessa looked over at her thin, wasted daughter. She started to say something, but there was really nothing worth saying. She went back to preparing her hog maws.

As the last day of the year wore down, everyone settled in to watch the silver ball fall at Times Square. Both television sets were on, with the volume on each one turned up to drown out the blast of fireworks and the roar of speeding cars from the streets. From time to time, what sounded like gunshots rang out, and everyone moved away from the windows.

A few minutes before midnight, Odessa walked slowly up the stairs to her bedroom. The long climb left her winded, and she felt drained from the burdens of preparing the next day's meal. But there was one more thing she had to do before she lay down to read her Bible and drift off to sleep for the last time that year. She opened her safe and withdrew her little .22-caliber Colt pistol. She checked the clip and saw that there was a bright, tiny bullet in place. Odessa had owned the gun for fifteen years, and she had fired it precisely fifteen times. Each New Year's Eve, she took it outside and squeezed off a single shot to mark the end of one year and the beginning of the next.

With the pistol tucked into her soft palm, Odessa walked heavily down the stairs, careful to hold the railing and to take the steps one at a time. She stepped over her bag of trash-picked clothes and twisted the storm door latch that Bo had repaired. It clicked firmly back into place as Odessa made her way onto the porch and felt the sting of the cold winter night. She bent low and looked out over the porch railing at flashes of light flickering up and down Allegheny Avenue. People were firing guns. Odessa stayed low, waiting for the last few minutes of the year to tick away. At the stroke of midnight, there were sudden new fusillades of gunfire all across North Philadelphia. Odessa braced her right wrist with her left hand and pointed the gun toward a spot in the night sky high above the naked limbs of the sycamores where they stood outlined against the dull square shapes of the row houses. She closed her eyes and pulled the trigger.

The bullet split the night and flew high above the rooftops. On and on it raced, carrying with it the whole long history of the Boones and the Williamses and all that they might become. Odessa tried to follow the path of the bullet to see what it foretold. She ached to know the future. She looked up at the painted sky and tried to see Brenda whole again, and fresh as before. She tried to see Bertha Boone vibrant and fussing, tending her collards and pulling fat perch from her fishing line. She tried to see Joyce in her graduation gown and Elaine leaving home for work downtown and Israel driving his old gray van to a nine-to-five office job. She tried to see Iesha at a job training computer and Danielle gently asleep and cool to the touch. She tried to see Jim inside one of the big safe schools in the Northeast and Kevin bent down over his schoolbooks and Delena tucked safely in her bed. She tried to see all her grandchildren and great-grandchildren living inside a vast high-gabled house set on a hill in the soft embrace of tall shade trees. She tried to see Darryl reading the Boone family Bible in her living room. And she tried to see Brian grown tall and strong with his eyes still searching and gentle, and his soul refreshed.

That bullet rose high for all of them, for all the cold and hungry children of the ghetto, for the desperate mothers on fixed income, for the homeless, for the gray-faced prostitutes and pipers, and for Odessa, too. She was weary, and she longed to rest. She turned away and let the bullet carry on for her. It raced across the heavens. She knew it would soar above the tired old city and never fall back to earth until there was peace in everyone's heart.

Survivors

S t. Edward the Confessor Church was formally handed back to the Archdiocese of Philadelphia by the KWRU war council at a public ceremony in downtown Philadelphia. No one from the archdiocese attended. Later the archdiocese had the church boarded up tightly. It now stands empty.

The Quaker Lace lot remained a trash-strewn urban brownfield. An arson at the western edge of the lot destroyed a corner grocery and hoagie shop where Tent City inhabitants had once been allowed to use the toilets.

A new Tent City arose on a vacant lot in North Philadelphia a few blocks southeast of the Quaker Lace lot. At least thirty homeless families lived there in shacks and tents, some of them built out of lumber and tarps from the Quaker Lace lot. The new Tent City was nicknamed Ridgeville, after Pennsylvania Governor Tom Ridge, a proponent of welfare cuts. Supporters of Tent City, among them Les the Pretzel Man, continued to deliver fresh food to the site.

Joanna Sorlien, the Main Line heiress, bought a former furniture warehouse on Kensington Avenue, with the intention of converting it into a boardinghouse for low-income, welfare-dependent people committed to KWRU's struggle for affordable housing.

A plan by Governor Ridge to eliminate medical benefits for 260,000 low-income adults in Pennsylvania was rejected by the state House of Representatives after protesters from KWRU and other organizations rallied in Harrisburg to condemn the cuts. The state legislature later passed a modified version of the plan. The new law ended medical assistance for 220,000 low-income, able-bodied adults with no children. Governor Ridge signed the bill into law one day after it had passed.

*   *   *

To protest further proposed cuts in welfare benefits, Cheri Honkala led a small group of KWRU members who walked 114 miles from Philadelphia to Harrisburg, where they camped out on the steps of the state capitol building for four weeks.

Cheri Honkala and Mariluz Gonzalez were convicted by a Philadelphia judge for blocking the highway during the KWRU welfare protest at Philadelphia's City Hall. The fine was waived. To pay her federal court fine of $250 for illegally camping at Independence Park, Cheri Honkala used the proceeds from a single night of topless dancing.

Despite eviction notices from HUD, Mariluz Gonzalez and Elba Gonzalez and their six children continued to live in the takeover house on Fairhill Street. In all, fifteen HUD takeover houses remained occupied by KWRU members. The union later used cash donations from two of the Main Line ladies to purchase two row houses in North Philadelphia. The war council voted to award one of the homes to Mariluz, Elba, and their children. The second home, located a block from the Quaker Lace lot, was awarded to Tara Colon. She and J.R. Rivera moved into the house along with their newborn baby girl, Sandra.

Yazmenelly Jimenez, the daughter of Elba Gonzalez, was crushed against a snowbank by a city bus as she waited for it to take her to school. Her leg was badly injured, but she recovered fully and was later named Student of the Month at McKinley school. Both Yazmenelly and Destiny, the daughter of Mariluz Gonzalez, were promoted to the next grade levels at McKinley.

The Kensington Welfare Rights Union obtained two Section 8 housing vouchers. The war council voted to award one voucher to Katie and Nancy Engle, who were able to keep Katie's grandchildren, Gina and Billy, living in the same rental home and attending the same school. The second voucher was awarded to Cheryl Mucerino, who was still without custody of her four daughters. She continued her duties as president of KWRU.

Leon "Chicago" Richards continued to live in a HUD takeover house in North Philadelphia. He spent most of his days, and many of his nights, at the new Tent City site, where he supervised the construction of wooden housing built in the shape of tepees.

Luis Torres, the homeless man with AIDS who briefly had left St. Edward's for a church hospice, died of a heroin overdose. He left behind three children and their mother, Beatrice, who recovered after nearly overdosing from the same heroin that killed Luis. Cheri Honkala led the eulogy at Luis's funeral, calling him "yet another young man taken too soon and too young by drugs."

In North Philadelphia, the police scandal in the 39th Police District deepened, with fourteen hundred criminal cases reviewed and 137 convictions overturned after six officers pleaded guilty to framing and robbing blacks and Hispanics, then lying about it under oath. At least 126 other people arrested on drug charges had their convictions overturned after Philadelphia judges refused to believe the testimony of agents from the state Bureau of Narcotics Investigation, the agency that had sent agents to film drug deals from inside the Quaker Lace factory.

State senator Roxanne Jones, who had shouted "Shame on you!" to legislators voting to pass Governor Ridge's bill cutting medical benefits, died at sixty-eight of a heart attack. Cheri Honkala and Tara Colon attended Jones' funeral dressed in black KWRU T-shirts that read "2 Legit 2 Quit."

Joseph "Skinny Joey" Merlino was acquitted of a drunk driving charge. "Going back to work," he told reporters who asked for comment. Later, *The Philadelphia Inquirer* published a front-page article reporting that the Drug Enforcement Administration had begun a drug conspiracy investigation of Merlino, who the newspaper said was already the target of a federal racketeering investigation.

John Kromer, director of the city Office of Housing and Community Development, refused to accept $11,000 due him in a city raise, saying he wanted to make a protest against impending cuts in federal housing programs.

William Parshall, Philadelphia's homeless czar, wrote a memo directing police to evict six homeless men living in Veterans Stadium, just before the major league baseball All-Star Game was to be played there. Instead, sympathetic police officers tipped off the men, who disappeared until the game was over. Later, Parshall announced that overcrowded city shelters would no longer accept homeless families. Some of the families turned away from shelters found makeshift homes on the rapidly expanding Tent City lot at Ridgeville.

Cheri Honkala continued to lead the Kensington Welfare Rights Union. She lived in her rented row house on Randolph Street with her son, Mark, who was promoted to the next level at his high school despite being threatened with expulsion for giving an exhibit on graffiti art at a KWRU meeting. Cheri continued to organize public protests against welfare cuts and to lead confrontational demonstrations at government offices and welfare centers. She spent most of her days on the Tent City lot and many of her nights dancing for tips in topless bars.

Odessa Williams's daughter Joyce graduated from her job training program. She wore a cap and gown at the graduation ceremony, just as she had envisioned, and her mother took color photographs. Joyce did not get the hospital job she had hoped for, but she did find a $7.50-an-hour job with an insurance company. She later quit the job because of the low pay and the expense of commuting to work, electing instead to enroll in a second medical computer training program. She gave up her apartment in West Philadelphia and moved, along with her son Geedy, into Odessa's row house on Allegheny Avenue.

Israel Williams took a temporary job at a factory in suburban Norristown, Pennsylvania, that made computer chips and weight sensors. When the job ended, he found a temporary job at a post office. When that job terminated, Israel returned to his long-standing occupation as a part-time burner. Israel married his fiancée, Monica, and the couple applied for a mortgage to buy a small house in Norristown. After the mortgage application was denied, Israel and Monica continued to live in the row house next door to Odessa Williams's home. Israel's four sons continued to live with their grandmother Odessa.

Odessa's daughter, Elaine, took a part-time summer job as a recreation supervisor at the Waterloo Playground. Her modest salary did not affect her welfare and food stamp payments. Elaine's son, Raysonno, or Pie, received probation after being arrested on a drug charge. When he was arrested again for probation violations, Elaine agreed with the judge in the case that Raysonno should be sent to a center for juvenile offenders. Later, Elaine's row house burned and she moved in temporarily with Odessa.

Odessa's granddaughter Iesha gave birth to her fourth child, a boy. She named him Curtis, after his father. Iesha immediately applied for an increase in her welfare benefits. She continued to rebuff all pleas from her mother, aunt, and grandmother to enroll in a welfare-to-work training program.

Iesha's daughter, Danielle, was diagnosed with a partially collapsed lung after she woke up vomiting and wheezing in Odessa's bed one night. She recovered. Her brother Khalil was diagnosed with leukemia. Doctors tested Danielle as a possible bone marrow donor.

Odessa's daughter Brenda continued to abuse drugs and prostitute herself. After she was arrested and jailed for drug possession and soliciting for prostitution, her mother borrowed $110 to bail her out. Afterward, Brenda did not keep her promise to Odessa to enter a drug rehabilitation program. When Brenda was arrested and jailed again, Odessa refused to pay her bail. Brenda spent the next five months in prison, where regular meals and the absence of drugs caused her weight to nearly double, from 97 pounds to 171 pounds. Her son Brian did not recognize Brenda when Odessa took him to visit her. When he at last recognized her, Brian refused to hug his mother, saying he wanted to punish her.

Bertha Boone, pronounced healthy after her doctors found no cancer in her eighty-one-year-old body, continued to live in her row house on Randolph Street. She spent her days caring for her two handicapped sons, tending her garden, and receiving visits from her children, grandchildren, great-grandchildren, and her newest great-great-grandson, Curtis.

Odessa's grandson Brian was promoted in the middle of the school year from second grade to third grade, based on exceptionally high achievement scores. He was awarded a school certificate for "outstanding behavior at lunchtime" after he retreated to the principal's office after a boy had tried to goad him into a fight. But despite continued therapy and medication, Brian's behavior deteriorated. After fighting with a classmate over a bowl of potato chips, he bit nearly halfway through his tongue, requiring several stitches. He was threatened with suspension after he overturned a snack table in class; he later told his therapist, Rebecca: "I wanted the other kids to think I was bad." After threatening to throw a brick at children on Seventh Street who had teased him about wetting his pants, Brian used the brick to smash the windows of seven parked cars. The owners demanded a total of three-thousand dollars from Odessa for repairs. For the fourth grade, Brian transferred to a school on Allegheny Avenue, where during his first month he was sent home for fighting.

Darryl Williams was promoted to prison trustee at Graterford while awaiting word on his application for early release. He was moved to minimum security quarters, where his mother was allowed to visit him with few restrictions, and to bring him home-cooked meals. Darryl specifically asked for onion rings, fried rice, and fried tomatoes from his grandmother's garden on Randolph Street.

Odessa Williams, saying she needed relief from the stress of life on Allegheny Avenue, took her four grandchildren and moved for several weeks into the home of her son Willie in suburban New Jersey. When she returned, she gave her bedroom to Joyce and began sleeping on the living room sofa, setting a pallet on the floor beside it for Danielle.

Odessa continued to trash-pick and fish to stretch her monthly budget. She continued to shop for bargains at discount stores and thrift shops. She continued to charge people for car rides to welfare offices and from grocery stores.

Odessa mourned the deaths of several relatives. Her nephew, Philadelphia Police Officer Robert Porter, was shot and killed as he rode in a police cruiser in West Philadelphia on the same night that another nephew, Gus, collapsed at age forty-nine of a heart attack as he played his regular Friday night pool game in a North Philadelphia bar. Odessa's great-nephew, Lamont "Cash" Bradham, was shot in the head and killed by a bullet intended for his cousin, Odessa's son Fred, during a traffic dispute. Another great-nephew, Anthony Smith, was left paralyzed by a gunshot wound inflicted while he was being robbed.

For lack of cash, Odessa postponed her plans for a Williams family reunion in Georgia and also canceled her planned trip to Disney World with her grandchildren.

All four grandchildren living with Odessa brought home superior report cards, and each one was promoted to the next highest grade level. The newest teachers for Jim, Kevin, and Delena reported to their grandmother that each one was a model student.

Odessa's beloved Chevrolet Caprice stopped running; for $150, a neighbor sold her a white 1974 Cadillac Coupe De Ville with a burgundy top.

Odessa's telephone service was disconnected for lack of payment after she wired her last $200 to Israel and Monica to pay for emergency expenses during their honeymoon in the Bahamas. She remained hundreds of dollars in arrears on her gas bill and continued to warm her home with a kerosene heater.

Odessa continued to receive her regular welfare, SSI, and food stamp payments. She watched on her trash-picked television set as Congress passed the welfare reform bill and President Clinton signed it. She did not worry about impending welfare cuts. She intended to let God deal with them.

Sources

1. TRASH PICKING

33. piped aboard a sinking ship: Roger Lane, *William Dorsey's Philadelphia & Ours: On the Past and Future of the Black City in America*. Oxford University Press, New York, 1991, p. 365.
37. make drug busts at the playground: Lt. John Gallo, Narcotics Field Unit, Philadelphia Police Department.
38. the man on Howard Street: Larry Copeland, "Taking back the playground," *The Philadelphia Inquirer*, May 28, 1992.
38. shove my foot right up: Dan Geringer, "He's a one-man army in war on urban decay," *Philadelphia Daily News*, July 2, 1992.
38. Roy's Ornamental Metal Work: Larry Copeland, "Phila. neighborhood takes back rec center," *The Philadelphia Inquirer*, July 2, 1992.
40. beaten with a baseball bat: Howard Goodman, "Bat-wielding family gets long terms," *The Philadelphia Inquirer*, Sept. 19, 1995.

2. QUAKER LACE

45. French artisans made doilies: Daniel Rubin, "Fire site once did fine business," *The Philadelphia Inquirer*, Sept. 21, 1994.
45. tattoos on both arms: Joseph A. Slobodzian, "Suspect says he was smoking as Quaker Lace was burning," *The Philadelphia Inquirer*, June 2, 1995.
46. pay to have Quaker Lace torched: Joseph A. Slobodzian, "Arson suspect says he was framed," *The Philadelphia Inquirer*, June 1, 1995.
47. first alarm was struck: Suzette Parmley and Jeff Gelles, "Fire destroys warehouse and 12 nearby homes," *The Philadelphia Inquirer*, Sept. 20, 1994.
47. a target zone for arson: Henry Goldman, Dianna Marder, and Wanda Motley, "Fire walls had been removed days before the huge Quaker Lace fire," *The Philadelphia Inquirer*, Sept. 21, 1994.
47. nearly three a day: Craig R. McCoy, "Among the worst seen in the city," *The Philadelphia Inquirer*, Dec. 24, 1994.
47. sign fee contingency agreements: Vanessa Williams, "In Second District war, accusations fly on TV," *The Philadelphia Inquirer*, Nov. 2, 1994.
47. people who lost their homes: Joseph A. Slobodzian, "Sentences no solace for arson," *The Philadelphia Inquirer*, Aug. 16, 1995.

51. twenty-seven thousand abandoned properties: Department of Licenses and Inspections, City of Philadelphia.

61. $20,000 a day from a single corner: U.S. Drug Enforcement Administration, Philadelphia Field Division.

62. driving through the neighborhood: Lt. John Gallo, Narcotics Field Unit, Philadelphia Police Department.

62. one out of every three households: Neill A. Borowski, analysis of U.S. Census data, Nov. 3, 1994.

62. $2.4 billion a year: Philadelphia County Assistance Office, "Open Line to Welfare," June 1994, p. 5.

62. had lost a quarter-million jobs: "Vital Signs, Campaign '95, Jobs & The Economy," *The Philadelphia Inquirer,* Sept. 24–28, 1995, p. 12.

63. waiting all day in lines: Thomas Ferrick Jr., "Marriott jobs draw long lines," *The Philadelphia Inquirer,* Nov. 18, 1994.

64. first General Poor Law: Philadelphia County Assistance Office, "A Welfare Chronology," June 1994, p. 59.

64. Roosevelt asked Congress: Social Security Bulletin, "Fifty Years of Service to Children and Their Families," Oct. 1985, Vol. 48, No. 10, p. 6.

64. more than 5 percent: Administration for Children and Families, U.S. Department of Health and Human Services, "State AFDC Activity," Dec. 28, 1994, p. 6.

65. 60 percent of all births outside marriage: The Twentieth Century Fund, "Welfare Reform," New York, 1995, p. 5.

65. a third of AFDC mothers in Pennsylvania: Department of Public Welfare, Commonwealth of Pennsylvania, "Characteristics of AFDC Cases," March 1994, pp. 1–11.

65. make welfare a way of life: The Twentieth Century Fund, "Welfare Reform," New York, 1995. pp. 8–10.

66. woman named Linda Taylor: "'Welfare Queen' Becomes Issue in Reagan Campaign," *The New York Times,* Feb. 15, 1976.

66. welfare checks were shrinking: The Twentieth Century Fund, "Welfare Reform," New York, 1995, p. 12.

3. CHECK DAY

76. highest murder rate in Philadelphia: Neill A. Borowski, analysis of FBI and U.S. Census data, Nov. 3, 1994.

79. 240,000 people in Philadelphia: Department of Public Welfare, Commonwealth of Pennsylvania, "Characteristics of AFDC Cases," March 1994, p. 12.

87. six cops from North Philadelphia: Mark Fazlollah and Joseph A. Slobodzian, "City Agrees to Pay $2 Million in 27 False-Arrest Cases," *The Philadelphia Inquirer,* July 16, 1996.

4. AN HISTORIC SQUARE MILE

98. twenty-four thousand homeless: William E. Parshall, Deputy Managing Director, City of Philadelphia, Nov. 30, 1995.

8. IN THE HOUSE OF THE LORD

161. number of Catholics in North Philadelphia: Ralph Cipriano and Connie Langland, "Archdiocese may be closing some of its poorer parishes," *The Philadelphia Inquirer*, Oct. 21, 1992.
162. refurbish a beach mansion: Ralph Cipriano, "Work on archdiocese villa financed by layman's gift," *The Philadelphia Inquirer*, July 9, 1993.

9. RIDING WITH THE DEVIL

183. students were from welfare families: "A District in Distress," *The Philadelphia Inquirer*, Oct. 23, 1994, p. G2.

10. MUST BE CHECK DAY

219. the essence of Cheri: John Woestendiek, "The Outsider. Activist Cheri Honkala breaks the law, bends the rules and bucks the system. But does she succeed?" *The Philadelphia Inquirer Magazine*, Dec. 3, 1995.
224. description from the 1870s: Archdiocese of Philadelphia, "St. Edward's Parish, School Centenary Celebration," Oct. 12, 1986.
227. percent of McKinley's students: "A District In Distress," *The Philadelphia Inquirer*, Oct. 23, 1994, p. G2.

11. A NECESSARY BUTT WHIPPING

230. nearly one of every three black men: The Sentencing Project, "Young Black Americans and The Criminal Justice System: Five Years Later," Washington, D.C., Oct. 1995.

12. SKINNY JOEY

254. legislators had just voted themselves: Robert Moran, "Ridge signs legislative pay-raise bill," *The Philadelphia Inquirer*, Oct. 20, 1995.
276. survived at least a dozen attempts: Thomas A. Gibbons Jr. and George Anastasia, "Hit plot targeted Merlino, police say," *The Philadelphia Inquirer*, June 10, 1995.
276. a 1989 armored truck robbery: George Anastasia, "Hit man's violent view of mob life," *The Philadelphia Inquirer*, Oct. 11, 1995.
276. the mob underboss for Philadelphia: George Anastasia and Ralph Cipriano, "Unwelcome cafe guests," *The Philadelphia Inquirer*, Oct. 26, 1995.
276. let them indict me: George Anastasia, "Stanfa trial's end was not end of mob probes," *The Philadelphia Inquirer*, Nov. 23, 1995.

EPILOGUE

347. scandal in the 39th Police District: Mark Fazlollah and Joseph A. Slobodzian, "City agrees to pay $2 million in 27 false-arrest cases," *The Philadelphia Inquirer*, July 16, 1996.

347. 126 other people arrested on drug charges: Mark Fazlollah, "Judge throws out conviction in BNI case," *The Philadelphia Inquirer*, Oct. 2, 1996.

347. Merlino was acquitted: Rita Giordano, "DUI charge doesn't stick on Merlino," *The Philadelphia Inquirer*, Jan. 18, 1996.

347. drug conspiracy investigation: George Anastasia, "Mob-busters expand pursuit of Merlino," *The Philadelphia Inquirer*, June 24, 1996.

347. $11,000 due him in a city raise: Craig R. McCoy, "City official gives back part of raise to offset fund loss," *The Philadelphia Inquirer*, Jan. 14, 1996.

347. evict six homeless men: Ralph Cipriano, "Plan to move vet's homeless strikes out when police balk," *The Philadelphia Inquirer*, July 10, 1996.

347. no longer accept homeless families: Peter Nicholas, "City shelters are too full for families," *The Philadelphia Inquirer*, July 6, 1996.

Index

About the Author

David Zucchino, winner of the Pulitzer Prize for reporting from South Africa and a three-time Pulitzer finalist, is foreign editor of *The Philadelphia Inquirer*. He lives in Berwyn, Pennsylvania, with his wife Kacey and daughters Adrien, Emily, and Natalie.